ANTONÍN DVOŘÁK

ANTONÍN DVOŘÁK

Musician and Craftsman

JOHN CLAPHAM

ST. MARTIN'S PRESS
NEW YORK

First published in United States 1966
Printed in Great Britain

Library of Congress
Catalog Card Number 66-17324

TO MY CZECH FRIENDS

Contents

Illustrations

ILLUSTRATIONS

Foreword

Of all Slavonic composers Dvořák stands nearest to the great Viennese classical tradition, yet (paradoxically) he is intensely national and as personal a composer as has ever lived. (This is a paradox within a paradox: so many 'national' composers seem to have sunk personality in nationality.) He is, as someone has said, 'the most *musical* composer since Schubert'—who, as the article reprinted on pp. 296–305 shows us, was his idol and whom he criticized in terms that often apply to himself—and the very ease with which he seems not only to have poured out melody but to have thought contrapuntally, so that even his mere doodling is apt to be in invertible counterpoint, has sometimes led (a third paradox) to undervaluation of his powers. It did not mislead Brahms, and I say 'seems' advisedly for, as Dr. Clapham points out on p. 32, the apparent spontaneity was often the result of very hard work. So was Mozart's 'spontaneity'; 'Deh vieni' in *Figaro* underwent quite as much reshaping as many of Beethoven's ideas.

Whether or not the world recognized the depth of Dvořák's genius, it was not slow to accept his music on the strength of its more obvious qualities. In his own country he was undervalued only by the over-zealous admirers of Smetana, who could bear no rival to their hero. But in Germany and Russia, and certainly no less in Britain and the United States, he was quickly accepted as a master and, whatever the changes of fashion among musical intellectuals, he has never lost the affections of the great musical public. Yet we have not studied him closely enough. His music seems too obvious, too immediately comprehensible, to need study. Fortunately some of our best English writers on music have not made that mistake; Stanford made it but his fellow-Brahmins—Hadow, Colles, Tovey—did not. It is true that Tovey, in the *Essays in Musical Analysis*, is sometimes playfully patronizing about the lesser Dvořák but he had 'no hesitation in setting Dvořák's second symphony [which we now number 7] along with the C major symphony of Schubert and the four symphonies of Brahms, as among the greatest and purest examples in this art-form since Beethoven'. Hadow selected Dvořák as early as 1894 as one of the three subjects, between Chopin and Brahms, of the second series of his *Studies in Modern Music*, and headed his essay with an apt quotation from Goethe:

> Es bildet ein Talent sich in der Stille,
> Sich ein Character in dem Strom der Welt.

Colles did Dvořák justice, though no more than justice, in the seventh volume of the old *Oxford History of Music* (1934) and in his chapter on the operas in Viktor Fischl's symposium, *Antonín Dvořák: his Achievement* (1943). Yet English Dvořák criticism, though good up to a point, is small in bulk. Add Alec Robertson's admirable short life-and-works in the 'Master Musicians' series (1945) to the books just mentioned, and you have it practically all. Moreover none of these writers understood Czech or possessed any but superficial knowledge of Czech culture, so that they had to take Dvořák's work very much at its face-value.

Here at last, in this book, we have a full-length study of Dvořák's music by an Englishman, familiar with all the extensive Czech literature on the subject, who has had access to the composition-sketches and the correspondence which throw so much light on a composer's method of work and his personality. It is the book we have long needed and I trust Dr. Clapham will follow it with a second, on Dvořák the man. Here he has wisely limited the biographical element to a brief outline, but Dvořák's personal simplicity was perhaps as deceptive as the apparent simplicity of his music. Certainly as a character he was as delightful as his music. He deserves a full-length biographical study as much as any musician, and he would richly repay such a study.

GERALD ABRAHAM

London, 1965

Preface

No single book can do more than emphasize a limited number of
facets of the life and work of a composer such as Dvořák, and
consequently although I have endeavoured to see the composer in
the round and to review his music as a whole, I have avoided trying
to produce an exhaustive study. As far as possible it has been my aim to
present some of the lesser known facts, and sometimes it has been found
possible to re-assess or add to what is already common knowledge by making
use of sources that had hitherto been overlooked. Until quite recently
practically no attempt had been made to study Dvořák's sketches. Professor
Sychra's work in this field is of the greatest importance for the penetrating
light it sheds on Dvořák's creation. Although it is natural that Sychra's and
my work on the sketches should overlap to some extent, we have studied
them independently of one another.

Since biographical details are often closely linked with Dvořák's music,
detail of this kind has been incorporated into the parts of the book where the
music is discussed. It thus serves to supplement the information to be found
in the first chapter. Some of this material has been culled from publications
that are not easily accessible, at any rate to English and German readers, but
the sources will be found listed in Appendix V. I offer no excuse for the
inclusion of so many Czech references in this bibliography, for almost all
of the most important printed sources are in this language, and this material
is a foundation for any serious study of Dvořák. Besides it was considered
right to make the bibliography as representative as possible.

Anyone who attempts to write a book on Dvořák inevitably owes a
tremendous debt to one man. The late Otakar Šourek, through his systematic
investigations and research and his untiring efforts and missionary zeal,
spread over almost half a century, amassed a wealth of authoritative material
on the Czech master for which we shall always be immensely grateful, and
which we can only ignore at our peril. It is most regrettable that there is no
translation of his four-volume *Life and Work of Antonín Dvořák* and his
volume containing nearly four hundred of Dvořák's letters, for these are
extremely important source books. Šourek's shorter biographies, which

have been translated, have far less value, and even the books on the orchestral works and chamber music which are available in German and English are abridged versions of the Czech originals.

I wish to express my deep gratitude to all those who have assisted me in my work, and especially to those without whose help my task would have been far harder or even impossible. I am grateful for the invaluable help and co-operation of the Czechoslovak Embassy in London, the Czechoslovak Ministry of Education and Culture, the Association of Czechoslovak Composers and the Antonín Dvořák Society of Prague, whose secretary, Dr. Karel Mikysa, who is also the director of the Dvořák Museum, has helped me in innumerable ways. To Dvořák's heirs, and especially to Mrs. Julie Dvořáková, I am deeply indebted for permission to study and publish extracts from their unique collection of manuscripts, sketches and letters. I am most grateful to Státní nakladatelství KLHU and Státní hudební vydavatelství for their very generous gifts of scores, and to Artia for their equally generous gifts of gramophone records and books, and also for the exceptional kindness I have been shown by Dr. Lubomír Dorůžka of the first two of these undertakings and to Mr. Josef Bernáth and Dr. K. Šlapák of the last-mentioned. I also gratefully acknowledge the financial support I have received from the Pilgrim Trust of the British Academy, from the University College of Wales (Sir D. Owen Evans Bequest) and from the University of Edinburgh.

I am exceptionally grateful to Jarmil Burghauser, who read the whole of this book in manuscript and offered expert advice and invaluable and penetrating criticisms. His interest in my book has enriched it considerably. I have made extensive use of his *Antonín Dvořák Thematic Catalogue*, which made a timely appearance before my work was too far advanced. I wish to thank Dr. Gerald Abraham for the encouragement he gave me, especially during the early stages of my work, to record my gratitude to Otakar Šourek for his friendly assistance, and to acknowledge my debt to František Bonuš for placing at my disposal his exceptional knowledge of the folklore of Czechoslovakia.

I also wish to acknowledge the help I have received from the following: the directors of the Royal Philharmonic Society for allowing me to have access to their archives, Laurence Swinyard and Novello & Co. for permitting me to study manuscript scores, B. A. de Nevers of Lengnick & Co. for the loan of scores, Alec Robertson, Geoffrey Turner of the Pitt Rivers Museum, Oxford, Professor Antonín Sychra, the late Josef Löwenbach, Mrs. Olga Klusáková, Dr. Frances Densmore, the Very Revd. Thomas Grassmann, director of the Mohawk-Caughnawaga Museum, Fonda, N.Y., Dr. Bruno Nettl, A. Hyatt King and the librarians of the British Museum, Dr. Alexander Buchner and the librarians of the National Museum, Prague, William Lichtenwanger of the music division of the Library of Congress, Washington, librarians of many cities of Germany, Switzerland, the United States and Britain, and many others besides. I am also grateful to the editor

PREFACE

of *The Musical Quarterly* and G. Schirmer, Inc., to the Council of the Royal Musical Association, and to the editors of *Music and Letters*, *The Music Review*, *Monthly Musical Record*, *Musica* and *Hudebni rozhledy* for permission to reproduce extracts from my articles.

Edinburgh, July 1965

NOTE ON PRONUNCIATION

STRESS

The stress occurs on the first syllable of a word, irrespective of whether the first vowel is short or long; so that in the name 'Dvořák' the first syllable is very short, but stressed, and the second syllable is prolonged without being emphasized.

Part One

THE MAN AND HIS ART

I

Biographical Sketch

Antonín Dvořák came of sturdy peasant stock. His great-grand-father Jan Dvořák (1724–1777) lived just beyond the north-eastern fringe of Prague at Třeboradice, where he combined farming with innkeeping. Eventually he died in the house in which he had been born. Six out of his family of ten survived infancy, the third of these being the composer's grandfather, Jan Nepomuk Dvořák (1764–1842). The latter became both publican and butcher, first at Vodolka (now known as Odolena Voda), and from 1818 at Nelahozeves, where the composer himself was to be born. All three sons of Jan Nepomuk pursued the same two means of liveli-hood as their father. František (1814–1894), the youngest of these and the tenth of the twelve children, helped to run his father's business, and took it over completely on the latter's death a year after Antonín was born.

The ancestors of the composer's mother lived in the region of Slaný, slightly further west, and were cottagers who tilled their plots of land, but her father, Josef Zdeněk (1775–1852), was steward at Uhy, near Velvary. Anna Zdeňková, his only daughter, became the wife of František Dvořák on November 17th, 1840.

Nelahozeves (Mühlhausen), a peaceful hamlet a dozen miles north of Prague, is situated on the banks of the Vltava near to Kralupy. It is domin-ated by the castle that came into the possession of the Lobkovitz family in 1623, and a few yards from the little church stands the house, formerly an inn and butcher's shop, where Dvořák was born. Today little is changed. Rural life continues in its quiet way very much as it did over a century ago, but there is now an inn on the other side of the road, the castle has become a museum and the composer's birthplace is a place of annual pilgrimage.

František and Anna Dvořák had nine children (and forty-four grand-children), the eldest of whom was the composer Antonín, born on September 8th, 1841. Some of his forbears had some skill in playing musical instru-ments, which was a normal enough accomplishment in Bohemian villages and towns during those times. His two uncles, Jan Křtitel and Josef, were reputed to play the fiddle quite well, and Josef played the trumpet in

3

addition. František himself played the zither and even wrote for it, although his modest compositions in dance forms are undistinguished. There is, however, no record of any outstanding musical talent and no hint that the family would one day produce a musical genius.

Antonín was taught to play the fiddle and to sing by Josef Spitz, the village schoolmaster and organist, who, according to his daughter's testimony, was able 'to play on all instruments'. The young boy's violin playing was popular with regular frequenters of the inn, but František regarded this as no more than a side-line. Naturally his son would follow in the traditional family business. Accordingly, having spent six years at school, Antonín left shortly before his twelfth birthday and became apprenticed to his father in the butchers' trade. In order to improve the lad's chances of success he was sent a year later to become a butcher's apprentice at Zlonice, where he stayed with his mother's younger brother, Antonín Zdeněk (b. 1823). His uncle, who was steward to Count Kinsky, treated him like a son, for he had no children of his own. This attractive Czech town, lying some twenty or more miles away by road to the west of Nelahozeves, offered chances of picking up a little German, which was an important point for one who was destined to become a publican, but the musical opportunities were very much greater. Josef Toman, schoolmaster, and organist and choirmaster of the church, was a baritone singer, and played the violin, trumpet and double bass in addition to the organ. Antonín Liehmann (1808–1879), a teacher of German and music and a typical Czech *Musikant*, was an excellent organist with a talent for improvisation, a good violinist and clarinettist who also played the French horn, and a prolific composer as well. Thanks to these two men, and expecially to Liehmann, Antonín's musical studies made great strides. He studied harmony and made rapid progress on the viola, organ and pianoforte.

When František, on his brother-in-law's advice, moved to Zlonice in an endeavour to improve his prospects by transferring his butcher's business there and becoming landlord of 'The Big Inn', both Antonín Zdeněk and Liehmann tried to persuade him to let young Antonín have a professional training in music, but their pleas fell on deaf ears. When the boy gained his journeyman's certificate on November 1st, 1856, he was packed off to Böhmisch-Kamnitz (Česká Kamenice), not far from Bohemia's common frontier with Saxony, to make good his deficiencies in the German language at the town school. While he was there, to his great delight, he was able to continue his lessons in music theory and in organ playing with the church organist, Franz Hancke, who also gave him opportunities to conduct his church choir. Antonín returned to Zlonice with his leaving certificate in the following summer.

Even had he wished to do so, František was in no position at this time to provide his son with a thorough musical training because his business in the town was not prospering. Fortunately for Antonín his uncle agreed to finance his studies, and this generous gesture, together no doubt with the lad's eagerness, resulted in František changing his mind and allowing his son to earn a living as best he could as a musician. In the autumn of 1857, at the age of sixteen, Antonín was enrolled as a student at the Prague Organ School, where he remained for the statutory two years. The Conservatory specialized in training executants, but the organ school was much better suited for those who hoped to become composers, and provided excellent tuition in practical studies as well. When Antonín arrived there K. F. Pitsch (1789–1858) was the director, but when he died the directorship fell to Josef Krejčí (1822–1881). The teaching was on sound orthodox lines and in general displayed a characteristic intolerance of the music of the so-called neo-romantics, Wagner and Liszt.

At first Antonín lodged with his cousin Marie Plívová (née Doležalová) in the Old Town, but as she had four small daughters her flat was overcrowded. A year later he moved to Charles Square to stay with his uncle Václav Dušek, who was an impoverished railway employee. It was at about this time that Antonín Zdeněk found it impossible to continue to support his nephew, and so the young student was obliged to try to make ends meet by taking pupils. A fellow student, Karel Bendl (1838–1897), who later became a well-known composer and conductor, helped Antonín considerably by allowing him to make use of his well-stocked library of scores, and also to play on his piano, for neither his cousin nor his uncle possessed one. By playing viola in the choral and orchestral concerts of the St. Cecilia Society he came into direct contact with music of the neo-romantic school, but the musical life of Prague offered him much greater riches. The many concerts and opera performances provided invaluable opportunities for him to become acquainted for the first time with many of the great musical classics, and the personal appearances of great artists like Liszt, Hans von Bülow and Clara Schumann, either as conductors or pianists, impressed him deeply.

On leaving the organ school Dvořák became violist in the Karel Komzák Band, which provided music three times a week in some of Prague's bigger inns and restaurants, and he attempted to improve his financial position by securing an organ post, but without success. When the Provisional Theatre was opened on November 18th, 1862, in order that there should be for the first time a stage specifically assigned for productions of Czech operas and dramas, the Komzák Band became the nucleus of the orchestra. The players, however, still continued their former engagements, and despite the additional work Dvořák received no more than his former small salary of eighteen gulden a month. The Komzák Band visited Hamburg in July 1863, but for Dvořák the greatest event of the year took place in February when he played in a programme devoted to Wagner's music and directed by Wagner himself.

During this period Dvořák composed a string quintet in A minor (1861), a string quartet in A major (1862) and several other works which he destroyed later. He changed his address sometime in the first half of 1864, joining forces with Mořic Anger, a colleague from the orchestra, and three other young musicians, but in the latter half of the following year he was obliged to return to his uncle's because he found the atmosphere too disturbing. That same year he began giving piano lessons to Josefina Čermáková, the sixteen-year old actress daughter of a Prague goldsmith, and soon fell deeply in love with her. His aching heart caused him to write a cycle of eighteen songs entitled *Cypresses*, but this effusion failed to soften her heart, to his extreme disappointment.

The year 1865 was a productive year, during which he composed two symphonies and a 'cello concerto in addition to the songs, but there were still no performances of his works to encourage him and spur him on to greater efforts, and years of struggle still lay ahead. He was not upset when his first symphony was lost. Numerous works were destroyed, but he still persevered. Even if he was following false trails and not making any obvious progress he was gaining in experience and learning from some of his mistakes. He was also witnessing a remarkable inflorescence of music that was essentially Czech, and taking part in the historic series of first performances of Smetana's operas that began with *The Brandenburgers in Bohemia* and *The Bartered Bride* in 1866 and included *Dalibor* two years later. This was indeed a powerful stimulus to him, just as it was to other Czech nationalists.

It is very probable that because of his unqualified enthusiasm for Wagner, Dvořák may have attended every production of his operas that was mounted at the German Theatre. To Dvořák the composer here lay a temptation that he found irresistible, and as a consequence the hand of the German master weighed heavily upon him at the beginning of the 1870s when his Wagner fever was at its height. Not only did his first opera *Alfred* and the first version of *King and Charcoal Burner* dog the musical giant's footsteps, but the three string quartets that he wrote at about the same time also show his strong influence. It was only gradually that Dvořák realized that this was an unwise path to follow, although the advice he received and the attacks made on Smetana for his Wagnerism were timely warnings. In any case, how could an inexperienced and struggling composer such as Dvořák was then hope to master Wagner's elaborate compositional methods and endeavour to reach Walhalla without sinking into the quicksands that lay in his path?

It is evident that Dvořák must have been having some success as a teacher, or he would not have resigned from the Provisional Theatre orchestra after nine years' service. Gradually a few of his compositions began to be heard. Some of his songs and the Adagio of a pianoforte trio were performed at

Ludevít Procházka's informal musical evenings, and his Piano Quintet in A, op. 5, was played at a matinée concert. On April 14th, 1872, Smetana conducted the overture to *King and Charcoal Burner* at a Philharmonic concert. The opera was rehearsed at the Provisional Theatre the following year, but to Dvořák's mortification it was declared unperformable and withdrawn. By the time he received this unpalatable news he was already well on the way towards a partial renunciation of Wagnerian influence and an acceptance of a good measure of classical ideals, helped by the example of Smetana. But naturally it needed time to bring about the fundamental transformation of his habits of thought, of his methods and style that now seemed necessary, and the replacement of a set of deep-rooted principles by a different set to which he had not previously given an adequate trial.

One of the first works that bears witness to a change of heart is the patriotic cantata, *The Heirs of the White Mountain*, which the Prague Hlahol Choir sang under the conductorship of Bendl on March 9th, 1873. The performance was an outstanding success, the first that Dvořák had experienced. A month or so later he was working on a third symphony, in E flat, and he followed this with a *Romeo and Juliet* overture, an octet and two string quartets (opp. 9 and 12). In the same year Starý published a set of his songs (op. 7).

Fortunately the difficulties that he encountered with his opera, although an unpleasant setback, did not seriously shake his confidence. On the crest of the wave of his first real success he and Anna Čermáková, a former pupil, a gifted contralto singer and the younger sister of his former love, decided to get married. The ceremony took place on November 17th, 1873. Three months later he became organist of St. Adalbert's church, and by that time he had half completed his fourth symphony, the earlier of the two in D minor. In May the young couple moved into a flat of their own, Na rybníčku, No. 14, not far from where Dvořák's uncle lived. Composition went on apace. Urged on very probably by Smetana's *The Two Widows*, he composed an entirely new version of *King and Charcoal Burner* in the summer of 1874, and this was performed with some success on November 24th, with Adolf Čech conducting. At the end of the same year he wrote the one-act opera *The Stubborn Lovers*, and immediately before this composed his seventh string quartet (op. 16). Smetana conducted his E flat symphony that same year at a Philharmonic concert on March 30th, and the scherzo of the D minor symphony was performed two months later, again under Smetana's direction. At the age of thirty-three Dvořák's prospects for the future looked more promising than at any earlier time, but it is probable that what made his wife and him happiest of all was the birth of their son Otakar.

7

Hearing that the State was offering a prize to young, talented and inpecu-nious writers, artists and musicians, Dvořák decided to compete and sub-mitted his E flat and D minor symphonies together with a chamber music composition, possibly the F minor string quartet. After waiting several months he heard in February 1875 that the jury had awarded him the hand-some prize of 400 gulden.[1] This encouraging news may have helped to make this a prolific year for Dvořák, a year in which he composed his fifth symphony (op. 76 in F), the grand opera *Vanda*, the string quintet in G, the piano trio in B flat, the piano quartet in D, the Serenade in E and four *Moravian Duets*. In the same year Starý published his string quartet in A minor, op. 16, and Wetzler issued his Potpourri based on *King and Charcoal Burner*.

One of his compositions of that year stands somewhat apart from the rest, for in it we can see a much stronger individuality, greater clarity of thought and singleness of mind, and a surer command of the means of expression than in anything he had composed up to that time. It seems certain that when Dvořák wrote his F major symphony he not only strove to create something finer than anything he had written before, but also that he discovered how this could be done. He still had far to go to reach his apogee, but at last he was a master of his craft with a distinctive character of his own.

Compositions continued to flow from Dvořák's pen. The G minor piano trio, the string quartet in E, fifteen *Moravian Duets*, twelve *Evening Songs*, the piano concerto and the *Theme and Variations* for piano were all written in 1876, and in the same year the *Stabat Mater* was sketched. This was then laid aside until the deaths within a month of each other of his son and daughter impelled him to return to it and orchestrate it. *Vanda* was performed but it was a failure. Early in the following year he composed a comic opera, *The Cunning Peasant*. Shortly before this, feeling that he was much more secure financially, Dvořák decided to relinquish his post as organist, a decision that he almost certainly reached after hearing the news that he was to receive the Austrian State Prize for the third time. Brahms had apparently been appointed to the Commission in succession to Herbeck in 1875.[2] In Novem-ber 1877 the by then childless couple moved to Žitná ulice 10 (Kornthorgasse

---

[1] At that time, in addition to his organist's salary of 126 gulden, he was earning 60 gulden a month by private teaching. The prize was worth about £40.

[2] According to the article that Hanslick wrote on Dvořák for the *Neue Freie Presse* (Vol. XVIII, New Series, pp. 58–59, 1880) 'It was not until Brahms had been summoned by Herr Stremayr, the Minister, to replace Herbeck that the recognition of Dvořák's talent took the necessary practical turn.' Since Brahms in writing to Simrock (12. XII. 1877) stated: 'In connection with the State Stipend, I have for several years been delighted with the works of A. D....', it may be presumed that he was then serving for his third year, having been appointed in 1875. Hanslick's state-ment appears to refute Šourek's view that Brahms was a member of the jury when Dvořák made his first application.

10), which then became their permanent home. In the following June their daughter Otilie was born.

At the time when Dvořák was about to be awarded the State Prize for the fourth time, Brahms saw clearly that this gifted Czech composer could not make headway in the musical world easily if his works were only published by small firms in Prague. He therefore wrote to Simrock of Berlin, his own publisher, recommending him to take Dvořák's *Moravian Duets* and perhaps other things besides. This started a chain reaction. Dvořák and Brahms, naturally, became firm friends, and remained so until the latter's death. Simrock commissioned the first set of *Slavonic Dances*, and published the duets. By writing a review of the dances and duets in glowing terms, the critic Ehlert brought the unknown Czech composer to the attention of the German people, and in just under a year after this notice had appeared Joachim, who had heard much about Dvořák direct from Brahms, gave the first performance of the string sextet in Berlin (9. XI. 1879) with the composer present. Had it not been for this kind action of Brahms it would have been impossible for Dvořák, despite the blossoming of his genius, to have gained such a firm foothold abroad in so short a space of time. Success in Germany opened the door to England, and that in turn eventually led to an invitation from America.

The period of this sudden change in Dvořák's fortunes coincides with a decisive change in his musical style, the adoption of a strongly national attitude, and a far greater use of the rhythms and spirit of the folk dances of his country than ever before. This factor appears to have facilitated the acceptance of his music abroad. It could be melancholy or bursting with life, and it was both melodious and colourful, but above all here was music that was new, different, that is, from what audiences were accustomed to, and with an instantaneous appeal. The *Slavonic Dances* whetted people's appetites but the more solid fare proved to be equally welcome. In September 1879 Taubert gave the first performance of the third *Slavonic Rhapsody* in Berlin. Two months later this work was conducted in Budapest by Erkel and in Vienna by Richter, who six months afterwards took it to London. The first and second *Rhapsodies* and the sextet and string quartet in E flat appeared in concert programmes in Vienna, Germany and England. Two more works, written in 1880, gained Dvořák further laurels, the *Gipsy Melodies* and the sixth symphony in D major. At this time he was at work on the violin concerto, and endeavouring to meet the criticisms of Joachim to whom he had turned for advice, but this work was not finished until a little later.

One work, however, which lacked obviously national characteristics was of considerable importance in gaining support and sympathy for Dvořák in foreign countries. This was the *Stabat Mater* which was sung in

9

the Hungarian capital in 1882, in London the following year, and which had crossed the Atlantic by 1884. The Czech composer's music was arousing so much interest that in Vienna, Dresden and Hamburg the possibility of performing one of Dvořák's operas was very seriously considered. Dresden and Hamburg presented *The Cunning Peasant* in the year Simrock published it. At the Saxon *première* in October 1882, which the composer attended, his opera was a triumphal success, which cannot be said of the Prague performance of four years earlier. Full of enthusiasm he wrote to Simrock: 'A pity, a pity that you weren't at Dresden! You would certainly have rejoiced heartily at the great success and the exemplary presentation, just as I have. Schuch prepared the opera splendidly.'

A fortnight before leaving Prague for Dresden Dvořák's new grand opera *Dimitrij* had been performed there for the first time and was very well received. Both Jauner, conductor of the Vienna Court Opera, and Schuch took note of this, but neither of them was prepared to risk a production. In Vienna, where there was strong anti-Czech feeling, Hanslick thought that Dvořák would be wise to drop his nationalism and become more cosmopolitan. If he abandoned Slavonic subjects and instead set German libretti, there seemed excellent reasons in Hanslick's opinion for thinking that he would emerge as a highly successful composer on the German and Vienna stage. Thinking along somewhat similar lines, and after discussing the matter with Hanslick, the Generalintendant of the Court Opera, Baron Hoffmann, offered the Czech composer two German libretti in 1884. At about the same time Brahms, who had been repaid immeasurably for his wisdom in moving to Vienna, may have made it plain to Dvořák that he would be well advised to do the same. At the beginning of August 1883 an invitation came from the Philharmonic Society of London inviting him to conduct some of his compositions at one of their concerts early in the following year, and he naturally accepted, but this did nothing to help him to resolve his operatic dilemma. The world was opening up to him. He was a simple, unspoilt man, but he must have felt flattered by the increasing attention that was being bestowed on him.

The crux of the problem rested with his conscience. It was natural for him to be ambitious, and being so he had set his heart on becoming a leading composer of opera, which made Vienna's overtures all the more tempting. But he was faced with the prospect of being disloyal to his own nation, and so betraying the national cause in which he so strongly believed. Even though he did not care to identify himself closely with either of the most ardently national Czech political groups, he had a profound love for and pride in his country.

When he was invited to be the honoured guest of the German Artists' Club in London he declined, explaining that he was not German. He preferred to avoid using the German language, unless there appeared to be no convenient alternative. He had the greatest difficulty in getting Simrock to print his first name on his music in the contracted form 'Ant.', in place of the German form 'Anton'. Simrock's lack of understanding in this matter caused Dvořák to retort: 'Don't make fun of my Czech brothers, and don't be sorry for me either. What I ask of you is only a wish, and if you cannot fulfil it then I have the right to regard that as an unkindness the like of which I have not found with either English or French publishers.'[1] As Simrock would not give way, Dvořák made himself even clearer in his next letter, in which he said: 'Your last letter with its humorous national-political explanation amused me greatly; I am only sorry that you are so badly informed. . . . But *what have we two to do with politics!* It is well that we are free *to dedicate our services to a splendid art*. And may the nations never perish that *possess art* and represent it, however small they may be. Forgive me for this, but I simply wished to tell you that an artist also has a fatherland in which he must have firm faith and for which he must have a warm heart.'[2]

Dvořák had a simple and unquestioning faith in God, yet he seems to have been a little shaken in his belief during this time of testing, for we notice that the phrase 'Bohu díky!' (Thanks to God) which he invariably wrote on the final pages of his manuscripts is missing in the F minor trio, the *Scherzo capriccioso*, the *Hussite* overture and the piano quintet, although it does occur at the end of the D minor symphony. This uncertainty is also reflected in some of the compositions of that time, or rather, it is seen in the hesitations and vacillations that occurred while he was at work on them, yet the works themselves are among Dvořák's greatest. The artistic and spiritual crisis that he was passing through made him see the art of creation in an entirely new light, and drew from him a profundity, a nobility and an epic grandeur which would have been impossible if he had not experienced such heart-searching.

Even though he found the temptations that lay before him very alluring, and it took him some three years to overcome them, there was only one satisfactory path for him to take. He had to remain loyal to Bohemia and his fellow countrymen.

During this period of crisis Dvořák paid four visits to England, where he was lionized and fêted as never before. He took with him on the first of these journeys the *Hussite* overture, the *Nocturne* for strings and the *Scherzo capriccioso*, which were all new to London. The overture was for the Philharmonic Society programme on March 20th, 1884, and the other two

[1] Letter of 22. VIII. 1885. The Dvořák-Simrock correspondence has been published by Altmann and Šourek; see Select Bibliography, II.

[2] 10. IX. 1885.

works for the Crystal Palace concert two days later. At the first of these concerts he conducted his sixth symphony and second *Slavonic Rhapsody*, and W. J. Winch sang two of the *Gipsy Melodies*. When these songs were repeated at the Sydenham concert Dvořák himself accompanied Winch. A few days earlier the composer conducted his *Stabat Mater* at the Royal Albert Hall. Dvořák had every reason to be satisfied with his visit. Apart from the great success of his concerts he had some excellent friends, and among them his host Oscar Beringer, the pianist, and Henry Littleton, head of the music publishing firm of Novello, Ewer & Co., who was extremely active personally in promoting concerts. Furthermore, he returned to Prague with commissions in his pocket for large choral works for the Birmingham and Leeds Festivals, and an invitation to return in the autumn to conduct some of his works at the Three Choirs Festival at Worcester. On June 14th he was elected an Honorary Member of the Philharmonic Society, and he was then asked by the Society to write a symphony for them. He therefore had enough work on hand to occupy him for eighteen months.

Being affluent for the first time in his life, he was able to realize an ambition that he had had for some time, to buy himself a house and a plot of land in the country. He acquired these at Vysoká where his brother-in-law Count Kaunitz had his estate, near the mining town of Příbram some forty miles to the south of Prague. During the winter months he remained in the capital, but from spring until autumn he was at Vysoká, walking in the forest early in the mornings, enjoying the peace and solitude of nature, rearing pigeons, chatting with peasants and miners about the village and at the inn, and either composing or simply resting according to his mood.

At Worcester on September 11th he conducted the *Stabat Mater* at the morning concert and his sixth symphony in the afternoon. He appeared for the first time in Germany as composer-conductor on November 21st when his *Hussite* overture and piano concerto were played in Berlin, with Anna Grosser-Rilke as soloist. The main purpose of his next visit to London was to direct the *première* of his seventh symphony in D minor at the fourth Philharmonic concert on April 22nd, 1885. This time he remained in London for a month and so was able to conduct his piano concerto when Franz Rummel played it at the Society's next concert on May 6th, and a week later he conducted Mr. Geaussent's Choir at St. James's Hall in the lately revised version of his *Hymnus*.[1] Since this work had only just been published by Novello, this was almost certainly the first performance in its final form. The Philharmonic audience was less enthusiastic about the seventh symphony than they were about its predecessor.

Dvořák's fourth visit was spent directing the final rehearsals and the first English performance of *The Spectre's Bride* at Birmingham, but he found

[1] *The Heirs of the White Mountain.*

time to visit Littleton's house at Brighton, where he was surprised and delighted to see the beautiful English ladies bathing *in public*. The concert took place on August 27th and was immensely successful. Both the public and the press were most enthusiastic, and Gounod's new work *Mors et Vita* was put in the shade. The *Sunday Times* described the concert as 'a great and unalloyed success'. The *Times* commented, 'Herr Dvořák, although he does not possess the graphic power and the orchestral resources of Berlioz or Liszt, has treated a difficult subject with the technical skill and earnest inspiration of a true artist.' When the cantata was repeated in London early in February, Ebenezer Prout, the *Athenaeum* critic, compared Dvořák's work with another written on a similar subject, Raff's *Lenore* Symphony. 'In both cases the appropriateness of the musical illustrations may be admitted,' he said, 'but Raff frequently becomes ugly, Dvořák never.' And he concluded with these remarks: 'That the work will take permanent rank among the masterpieces of musical art there cannot, we think, be a shadow of doubt.'

The growth in Dvořák's stature that we have noticed in the compositions of these last years was due partly to the influence of Brahms, whose presence is sometimes felt either directly or indirectly. Also there is rather less obvious use of national features, unless, for instance, a movement takes on the character of a *furiant*. In the years that followed Dvořák once again adopted a strongly national outlook, but if we compare the second set of *Slavonic Dances* with the first we find that the prevailing tone is now rather more serious. Dvořák was still capable of unbridled exuberance, as in the Scherzo and Finale of the piano quintet, but the experiences of those difficult years can be seen to have enriched his musical idiom, even in the lighter forms. These tendencies continued for six years, a period that embraces *The Jacobin*, the E flat piano quartet, the G major symphony and the *Dumky* Trio, as well as two liturgical works that transcend national frontiers.

During the first half of 1886 the composer was busily engaged on the oratorio *St. Ludmila*, which he was writing for Leeds, but once that was finished he turned to the new *Slavonic Dances* that Simrock had been pestering him to write for so long. Dvořák was again given a tumultuous reception by his English friends when he conducted the *première* of his oratorio on October 15th; in fact, as he himself told his friend Rus, 'at the end of Part I the whole audience, chorus and orchestra burst out into such cheers that I felt quite queer.'[1] However, the success of the work in England was short-lived. Dvořák conducted it twice in London, but practically no attempt to perform it was made by the provincial choral societies.

Although Dvořák had made such an enviable reputation for himself, especially abroad, and was esteemed very highly by so many distinguished musicians of the time, yet, as the following extract from a letter to a Příbram

[1] Letter from London, 18. X. 1886.

13

choirmaster shows, he still remained at heart a modest and humble peasant. 'I must confess to you candidly', he wrote, 'that your kind letter took me a little by surprise, because its excessive servility and humility make it seem as if you were addressing some demigod, which of course I never was, am not and never shall be. I am just a plain Czech musician, disliking such exaggerated humility, and despite the fact that I have moved a bit in the great musical world, I still remain just what I was—a simple Czech Musikant.'[1]

In 1887 Dvořák's mind turned towards earlier compositions. He rewrote a substantial part of *King and Charcoal Burner*, and also brought his brilliant *Symphonic Variations* out of cold storage, where they had unaccountably lain for nine years. When he offered this work to Richter the latter accepted it with alacrity, and was rewarded with a triumphant success when he presented it in London on May 16th. At about the same time Dvořák also revised several compositions of the sixties. His new works included the Mass in D, the piano quintet and *The Jacobin*, an opera he was engaged on until the autumn of 1888. When Tchaikovsky visited Prague in February that year the two composers became firm friends, and they were able to renew their friendship at the end of November when the Russian composer returned to conduct his fifth symphony and *Eugene Onegin*. In March Dvořák conducted his *Stabat Mater* in Budapest. He visited Dresden a year later to conduct three of his compositions, including another work that he had revised, the fifth symphony in F, which had already been heard abroad as early as April 7th, 1888, when Manns performed it at the Crystal Palace.

His new opera was performed and warmly received in February 1889.

In June he was honoured with the Austrian Order of the Iron Crown, and consequently paid a special visit to Vienna a few months later to have an audience with the Emperor Franz Josef I. Between these two last events he composed the E flat piano quartet and one of his happiest works, the eighth symphony in G major. At the end of October he visited Berlin for the first German performance of his seventh symphony, with Hans von Bülow in command. This was another triumph for the composer.

Having been invited to Russia by Tchaikovsky, Dvořák spent the month of March 1890 in Moscow and St. Petersburg. He conducted his F major symphony, first *Slavonic Rhapsody*, *Symphonic Variations* and *Scherzo capriccioso* in Moscow on the 11th, and at St. Petersburg on the 22nd the D major symphony was performed and the *Scherzo* repeated. His music was received with less enthusiasm than he had become accustomed to in England and Germany, but he had strong support from Moscow's German community. He was given a silver coffee service as a souvenir of his Moscow visit. At Petersburg a silver goblet was presented to him at a banquet given by the

---

[1] Letter to Bohumil Fiedler, 9. I. 1886.

Czech Aid Society, and on the eve of his departure he was the guest of honour at a Russian Musical Society banquet.

A month later he paid another visit to the Philharmonic Society of London to conduct the first English performance of his G major symphony. He was very busily engaged for most of that year composing his *Requiem Mass* for Birmingham. After having refused a previous invitation to join the staff of the Prague Conservatory he agreed to do so in October, and took up duties there early the following year. Further honours were heaped upon him. He received the honorary degree of Doctor of Philosophy of the Charles University, Prague, in March 1891. On June 15th he conducted his G major symphony and *Stabat Mater* at Cambridge, and, having thus demonstrated his academic fitness, the degree of Doctor of Music *honoris causa* was conferred on him the next day. He was embarrassed to find that all the speeches were in Latin, which he did not understand, but he consoled himself later with the thought that it is better to compose a *Stabat Mater* than to know Latin.

Hitherto Simrock had published most of Dvořák's compositions, for according to their contract of 1879 he had the option to purchase any new work of Dvořák's prior to its being offered to another publisher. Simrock had given Dvořák 300 marks for the earlier set of *Slavonic Dances*, which, bearing in mind that the composer was unknown in Germany at the time, was a fair enough price; but for Simrock the work proved to be a gold mine. After Dvořák had become internationally famous the publisher offered him 3,000 marks for his D minor symphony, but the composer told him that another firm was prepared to offer more. After hearing Dvořák and Hanslick play the piano duet version of the symphony Simrock agreed to double his original offer, but at the same time he pressed Dvořák to write some more of those lucrative *Slavonic Dances*. When the time came for the composer to fall in with his publisher's wishes he was rewarded with another 3,000 marks.[1] Simrock tried to encourage the Czech composer to write more songs and pianoforte pieces, because experience showed them to be a better commercial proposition than symphonies, big choral works and chamber music.

The relationship between the two men had been strained before, but in 1890 during the negotiations for the publication of the G major symphony it reached breaking point. In his reply to Dvořák's letter of January 3rd Simrock stated his case as follows:

[1] Burghauser informs me that Simrock paid 2,000 marks for the D major symphony, and that for the F major symphony, together with opp. 77–81 collectively, Dvořák received 6,000 marks. It seems probable that the composer did not value his E minor symphony nearly as highly as the one in D minor, for he sold it to Simrock for the same amount as the D major symphony, one-third the price of the D minor, even though it had been far more successful.

If only I did sufficient business with your symphonies to be repaid for my enormous expense! But this is far from being the case! and I am thousands down on them. That is how it is—and nothing can change it What use is it if I make money on one or six works and lose it again on four others? I can't carry on my business like that! If the performances are successful the composer always thinks his work will sell. You were successful here over Bülow's performance of your D minor symphony, but subsequently not a single copy, not even a piano duet version, was sold. Bülow has been performing the *Hussite* overture for years—despite opposition! The public never likes it—I've already observed this six times. He doesn't play your overture *My Home* (which the public would enjoy!) —and it is the same with other works! For a long time I had to urge him to perform the second symphony before he finally did so! On the other hand the third (in F major) was sent back to me after the rehearsal 'This cannot be performed'! And this third symphony has never yet been performed anywhere in Germany and Austria! The same is true of the *Psalm* op. 79. So unless you also give me small and easy piano pieces (and even these will sell almost exclusively in Bohemia, as, for instance, op. 85) it won't be possible to publish big works.

Dvořák assumes in his letter of February 17th that Simrock is no longer considering buying his symphonies, and states that if the publisher will not accept his symphony by the autumn at the latest he will be obliged to look elsewhere. Since no offer was forthcoming he wrote again on October 7th, saying that he would have to try to find another purchaser for his works in view of the enormous cost of educating his children. The quarrel reached its climax two days later when Dvořák sent the following letter to Simrock:

Since you have thought it right once more to reject my symphony I shall not offer you any big expensive works in future, for I shall know in advance, because of what you say, that you cannot publish such works. You advise me to write small works; but that is difficult, for how can I help it if no theme for a song or a piano piece comes into my head? Just now my mind is full of big ideas—I shall do as God wills. That will be best.

Simrock attempted to parry this threat by invoking their agreement of 1879, which made Dvořák extremely angry. In reply he pointed out that, quite apart from the symphony, he had been waiting for almost a year to hear if Simrock would take his Mass. The rupture was now complete, and for more than a year no letters passed between the two men. Dvořák therefore offered the symphony to Novello, who published it in 1892 and issued his

Mass early the following year. It would appear that the business acumen that Dvořák displayed was due in large measure to his wife.

In the spring of 1891 Dvořák received a telegram from Vienna enquiring if he would accept an important post in New York, but he showed no interest at the time. Mrs. Jeannette Thurber, a very persevering woman and the wife of a wealthy grocer, was behind this offer. When she arrived in Paris she arranged for the following telegram to be sent to the composer on June 5th: 'Would you accept position Director National Conservatory of Music New York October 1892 also lead six concerts of your works.' This arrived before he left for Cambridge, but on his return he found a letter awaiting him giving fuller particulars, and the position was clarified further six weeks later when the contract arrived. He would have three hours teaching a day, prepare four students' concerts, conduct six concerts of his own music in American towns, have a four-month vacation and receive 15,000 dollars per annum. At first he felt inclined to accept the concert engagements, but not the directorship, but that did not suit Mrs. Thurber. During the second half of November,[1] after making several amendments to the contract, he agreed to accept the position for two years, although he still had some misgivings about his prolonged absence from the land he loved so dearly, and his separation from his family.

Dvořák interrupted his work on the three overtures, *In Nature's Realm*, *Carnival* and *Othello*, in order to conduct his *Requiem* at Birmingham on October 9th, 1891. Again he scored a great success, even though the performance left something to be desired. During the first five months of the year of his departure for America he undertook a farewell concert tour with Ferdinand Lachner, the violinist, and Hanuš Wihan, the 'cellist. The main item of their programmes in the thirty-nine towns of Bohemia and Moravia that they visited was the *Dumky* Trio, but they also played the violin *Mazurek*, a Rondo written especially for Wihan and some arrangements of Dvořák's music. Some light is shed on the Czech composer's character by two events of that summer. Showing indifference to the accumulation of fresh laurels, he did not bother to travel to Vienna for the first performance in the Austrian capital of his opera *Dimitrij* on June 2nd. Just as characteristically, while his fiftieth birthday was being celebrated in Prague in the previous year he had remained at his beloved Vysoká. On the other hand, two days before the Vienna performance he was deeply affected by the Příbram mining disaster, for he knew personally many of those who worked underground.

[1] Mrs. Thurber wrote on Nov. 20th: 'Will you kindly mail me yr. contract with the alterations you desired—as I should like to have your signature as soon as possible.' Her letters to the composer are in the possession of Dvořák's heirs.

Dvořák was due to arrive in New York when the Columbus Fourth Centennial Celebrations were in progress. The President of the National Conservatory, Mrs. Thurber, had requested him to write a commemorative work, and in her letter of July 10th, 1892, she said: 'As for the Columbus Cantata I do hope you will find it convenient to write something for the 12th October. *The American Flag*, which was sent to Mr. Littleton,[1] would be most appropriate.' It would have suited Dvořák to have had Rodman Drake's poem sooner than this, but to ensure that he had a new work completed in time he made a setting of the *Te Deum*. He began work on the cantata at the beginning of August, but when he was about to depart the work was still only in sketch form. On September 10th he left Prague for America with his wife, their eldest daughter and son, Otilie aged fourteen and Antonín who was five years younger. He also took with him Josef J. Kovařík, an American-Czech violinist who had just completed his studies at the Prague Conservatory, and who was very soon to become a member of Dvořák's staff in New York. They embarked at Bremen on the 17th and landed in New York ten days later.

Besides the formal welcomes that Dvořák was given on his arrival, he was besieged by journalists who wanted to find out all manner of insignificant details about the great composer who was now in their midst. One of the published descriptions of him reads as follows:

> He is not an awesome personality at all. He is much taller than his pictures would imply, and possesses not a tithe of the bulldog ferocity to be encountered in some of them. A man about 5 ft. 10 or 11 inches, of great natural dignity, a man of character, Dvořák impresses me as an original, natural and—as Rossini would say, to be natural is greater than to be original. . . . He is not beautiful in the forms of face, but the lines of his brow are so finely modelled, and there is so much emotional life in the fiery eyes and lined face, that when he lightens up in conversation, his face is not easily forgotten.[2]

Mrs. Thurber knew well how to gain publicity for her enterprise, and she had no difficulty in fanning the flames of controversy later by encouraging Dvořák to air his views on the founding of a national American school of composition, which was one of her loftiest dreams and a powerful reason for inviting the Czech musician to America. Her National Conservatory, however, proved to be different from what Dvořák imagined it to be, for no diplomas were awarded, and fees were only charged to those who could afford to pay them. He was in complete sympathy with Negroes being given free tuition.

[1] Alfred Littleton. His father died in 1888.
[2] Reprinted in *The Musical Standard*, 22. X. 1892.

He settled down in New York, often visited the Central Park, and, finding it far from easy to pursue his hobby of train-spotting, he made, instead, an effort to see all the larger boats leave for Europe, and if possible to board them on sailing days, examine them from stem to stern and chat with the captain and his officers. His thoughts turned homewards very frequently, and sometimes his heart was heavy because he was so far away. On October 9th the New York Czech Circle gave an immense banquet in his honour. The *Te Deum* was not performed three days later as planned, but was included in a concert of the composer's compositions on the 21st. At the end of the following month Dvořák conducted his *Requiem Mass* in Boston. Having completed *The American Flag* early in January, he began work on his ninth symphony, finishing it on May 24th. He had originally intended to return home for the vacation. Edward Rosewater, the Czech-born owner of *The Omaha Bee* (a daily newspaper), invited him to stay with him. But when Kovařík talked to him about Spillville, a little Czech settlement in the north-east corner of Iowa, eleven miles from the nearest railway station, and where his father was schoolmaster, organist and choirmaster, Dvořák made up his mind to spend the summer there among his compatriots, and to arrange for his sister-in-law to bring the four other children to the United States for the holiday period.

The children arrived on May 31st, and three days later they all started on the long journey to Spillville, spending ten hours in Chicago on the way. Dvořák felt at home at once in the peaceful village. On the following morning those who attended the little church of St. Wenceslas for seven o'clock mass, which was celebrated daily without music, were astonished to hear the familiar hymn 'Bože před tvou velebností' (O God before Thy Majesty) played on the organ by their visitor. During the remainder of his stay Dvořák made a point of playing this and other well-known hymns daily at mass, and the congregation joined in enthusiastically. Finding the atmosphere of Spillville so delightful, he was immediately inspired to compose, and within two months produced finished scores of the quartet in F and the string quintet in E flat.

At Spillville his wrath with his publisher melted. By standing up for his own rights, and by refusing to make the first move to heal the breach, he had taught Simrock a lesson. He now offered him almost everything he had and stated his price: the three overtures, 2,000 marks; *Dumky* Trio, 2,000 marks; E minor symphony, 2,000 marks; the 'cello Rondo, the quartet in F and *Silent Woods* for 'cello, 500 marks each. Simrock took all of these works. When Dvořák heard later that Brahms had agreed to do the proof-reading in order to expedite publication, he was deeply touched, and in writing to Simrock on February 5th, 1894, said: 'I can scarcely believe there is another composer in the world who would do as much!'

Early in August Dvořák travelled to Chicago, and on the 12th, which was 'Czech Day' at the World Exhibition, he conducted his G major symphony, three of the second set of *Slavonic Dances* and the overture *My Home*. In the evening he was fêted by the Chicago Circle of Czech Musicians. He again left Spillville on September 1st to pay his promised visit to Rosewater at Omaha, where another banquet was arranged for him. From there he went to St. Paul, Minnesota, to visit Father Rynda, a Moravian, and met many of his countrymen among the 3,000 guests at the banquet with which he was honoured. But possibly his visit to the beautiful Minnehaha Falls on the 5th made the deepest impression. The family finally left Spillville on the 16th, going first to Chicago and then to Buffalo, from where they went to see the Niagara Falls. After he had gazed at the falls for several minutes, Dvořák exclaimed: 'Damn it, that will be a symphony in B minor!'

It was not easy for Dvořák to settle down again in New York after the idyllic life at Spillville, and both he and his daughter suffered from serious attacks of nostalgia. For his hundredth opus he wrote the Sonatina for violin and piano especially for his children, a charming gesture, but he was anticipating a little, for at the time opp. 98 and 99 had not been composed. After this he made a few preliminary sketches for a project that Mrs. Thurber was urging him to undertake, an American opera on the subject of *Hiawatha*, but owing to the delays over procuring a suitable libretto he made hardly any progress.

He became particularly friendly with Anton Seidl, the conductor, with whom he had many stimulating discussions on musical matters. He asked his friend to conduct the first performance of his new symphony, and Seidl did so at the New York Philharmonic Society's concert at the Carnegie Hall on December 16th, 1893, preceded by a public rehearsal a day earlier. As this was the first work Dvořák had written on American soil, and it represented the beginning of a new stage in his development, one in which he made some use of 'American' features, and as the *première* was one of the most outstanding triumphs of his life, it was, as the Americans themselves appreciated, an event of historic importance. Shortly afterwards the other two works were performed, the string quartet in Boston on January 1st and the string quintet in New York a few days later. Dvořák composed the *Biblical Songs* in March, and then set about revising *Dimitrij*.

In the previous November he was faced with the need to come to a decision about the possible renewal of his contract with Mrs. Thurber for another one or two years. There were considerable financial advantages in remaining, as he pointed out on November 16th in a letter to the Director of the Prague Conservatory, Dr. Josef Tragy, who was allowing him leave of absence, but he wished to be guided by his chief's advice. He was extremely reluctant to tie his hands irretrievably, and Mrs. Thurber was obliged to wait several months for his answer. But she herself may be held indirectly responsible for the delay. As her letters to the composer show, Dvořák was receiving his salary rather irregularly.[1] Undoubtedly one of his main reasons for refusing to commit himself was that he had a deep longing to be back in Bohemia once again, but he gave other reasons to Mrs. Thurber.[2] At last he decided to return to the United States for a six-month period, November 1st to April 30th, and signed the contract on April 28th, 1894.[3] On the same date Mrs. Thurber gave him a promissory note in the following terms: 'It is hereby understood and agreed that unless you received the $7,500 due you, on your salary of the present scholastic year, on or before October 6th, 1894, the contract for further services as Director of the National Conservatory of Music dated April 28th, 1894, may be annulled at your pleasure.'

As the time approached for Dvořák's return to New York he became somewhat anxious as to whether Mrs. Thurber would fulfil her promise, and a series of cables passed between them. On September 8th she assured him that she would send him the steamer tickets and the balance of salary by the appointed date, but a month later half the arrears of his stipend was still owing.[4] Dvořák's displeasure is shown by the cable he sent on October 12th: 'May be cannot come without receiving all.' However, he was prepared to accept this rather unsatisfactory state of affairs, and on the 16th he departed for New York, taking with him his wife and their second son Otakar, who was nine years old at the time. They sailed in S.S. Bismark from Hamburg on the 18th, and on November 1st he resumed his duties at the National Conservatory.

[1] On March 17th, 1894, she wrote to him as follows: 'You doubtless know that owing to the hard times everyone has had more or less difficulty to meet their obligations. This explains the delay in the prompt payment of your salary this season. I can give you a note payable October 15th for $7,500—with interest at six per cent— the balance due you I will try to give you before sailing. I will be able to give you some money next week.' And on April 21st: 'I think your answer is rather unkind. We will not discuss the contract until the settlement is made— $3,750.'

[2] In a letter to Mrs. Thurber dated 5. IV. 1894 he said: 't[h]ough I personally care very little for worldly things, I cannot see my wife and children in trouble', and he even threatened to 'publish my situation to the world' if he was not given his salary according to the terms of his contract. We can detect the hand of his wife in this, but it is almost inconceivable that Dvořák would ever have carried out such a threat.

[3] Šourek was under the impression that he returned to Europe without having signed this second contract, but this is not so. The date of signing has been established by Dr. Robert Aborn, who has found the contract, and to whom I am indebted for this information.

[4] Her message of October 9th reads: 'Cabled 3,750 dollars pay other half on arrival.' The letters and cables from which the above quotations have been taken are in the possession of Dvořák's heirs, who have kindly given me permission to use them. This correspondence is published more fully in my article 'Neznámé dopisy Antonína Dvořáka' in *Hudební rozhledy* XVIII, 4, Prague 1965.

During his second stay in America Dvořák was less happy than before. He remained in New York, and consequently there were no experiences to match those he had had in the two previous years. He missed his family and his friends, and his thoughts often travelled back to his homeland and especially to Vysoká. Almost as soon as he arrived he was made an honorary member of the New York Philharmonic Society, and in February he was similarly honoured by the Gesellschaft der Musikfreunde of Vienna. In the superb 'cello concerto that he wrote during the winter months there is scarcely a trace of 'Americanism', which suggests that although he still believed that American folk music should serve as the basis of American national music,[1] personally he wished to compose music that was wholly Czech.

Dvořák had little thought of continuing in his New York post after the end of his third year, but the ever-optimistic Mrs. Thurber booked passages for him, his wife and four daughters for October 17th, presumably because he had not given a clear-cut refusal to Miss Adele Margulies, who was negotiating on Mrs. Thurber's behalf.[2] In September 1896 Mrs. Thurber tried again to entice him to America, and in December, without sufficient justification, the *Wiener Tageblatt* published the news that he was returning. He toyed with the idea of going for two months. In 1897, in May or possibly April, he received from her a draft copy of a contract for an engagement from April 1st to June 1st in the following year, but he did not complete this. In his subsequent negotiations with Miss Margulies he was prepared to bind himself to very little, and in his last letter to her (20. VIII. 1897) he said in exasperation: 'It is enough to drive one to despair the way you want to drag me in! I have already told you that you may announce my name, but I do not want to be under any obligations to the public and Mrs. Thurber as a result!' After that we hear no more of the matter.

It was a wonderful relief to Dvořák to be home again. He spent the first few months resting, meeting Hanslick and Simrock at Karlovy Vary (Carlsbad), visiting Judge Rus at Písek and other friends besides, revisiting the Bohemian Forest, and enjoying a quiet life at Vysoká with his family and his pigeons. He wrote nothing new. Only after resuming his work at the Prague Conservatory in November did he begin composing again, first the G major quartet, and then the quartet in A flat on which he had made a start before leaving America. In December he went to Vienna where he saw Brahms and Richter. He returned there two months later for the latter's performance of his ninth symphony, and yet again at the end of March

[1] A comprehensive exposition of his views appeared in his article 'Music in America', published in *Harper's Magazine*, 1895.
[2] Letter from Mrs. Thurber to Dvořák, 18. VII. 95.

to conduct *The Spectre's Bride* at the Ljubljana Choral Society's charity concert.

A few days earlier he had been to London, for the last time, to conduct the world *première* of the 'cello concerto, but he now found London had fewer attractions for him than before. He complained of the atrocious March wind and the interminable rain, and he could not get any food or coffee to his liking until he was invited to Novello's.[1] He is reported as having said: 'A good meat soup is the foundation (of a meal) like the basses in the orchestra, and I could never get a good foundation of soup in England.'[2] His main consolation was that both the public and the critics thought very highly of his new work.

On the last of the above-mentioned visits to Vienna he went with the Bohemian Quartet to visit Bruckner, who was already a sick man, and also to see Brahms. Brahms tried hard to persuade him to move to Vienna, and to become a professor of composition at the Conservatory, doubtless in the hope of counterbalancing the influence of Bruckner. Since Dvořák would have found it too expensive to live with his family in the Austrian capital, Brahms magnanimously offered to put his personal fortune at the disposal of the Czech musician. But Dvořák, deeply moved, loved his country too much to accept. It was on this same occasion, as Suk has related in his memoirs, that Brahms, in referring to Schopenhauer, talked of his own agnosticism. This may not have been the first time that Dvořák had heard his friend express such views, but he left his flat in shocked silence. When at last he spoke, he said: 'Such a man, such a fine soul—and he believes in nothing, he believes in nothing!'

At the beginning of 1896, in his fifty-fifth year, Dvořák began the composition of a series of symphonic poems, a type of work that was quite new to him. By the end of April he had completed *The Water Goblin*, *The Noon Witch* and *The Golden Spinning Wheel*. *The Wild Dove* followed several months later during the period in which the first three works were being heard in public for the first time, under the direction of Henry J. Wood and Richter in London. The fifth work, *Heroic Song*, was not composed until the second half of 1897. These works represent the penultimate stage in the Czech master's development, and to some extent paved the way for the final phase, in which he was wholly immersed in opera composition. Even before he began work on *Heroic Song* he was dealing with operatic problems, for he had begun a thorough revision of *The Jacobin*. The two string quartets that he wrote late in 1895 were in fact the last of his compositions to stem from classical forms as examples of absolute music.

[1] Letter to J. Geisler, 18. III. 1896. He had evening meals presumably with Alfred Littleton.

[2] Ludmila Wechte, *Culture Forum*, VI, 38. New York, 1923.

Just as he was starting to compose *The Wild Dove* Dvořák asked Simrock for news of Brahms, for he had heard that he was seriously ill. He talked of going to visit him, but hesitated to do so. At last he went during March 1897, and some three weeks later he returned for the sad occasion of the funeral of the man who had been such a wonderful friend to him, and to whom he owed so much. A few months later he lost another friend when Karel Bendl died. Several weeks after this he heard that he had been appointed to succeed Brahms on the jury that recommended Austrian State Prize awards.

A programme of the Czech composer's compositions was conducted by Mengelberg at Amsterdam on February 13th in the following year. The Bohemian Quartet happened to be in Holland at the time, and reported to Dvořák that the entire concert was an outstanding success. Dvořák's pupils were already gaining recognition at home and abroad, Josef Suk and Vítězslav Novák as composers, and Oskar Nedbal, viola player of the Bohemian Quartet, as a conductor. Suk, who lived with the Dvořáks, had fallen in love with Otilie Dvořáková. November 17th, 1898, was a particularly happy day, for the two young people's wedding was arranged to coincide with the silver wedding of the bride's parents. Eight days later the Emperor Franz Josef bestowed a great honour on Dvořák, when he gave him the Medal of Honour for *litteris et artibus*, a distinction that had only previously been granted to Brahms. The Czech master was delighted with the 'great golden platter', as he called it, that he was expected to wear suspended from his neck.

A few months earlier the composer had found an opera libretto that suited him admirably, a Czech fairy tale that had pronounced comic aspects. In this new work, *Kate and the Devil*, he made a severely limited yet significant use of Wagnerian methods, which he had shunned for many years, except on a limited scale when revising scenes in his two previous operas. By now he had good reason to believe that he could succeed along these lines, and he was convinced that it was the right path for him to follow. In his next two works for the stage he went even further in the same direction. Apart from one significant break in his work, a journey to Vienna for the sake of attending Mahler's performance of his *Heroic Song*, progress on the opera proceeded smoothly, and by February 1899 he had completed it. Nine months later he witnessed a very successful performance of the work at the Prague National Theatre.

Dvořák now had no thought for any other type of work, and having finished his opera he immediately began to look for another libretto. During this interval he went to Berlin to hear *Heroic Song* under the direction of Nikisch, and a month later he was on his way to Budapest. He was the pianist in a concert of his own chamber compositions in the Hungarian capital on

December 19th, and on the day following he conducted there *Carnival* over-ture, *Heroic Song*, and his 'cello concerto, with Wihan as soloist, at a concert of the Philharmonic Society. Soon after this his disciple Nedbal was having such success conducting his *New World* symphony at the World's Fair in Paris, at St. Petersburg, Berlin and elsewhere, that it was becoming unneces-sary for the composer to present his own works. When Dvořák was given the opportunity to conduct the Czech Philharmonic Orchestra on April 4th, 1900, he chose to perform the *Tragic* overture of Brahms, Schubert's *Unfinished* symphony, Beethoven's seventh symphony and his own *Wild Dove*.

Within a short time Dvořák had begun the composition of *Rusalka*, another fairy tale opera, but a tragic one this time. It was finished before the end of November, in time for it to be put into production that season. The first performance, which took place on March 31st, 1901, achieved the kind of result he had been working towards for years, for it was the greatest triumph he had ever had with a work for the stage. At last he had written an opera that was accepted by his countrymen as a great national work of art that could take its place beside the best-loved operas of Smetana.

Further honours came the way of the venerable Czech master. He was made a member of the Austrian House of Peers, but he only once availed himself of his privilege by attending a debate. In July 1901 he became the nominal head of the Prague Conservatory. He absented himself from the festivities arranged to celebrate his sixtieth birthday, paying Mahler a visit at that time in order to give him the score of *Rusalka* in preparation for a possible production in Vienna. However, he was unable to avoid seeing and hearing the torchlight procession and serenade in the street below his flat, which took place early in November when the cycle of his operas at the National Theatre was at an end. Although he could not bear all this fuss, he was touched by his admirers' fervent shouts of 'Long Live Dvořák!' He discovered that he had been tricked into being present at the morning National Theatre meeting and the evening Artistic Circle concert and banquet arranged to honour him on November 10th, but expressed the opinion that he would in all probability survive them. Little more than a month later Otilie presented him with a grandson.

Having at last secured a libretto on the subject of *Armida* from the distin-guished poet Vrchlický, after an interval of fifteen months and for the last time Dvořák turned to the composition of a major work. His opera was com-pleted towards the end of August 1903, and preparations for its production were put in hand almost immediately. This time the composer met with misfortune, for the rehearsals did not go at all smoothly, and he was dissatis-fied. He attended the first performance on March 25th. It must have been quite clear to him that the production was a failure, but he was obliged to leave early because of a pain in his side.

This was the first clear sign of Dvořák's final illness. Five days later, however, he was well enough to go out. He went to the Franz Josef station to look at the trains, but unluckily caught a chill. By April 5th his condition was serious enough for his doctor, Professor Hnátek, to call in a colleague for a second opinion, and a fortnight later the composer's condition had deteriorated considerably. It seems clear that he was suffering from generalized arterial degeneration with some involvement of the kidneys, but if there were any subsidiary contributory causes for his serious physical condition these did not emerge with any clarity at the time.[1] On May Day, a traditionally festive day, Dvořák was feeling decidedly better, so that his doctor permitted him to join the family for lunch, He enjoyed his soup, sitting in his customary place at the head of the table, but almost immediately after that he felt ill again, and had to be helped back to bed. Before the doctor arrived he had expired.

The funeral service took place on May 5th at the church of St. Salvator. While the Introit of Dvořák's *Requiem* was being performed from the colonnade at the top of the steps of the National Theatre the cortege paused, and then it proceeded on its way to the Vyšehrad burial ground, the historic and legendary site high above the Vltava where many famous Czechs of modern times are laid to rest. Zdeněk Knittl, the administrative head of the Conservatory, pronounced the funeral oration. At the memorial service held two days later at the Týn church, Mozart's *Requiem* was sung. Warm tributes to the memory of the great and much loved Czech musician poured in from his friends and admirers in many parts of the world.

---

[1] In the light of the evidence we have it does not appear to be certain that Dvořák was suffering from uraemia. Otakar Dvořák attributed his father's deterioration on April 18th to an attack of influenza, but it is possible there may have been some other cause. I offer this explanation after seeking the advice of an eminent authority on vascular disease.

II

Methods of Work and Features of Style

Let us consider briefly some of the impressions that Dvořák's music makes on us. He never seemed to be at a loss for an idea, or how to use the ideas that occurred to him, in fact sometimes as one beautiful idea led to another he found it difficult or even impossible to part company with them and bring them to a timely close. We can see this in the Adagio of the 'cello concerto. He had a rich store of melody, and colourful and effective scoring seemed to come naturally to him. Having in addition the priceless gifts of vital rhythm and rhythmic propulsion he could do much more than sustain the interest with ease throughout a generously proportioned movement: he could infect an audience with a feeling of exhilaration and carry them along with him willy-nilly. Hely-Hutchinson pointed out[1] that Dvořák, by means of his supremely self-confident inspiration, could in fact successfully achieve what was thought to be impossible. He cites the dramatically illogical repetition of the words:

> *And all that heard them said, in fear,*
> *There is a spectre somewhere near.*

in *The Spectre's Bride*, where they are spread over more than sixty bars, and states that this absurdity does not matter because the magic of the music holds the audience.

The impression we get is similar to that given by Schubert, that his inspiration flowed spontaneously and that he could pour out music as Boccherini is supposed to have done, simply by turning a tap. Hely-Hutchinson summed up this viewpoint aphoristically when he stated: 'Dvořák was a musician first, last and all the time; and at his best he neither thought, nor reasoned, nor wondered, but *knew*.' Even though Stanford couched his phrases in decidedly derogatory tones when he said that Dvořák was 'a child of nature, who did not stop to think, and said on paper anything which came into his head',[2] the general assumption is the

---

[1] 'Dvořák the Craftsman', *Music and Letters*, XXII, 4 (1941).
[2] *Pages from an Unwritten Diary.*

same, that Dvořák did not need to think because his 'inspiration' took control.

For many years this quite widely held opinion went unchallenged, and only recently has an attempt been made to test its validity. Now that this has been done it is clear that the belief was unfounded, and that it has been arrived at intuitively simply because on the evidence of Dvořák's music it appeared to be true. None of those who subscribed to it took the trouble to investigate the matter for themselves, and all were deceived by the naturalness and fluency of Dvořák's style. Nevertheless it says a great deal for Dvořák's genius that he could make his music sound so spontaneous even when he was obliged to struggle with his material.

Dvořák was not an exceptionally fast worker, and we find that his later compositions occupied him for longer periods than his earlier ones. The D minor symphony and the 'cello concerto each took a little more than thirteen weeks to write, compared with five and a half for the F major symphony and as long as four and a half months for the *New World* symphony. He took a minimum of six months over a cantata or an opera, and between nine and a half and seventeen months in four instances. He expected to take anything from a month to six weeks over a chamber composition, and it was quite exceptional for him to complete a late work like the F major quartet by the sixteenth day. Since his wife found that discarded sheets of manuscript paper made convenient fuel on her baking days, many of Dvořák's sketches must have been destroyed in that manner, but fortunately a number of them have survived. Some of these merely consist of brief jottings on odd scraps of manuscript paper. But almost all those of the American period are in books which include many themes, some in a very unpolished state, which he wrote down just as they occurred to him, and also, in abbreviated form, complete drafts of several entire works.

We have little difficulty in recognizing what is in all probability the earliest form of the main theme of the *New World* symphony's finale, even though the time signature, rhythm and phrase structure differ from the familiar version:

Ex. 1.

Allo moderato

As it happens, it took Dvořák very little time to get extremely close to the theme as it appears in the symphony, for on the same page it is shown in common time, identical in every way except for a syncopated crotchet, minim, crotchet rhythm in the second bar. He got a little closer still when drafting the Finale, but then decided to subdivide the bars and change the time signature to $\frac{2}{4}$, and in this version we find he hits upon the exact rhythm of the final version at this point, although a triplet appears just before the end of the phrase.

A much cruder undated sketch exists showing presumably the first draft, or at least a very early one, of the opening bars of the Scherzo of the A flat quartet. This differs so greatly from the ultimate version that it is probable that there may have been intermediate sketches made between this and the sketch for the complete movement that bears the date December 19th, 1895, which in its main essentials hardly differs at all from the definitive version. The first bars of the early draft, and the equivalent part of the published version are shown in Exx. 2a and 2b. The early sketch was doubtless intended for a scherzo, but this could not have been a *furiant*. The rhythm is unimaginative, and bars 5–8 not only mark time but appear to be a recollection of the equivalent bars in the Scherzo of the F major quartet,[1] which was a good enough reason for rejecting them.

We can easily imagine that ideas frequently occurred to Dvořák in a rough and ready state like this, and that he wrote them down at once without thought. Alternatively he may have had an elusive idea at the back of his mind, and what he first wrote represented a quite inadequate attempt to crystallize this thought. Sometimes, on the other hand, he deliberately avoided attempting to work out a satisfactory rhythmic pattern in his desire to write down as speedily as possible a very rough approximation of the thought that occurred to him, an approximation that would serve adequately as a reminder. We must appreciate that at this early stage he did not attempt to record any accompaniment or counter-melody that might serve to enliven his theme. Yet it is not wholly unthinkable that he might have considered writing a monotonous rhythm for several consecutive bars, for he had done this in the Scherzo of the E flat quintet, although it would perhaps have been unwise to have repeated this a second time. Whatever the true explanation may be for the inadequacy of this and other early drafts of his, we need not suppose that Dvořák was under the slightest illusion that what he committed to paper was already suitable for use. He would have realized the need to work on it and improve it out of all recognition until he reached the point when he was satisfied with it.

At other times Dvořák was unsure what was the most suitable time signature. Having made a sketch for the greater part of the double theme which, with only slight modifications, he used six months later for the variations of his E flat quintet, he then experimented with the second part

[1] In the first sketch of the quartet theme the resemblance is much closer: the time is quadruple, not triple, and the note D does not occur.

Ex. 2a.

Ex. 2b.

of it, transforming it from a presumably rather slow triple time to an *Allegro* in duple time and completing it in the new metre. Later it was unnecessary to do very much more than decide on a suitable key, convert it back to triple time and reduce the speed, for his first thoughts were better.

Nelahozeves, Dvořák's birthplace, from the north, showing the castle of the Lobkovitz
family, the church and the R. Vltava. Engraved by A. Lewy in the 1870s

Česká Kamenice (c. 1840), where Dvořák was sent in 1856 to improve his knowledge
of German

The Organ School, Prague, in the 1870s. Dvořák studied there from 1857–59

Programm
zur grossen Musikaufführung
unter persönlicher Leitung
von
Richard Wagner.
8. Februar 1863.

1. Eine Faustouverture.
2. a) Versammlung der Meistersingerzunft. (für Orchester allein) neu.
   b) Pogners Anrede an die Versammlung, gesungen von Herrn *Rokitanský*, neu.
3. Vorspiel zu den „Meistersingern", neu.
4. Vorspiel zu „Tristan und Isolde".
5. Siegmunds Liebesgesang, (gesungen von Herrn *Bernard*) neu.
6. Ouverture zu „Tannhäuser".

Sämmtliche Compositionen von Richard Wagner.

Die Herren *Rokitanský* und *Bernard* haben aus besonderer Ge-
fälligkeit die obgenannten Parthien übernommen.

Program
k velké hudební produkci
osobním řízením
Richarda Wagnera.
8. února 1863.

1. Ouvertura k Faustu.
2. a) Shromáždění cechu mistrných pěvců, (pro orchestr samý) nové.
   b) Pognerovo osloveni shromáždění, nové, zpívá pan *Rokitanský.*
3. Předehra k „mistrným pěvcům," nová.
4. Předehra k „Tristanu a Isoldě."
5. Milostný zpěv Siegmunda, zpívá pan *Bernard*, nový.
6. Ouvertura k „Tannhäuseru."

Veškrá skladby Richarda Wagnera.

Pánové *Rokitanský* a *Bernard* převzali z obzvláštní ochoty
nadzmíněné úlohy.

Programme of the Wagner concert in Prague in which Dvořák played under the German composer's baton

The Trio theme of the same work is shown in ⁶⁄₈ time in two preliminary sketches, one in B flat minor and the other in B minor, the former being marked 'Largo'. Internal evidence strongly suggests that the one in B minor is the later sketch even though it appears first in the book. In each case the second phrase ends rather stolidly on dominant harmony in the relative major, instead of glancing back towards the tonic. The germ of this theme, however, seems to have been jotted down in the sketch book three pages earlier, where it appears in very rudimentary form in D flat major and ²⁄₄ time, with the indication that it was intended for the Trio of a quartet. In the published work this theme is in B minor and ¢ time.

On the page immediately before the continuous sketch for the Sonatina for violin and piano is seen a suggested melody for an Andante movement of a piano sonata, but which in fact became the continuation of the opening melody of the Sonatina's second movement. Here again a transformation of rhythm took place, and Dvořák found it necessary to make numerous other improvements, but despite this the preliminary sketch foreshadows most of the main features of the Sonatina theme. The intermediate versions are not shown here, but only the first, if this really was the first, and the last (Exx. 3a and 3b).

Ex. 3a.
Andante

* These notes were originally reversed

In many respects the earlier form already makes a satisfactory, unified and well-balanced melody, but it was conceived as a beginning rather than as a continuation, and being wise after the event we miss the expansion and extension of the second part. The second cadence is obviously too angular, and the end, which is very similar to that of 'Onaway! awake, beloved!'[1] is

[1] See p. 282. The key is also the same, and D flats are a prominent feature in each case.

Ex. 3b.

reached rather too hastily. Dvořák may have decided to make the beginnings of the phrases correspond exactly partly because the Sonatina was a simple work written expressly for his children.

Professor Sychra has done an extremely valuable service in drawing attention to the slow crystallization of the main theme of the Finale of the G major symphony. This is the classic instance of Dvořák having no conception at first of what kind of a theme he wanted, and having to take a considerable amount of trouble before he arrived at anything bearing a strong resemblance to the melody as we know it in its final form. Nothing could be further from the truth in this case than the statement that the finished product came to him freely and spontaneously. It is extremely doubtful if anyone would have recognized Dvořák's first sketch (ex. 4) as having any connection with the movement in question if the sheets had not borne the inscription 'Finale—Thema—Simfonie' and if this sketch had not appeared together with five other short sketches, some of which approach a little closer to the melody he eventually used. No key signature is shown, but two of the jottings are labelled 'G dur'. It is true that notes 4–7 of this first theme are not far removed from the notes in the third bar of the final version, and also that the descending sequence is foreshadowed, but the choice of intervals and more especially the repetitions of pairs of notes give it quite a different character:

Ex. 4.

into E minor

In the second sketch for this theme Dvořák established the two detached notes that occur at the outset, but in this and subsequent drafts these do not ascend through notes of the tonic triad, but dwell on the fifth note of the scale, an emphasis that was brought out far more strongly later by the introductory trumpet passage. Whereas the first version moved towards E minor, the second, fifth, seventh and eighth closed after a few bars on the tonic, and the sixth, ninth and tenth (i.e. the last) left the phrase open by moving to the dominant. In most of them there are descending sequences, but in the fifth the sequences rise. For some time Dvořák persisted in making his third note less than a bar in length, but at the seventh attempt he made it a minim tied over the bar-line, and substituted a C natural for the C sharp. This is the turning-point of his efforts, for from then on he began to realize what he had been seeking. The second, sixth, seventh and final versions of the theme are shown below:

Ex. 5a.

Ex. 5b.

Ex. 5c.

Ex. 5d.

There is good reason for wondering just how often Dvořák had as much difficulty in formulating a theme as we have seen here. Although numerous sketches that survive throw fascinating light on his methods of work, many have been irretrievably lost. Consequently it is impossible to be sure, even in the best documented cases, that we have all the evidence before us, and in other cases we know that much is missing. Besides the Czech composer doubtless did some of his sketching in his head.

By the time that he had become fairly confident as to how a melodic theme ought to begin, it was still quite likely that, as he continued it, commonplace features would creep in which would have to be eliminated later, or, alternatively, he might take a wrong turning and so be obliged to retrace his steps and start again. When he was sketching the 'cello concerto he was able to give the second subject much of the beauty that it has in its definitive form, but with certain notable exceptions. Since he did not think of the charming idea of repeating bars 11–12, he failed to avoid a succession of four-bar phrases. In the eighth bar of the horn melody he quickly eliminated his undistinguished first thought and substituted the telling octave rise, but he ended his fourth phrase rather stiffly. He still had no thought of approaching F sharps romantically by way of E sharps, and, unwisely, he made his first, second, and fourth phrases begin not only with a rising sixth but with the same two identical bars. Apparently he did not hesitate for a moment over the decision to short circuit the recapitulation, for the sketch shows unequivocally the development leading directly into the second subject in B major.

Dvořák was rather more hesitant over the concerto's slow movement. It is not easy to decide what was the exact sequence of his train of thought, but certain points are clear. Instead of beginning with the expected four-bar phrase, he prolonged this with an additional bar, and at the end of the second phrase closed in B minor instead of evading the modulation. Between the entry of the soloist and the new clarinet theme (bar 15 in the published score) an additional phrase appears that he later considered to be redundant. After the equivalent of bar 28 there are eight bars crossed out followed by some alternative bars that are no nearer to the final version. A photograph of this page of the sketch is shown opposite page 129.

Having reached the point where the stormy G minor section was due to begin Dvořák turned aside to improve the end of the first movement, and then began the slow movement once again, starting this time with a four-bar phrase. The second phrase is still very unlike his final thoughts, but by touching B minor only momentarily there are signs of progress. On the other hand he wrote a curiously ornate ninth bar, and provided an almost wholly diatonic continuation to the clarinet melody, instead of the vague but wonderfully imaginative chromatic passage that appears in the previous draft (bars 22–28). He ultimately decided that in both these cases his earlier thoughts were better.

In the F major string quartet there is another instance of reversion to original intentions, and this again indicates that ideas that came to Dvořák spontaneously, however valuable or inspired, nevertheless needed to be considered critically in case an alternative solution could be found that he considered to be an improvement. When sketching the first movement he wrote the earlier part of the second subject in A minor and the later part in A major, in which key he continued for sixteen bars. He then thought it would be preferable to have the whole of this section in the minor key, and so indicated the change without working out all the details. However, when preparing the score, he reinstated his original key plan, possibly without making a fresh sketch, even though his first draft is no more than an artist's cartoon, and merely blocks in the rough trend of the music without any attempt being made to give it rhythmic animation.

Sometimes Dvořák sketched a whole movement or even an entire work before beginning to write it out in score. At other times the work of sketching and scoring went on simultaneously, as in the case of the *New World* symphony, the score of which was begun a month after the sketch and was completed twelve days after the latter was finished. Dvořák's continuous sketches are written on a single stave, or sometimes on a pair, and, as the facsimile shows, give occasional hints of possible instrumentation and some indications of intended harmonies and keys. Deletions and substitutions are common. It is most exceptional to find vacillations and alterations occurring with the same frequency in the later stages of composition, although this is certainly the case in *The Jacobin*, and in the manuscript score of the F minor trio the changes were so extensive and far-reaching that it became necessary for the composer to prepare another score, in which he incorporated a number of fresh modifications.

His first requirement was a theme, and if, as in the Scherzo of the F minor trio, he could not decide on a satisfactory form for this he was handicapped at the start. Having found a theme it seems probable that he allowed this to grow naturally and to suggest other ideas. He would continue until he noticed that he had made a false move, perhaps several bars previously, one which obliged him to stop and to try to remedy the mistake. He was rather inclined to introduce new themes too soon and sometimes too abruptly, so that it became necessary for him to expand his earlier ideas substantially and provide more satisfactory transitions, work which could not necessarily be completed successfully at the first attempt. It is curious to find that he contemplated including a Dolce G major theme in the Scherzo section of his D minor symphony, where it would have very seriously impaired the impetus of this splendid movement, but fortunately he soon realized his error. It reappeared as the theme of the movement's Trio.

Transitions and developments were liable to give trouble and to require redrafting. As the sketches for the Finale of the same symphony show very clearly, Dvořák found it extremely difficult to avoid being bogged down in the development section. He was obliged to discard his first attempt and turn temporarily to another matter, and when he made a second draft, he was, in many respects, still unable to approach closely to his final version. In the sketch of the slow movement the recapitulation takes place as expected in the tonic key, F major, but in the first and second versions of the full score of this movement it occurs in A major instead, the first ten bars of the main subject being omitted in the second of these. Possibly it was after the first performance that the composer made a great improvement, when revising this movement once again. This time he retained the eleven-bar pedal on E that prepares the ear for A major, but transposed the shortened recapitulation back to the original key, thus catching us completely off guard.

Ten of the themes of the *New World* symphony, together with more than a dozen other themes, appear in the earliest of the American sketch books, on the pages immediately before the continuous sketch of the symphony begins. The only important one missing is the main theme of the Finale, but this is found in another book. In several cases Dvořák tried to complete the whole of the paragraphs in which the themes might appear, in fact he did so with the themes that later headed the first three movements of the symphony, as well as with some others for which he never found a use. That all these themes were for the most part written down haphazardly, without any clear purpose in view, may be seen by the odd assortment of keys and the miscellany of styles. Yet in certain cases he must have known what their subsequent purpose might be. The theme he first thought of as a march was immediately transformed into a minuet, and then was not used in either form, but the one he visualized as appropriate for the Rondo finale of a piano concerto was given a similar function as a subsidiary idea in the last movement of his symphony.

The original draft of the main theme of the first movement does not appear until the eighth page. Little attempt was made to avoid stiffness in the rhythm, and the first bars are marked for violins, not for the horn. The *tutti* is not pressed home, but most important of all, the key is F major, not E minor. Nevertheless the whole passage already foreshadows almost all the more important features of the first thirty-nine bars of the Allegro molto, including the arrival of the first *tutti* a bar earlier than would normally have been expected (Ex. 6). In the continuous sketch for this movement most of the discrepancies were cleared away, but the *tutti* bars gave Dvořák some trouble.

36

Ex. 6.

In this movement, which may be taken to be reasonably typical of his compositional methods and of the types of problem that were likely to arise, he was unable to decide how to approach his second subject, and so passed on leaving almost thirty bars unaccounted for. He was able to get the proportions of his second subject approximately right at the first attempt, but having reached the double bar he rejected two dozen or more bars leading up to the flute melody. Subsequently he decided to jettison the remaining bars and the whole of his development, more than two pages of sketch and well over a hundred bars of music.

Reference will be made in the chapter on the symphonies to the strong element of chance that determined that the key of the *New World* symphony's Largo would be in D flat major, instead of C major, and that the succession of chords heard in the opening bars would effect a transition from the key of the first movement to D flat.[1] It remains to add a few details. On the second page of the sketch book appear the first draft of the complete melody for cor anglais and violins in D flat major, a rudimentary version of

---

[1] See pp. 90-91. For fuller discussion of the sketches of the *New World* and D minor symphonies and the F minor trio, see *Musical Quarterly*, LXIV, 2, *Music and Letters*, XLII, 2 and *Musica*, XIII, 10 respectively.

the beginning of the subsidiary theme in C sharp minor, some comments on how the movement would continue, and finally the somewhat cryptic notation that is shown here, labelled 'záverek' (conclusion) and with the words 'zvětšené trojzvuky' (augmented triads) written underneath:

Ex. 7.

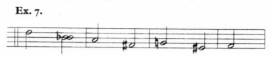

If we assume that this was intended for the final bars of the slow movement in D flat major, a key signature of five flats may be inferred. The double note was probably unintentional and may be ignored. The last note would in all probability have been a note of the chord of D flat, completing a four-bar phrase, in fact either an F (treble clef) of A flat (bass clef). If it were the latter it could hardly have been the lowest part, and it is unlikely to have been an inner part. Consequently, the sharp against the penultimate note would appear to be incorrect and to have been intended as a natural. If there is justification for these assumptions, then the following harmonizations may be considered to be two possible solutions to the problem:

Ex. 8a.

Ex. 8b.

The chord progression is seen taking shape four pages later in the sketch book, in G minor, a key closely related to B flat, which may have been the key of ex. 7. The passage includes only one augmented triad, and does not resemble the final version at all closely:

Ex. 9.

38

Just before the end of the sketch of the slow movement, and marked 'Tromboni' and '*pp*', we find in single notes the exact melodic shape of the chord passage as it appears in the printed score, but it was an afterthought of Dvořák's to include it at the beginning of the movement and again at bar 22. Furthermore the sketch shows that although the composer intended to have a brief dramatic trombone entry before the return of the cor anglais melody, it was again an afterthought to introduce the main theme of the first movement at this point.

Quite often certain national characteristics are seen rather more conspicuously in Dvořák's sketches than in his completed compositions. They came instinctively to him, but when shaping and polishing his work the composer-craftsman found that some of these features would not fit well into his scheme, and that he could improve upon others. Despite this numerous national characteristics remain. He realized that Moravian modulations, which in normal circumstances modulate from a minor key to the major key a tone lower, were useful occasionally in songs, duets and short instrumental pieces, but much less suitable for inclusion in symphonic works. In the earliest sketches the G minor theme in the *New World* symphony's first movement modulates to F major in the fourth bar, but this was soon changed. It must be unique, however, for a theme that lacked a Moravian modulation in the first two sketches to be given one as soon as it was thought of as part of a symphonic movement, as we notice with this theme from the Finale of the same work:[1]

Ex. 10.

The supporting harmony clearly shows this to be a modulation from E minor (Aeolian mode) to D major.

A survey of Dvořák's music seems to show that one modulation took precedence over all other modulations to keys that are not closely related to the key just quitted. This modulation can be traced back to the *Cypresses* song cycle of 1865, and it appeared after that during every important stage in the Czech composer's career. Basically the modulation leads from a major

[1] An example of this modulation is seen in the Moravian folk-song quoted as Ex. 7 (b) on p. 141. It is found in Dvořák's music in op. 20, no. 3; op 32, no. 5; op. 46, no. 7; op. 59, no. 10; op. 72, no. 4; op. 77/II and op. 85, no. 11.

key to another major key a minor third higher, but variations on this lead through a similar interval from a major to a minor key, from one minor key to another, and also from a minor key to its relative major. Although the last-mentioned modulation has less intrinsic interest for us, it was occasionally linked in Dvořák's mind with the other modulations, as may be seen from the modulatory series G minor—B flat major—C sharp minor—E major that he thought of including in the first movement of the D minor symphony, before he discarded his sketch for twenty-six bars of coda in which it appears.

The minor-relative major relationship offered a simple means of effecting the modulation, for by changing the mode of the original key from major to minor the modulation became a routine matter. This method is used to modulate from B flat to D flat and E and from A flat through B to D in the first movement of the B flat trio, op. 21, and to reach the second subject in the G major quartet.[1] It was quite normal for Dvořák to complete the modulation from one major key to another in three chords. If for instance he wished to go from C to E flat he would merely interpose a chord of B flat major between the two tonics. An alternative method that he favoured was simply to leap from one key to the other without preparation of any kind. An excellent example of this is seen in the Scherzo of the string quintet in E flat, where he changes abruptly from B major to D major just as he is about to present new material. Elsewhere in Dvořák's music the change of key is utilized for sequential repetitions, as in the Finale of the D minor Serenade (bars 227–243), or partial repetitions, as in the Finale of the piano concerto (bars 103–126), the first bars of which are quoted below as ex. 14. At the beginning of *The American Flag* eight bars that modulate from F minor to A flat major are immediately repeated at the higher pitch, giving a further tonal shift from A flat minor to C flat major. In order to secure an intensification of emotion in choral works Dvořák sometimes favoured the sequential method on a bigger scale, as we see in the Hostias of the *Requiem*, and again in the third number of *The Spectre's Bride*, where a score of bars are repeated a minor third higher.

In view of Dvořák's fondness for this key relationship[2] it is not surprising to find that the Scherzo and trio of the F major symphony are in the keys of B flat and D flat. However, he avoided using the flattened mediant for second subjects of movements in major keys, except rather briefly in the C major and G major quartets. Several of his second subjects are in the mediant and

[1] The same method is used in the slow movement of the 'cello concerto in bars 50–57, and in the first movement of the piano quintet in bars 221–235.

[2] It is advisable to be extremely suspicious of the Slovak folk-song 'Ty Nitranské hodiny', the third phrase of which is in a key a minor third higher than the rest of the song. It is undoubtedly modern in origin. This modulation is a striking feature of Rossini's *Barber of Seville* overture.

submediant keys. His choice of F major in the G major quintet and B flat for the ill-fated quartet in A minor, op. 12, was quite exceptional.

A succession of four unresolved dominant sevenths rising by minor thirds in the Poco Adagio of the B flat symphony, op. 4, shows another aspect of this key relationship. In certain other works two such dominant sevenths are found to alternate, thus producing a temporary ambiguity of key, as in a celebrated passage in Schubert's Great C major symphony and a few bars of the first chorus of the Brahms Requiem.[1] Dvořák, however, achieves his greatest successes as regards suspense and surprise by entirely different means. Having made elaborate preparations in the *Carnival* overture for a modulation to E he follows these with the passage quoted here, at the end of which the ultimate haven appears to us to be incalculably remote:

Ex. 11.

<hr>

[1] In *Boris Godunov* the bells peal out on dominant sevenths that are an augmented fourth apart.

41

A very different, cryptic passage is shown as ex. 15 on p. 70.

Possibly taking a hint from Schubert, Dvořák occasionally ended a song or piece in a different key from that established at the beginning. He also started several movements obliquely in some key other than the tonic.

Like Schubert, Dvořák delighted in changes from major to minor and minor to major. This device may not be so pronounced a characteristic of his music as it is of Schubert's, and besides, he seldom resorted to it in song composition, a field in which, in the Viennese composer's hands, it is seen to play such a vital role. Dvořák apparently made use of it partly because it provided him with a valuable extension of tonality, but also because of his liking for variety of mood and colour. It is possible that Dvořák's very warm admiration for Schubert may have stimulated him to some measure of imitation, but if this is so then he would no doubt have been conditioned to it by the occasional presence of mode changes in his native folk-lore. There is something Schubertian in the way Dvořák begins repeating a melodic phrase in the opposite mode in bars 41–48 of the first movement of the D minor quartet, and yet the passage is also essentially Dvořákian. Usually he treats the change in a more individual manner; in any case we need hardly expect to find anything resembling the dramatic changes of mode in Schubert's G major quartet. In Moravian and Slovak folk-song it is more common for contrasting sections of a melody to be in different modes. But sometimes, as in the Moravian song 'Pod synečkem zticha koně kráčé',[1] changes of mode occur with greater frequency:

Ex. 12.

In the *Dumky* trio's second movement, which is in C sharp minor, the 'cello's answering phrase in the tonic major provides a fleeting yet unexpectedly warm glow that contrasts vividly with the prevailing mood of despondency.[2] A remarkable and unique series of rapid changes from one mode to the other occurs in the postlude of the song 'Mé srdce často v bolesti' (op. 2, no. 3), but only in the revised version of the early 1880s. In this case the mutations are due to successions of chromatic passing notes and the effect is kaleidoscopic (Ex. 13).

During the opening melody of the A major piano quintet the 'cello descends through the flattened seventh and sixth degrees of the scale, and although this does not effect a change of mode immediately, the melody ends in A minor and the next theme commences in that key. So many flattenings occur in the first few bars of the C major quartet, notably added sixths on minor triads of C and F, that it is not until the second theme arrives (bar 24) that the brilliant sunshine of C major breaks through the clouds.[3] In the Finale of the piano concerto there appears a much more artistic variant of the naïve E flat major theme of the Finale of the string quintet in G, and in this we can again see how harmony, diminished sevenths in this case, can produce an ambiguity that creates the impression of a change of mode (Ex. 14).

In the last example the melody uses a 'gipsy scale', such as is found in some of the folk-songs of Slovakia but was rarely used by Dvořák. The

---

[1] F. Sušil: *Moravské národní písně*, 3rd edn., 1860.
[2] See ex. 9, p. 208. Quick changes from one mode to the other in the E flat piano quartet are shown in ex. 7, pp. 203-4.
[3] The first bars of this theme are shown in ex. 13 on p. 176.

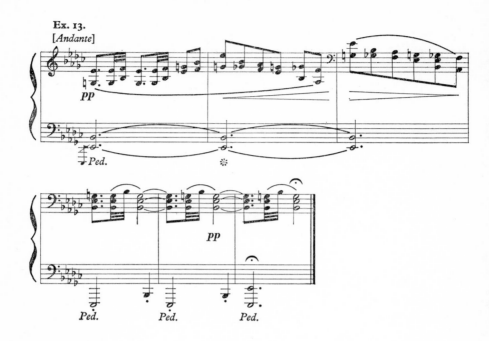

Ex. 13.
[Andante]

Ex. 14.

main theme of the Finale of the D minor symphony,[1] however, is founded on a similar series of notes, and the second of the *Romantic Pieces*, op. 75, is based on a portion of the same scale, the first five notes of a minor scale but including a Lydian fourth. This last example may have been influenced by the Czech folk-song 'Líto, líto přichází', which begins with the same intervals and is to be found in Erben:[2]

Ex. 15a.

Ex. 15b.

Dvořák was more inclined to introduce Lydian fourths in major keys, as for instance in the fourth *Humoresque*, the theme of the *Symphonic Variations*, the Romance of the *Czech Suite*, and also in the coda of the third movement of the D minor Serenade,[3] although in the last of these the harmony is seen to conflict temporarily with the major mode and the fourth is in reality a prolonged appoggiatura. Both types of fourth, Lydian and perfect, occur in the *Symphonic Variations* and in the Romance, just as they do in a number of the folk-songs of Czechoslovakia. The same thing occurs in *The Wild Dove* and the first version of *King and Charcoal Burner*,[4] and in both these instances there seems to have been a distinct association in Dvořák's mind between the alternation of these fourths and the representation of bagpipes, perhaps due to the pitch of the fourth note on the chanter of this instrument failing to correspond with normal tuning. Even in the *Symphonic Variations* and the Romance we find pedal notes suggestive of a drone.

It came perfectly naturally to Dvořák to repeat the opening motif of a theme, as in ex. 10 above. We find him doing this repeatedly, and probably more frequently than any other composer of equal status. This may well be due to the influence of folk-song, for it is quite common for the initial bar in Czech and Moravian song to be sung twice, thrice and sometimes even

[1] See ex. 28 on p. 82.

[2] *Prostonárodní české písně a říkadla, s nápěvy*, 1842.

[3] For the three last-mentioned passages see exs. 17, 15 and 13 on pp. 152, 149 and 148. Ex. 9 on p. 168 not only shows the less common Moravian modulation from one major key to another, but also includes a Lydian fourth in the second key.

[4] Quoted as ex. 16 on p. 124 and ex. 2 on p. 270.

four times in succession. We see this trait in 'Quis est homo' and 'Inflammatus' in the *Stabat Mater*, in 'Songs my mother taught me' and no. 7 of the *Gipsy Melodies*, in the slow movement of the string quintet in E flat, in the first movement of the A flat quartet, in the twelfth *Slavonic Dance*, in the pentatonic 'Nature' theme of the three overtures and the first movement of the G major symphony,[1] to mention only some of the more familiar examples. It seems unlikely to have been a coincidence that the *Slavonic Dance* theme just mentioned bears a direct relationship to the Czech song 'Já tu nebudu!' for Erben published this song and Dvořák must have been familiar with it:

Ex. 16.

To repeat bars in the middle or at the end of a phrase is perhaps less typically Czech, for this certainly occurs in German and Schwabian folksong as well as in that of Czechoslovakia, and it is also seen in Schumann's 'Wiegenliedchen' and in three of Haydn's 'Paris' symphonies.[2] This type of repetition occurs less frequently in Dvořák's music than repetitions at the beginnings of phrases, but it is found in the fifth, sixth and seventh symphonies, and is associated with village characters in *The Cunning Peasant* and *Kate and the Devil*.[3]

As Gerald Abraham has pointed out,[4] there are several characteristic leaps and melodic curves that Dvořák wrote instinctively and repeatedly. Some of these, but not all, emanate from folk-song. Even though these curves may be grouped into certain distinct basic types, the Czech composer was able to present them in a variety of forms and guises, and he only rarely repeated himself. One of these personal fingerprints, an upward leap of a fourth from the dominant to the tonic and back, usually followed by a gradual descent, may be seen in the Dumka of the E flat string quartet, the Finale of the sextet, the first *Slavonic Rhapsody*, the motif associated with Bohuš in *The Jacobin*, two themes in the *Czech Suite* and the third *Slavonic*

[1] The 'Nature' theme and one of the themes from the symphony are shown as ex. 4 on p. 113 and ex. 30 on p. 84. In each of these cases the repeated motif consists of only two notes. Ex. 30 reminds us of a *Rhenish* symphony theme.
[2] No. 82, I; No. 84, I; No. 85, III.
[3] For the latter see ex. 6a on p. 283.
[4] 'Dvořák's Musical Personality' in V. Fischl: *Antonín Dvořák: his achievement*.

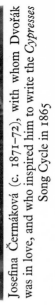

Josefina Čermáková (c. 1871–72), with whom Dvořák was in love, and who inspired him to write the *Cypresses* Song Cycle in 1865

Antonín Dvořák, c. 1866

Josefina and Anna Čermáková
(seated) c. 1871–72. Dvořák marrie
Anna in 1873

Na příkopě, one of the main thoroughfares of Prague, c. 1870

Dance.[1] A variant curling up again after the downward leap is seen in the first movement of the B flat symphony (in the codetta), the Minuet of the D minor Serenade and the *furiant* section of the Dumka of the above-mentioned quartet. The origin of this melodic shape lies in folk-lore, and without doubt Dvořák was most familiar with one particular song that embodies it, 'Hajej, můj andílku' which is found in Erben and was borrowed by Smetana for the lullaby in *The Kiss*:

Ex. 17.

An upward leap of any interval from a third to an actave followed by a gradual descent is another characteristic trait. A search among the folk-songs inevitably brings to light certain parallels with each of these basic figures, but the diversity of treatment they receive in Dvořák's hands, which underlines their remoteness from such primitive models, is of far greater interest to us. Of the examples that start with a leap of a fourth, the theme of the third *Slavonic Rhapsody* is the most majestic.[2] In the first bars of *The Spectre's Bride* a similar figure, coloured with foreboding,[3] appears in a minor key, but in the twelfth number of this cantata the same figure changed to the major serves to show the girl reassured by her strange lover. A dreamy syncopated version appears in *Silent Woods* (op. 68, no. 5), and it is seen again in the piano quintet, but in this case the sixth note of the scale is given a significant and expressive emphasis.

Figures that include the larger leaps may sometimes be treated with nonchalance, as we see in the first *Slavonic Dance*, and more especially in the string quintet in G.[4] The second *Slavonic Dance* shows two entirely different aspects of this type of melody, one plaintive and the other vivacious.[5] The same figure becomes wistful in the Trio of the Tempo di Valse in the

[1] For extracts from these last two works see exx. 15 and 16 on p. 149 and ex. 6b on p. 139, the latter being derived from the folk dance shown in ex. 6a.

[2] See ex. 4b, p. 134.   [3] See ex. 2, p. 248.

[4] This provides several instances: the initial figure in the Introduction leaps a sixth, fifth, seventh and later an octave; the second subject starts with an octave leap; the Finale's main theme has a similar figure starting with a sixth and the E flat theme begins with an octave.

[5] For the latter, see ex. 5b on p. 138.

Serenade for strings, and expresses strong yearning in the final bars of the third movement of the D minor Serenade.[1] As we would expect this figure also holds great possibilities for dramatic expression. Later transformation shows that despite its initial arpeggio figure the principal finale theme of the F major symphony falls into this category, and so does the theme used for variations in the *Terzetto*, but the finest examples are seen in the F minor trio and the D minor symphony.[2] Undoubtedly one of the most beautiful examples is to be found in the passage that derives from the song 'Leave me alone' and appears in the coda of the 'cello concerto.[3]

Much more might be said concerning small figures that crop up frequently in Dvořák's music: turns, triplet figures, what Gerald Abraham aptly calls the 'knight's move', the 'Three Blind Mice' cadence that springs directly from folk-song, and so on. Yet it is advisable to try to avoid endowing such small details with too great a significance, for fear they may draw attention away from more important aspects of the music. Perhaps in certain directions too much may have been said already. The rising and falling fourth, for instance, is not very often prominent in Dvořák's work, even though it is clear that it had some significance for him. Although the use of the Lydian fourth is not without interest, it is in fact quite untypical of Dvořák, and consequently it gains in effect by being seldom used. It does not betray any ingrained habit of thought as it does with Sibelius.

One point, however, must be mentioned. In both the Czech and Slovak languages, except in Lachian dialect, the stress invariably falls on the first syllable of a word unless this is deprived of its stress by a preposition that precedes it. Furthermore, sentences hardly ever start with unstressed single-syllable words. It follows from this that it is rare to find a folk-song that starts with an anacrusic metre. Thanks to Dvořák's familiarity with and great love for the folk-lore of his native land, it became second nature to him to write themes that start on the first beat of a bar, and although he undoubtedly added up-beats to some of his themes later, a very large number of themes must have lacked them when he first conceived them. There is support for this view in the first pages of the earliest of the American sketch books, where we find only one unambiguous rejection of this powerful impulse, the theme for the scherzo of the *New World* symphony, which starts on a second beat in $\frac{3}{4}$ time, and one theme to which he subsequently added an up-beat, the Trio theme of the same work. Anacrusic themes are naturally much more common in Dvořák's music than in the folk-songs,

---

[1] See ex. 11a, p. 146, and ex. 13, p. 148.
[2] For quotations of all these passages see exx. 13 and 14 on p. 69, ex. 15 on p. 179, ex. 5, p. 199, and ex. 28, p. 82.
[3] See exx. 12a and 12c on pp. 107-8.

but it is possible that only approximately one-quarter of his themes are of this type.

When repeating themes he often made some slight rhythmic or melodic modification, or alternatively he added a decoration, which suggests that he did not look upon his material as rigid and immutable and that he welcomed some measure of variation. This makes the task of editors more difficult, for in some places where there appear to be discrepancies in a manuscript they cannot necessarily be 'corrected' from a parallel passage. Even though Brahms's remark about unduly hasty writing would have been heeded by Dvořák, he must have found it difficult sometimes to make his pen keep pace with his lively imagination. Nevertheless we cannot be certain whether this provides the clue to the occasional consecutive fifths that he wrote, or whether in these few instances alone the conventional taboo was a matter of indifference to him. Although he did not very often write in traditional contrapuntal styles, he had a genuine flair for certain types of contrapuntal writing, notably the enrichment of the texture with counter-melodies. He also had a full realization of the need to give each of his individual lines an interest of its own, which offers attractions for the performers as well as the listeners. Besides this he had an instinctive and sometimes subtle ability to combine opposing rhythms, beside which some of the efforts of Brahms appear laboured.[1]

Dvořák's orchestration can on occasion be both unexpected and effective, as we see in the *New World* symphony's Scherzo when the 'cellos play below the double basses, and in the previous movement where the final four-note chord is played by double basses alone, or when in the third *Slavonic Rhapsody* a solo violin plays high above a quartet of horns and a kettle drum. But we call to mind more readily the many entrancing passages for woodwind and solo horn, and his occasional use of darker orchestral hues, and notably the cor anglais and bass clarinet. In particular there are some wonderfully imaginative solos for a flute: the arpeggios leading up to trills in the first movement of the D minor symphony, and the pathetic interjections at the end of the same movement; the arpeggio passages during the violin solo in the Adagio of the G major symphony, the vivacious variation in the Finale, and especially the delightful broken octave decorations later in the movement; the luminous solo against a dark monotonous cor anglais background in the slow interlude of the *Carnival* overture; and also the supremely beautiful duet between 'cello and flute, supported by

---

[1] Compare for instance the first sixteen bars and the coda of the first movement of Brahms's quartet in B flat, and the last twenty-one bars of the first movement of his A minor quartet, with the beginning of the second section of the Scherzo of Dvořák's D major symphony (ex. 21, p. 75) and the opening bars of the Vivace of his D minor symphony (ex. 27, p. 81). When there is an absence of conscious struggle, as in the initial bars of the A minor quartet, the result is delightful.

tremolo strings and a solitary clarinet in the Molto sostenuto of the
opening movement of the 'cello concerto. However, we must not
overlook the enchanting piccolo solo in the Trio of the D major
symphony.

There is often an outstanding resilience in Dvořák's dynamics, and many
are the instances of impulsive crescendos from *p* or *pp* to *f* within the time-
span of a single bar, just as there are equally sudden diminuendos. This
natural volatility of Dvořák's also results in rapid changes of emotional
feeling, speedy transitions from one mood to another in preference to abrupt
changes, and transmutations such as these can make a direct appeal to the
heart.

Dvořák's harmonic vocabulary undoubtedly owed a little to the chromatic
harmony of Wagner and Liszt, yet we find that when he wrote chromatically
it was normal for his music to remain highly personal. Had the two cadential
bars been added to the extract from the piano concerto shown above (ex. 14),
the melodic shape and the appoggiatura rising a semitone would have caused
many a reader with perfect justification to have exclaimed 'Liszt!' Far more
often, however, the appoggiaturas we encounter are essentially Dvořákian,
as are those in the Scherzo of the D major symphony[1] and the Lento of the
E flat piano quartet,[2] in the first movement of the E flat quintet (bars
251–4 especially) and the second theme in the A flat quartet, and in bars
158–165 in the first movement of the 'cello concerto and a distantly related
passage at the end of *Rusalka*.[3] A second type of appoggiatura occurs when a
melodic line curls around the harmonic framework, as in several passages
in the second *Legend* and in some far finer bars in the Poco adagio of the
D minor symphony.[4] The unquestionable genius that this passage displays
depends upon a variety of factors, not the least of which is the choice of
contrasting sonorities and registers. How differently, for instance, do the
repeated chords sound when given to trombones, clarinets, bassoons and
plucked double basses in the second bar, and oboes, a horn and plucked violins and violas in the third. Contrasts of timbre and pitch may also be seen
in an astonishing passage in the Finale of the same work, one in which
appoggiaturas again occur.[5]

In several instances dissonances are heightened by the use of pedals in
combination with appoggiaturas. We observe this, for example, at the end of
the opening movement of the D minor symphony at a point where diminished sevenths twice descend a tone,[6] and also in the following passages in the
Lento of the A flat quartet, where in each case the basic chord is again a
diminished seventh, and in the first the A flat is the pedal:

[1] See ex. 20, p. 74.   [4] See ex. 26, p. 80.
[2] See ex. 8, p. 205.   [5] See ex. 29, p. 82.
[3] See ex. 9, p. 288.   [6] See ex. 25, p. 79.

Ex. 18a.

Ex. 18b.

A chromatic seventh is used in a similar context when the crisis is reached at the end of the *New World* symphony. This chord, although notated as D, E sharp, G sharp, C natural in the key of E, makes better sense if thought of as D, F, A flat, C, a chord that includes the flattened second and fourth and the minor sixth and seventh degrees of the scale.[1]

Chromatic inflection of notes in a downward direction has already been referred to in discussing changes of mode, but we are now confronted with an extreme example of a procedure that was quite common in Dvořák's work, and one that needs to be recognized as an important integral part of his style. He so frequently used the minor sixth in a major key, sometimes light-heartedly as in the polka-style second subject theme in the E flat string quartet, that sometimes it almost acquired a diatonic function. But inflections of this kind assumed the greatest importance when they were used as an aid towards the expression of pathos and tragedy, for instance in the *New World* symphony passage just mentioned, following in the wake of a *tierce de Picardie*, in the D minor symphony passage already cited, where the 'cellos descend through E flat, D flat and B natural (i.e. C flat) in the tonic key, in the F minor trio,[2] in *Rusalka* and *Armida* at the points where the hero and

[1] See ex. 36, p. 92. It could possibly be argued that the chord is a tonic minor thirteenth.

[2] Ex. 5 on p. 199 shows one of the many instances that occur in this work.

heroine are about to die, during the final confession and prayer of the maiden in *The Spectre's Bride*, and in many other places besides.

Just as Wagner chose to conclude *Götterdämmerung* in D flat major, so too Dvořák favoured the more extreme flat keys for critical points or culminations in his big vocal works. The turning point in *The Jacobin* and the climax of *Rusalka* are both in the key that was chosen by Wagner, whereas the prayer in *The Spectre's Bride* and the end of *Armida* are in G flat major, and the *Requiem* ends as it began in B flat minor.[1]

Dvořák was affected by a wide range of influences, but almost always he was able to absorb these influences and make them a part of his own musical personality. The extremely potent impact of Wagner and the lesser pull of Liszt were counterbalanced to a very great extent by his tremendous admiration for the Viennese classics and his friendship with Brahms. He was fortunate not to be exclusively linked with one or other of the two antagonistic contemporary schools of musical thought, and to receive support from both sides. He was free to take what suited him from either camp: for example, on the one hand the principles of classical design, which he infused with a romantic spirit, and on the other the new symphonic poem of Liszt and the *leitmotiv* of Wagner. As has already been shown, his music was strongly imbued with a number of features that derived from the folklore of his fatherland, and which helped to give his music a decidedly nationalist colouring. So strong were these native influences, that even during the first two years of his stay in America, when he was strongly drawn towards Negro spirituals and acquired an American veneer, he still remained for the most part a characteristically Czech composer.

Although he was not invariably successful when writing in classical forms, when he was at his best he showed outstanding mastery in this field, whereas his contemporary Grieg was singularly unsuccessful except in miniatures. He wrote in all the branches of music that were open to him. He had tremendous success with choral music during his heyday, and ultimately in his own country he achieved the kind of recognition as a composer of opera that he had long coveted. Today his instrumental compositions take pride of place over his vocal work, but it is essential to know the latter if we are to understand Dvořák adequately, and a number of his vocal compositions will be found to contain some of his sublimest music. It is unfortunate that he is known to most people by a mere handful of works, and particularly so since several of those that are most familiar are neither wholly typical nor represent him at his greatest. Besides, such a limited number of works cannot possibly give a true impression of his many-sided genius. Further misunderstanding arises when, as frequently happens, his music is performed outside

[1] It may be worth noting that Janáček's *Cunning Little Vixen* and *Excursions of Mr. Brouček* finish in D flat major, and his *Katya Kabanová* ends in B flat minor.

his own country without sufficient appreciation of its true character. That it should sometimes be made to resemble the music of Brahms is ludicrous, and betrays only too clearly a complete lack of understanding of its Slavonic spirit.

Dvořák emerges unquestionably as one of the most distinctive and distinguished musical personalities of his generation, and he has a place of honour alongside Brahms, Bruckner and Tchaikovsky as one of the three or four greatest composers of symphonic works of his time. In the field of chamber music, however, he had only one serious rival, if it is possible to use that word, for who else apart from his good friend Brahms applied himself so assiduously and left so rich and unique a heritage in this branch of music as Dvořák?

His great musical gifts, however, were of quite a different order from those of the composers just referred to. His music covers a wide emotional range, but it was not often that he showed an inclination to sustain a mood in the classical manner, as Brahms did. Dvořák had greater melodic, rhythmic and colouristic gifts than his friend, but less intellectual control over the growth and design of his music. We find nothing of the sustained exaltation and monumentality of Bruckner, nor the fascination for chromaticism and modulation that that composer sometimes displayed. Quite early Dvořák had sensed the dangers of excessive length, and recognized that he personally was much better fitted to write works of classical proportions. Tchaikovsky, as the only other Slavonic composer of this small group, has a certain affinity with Dvořák, but he was capable of expressing more intense emotion and concentrated passion. He had, in fact, an uncanny knowledge of how to drive home a dramatic point in the most compelling manner, and consequently he was more capable than the Czech composer of displaying an overwhelming sense of power.

Dvořák has more in common with Schubert than with any of these three composers. Both men possessed a similar gift of motivic development and rhythmic propulsion, and there often prevailed in their music a spirit of optimism. Even though Dvořák's melodic gifts were not quite the equal of the Viennese master's, he was without question an outstanding melodist. Their music gives the impression that they were both God-given composers, although neither was in fact quite as spontaneous in musical composition as has for so long been imagined. It seems reasonable to assume that Dvořák must have felt that he had a spiritual kinship with Schubert, an affinity that transcended nationalities, though not races, owing to Schubert's Moravian and Silesian parentage. Dvořák spoke of Beethoven with awe, but of Schubert he spoke with love.[1]

[1] The article that Dvořák wrote on Schubert will be found reprinted at the end of this volume.

Part Two

INSTRUMENTAL WORKS

III

The Symphonies

Confusion arises over the numbering of Dvořák's symphonies, for the simple reason that only five were published during his life-time and given the numbers 1 to 5. Of these, 'No. 3' was composed before 'No. 1', but it was published, following some very minor revisions, after 'No. 2'. The composer numbered his symphonies from one to eight, but in doing so ignored his first symphony, which he had lost. All nine symphonies have been published and recorded. To avoid hopeless confusion it is essential to adopt the chronological numbering that was proposed long ago by Šourek. The nine works are as follows:

1. Symphony in C minor, *The Bells of Zlonice*. 1865.
2. Symphony in B flat major, op. 4. 1865.
3. Symphony in E flat major, op. 10. 1873.
4. Symphony in D minor, op. 13. 1874.
5. Symphony in F major, op. 76 (originally op. 24), 'No. 3'. 1875
6. Symphony in D major, op. 60, 'No. 1'. 1880.
7. Symphony in D minor, op. 70, 'No. 2'. 1884–1885.
8. Symphony in G major, op. 88, 'No. 4'. 1889.
9. Symphony in E minor, *From the New World*, op. 95, 'No. 5'. 1893.

THE BELLS OF ZLONICE

The first symphony, composed between February 14th and March 24th, 1865, was entered for a competition in Germany, but it was not sent back to Dvořák, and he failed to ask to have it returned. In 1923 it was discovered in the possession of the late Dr. Rudolf Dvořák, who was no relation to the composer. He had bought the score from a secondhand dealer in Leipzig during his student days. Although the manuscript has no title, the composer is said to have referred to the work as 'The Bells of Zlonice', in recollection of the two boyhood years he spent under the schoolmaster-musicians, Josef Toman and Antonín Liehmann, in this most attractive little town. He often played on the two-manual organ, so the sound of the church bells had a special significance for him. There was, however, no attempt made to recapture the sound of the bells in the symphony; they were merely a symbol.

It is possible that Dvořák chose the key of C minor for this work because at Zlonice he felt uncertain about his future. He had been sent there to become a butcher's apprentice, but he found Zlonice gave him good opportunities to increase his knowledge of music, and this proved to be the greater attraction. It should also be recalled that the symphony was composed during the period of his unrequited love for the actress Josefina Čermáková, his future sister-in-law. Perhaps the cheerful mood of the Finale represents his unwarranted optimism over the outcome of his passion, but it may on the other hand be a natural reaction following prolonged brooding over his lack of success. As an ardent admirer of Beethoven he may well have chosen the same keys for the four movements as those of that master's fifth symphony. C minor is uncommon in Dvořák's music. According to the numbering of the pages, Dvořák would appear to have written the Scherzo last, as an afterthought, but the evidence is inconclusive.[1]

All the movements start with brief introductions. The first of these is like a call to attention, and its theme has the character of a motto, but it is only used in two of the movements:

Ex. 1.

This striking motif reappears in the development of the first movement, and, through a miscalculation of the composer's, it returns in an unexpected tonality at too early a stage in the Finale. A drum rhythm found early in the movement is also used again in the Finale, but it is hardly conspicuous enough to assist in the unification of the work. The somewhat chorale-like introduction to the Adagio, which borrows a pair of chords from Wagner's 'Tarnhelm' motif, is used later in a fugato. The introductions to the remaining movements merely state the principal themes, the Scherzo theme being in augmentation, and neither seems really necessary. In the second symphony, once again all the movements have introductions, but they fulfil their function much more satisfactorily than here.

---

[1] The pages of the Scherzo are numbered from 1–44, but pages 37–40 form part of the two sheets on which the Finale begins (pp. 133–136).

The first movement of *The Bells of Zlonice* has some striking moments, some attractive brief turns towards tonalities with more flats, and in general an abundance of invention and rhythmic vitality. When composing this movement Dvořák had insufficient understanding of the function of key in sonata form, and in consequence was unable to keep away from the tonic key for long in the development. The coda works up to a powerful climax, and shows that this young composer possessed a valuable gift, the ability to drive his music onward with an impelling force. The adagio is particularly rich in themes, and is notable for the beauty of its long melodic lines that modulate freely, and for its rich texture. This movement has a lovely spacious opening, and is beautifully shaped in its closing pages, but is inclined to be diffuse. Dvořák uses the oboe so often and so successfully as a solo instrument here, as well as in the first and last movements, that one suspects that it must have been his favourite instrument at that time. In the tuttis he is inclined to overload his score.

It is interesting to see how Dvořák was able to maintain the momentum in the Scherzo, despite the frequency of two-bar phrases. He was not so successful over this in the Finale, and was less able to avoid the common-place, as for instance when he concentrates on the first three notes of his yearning secondary theme, and when he alters its character:

It would be preferable if the work as a whole were more concise, but nevertheless it gives evidence of the composer's fertile imagination and promise for the future.

SYMPHONY NO. 2 IN B FLAT

The second symphony was composed between August 1st and October 9th, 1865, only about six months after *The Bells of Zlonice*, but it was not performed until March 18th, 1888, when it was conducted by Adolf Čech. Dvořák revised the symphony during 1887, rewriting some parts, reducing the length of the first and last movements considerably, and making innumerable small changes. Some alterations, however, may possibly have been made earlier than this, while it is certain that other modifications were made shortly before the first performance. The revisions include the removal of pages from the full score, several of which have been preserved. These contain 69 bars of the development of the first movement, and 70 bars of the exposition and 113 bars of the recapitulation of the Finale. Besides this, other cuts were indicated, the balance of parts was improved, and the scoring was thinned out in many places, brass parts being either reduced or omitted. Some countermelodies were added during revision. The whole work would have originally taken about 55 minutes to perform.

As a consequence of the revisions the symphony represents two different periods in Dvořák's life, but it is a surprise to see what an advance the original conception was over his first symphony. Some of the composer's ideas are quite impressive, even if he was unable to maintain this level of inspiration. The first bars of the work set the atmosphere for the whole movement, and the big crescendo hints at the latent power it contains:

Ex. 3.

These thirteen bars are immediately repeated a major third higher. The melody in bars 9–12, which anticipates the principal theme of the movement, was added during revision to replace the repetition of the opening four-note motive in diminution at this point, but the rest, including the shift to D major, remained practically as Dvořák first conceived it. In the same movement we notice frequent repetition of a motive, after the manner of Beethoven's *Pastoral* symphony. Dvořák must have been carried away to have inserted an extra 93 bars in the recapitulation, and it is a relief to learn that he agreed to half of these being cut.

It was necessary to perform drastic surgery on the last movement, for the exposition was unsuitable for recapitulation without considerable changes being made, and needed compression most of all. Having made a big cut, Dvořák left the recapitulation with a large amount of development sandwiched between a brief reminder of the main theme in the tonic key and a section of the second subject that is heard in remote keys. It is sometimes possible to recognize strokes of genius in Dvořák's and Schubert's use of unexpected keys in expositions and racapitulations, but in recapitulations it is natural to expect a much stronger bias towards the tonic key than here, and the movement is unsatisfactory without this. Dvořák's chief problem in 1865 was the mastery of sonata form.

He found it was necessary to make far fewer alterations when revising the two middle movements. The Poco adagio, in which the long expressive melody over a steadily moving bass is the most memorable feature, represents the highest peak reached by the composer at that time, even though there are misjudgements in the middle of the movement. We may be aware of the slight influence of Wagner, but this has fertilized Dvořák's imagination, and helped him to express more fully his own inner thoughts and feelings.

Thirty-five years after the completion of this symphony, the composer returned to the Finale, either consciously or unconsciously, and borrowed a few bars from it for the culmination of his opera *Rusalka*. The passage from the symphony is shown first:

Ex. 4a.

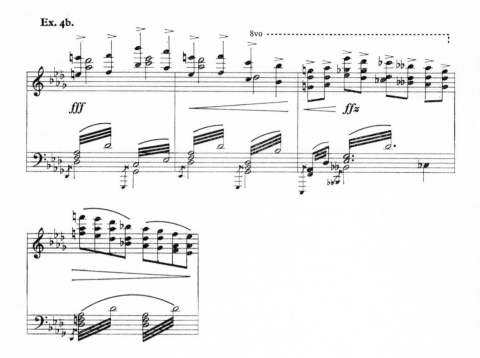

Ex. 4b.

František Bartoš asks: 'Is this identity of motif accidental or intentional? Can it indeed be unintentional? And is not then the catharsis of *Rusalka* the final reconciliation and resolution of all those spiritual conflicts which are so distinguishing a feature of Dvořák's youthful works from the year 1865?' Rising appoggiaturas are found from time to time in Dvořák's music, and seem sometimes to have been associated in his mind with human and divine love.[1] But Dr. Bartoš's questions are likely to remain unanswered, for we shall never know for certain that Dvořák recalled even subconsciously the inner struggles of that early period when writing those final pages.

[1] Among passages in Dvořák's songs where rising appoggiaturas occur, there are three instances where the words refer to the love of God and of humans, but there must be very many more such references that do not use rising appoggiaturas. In one case where these appoggiaturas are found (op. 50, no. 2) the sense is entirely different. In the passage cited from *Rusalka* the words are as follows:

> *For your beauty, for your human love,*
> *By that strange and restless passion ruled,*
> *For all that by which I am accursed,*
> *Human soul, may God be merciful.*

but a rising appoggiatura with a contrary meaning is found in the same opera in the 'water magic' motif. Clearly, Dvořák was inconsistent. For Bartoš's views, see the Introduction to the Complete Edition score.

THE SYMPHONIES

SYMPHONY NO. 3 IN E FLAT

The period that separated Dvořák's second symphony from his third, seven and a half years in the life of a composer who was slow to mature, was sufficient for him to learn how to attain a good measure of structural coherence. The failure to have his second opera staged was more than offset by the public recognition which he received for the first time when his cantata, *The Heirs of the White Mountain,* was performed successfully in March 1873. This gave him good reason to have confidence in himself. The symphony in E flat, from which the opus no. 10 was later withdrawn, was completed by June 4th that year, but remained unpublished until 1912.

The noble sweep of the principal theme (ex. 5), turns of melodic phrase, harmonic characteristics, the inclusion of a cor anglais in the first two movements, a harp in the second and a tuba in the Finale, and in some instances the method of writing for the instruments, all betray a continuing, but diminishing, admiration for Wagner.

Ex. 5.

The last movement owes more to Beethoven, and, in its metamorphoses of the main theme, to Liszt. The first movement was very thickly scored, while the last was conceived with more clarity and imagination. Here the composer's handling of unmixed tone colours, his discreet blending of instruments and the cheerful tinkling of the triangle, gave hints of his genius in a direction in which he was shortly to be pre-eminent.

In this work, Dvořák's only symphony in three movements, he proclaimed his right to be unorthodox in form. Having briefly recapitulated the first subject of the opening movement, he somewhat unaccountably develops his themes once again before reaching the second subject. The Adagio molto is restricted in tonality, and suffers from a pompous middle section in D flat, the tonic major. The Finale, which can hardly be said to be in sonata form and certainly is not a rondo, overemphasises the subdominant key early on, but its gay mood disarms criticism.

There is some semblance of unification in the first two movements, but no conscious attempt has been made to draw the Finale within their orbit; instead that movement has strong inner unities of its own. The groups of six semiquavers in the main theme quoted above are used in the Adagio, more as a rhythmic element than as a melodic factor, and the concise rhythmic germ in the same theme's tenth bar, shown bracketed, is given prominence in the second movement by the horn. Less obviously, the rhythm on tonic and dominant in the opening bars of the symphony reappear in the bass in the middle section of the Adagio. The first movement's second subject theme is accompanied by the first bar of the main theme:

Ex. 6.

and the steady descent through a fourth, which is its essence, originated in the melody and bass of bars 4–6 of the same theme. A related scalic descent is found in a subsidiary theme of the Adagio, which was borrowed later for the sixth of the *Legends*, op. 59:

Ex. 7.

Dvořák's seriousness of purpose and his growing command over his resources are conspicuous in this work. They could hardly have failed to impress the Commission appointed to award the annual State Prize for young, talented and poor writers, artists and musicians in the Austrian half of the Empire when Dvořák submitted his third and fourth symphonies together with an unidentified chamber work. The judges were Hanslick and Herbeck, Director of the Imperial Opera. Dvořák was awarded 400 gulden, and continued to win the prize for four more years. An important outcome of these successes was that after Brahms became a member of the Commission, his close friendship with Dvořák began.

THE SYMPHONIES

Symphony No. 4 in D Minor

Dvořák's next symphony, originally op. 13, is in the same key as the great symphony op. 70. It was composed between January 1st and March 26th, 1874, little more than half a year later than the third symphony, and, rather significantly, immediately after the string quartet, in A minor, op. 12, which marked a crisis in his career, and which is referred to elsewhere in this volume. The symphony comes therefore at the beginning of a decisive reaction against the influence of Wagner and Liszt, but evidence is still shown of unorthodox structural procedures, and Wagner's influence is strongly felt in the Andante. Like the third symphony it was published posthumously.

The work opens with a rolling ostinato figure in the bass, and a signal theme, which might have been written by Bruckner, if it were not heard in Czech fashion three times before the succeeding thought is persuaded to appear:

Ex. 8.

Both the ostinato and the signal return at the end of the Scherzo, but this is the only instance in this work of themes recurring in later movements. The form of the first movement is curious. After an innocuous development section there are only nineteen bars of recapitulation starting with a secondary theme, and then as if to make up past deficiencies Dvořák plunges into the most powerful working-out of his themes.

The theme of the Andante starts with the same harmony and tonality as the second portion of the Pilgrims' March in *Tannhäuser*, and the whole of this seventeen-bar theme, solemnly announced by clarinets, bassoons, trombones and horns, is strongly influenced by Wagner, notably in its constantly shifting and seldom defined tonality. A theme of this kind has rarely been used for variations, and Dvořák evidently found his task difficult, for he sooon sought refuge in development.[1] Having dodged the problem of a Scherzo altogether in the previous symphony, Dvořák wrote one here

---

[1] The last movement of his *Terzetto* also has a rapidly modulating theme used for variations, but the character is entirely different.

which opens with a ferocious ejaculation and a striking chord motif. A lyrical subsidiary thought, borrowed later for the sixth of the set of pianoforte duets, *From the Bohemian Forest*, has suggested the melodic shape of the Trio theme:

Ex. 9a.

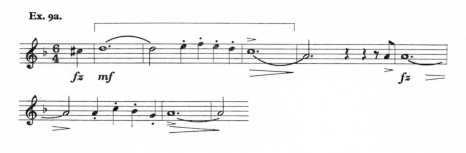

Ex. 9b.

For his Finale the composer used a large scale ternary scheme, and except for fleeting references to a melodic idea, based the whole movement on the following epigrammatic theme:

Ex. 10.

Although he could generally be relied upon to sustain interest throughout a movement by relying on his innate sense of rhythmic propulsion, a virtue also possessed by Schubert, in this movement he found his theme rather inflexible, except when developing it, with the result that in one long section, recapitulated later, two-bar phrases are very much in evidence. The bias of the principal theme towards the relative major is counteracted by the melodic theme, which is in the tonic major. The symphony is written for the normal full orchestra including three trombones, with a harp and extra percussion added for the Scherzo. The scoring is more satisfactory than hitherto.

THE SYMPHONIES

SYMPHONY NO. 5 IN F MAJOR

Little more than a year separated Dvořák's fourth symphony from his fifth, but it was a period of great activity during which he composed two operas, four chamber works, a Rhapsody, a Serenade and a Nocturne for orchestra, and the first of the *Moravian Duets*. At the same time he was greatly encouraged to learn early in 1875 that he had been awarded the Austrian State Music Prize, and this undoubtedly spurred him on to greater efforts. But Dvořák had also gained a much clearer idea of the paths that suited him best in the sphere of symphonic and chamber music, and consequently the new symphony shows an important advance beyond the best of his earlier works. The retreat from Wagner was complete, and henceforth the work of the Viennese composers was to serve as his principal model. But at the same time, with the strengthening of his individuality, he had at last reached maturity—at the age of thirty-four. The full score of the symphony in F occupied him from June 15th to July 23rd, 1875.

It is chiefly around this work that the confusion in numbering of the symphonies and arbitrary use of opus numbers centres. Fritz Simrock, being an astute business man, knew perfectly well that if Dvořák's works were published with high opus numbers they would be more likely to sell than those with low numbers. He published two of Dvořák's symphonies in 1882 and 1885 as nos. 1 and 2 with the opus numbers 60 and 70. He was then offered the F major symphony, of earlier date than either of these two, and, paying no heed to Dvořák's protests that the work was actually his op. 24, published it in 1888 as no. 3, op. 76.[1]

During the autumn of 1887 Dvořák made quite a large number of minor corrections to the symphony, many of them being improvements to the instrumental layout. It is presumed that he made a cut in the Andante con moto at an earlier date, but this appears to have been the only structural alteration that he considered necessary. The symphony received its *début* in Prague on March 25th, 1879, with Adolf Čech conducting. It is possible that August Manns may have given the first performance of the symphony in its definitive version at the Crystal Palace on April 7th, 1888. Dvořák asked if he might dedicate the work to his friend Hans von Bülow, who was doing much at that time to make the composer's orchestral works known, and especially the *Hussite* overture and the seventh symphony. Dvořák received the following reply:

[1] It was during this period that Simrock published the string quintet in G (op. 18) as op. 77, the *Symphonic Variations* (op. 28, but temporarily allotted the number 40 later) as op. 78, the *149th Psalm* (op. 52) as op. 79 and the E major string quartet (op. 27) as op. 80. Several other works have misleading opus numbers, but these numbers are usually a fairly reliable guide to the approximate order in which Dvořák composed his works.

Most honoured Master!

A dedication from you—next to Brahms the most divinely gifted composer of the present time—is a higher decoration than any Grand Cross
from the hands of any prince. With most heartfelt thanks I accept this
honour.

With most sincere esteem,
Your devoted admirer,
Hans v. Bülow

Hamburg, Nov. 25th, 1887.

The F major symphony is another work that might very well be described
as pastoral, provided this description is not applied to the Finale. The first
movement opens in a leisurely way with a theme for two clarinets that keeps
strictly to the tonic chord until the cadential bars arrive:

Ex. 11.

In this simple yet magical manner the bucolic scene is set. After a vigorous
new theme has been announced in the tonic key the tonality shifts to A minor,
a key that has especial significance in this symphony, because this is the key
of the Andante, and in the Finale the initial trend is reversed, being from
A minor to F major. As soon as the tonic key is restored the transition begins,
and leads to this wayward theme in D major:

Ex. 12.

so wayward, in fact, that it soon continues to flow precariously on the verge
of the original key.[1] But, as Tovey liked to express it, 'another accessory
figure, by asserting a much remoter key (B minor), saves the whole story
from premature marriage-and-living-happily-ever-afterward.' All these

---

[1] For twenty-eight bars the dominant seventh of F exerts a powerful influence.

themes are used in the development. The coda ends similarly to the beginning of the recapitulation, in a more tranquil mood than the beginning of the work, with farewell references to the opening theme.

The Andante con moto foreshadows the plaintive *dumka* movements of later compositions. In Dvořák's skilled hands its theme is made to flow onwards quite naturally with the aid of an overlap of phrases, toying with the opening figure, changes of scoring, accompaniment, tonality, harmony, and other means, so that it always remains fresh. Dvořák liked concentrating on one idea, and here he does so by deriving demi-semiquaver accompaniments for the melody from the first four notes of his theme. The demi-semiquavers and snatches of the main melody are also worked into the contrasting middle section. After a brief pause Dvořák with great originality, but unnecessarily, resumes his Andante theme for several bars on what might be augmented sixth harmony. The chord, however, turns out to be the dominant of B flat major, and the bars lead directly into the Scherzo in the new key. The movement whirls along vivaciously, until the Trio provides a breathing space.

Beethoven, Schubert, Schumann, Brahms and Dvořák all showed interest in commencing Finales in foreign keys, but none of them held the 'correct' key at bay for more than a fraction of the time that Dvořák did in the F major symphony. Whereas Beethoven and Schubert treated the matter as a joke, Dvořák is serious here. Although the tonality shifts, as one might expect with Dvořák, A minor is emphasized three times by the principal theme:

Ex. 13.

before it reappears in a new form in G minor:

Ex. 14.

A lovely mysterious harmonic passage, first with violins and then with flute and oboe playing bell-like pedal notes high in the treble:

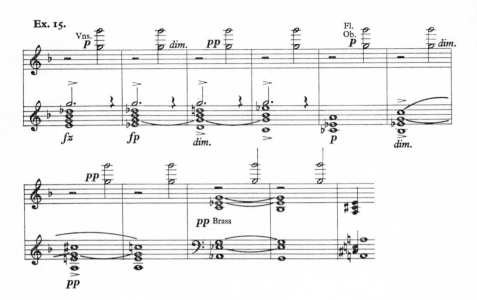

and then mounting close imitations of the main theme lead at last to the return of the second version of the theme, in F major, which key is then firmly fixed in the mind. The second subject group, beginning with a passionate melodic theme and continuing with an ethereal motive, transports us to the extremely distant key of G flat major.

The development is one of the most tempestuous and powerful that Dvořák ever wrote, and it includes this delightful transformation of the second and third bars of the main theme, for two clarinets:

Although not specially marked so, this should be played at an easier pace. As the last climax subsides, a bass clarinet is used for the first time, to follow the oboe in bringing back the first theme quietly in A minor. In the recapitulation F major is reached much sooner than at the beginning of the movement, and the bell-like passage is replaced by another that faintly echoes some of the harmonies of Wagner's 'Magic Sleep' motif. Following the ethereal theme, a chord of F major is quietly held while arpeggios for the strings ascend, and then bars 9–12 of ex. 11 from the first movement return. The beginning of the symphony has been suggested in the most subtle manner, for, despite the new scoring, the tranquil chord alone recalls the mood of the first movement, and it was therefore unnecessary to recall the most vital part of the main theme. After this there is no surprise when a trombone plays the missing part of this theme some fifty bars later, and conductors should see that the trumpets do not obscure it.

The Finale of this symphony reaches out much further than anything Dvořák had written before, and it is not only the most outstanding part of the work, but also one of his finest symphonic movements. It causes the symphony to go out like a lion after coming in like a lamb.

SYMPHONY NO. 6 IN D MAJOR

Five eventful years elapsed before Dvořák again wrote a symphony. During that time the *Moravian Duets*, the first set of *Slavonic Dances*, op. 46, and several other important works were published. Dvořák also continued to win the Austrian State Music Prize, and began to gain recognition abroad, first with his *Slavonic Dances*, and then with his *Slavonic Rhapsodies* and sextet. When the first Vienna performance of his third *Rhapsody* was given by Hans Richter on November 16th, 1879, the composer was present and received a great ovation. Richter was delighted and embraced Dvořák. The composer promised to write a symphony for the Vienna Philharmonic Orchestra and Hans Richter, but he did not start work upon it until several months later. The sketch was begun on August 27th and finished on September 20th, 1880, and the full score was prepared between September 27th and October 15th. The composer took the score to Vienna in November and played the work to Richter, who was so delighted that he kissed Dvořák after every movement, as the latter related to his friend Göbl. The composer dedicated the symphony later to the Viennese conductor.

Dvořák expected his work would be heard in Vienna on December 26th, but Richter wrote to explain that, owing to his orchestra being so over-worked, he was obliged to postpone the performance of Dvořák's 'beautiful composition' until early in March. He added: 'If you are able, entrust me with the *first* performance of your magnificent work.' When Richter wrote again at the beginning of March asking for a further postponement on account of his wife's confinement, his children suffering from diphtheria, his mother's death and pressure of work, Dvořák began to think there were other reasons why the symphony could not be presented. He found out that some members of the orchestra who were consulted when programmes were being arranged objected to playing music by a new Czech composer in two successive seasons.[1] Adolf Čech gave the *première* in Prague on March 25th, 1881, and after the symphony had been published Manns performed it at the Crystal Palace on April 22nd, 1882, and Richter on May 15th the same year at St. James's Hall, London. Richter never conducted it in Vienna, and it fell to Wilhelm Gericke to present it there at a Gesellschaft der Musikfreunde concert on February 18th, 1883. Richter retained his enthusiasm for Dvořák's music, and in two decades performed sixteen different works by the Czech master in the Austrian capital.

Several writers have referred to a number of similarities between Dvořák's D major symphony and Brahms's symphony in the same key, composed three years earlier, but Julius Harrison in an admirable essay on Dvořák's symphony,[2] besides discussing the similarities, makes the following comments on the differences: 'Brahms', he says, 'takes a D major triad as a kind of thesis in triplicate, from which, by means of the melodies resulting from that triad, he proceeds step by step to a logical conclusion. Dvořák takes an odd bit of sound, a mere dominant-tonic progression (perhaps the commonest thing in music), something that could go anywhere or nowhere, something of a character more terminal than initial, and then, to our great delight fashions it into a movement structurally classical, yet thematically having the nature of a lovely improvisation.' Tovey remarked: 'the very first line presents us with those intimations of immortality that make the child sublime,' and adds: 'Dvořák moves with great mastery and freedom; the scale and proportions are throughout noble, and if the procedure is often, like Schubert's, unorthodox and risky, it is in this case remarkably successful.'

Dvořák's first movement is in triple time like Brahms's movement, and the main theme of each work moves to the chord of E minor in the tenth bar, but Dvořák modulates to that key:

Ex. 17.

<hr />

[1] Richter had repeated the third *Slavonic Rhapsody* in Vienna on 29. III. 1880. The Vienna Philharmonic played six Dvořák works during the years 1882–1887, two being played in the last year but none in 1884.

[2] Fischl: *Antonín Dvořák: his achievement*, pp. 272–282.

and Brahms does not. The syncopations of Dvořák's opening bars are found in the Brahms symphony in the neighbourhood of the transition, and the *furiant*-like broadening of time values just before Dvořák's restatement of the main theme in bars 43-46, appears just before the second subject in Brahms's work. These, however, are small points. No one could imagine the quaver and semiquaver passage heard with the first part of the second subject to be the work of any other composer than Dvořák:

Ex. 18.

Dvořák unexpectedly chose the submediant for this group, and after beginning in the minor mode changed to the major.

The restrained first half of the development concentrates on the principal theme, and leads to a charming passage stemming from a figure associated with the main theme. This is given to pairs of flutes and clarinets accompanied by tremolando strings playing *sul ponticello*, which is extremely rare in Dvořák's music:

Ex. 19.

The powerful continuation of the development leads eventually to C sharp major, under the cover of which the recapitulation emerges quietly in D major. The imposing coda of eighty-one bars adds to the majesty of the movement.

The Adagio in B flat major has several points of resemblance with the Adagio molto of Beethoven's ninth symphony. The keys are the same, both movements start with brief imitative introductions, in each case wind instruments echo the ends of phrases played by the strings, and both movements modulate to D major, but, unlike Beethoven, Dvořák only presents a brief thematic germ in that key and then moves elsewhere. The Czech master's movement centres around an extended lyrical melody first used in his early string quartet in B flat (see p. 160), and which recurs twice here in slightly varied guise. The movement is practically monothematic. In the development that occurs after the first repetition of the melody, Dvořák uses astringent harmony in *ff* and follows it with mysterious *pp* modulations. Once again in the coda the spirit of Beethoven's movement is recalled.

The Scherzo is Dvořák's finest *furiant* up to that time. Sometimes, as at the beginning, the bars with strong cross accents and apoggiaturas are separated from the normal triple time bars:

Ex. 20.

but a few bars later the rhythms conflict with one another in the most exciting manner[1] (Ex. 21). Cross accentuation is dropped during the Trio. In this delightful idyll the piccolo reaches for the heavens while woodwind and a

[1] The notation is mine.

Ex. 21.

horn sustain the harmony and 'cellos pluck spread chords. This must be one of the most poetic passages ever written for a piccolo.

The symphony ends with an Allegro con spirito, a large scale sonata structure. Julius Harrison has drawn attention to part of the main theme that comes from the principal theme of the first movement, and which may have been an unconscious reminiscence. It is shown bracketed here:

Ex. 22.

Tovey says the Finale is 'a magnificent crown to this noble work, and is admirably endowed with that quality that is rarest of all in post-classical finales, the power of movement.' There is plenty of exuberance in the Finale, but not much nobility. Dvořák was unwise to use such heavy dynamic markings—more than two-thirds of the movement is marked *forte* or even louder—but if these are suitably modified the movement can be most effective.

SYMPHONY NO. 7 IN D MINOR

Dvořák's next symphony was his last work to show unmistakable signs of the crisis he passed through during the early 1880s. The interest in the composer's operatic work shown in both Vienna and Dresden did not result in his writing operas with German libretti after all, for the nationalist in him finally decided that that would be impossible. That the decision was hard to make can be read in the content of this symphony. It is written on an epic scale, is fundamentally tragic, and judging by the sketches, it cost the composer greater effort and more heart-searching than any comparable work of his. These circumstances help to make it the greatest of his symphonies, but there were other reasons why he endeavoured to create an outstanding work.

After his first highly successful visit to London in March 1884, when several of his works including the D major symphony were performed, Dvořák was invited to compose a symphony for the Philharmonic Society and to conduct the first performance. He regarded this as a great honour and wanted to make sure that his work would be worthy of performance in London. On 22. XII. 1884 he wrote to his friend Rus: 'Just now a new symphony (for London) occupies me, and wherever I go I think of nothing but my work, which must be capable of stirring the world, and may God grant that it will!' Even if the invitation had not come from London, sooner or later he would have been bound to write another symphony, finer than the D major, for he was greatly impressed by Brahms's new F major symphony, which he travelled to Berlin expecially to hear at the end of January 1884, and he wished to compose a work equally great. When he wrote to Simrock in February 1885, he said: 'I have been engaged on the new symphony for a long, long time; after all it must be something really worth while, for I don't want Brahms's words to me, "I imagine your symphony quite different from this one (the D major)" to remain unfulfilled . . .'

The sketches were begun on December 13th, 1884, but it is uncertain when they were finished. In any case additional sketches which have not been found must have been made, for there are several sections of the extant sketches which differ too greatly from the final version to serve as a basis for the preparation of the full score, and besides the last movement caused trouble and was left incomplete.[1] The full score has no date at the beginning,

---

[1] The sketches are described in detail in *Music and Letters*, XLII, 2.

but was completed on March 17th, 1885. The first performance took place at the St. James's Hall on April 22nd that year. During June the slow movement was revised. Dvořák was present when Hans von Bülow gave splendidly successful performances of the work in Berlin on October 27th and 28th, 1889, and he was so delighted that he stuck the celebrated conductor's portrait on the title page of the score, and underneath wrote the words: 'Praise to you! You brought this work to life!'

The mood and range of the first movement are hinted at darkly in the theme muttered by violas and cellos at the beginning of the work:

Ex. 23.

The strongly marked feeling of foreboding is emphasised here by the repetitiveness of the theme, by the flattened sevenths, and by the hopelessness invoked by the diminished seventh on which the first phrase finishes and over which the theme is continued by a pair of clarinets. The main theme, originally suggested to the composer when he witnessed the arrival in Prague of the festival train from Budapest,[1] needed to be moulded to conform to the high aims he had for this symphony. He did not think of using the diminished seventh at first: this was one of those great inspirations that helped to transform the movement as it was taking shape. Two turbulent themes appear in G minor, the second of them being a close relative of the principal allegro theme of the *Hussite* overture (see p. 113). A new theme makes way for a delightful dialogue between horn and oboe in the unrelated key of E flat major, stemming from the earlier part of the same theme. This is interrupted by the important rhythm (b) from the main theme, which leads to a short restatement of four bars of the theme itself, with rhythm (b) now replacing rhythm (a).[2] After a short period of groping, the second subject appears in B flat major.

[1] As Sychra has pointed out, this train brought several hundred anti-Hapsburgian patriots to the National Theatre Festival, and was fêted as it passed through Moravia and Bohemia.

[2] When sketching the opening bars of the symphony Dvořák was very uncertain in which bars to use (a) and (b) respectively, and he changed his mind several times. Sure of himself at last, he reserved this more powerful emphasis for the restatement.

Ex. 24.

The beginning of this melody may have been an unconscious recollection of the main Andante theme of Brahms's second piano concerto. The key is the same, but the metre is more like another of the *Hussite* overture themes, the one derived from the St. Wenceslas plainchant, and even the melodic shape is not far removed from this (see p. 112, ex. 2b). From the fourth bar onwards the melody is entirely individual. There follows what Tovey has described as 'one of Dvořák's greatest musical paragraphs', a wistful melody for violins accompanied by woodwind arpeggios and flute trills that expands and rises passionately to a climax. The remainder of the exposition is built on the two quoted themes and the first '*Hussite* theme', which are finely combined at the greatest point of tension. There is no repeat, although there are still traces of Dvořák's intention to include one.

The development is one of the most concise in the Czech master's music,[1] and may well be his greatest. As is so often the case Dvořák seizes upon his second subject first before concentrating on the far greater potentialities of his principal theme. A sudden twist of tonality brings back the tonic key unexpectedly at the climax, and with it the most brilliant short-circuiting of more than fifty bars of the first subject, due once more to one of the composer's inspired afterthoughts. Picking up the recapitulation at the emphatic restatement of the main theme, the second subject is reached almost at once, and except for the omission of a repeat is heard in full. In the coda another great climax is reached, and when this collapses the main theme is pierced with tragic harmonic sword-thrusts (Ex. 25). The movement ends in a spirit of resignation.

The Poco adagio in F major shows Dvořák's mastery in another way. There is no need for concern about the clear-cut cadences in the fourth and eighth bars of the beautifully shaped opening, for after these the music flows on, gradually increasing in chromaticism and gaining in intensity,

[1] Tovey calls it 'this shortest of all Dvořák's developments', but failed to verify his statement. The development of the first movement of the sextet is even shorter.

Žitná ulice, 10 (now No. 14), where Dvořák lived from 1877
until the end of his life. A contemporary photograph

St. Adalbert's church, Prague, where Dvořák was organist
from 1874–77. From a painting c. 1860–70

Antonín Dvořák c. 1881. Engraving, after a photograph

Antonín Dvořák c. 1877–78

Ex. 25.

until it passes through a passage of amazing pathos, which needs quotation, and comes to rest on a tonic pedal while a solo horn converses diatonically with woodwind instruments. The poignant melody for violins and cellos with drooping diminished sevenths and major sixths and the solemn chords given in alternate bars to trombones, clarinets, bassoons and pizzicato double basses, and to oboes, a horn and *pizzicato* second violins and violas, shows extraordinary imagination on Dvořák's part, and must be without any musical parallel (Ex. 26).

The pair of minor triads (E♮ = F♭) with added sixths may have been suggested by similarly placed pairs of chords (dominant sevenths with apoggiaturas) in bars 57–62 of the Andante of Brahms' third symphony. Both passages obscure the tonality, but Brahms gives an impression of aloofness while Dvořák makes a deep emotional appeal. The middle section begins with a brief stormy passage in the tonic minor that leads to a steeply falling and rising melody for the clarinet in D flat major, which is then passed to other instruments, moves to other keys and reaches a climax. A long pedal E in the bass suggests preparation for a modulation to A major, which was at one time the key chosen by Dvořák for the commencement of the recapitulation. However, an interrupted cadence effects a swift and unexpected return to F major, and the forward momentum is maintained by the omission of the first ten bars of the movement. When the tragic melody returns, flute oboe and clarinet add the stately countermelody shown in the previous

7

Ex. 26.

illustration. The music becomes much more impassioned, the missing opening phrase of the movement returns quietly, and finally there are reminders of the clarinet melody.

Even though the Scherzo is written in $\frac{6}{4}$ time it is virtually a *furiant*, for the characteristic conflict of $\frac{3}{2}$ and $\frac{3}{4}$ rhythms is much in evidence, and the composer originally wrote a substantial part of the movement in $\frac{3}{4}$ time (Ex. 27). Surprising as it may seem, Dvořák, who one might expect could toss off dance movements with the greatest of ease, found the composition of this movement a tough proposition. He crossed out completely the first two pages of his sketch, and, having started again, was then compelled to reject half of the next page. The outstanding success of this movement cannot

Ex. 27.

be questioned. After the exhilaration and verve of the Scherzo proper, tempered by its minor tonality, the Trio in G major provides a fascinating contrast, and seems to transport us to the tranquil yet throbbing life of woodland and meadow. Contrary to his original intention, Dvořák cut his *da capo* very short and added a long coda. After a deliberately halting start this last section gives us a superbly tragic cry from the violas, builds up its climax on a repeated rising scale in the bass, and shows the composer's splendid awareness of the spirit of the work as a whole.

The mood of tragedy is heard immediately in the Finale. Its main theme was foreshadowed in the slow movement of the F minor trio, but now the underlying scale includes two augmented seconds and a diminished third, which help to give it much greater intensity (Ex. 28).

The last three notes become the starting point for a chorale-like theme that follows immediately. After a while a much used rhythmic fragment emerges as the first of the transition themes. The second subject begins with a graceful but rather light-weight melody for cellos in A major. In the closing section the singing becomes more and more ardent until at the beginning of the development the insistent rhythm of dotted crotchets and quavers banishes the ecstatic feeling.

Almost at once the surprising passage shown in ex. 29 occurs. If the first chord of *Tristan*, demoted, was the springboard, how different is the sequel!

Ex. 28.

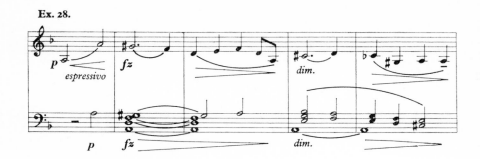

Ex. 29.

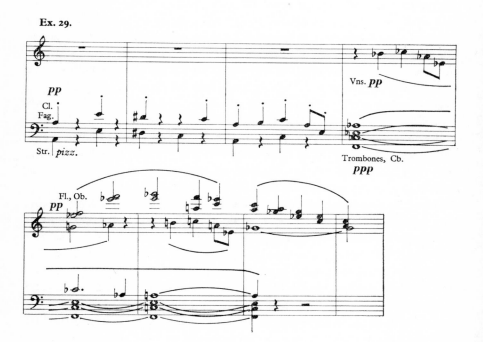

Some of the remainder of the development fails to shed much fresh light on the musical material, and disappoints after the promising opening. The recapitulation is shortened, the rhythmic theme being omitted altogether until the coda. Here Dvořák is conscious once again of his responsibilities, and the work ends majestically in the tonic major.

SYMPHONY NO. 8 IN G MAJOR

Dvořák's next symphony was composed mainly at his house in the country at Vysoká during a period of contentment. He began sketching themes on August 26th, 1889, made the continuous sketch of the four movements between September 6th and 23rd, and prepared the definitive score from September 6th to November 8th. The score bears the inscription: 'For being admitted to membership of the Emperor Franz Josef's Czech Academy of Science, Literature and the Arts', an honour he received in April 1890. Dvořák conducted the first performance on February 2nd, 1890, in Prague. He conducted it again at a Philharmonic Society concert in London on April 24th, at Frankfurt-on-Main on November 7th, and at Cambridge on June 15th, 1891, the day before he received an honorary doctorate.

During 1890 his relationship with his publisher, Simrock, deteriorated seriously. More than ten years earlier Dvořák had agreed to offer every new composition to Simrock first, but he was dissatisfied when he was only offered 1,000 marks for this symphony and told short pieces would be more acceptable. This dissatisfaction was only natural, for the Berlin publisher, after some bargaining with Dvořák, had paid him six times as much for his D minor symphony. Eventually the new work was published in 1892 by Novello of London as 'No. 4'.

Richter performed the symphony in London on July 7th, 1890, and planned to give it in Vienna that year. Dvořák was very touched by his devotion, and wrote to him on October 16th: '. . . I feel myself, honoured Friend and Patron, eternally indebted to you. May God reward you for it! There is nothing I can do—only my heart and my feelings say: "Keep to the path that leads to the highest point of noble art, and thus you will be able to repay in the greatest measure".'

Richter was obliged to postpone the Vienna performance until January 4th, 1891. Dvořák excused himself from attending as he had just been appointed professor of composition at the Prague Conservatoire, and did not feel able to be absent just at the time when he was due to take up his duties. Šourek, however, senses that he may have been annoyed by the delay. Richter wrote as follows after the concert:

Dear bad Friend,

You would certainly have been pleased with this performance. All of us felt that it is a magnificent work, and so we were all enthusiastic. Brahms dined with me after the performance and we drank to the health of the unfortunately absent father of No. 4. Vivat sequens!

Your devoted,

Hans Richter

The success was warm and hearty.

While composing this work Dvořák had no symphony of Brahms in mind as a stimulus to high endeavour; on the contrary he allowed himself to experiment, and the result is hardly satisfactory in the Finale. Yet in many ways this is a lovable work and thoroughly Czech. The label 'English', due to its publication in London, is unnecessary and misleading. There is no substance in Tovey's assertion that the symphony shows 'traces of an effort to meet with what the composer took for English musical taste'. The D major and D minor symphonies had been most warmly received by the English public, yet Dvořák did not attempt to write a work in any way similar to those. The G major symphony was written not for England but to satisfy Dvořák himself.

The novel and effective feature of the first movement, and one of the composer's second thoughts, lies in the noble introductory 'cello melody in G minor, which returns before the development, and reappears on the trumpets richly accompanied just before the recapitulation. The first subject has two greatly contrasted ideas, the first a light and rhythmic pentatonic theme for the flute which is followed by tender echoes for strings, and the second a solemn melody for violas and 'cellos in harmony, which grows out of bars 8–10 of the Introduction. It is accompanied not only by a figure associated with the flute theme, but by part of that theme itself, so that the antithesis is resolved. The second subject and closing section are in the mediant minor and major, but the key is not established by the first theme:

Ex. 30.

Both this and the next theme start with a three-fold repetition of the first notes, in the manner of some Czech folk-songs.

The second subject is not used in the development. There is a delightful interlude in F sharp major with the flute playing a charming countermelody while clarinets and violas have the solemn theme. After this, close imitations of the same theme in diminution lead to a big climax. A turbulent combination of the two first themes follows, which reaches a crisis on no ordinary diminished seventh chord, after which the introductory melody sails in majestically. Again Dvořák telescopes his first subject drastically, and neither the solemn theme nor the diffident theme just quoted are heard again.

The comparison often made between the Adagio and Dvořák's pianoforte piece, *In the Old Castle* (op. 85, no. 3), does not seem to me to be particularly apt. Kretzschmar imagined he heard 'solemn church music, serenades, sprightly march sounds from afar, elements utterly diverse ... most happily brought together',[1] but there appears to be no means of knowing if the composer had a definite picture in mind. Dvořák's sketch shows that he intended the movement to commence in C major, but later, without altering the written notes, he added a key signature of three flats, which changed it to E flat major:

Ex. 31.

Except for this beginning, which even touches D flat major momentarily, the movement is in C major with chromatic depressions, a mixture of sunlight and dark shadows:

Ex. 32.

---

[1] Kretzschmar denied that this symphony was symphonic, and relegated it to a place beside the Slavonic Rhapsodies. *Vide:* 'Führer durch den Concertsaal'.

The four rising notes at the beginnings of the phrases return again in the middle section, which is in unclouded C major. In this part we seem to hear a cimbalom[1] playing descending scales in sixths while flute and oboe sing joyfully. The opening bars return *ff*, not in E flat as before, but in C major, and then all is hushed until a horn bursts forth dramatically in a remote key. For a while there is some agitated development, which eventually gives way to a coda in which most of the important themes have a place.

The Allegretto grazioso in G minor is a waltz that needs to be taken at a moderate pace to avoid loss of detail. The first phrases are skilfully extended to ten and eleven bars. The Trio theme in the tonic major is taken from Dvořák's opera *The Stubborn Lovers*. Finally this is transformed into $\frac{2}{4}$ time for the molto vivace coda. The last movement consists of variations on a theme announced by the 'cellos, but has an interlude in C minor. The key scheme is rather monotonous, and there are moments of bombast that need careful handling. The flute variation, subtly linked with the theme, is particularly attractive. A trumpet heralds the theme, and anticipates some of its melodic curves. The theme, like the main theme of the first movement, starts with three rising notes of the tonic triad. Julius Harrison, who in writing about this symphony suggested that Dvořák would have had 'little time for second thoughts on anything', would have been surprised to learn that the composer made ten sketches before he was satisfied that he had a suitably shaped theme for this finale.[2]

SYMPHONY NO. 9 IN E MINOR, 'FROM THE NEW WORLD'

While sketching the second movement of his last symphony Dvořák wrote these words to Geisler (24. I. 1893): 'It seems to me that American soil will influence my thought beneficially, and I could almost say that something of that kind is already heard in the new symphony.'

On April 12th he wrote to Kozánek: '. . . I have just finished a new symphony in E minor. It pleases me very much and will differ very substantially from my earlier compositions. Well the *influence* of America can be felt by anyone who has "a nose".' The influence that he mentions refers to his interest in Negro spirituals and the plantation songs of Stephen Foster, and also in the songs of the North American Indians. Later on he wrote as follows:

> The music of the people is like a rare and lovely flower growing amidst encroaching weeds. Thousands pass it, while others trample it under foot, and thus the chances are that it will perish before it is seen by the one

[1] In eastern parts of Czechoslovakia the traditional band for dancing consists of three violins and a small double bass, to which are added a clarinet and cimbalom.
[2] See pp. 32-33.

discriminating spirit who will prize it above all else. The fact that no one has as yet arisen to make the most of it does not prove that nothing is there.[1]

In order to become better acquainted with the spirituals he invited a Negro student at the National Conservatory of Music in New York, Harry T. Burleigh, to sing to him on several occasions. The spirituals and Foster's songs impressed him deeply. It was less easy to become familiar with Indian music. He was given transcriptions of some songs, he visited Buffalo Bill's Wild West Show, and after judging musical works entered for competitions, said, 'here and there another spirit, other thoughts, another colouring flashes, in short Indian music, something á la "Bret Harte".'[2] In an interview with the *New York Herald* (15. XII. 1893) he stated that he had found the music of the Negroes and Indians practically identical. '. . . the music of the two races bore a remarkable similarity to the national music of Scotland. In both there is a peculiar scale, caused by the absence of the fourth and seventh, or leading note. In both the minor scale has the seventh and invariably a minor seventh, the fourth is included and the sixth omitted.' Consequently he studied the Indian melodies carefully in order to absorb their spirit, and declared:

> It is this spirit which I have tried to reproduce in my new symphony. I have not actually used any of the melodies. I have simply written original themes embodying the peculiarities of the Indian music, and using these themes as subjects, have developed them with all the resources of modern rhythms, harmony, counterpoint and orchestral colour.

The further one goes in this matter, the more uneasy one becomes. It is not possible to discover the nature and spirit of Indian music by studying a few simple transcriptions prepared before the art of transcribing had been placed on a solid scientific basis, and it is doubtful what he might have gained from a visit to the Wild West Show. It is clear that in comparing the music of the two races Dvořák concentrated his attention on their scalar characteristics, but he does not appear to have realized that pentatonic scales are more common in Negro than in Indian music.[3] Up to a point there

[1] Harper's Magazine, February 1895.
[2] Letter to Josef Hlávka, 27. XI. 1892.
[3] Frances Densmore, an indefatigable collector of Indian song from numerous parts of the United States, found on the average that only twenty per cent of the songs used the major pentatonic scale, but among the Ojibways (Minnesota), the Omahas (Nebraska) and the Menominees (Wisconsin) the percentages range from twenty-six to thirty-one. Eight per cent use the minor pentatonic scale. Seventeen per cent of the songs use only four different notes of the scale, and there are songs that use no more than one or two notes. Densmore's cumulative tabulations are found in her 'Yuman and Yaqui Music', Washington, 1932.

is some agreement here, but melodically, structurally, in the method of performance and even rhythmically the differences are very great. Negro songs by comparison are far more sophisticated. Krehbiel sweepingly asserted, 'as to Indian music, I do not believe that the Doctor ever saw or heard a single song of our aborigines'. It is quite clear that Dvořák was much more strongly influenced by Negro melodies than by Indian song, but his symphony, it must be emphasized, is far more Czech than American.

About thirty years before visiting America Dvořák had read Longfellow's *Song of Hiawatha* in a Czech translation. On arriving in New York he became seriously interested in composing an opera on this subject, but he did not get beyond a few preliminary sketches. The funeral of Minnehaha in the forest, however, inspired the Largo of the symphony, and the Scherzo was suggested by the feast in *Hiawatha* at which the Indians dance. At times Dvořák suffered from severe nostalgia when he was so far from home, and this feeling affected the Largo, and also the slow movement of the string quartet in F.

Dvořák began to sketch his themes on December 19th, 1892. The continuous sketch was begun on January 10th, 1893 and finished on May 12th. The first page of the full score is dated February 9th, and on the last page is written: 'Praise God! Finished on May 24th, 1893. The children have arrived at Southampton. Antonín Dvořák. A cable arrived at 1.33 in the afternoon.' The exciting news of his four children's progress on their way to the United States for a summer holiday was too much for the composer: when the work was first rehearsed he discovered that he had forgotten to add parts for the trombones in the last bars. The title *From the New World* was added just before the score was delivered to Seidl, who conducted the first performance. Dvořák explained that all this meant was 'Impressions and greetings from the New World'.

The composer was not present at the 'public rehearsal' on the afternoon of December 15th, 1893, but he attended the world *première* at the Carnegie Hall, New York, on the 16th, and received a tremendous ovation. Writing to Simrock he said: '. . . I had to show my gratitude like a king? from the box in which I sat. It made me think of Mascagni in Vienna (don't laugh!).' The symphony was performed at Boston on December 30th with Emil Paur conducting, and Seidl presented it at Brooklyn on January 11th, 1894. It was given its first European performance by Mackenzie in London on June 21st, and its first Czechoslovak performance by Labitzký at Karlovy Vary (Karlsbad) on July 20th that year.

Most of the themes used in the *New World* symphony are found in early forms in one of Dvořák's American sketch books, but only those for the slow movement make their first appearance in the same keys as in the symphony. A preference is shown for themes in flat keys, and the main theme of the first movement is given in F major, so that it is possible that the composer may have thought of writing the work in that key, with the slow movement in D flat major, the flattened submediant, which was quite a normal choice for him. More will be said presently on why this remote key was retained after E minor was selected as the key of the symphony.

The main theme of the first movement:

Ex. 33.

is foreshadowed in the slow Introduction, which moves dramatically from melancholy to passionate ejaculations. The primitive repetitions of the answering phrase give a foretaste of what we shall hear in the Finale. The *tutti* restatement of the theme comes sooner than is usual with Dvořák. It leads on first to a compact theme accompanied with pedal notes in G minor, which is roughly inverted in its second half,[1] and then, after a risky return to the tonic key, proceeds to the G major theme for the flute in its lowest octave, that reminds most people of '[Swing low, sweet] chariot, coming for to carry me home'. It may be a coincidence that the next two bars are similar to part of the refrain of 'The Little Alabama Coon', which was published in the year the symphony was written. Mercifully Dvořák did not use Hattie Starr's mawkish answering phrase, but wrote an original ending. The whole melody is one of the Czech master's freshest creations:

Ex. 34.

It is strange to find the beginning of the development making straight for E major. The drama begins when the trumpet cuts through diminutions of the flute melody with a variant of the same theme in F major and a trombone replies with the main theme in ambiguous diminished seventh form. The themes follow one another naturally because their rhythms are so similar.

---

[1] In its original form it was inverted exactly, with the possible exception of a doubtful note in the third bar, so instead of showing a flattened seventh in a minor key it made a 'Moravian modulation' to the major key a tone lower. For further information on this symphony see my article in *The Musical Quarterly*, XLIV, 2.

After passing through F sharp and E flat minors the tonic key is reached, but this is a false alarm and the key soon vanishes. A series of sequences with the main theme superimposed on dominant sevenths rising by semitones leads unobtrusively to the recapitulation. There is a little shortening of the first subject, and then Dvořák brilliantly departs from custom by presenting the second subject in the remote keys of G sharp minor and A flat major. He was quite sure of himself over this, for these keys are shown in the sketch without any of the usual hesitations and changes of mind. This master stroke enables him to achieve another stroke of genius, an unexpectedly sudden change onto a six-four chord in A major, which is made to blaze forth gloriously while the two themes quoted above are combined.[1]

The two most interesting things about the Largo are the melody for the cor anglais, which is almost as famous as the composer's *Humoresque* in G flat and has been turned into the song 'Goin' Home', and secondly the series of chords with which the movement is framed. The theme has an unmistakable Negro flavour about it, and bears a remarkably close resemblance to A. Johnson's 'Massa Dear', but this was probably inspired by Dvořák's melody. The slight similarities that may be observed between the Largo theme and the Macintosh lament, 'Cumha Mhic an Toisich', may well be fortuitous. The cor anglais enhances the Negro characteristics of the song, but at first Dvořák thought of giving it to a clarinet and flutes. H. C. Colles, who was fortunate enough to hear Burleigh sing a number of the spirituals he sang to Dvořák, thought the composer had chosen the cor anglais because of all instruments it resembled the quality of Burleigh's voice most closely.

Dvořák wrote the Largo in continuous sketch in the submediant key, C major. While at work on it he decided to add some minim chords he had been experimenting with, and use these as an introduction and twice later in the movement. The chords began and ended with chords of C major, and were almost in the same form in which they appear (transposed up a semitone) when heard for the second and third times in the definitive version. Later the composer discovered that if he transposed the chords into E major and changed little more than one chord, the last, they would give him a modulation from the tonality of the first movement to the key in which he had originally conceived the cor anglais melody, D flat major. Consequently he transposed the movement into D flat when preparing the full score, and gave us the miraculous modulation that has been so highly praised by many commentators. The two versions of the chords are shown here:

[1] The change is achieved in three chords: tonic triad of A flat; dominant seventh of D flat in last inversion; second inversion of A major. After eight bars this last chord which has become minor, is followed by the augmented sixth and then by an interrupted cadence in E minor. This is strong harmony.

Ex. 35a.

Ex. 35b.

In the minor middle section new themes for flute and oboe together and for clarinet are heard twice over with changes of scoring, and then a vivacious new theme in the major interrupts the elegiac mood, and tends to confirm the impression that Dvořák was sometimes too prodigal with his ideas. Perhaps there is a good reason for the theme's inclusion, for its function is somewhat similar to that of Macbeth's drunken porter. He provides comic relief immediately before the murder of Duncan is discovered, and this theme whips up a feeling of gaiety just before the brass solemnly proclaims the two first movement themes and the cor anglais melody in combination. This movement, which hardly ever leaves the tonic key, ends in the funereal mood in which it began.

The only Indian feature of the Scherzo is the accompaniment in repeated crotchets in the opening bars, but the curious chord heard at that time, a secondary seventh on the tonic in E minor, was a freak of Dvořák's. We can imagine Pau-Puk-Keewis whirling around in the pseudo-canon for woodwind instruments. The Poco sostenuto does not mark the beginning of the Trio, but the middle section in the tonic major of the ternary Scherzo proper. A transformation of the main theme of the first movement, given to horns and bass instruments and occurring at the end of the Scherzo section, may not be noticed. This theme is heard twice more in the transition to the C major Trio, and the same theme's last three notes become an important accompaniment figure. The Trio appears to be in the style of a *sousedská*.[1] In the coda both the first movement themes return, the second being reserved for the climax.

The Allegro con fuoco is in sonata form, but with a repetitive fantasia that is afraid to allow the tonic key out of earshot in place of a development. This is not a very happy solution to the problem. The main theme in E minor,

[1] This is not marked *meno mosso*, but a slower pace is necessary.

announced by the trumpets, is a broad and noble melody with much more *alla breve* feeling about it than common time. An animated but repetitive theme follows in the same key, to be followed after a brief transition by the beautiful second subject melody for solo clarinet. It is disappointing to see how Dvořák, master of movement that he was, cobbles his bars together in the fantasia. Tovey comments that the Three Blind Mice of the closing section refuse to run. Add to this the stagnation of key, and the by now inevitable reappearance of themes from earlier movements, in this case from the Largo, the Scherzo and finally the first movement, and we see how the composer's judgment was impaired.[1] But there are compensations to follow. In the recapitulation the first subject is drastically curtailed and a miraculous series of descending first inversion triads wafts us to the second subject. The mice are replaced by echoes of the delights of Venusberg in the closing section. During the coda the main first movement theme rears its head angrily, the introduction to the Largo, now in E minor, 'strides over the world like Wagner's Wotan when he rides the storm' (Tovey), the cor anglais and Scherzo themes pair off once more, and the main themes of the first and last movements are combined, causing what is for Dvořák exceptionally astringent harmony:

Ex. 36.

---

[1] The rudimentary nature of the writing is probably due to the influence of folk music of America, and may be regarded as characteristic of the composer's most typically American works.

IV

The Concertos

Dvořák destroyed most of his compositions of the 1860s, but a few key works survived the flames, the most notable being the string quintet and string quartet of 1861–1862, and the two symphonies, the *Cypresses* song cycle and the 'cello concerto in A major of 1865. The composer regarded his first symphony as lost. Later on he showed sufficient interest in the songs and the second symphony to return to them and revise them for publication or performance, but the 'cello concerto remained in its early form with pianoforte accompaniment, and was never orchestrated by the composer. The work was rediscovered in Württemberg in 1925, and was edited, scored for orchestra and published by Günter Raphael.

Raphael pointed out that the original version of the concerto by no means gives the impression of being definitive, and yet it might have served Dvořák adequately as the detailed sketch upon which he could base his full score. The solo 'cello part is shown in full, but in the piano part we notice a dearth of thematic interest in the solo sections. It may be presumed that the composer did not intend to indicate all the significant features of the accompaniment in the piano score, and that, as was his custom later, he would have seized upon opportunities to enrich his score as he continued to work upon it, probably making modifications to the 'cello part at the same time.

Why did he leave the work unscored? The explanation that springs most readily to mind is that he was not sufficiently confident that the unorthodoxy of his first essay in concerto form was satisfactory, and that this, like several earlier works, would have to be regarded as experimental. He completed the piano score on June 30th, 1865. Ten days later he was immersed in his song cycle, and no sooner had he finished that than he became caught up in the creation of a symphony of even greater promise than *The Bells of Zlonice*. Perhaps if Ludevít Peer, to whom the concerto was dedicated, had urged the composer to complete the work, Dvořák would have undertaken to orchestrate it, and possibly revise it at the same time, but it seems unlikely that Peer was sufficiently impressed by it to do so.

Raphael, fully aware of his heavy responsibility in attempting to present a performing edition of Dvořák's immature concerto, claimed that he had at all times striven to conform to Dvořák's thematic, harmonic and technical style in making modifications additions and cuts, besides preserving the spirit of the Czech composer's orchestration.[1] It will be readily admitted that substantial changes were desirable, and that Dvořák's concerto was unsatisfactory from several points of view, but the liberties that Raphael has allowed himself to take show his claim to be hollow, as the following examples will show. The harmony, phrase shapes and figuration in his version of the first bars for the solo 'cello in the Rondo deviate considerably from Dvořák's original:

Ex. 1a.   DVOŘÁK

Ex. 1b.   RAPHAEL

In the first movement Raphael's version of the beginning of the second subject, with its three-bar phrases, syncopations in the answering phrase, extreme chromaticism and dominant pedal in the bass, is a travesty of the composer's intentions and style. When Dvořák repeated this section shortly afterwards he did indeed have a dominant pedal and treble instruments moving in thirds, but the pedal occurred in an inner part and there was hardly a suggestion of chromaticism. Dvořák's first version is shown in exx. 2a and 2b. Raphael said he had reshaped (Neugestaltung) the concerto, but it would be more accurate to describe it as reshaped and newly composed.

The form of Dvořák's first movement is far from satisfactory. Except for the principal theme, the material of the first tutti is neither used in the first

---

[1] Raphael goes as far as to state that the original version would take no less than one and a half hours to perform, whereas, in fact, it would not have lasted more than about fifty-two minutes.

Antonín Dvořák in 1892

The Carolinum, Prague. The university conferred an honorary doctorate on Dvořák in March 1891

Antonín Dvořák c. 19

Family group at Vysoká, c. 1901. Front row: Aloisie, Antonín (son), Marie Štěpánková (niece of Anna Dvořáková); middle row: Marie Bohdanecká (daughter of Judge Rus), Dvořák, Anna (wife); back row: Anna (daughter), a friend, Magda

solo, nor in the development or the recapitulation. This tutti is in clear-cut ternary form, while the second tutti consists solely of twenty-two bars borrowed from the opening, the themes of which are then summarily dismissed, and not heard again until the coda of the Finale. There is practically no attempt at development, but it is interesting to note that Dvořák tried his hand at short-circuiting his recapitulation by omitting the whole of the first subject, reminding us of the brilliant compression at a similar point in his more famous 'cello concerto. The short cadenza comes, rather curiously, at the end of the exposition. The most serious defect in the movement is due to the composer's apparent failure to recognize the need for

Ex. 2a.

DVOŘÁK

8

Ex. 2b.   RAPHAEL

alterations of tutti and solo. It is astonishing to find that the second solo extends over the whole of the free fantasia and the shortened recapitulation, and then continues unbroken to the end of the Andante cantabile. Although the first movement leads into the second without a break, there is no thematic connection between them.

The Rondo is an independent movement, but forty bars from the opening tutti of the first movement reappear (in the coda) for no very good reason, and a few bars later a first movement theme, that had not been recapitulated along with its companion themes, returns like a long-lost friend, and is followed by other reminiscences. In this concerto Dvořák displays an unbridled fecundity, especially in the first movement, and some themes reappear at short intervals in new guises. The Andante shows Dvořák's gift for writing a sustained and expressive melodic line, which we also notice in his symphonies of the same year. The accented crotchets in $\frac{6}{8}$ time at the beginning of the Rondo, and used later in the movement, provide cross-rhythms reminiscent of the *furiant*. This last movement is relatively orthodox and is the most satisfactory in form. Example 1a gives some indication of its rhythmic zest.

PIANOFORTE CONCERTO

Eleven years passed before Dvořák attempted to write another concerto, and on that occasion the task was completed. Much more interest was shown in new Czech music by the virtuoso pianist, Karel ze Slavkovských, than by other instrumentalists of that time, and so Dvořák decided to compose a concerto for him. The full score was prepared during August and the first half of September 1876, a year after the F major symphony, immediately after the *Moravian Duets*, and when he was brooding over his *Stabat Mater*. Slavkovský performed the work in Prague on March 24th, 1878, and it was repeated with success by Oscar Beringer at the Crystal Palace on October 13th, 1883. Beringer had written to Dvořák some time before[1] asking him to compose a piano concerto for him that he could play at the Crystal Palace, at Philharmonic concerts and possibly in Germany as well, without being aware that Dvořák had already written one.

Besides being a viola player and organist, Dvořák was a pianist worthy of appearing in public with distinguished soloists in performances of his own chamber music. He took some time, however, to adapt his musical thought to a keyboard style, a style that came less naturally to him than writing for strings. He had composed three chamber works with pianoforte and a number of songs and duets shortly before starting on the concerto, but it was a far cry from any of these to a virtuoso work for a pianist. In the circumstances Dvořák did remarkably well, and he was able to express his own individuality in the greater part of the work, while making the example of Beethoven his mainstay, and incorporating a Chopinesque filigree in the Andante sustenuto and occasional suggestions of Brahms elsewhere. It is a pity he did not seek the advice of Slavkovský when at work on the concerto, for the layout of the solo part is often ineffective, and at times the work appears to have been conceived for a player with two right hands. Josef Suk, the composer's son-in-law, told Harriet Cohen[2] that Dvořák recognized the impracticability of the pianoforte writing, and fully intended to re-draft much of the solo part, but always postponed doing so. Several revisions of the piano part have been made by others, and notably by Wilém Kurz, whose version appears under Dvořák's in the Complete Edition score.

The piano concerto in G minor, op. 33, was written on traditional lines, with the customary introductory and anticipatory tutti to the first movement, but Dvořák avoided any anticipation of the second subject group in this section. The movement is serious and noble in tone and symphonic in character, with the piano playing an important but not a dominating role. In the second subject group there are two themes, the first elegant and with a touch of humour, and the second consisting of a chorale-like phrase, succeeded by a sparkling reply from the piano. The first of these lightens the mood from time to time, but the foundation of the whole movement lies in the main theme (Ex. 3), and in the coda this theme takes on an unexpected power within the framework of the diminished seventh. The Andante in D major is meditative and rhapsodic, and typical of the composer in a romantic mood.

[1] The letter is dated July 8th, but Beringer omitted the year (1883).
[2] Fischl: *Antonín Dvořák: his achievement*, p. 129.

Ex. 3.

For the Finale Dvořák wrote a sonata rondo with a pair of themes for the rondo subject. These return simultaneously at the beginning of the recapitulation:

Ex. 4.

a fact that Edwin Evans[1] seems to have overlooked when he compared the first with the introductory theme in the Finale of the G major symphony. In

[1] Fischl: *Antonín Dvořák: his achievement*, p. 89. Lionel Salter follows Evans's example in his contribution to Ralph Hill's *The Concerto*.

the piano concerto this theme is no mere introduction: it is an important factor in the interplay of ideas in the movement as a whole. The second theme is announced by the soloist in F sharp minor and is not heard in the 'correct' key of G minor until twenty-seven bars later. Continuing to be capricious, Dvořák recapitulated this theme normally in the tonic key, and then repeated it in the remote key of B major. There appears to be a conflict of tempi between these two themes, the first being faster than the second, but if an elasticity of tempo is adopted, such as is often found when Czechs perform music of their own country, then each of these themes can be played at its best speed.[1] Josef Suk believed that the composer intended the speeds of the movements to be slower than those indicated by the metronome marks, but this is rather difficult to understand. The second subject, derived from a theme in the string quintet in G, op. 77, has a habit of slowing down after a few bars each time it is heard, but it is less tiresome in this respect than the Grieg piano concerto.

Dvořák's work should not be allowed to drop completely out of the repertoire, for, even if it is not on the same level as his next two concertos, it contains much of the genuine Dvořák, and consequently when performed by sympathetic musicians has much to commend it. It might be remembered, too, that Brahms did not pay much attention to what lay conveniently under the hands when composing for the pianoforte.

Violin Concerto

Dvořák wrote his violin concerto in A minor after composing the first set of *Slavonic Dances*, the *Slavonic Rhapsodies*, the *Czech Suite*, the string sextet, and the string quartet in E flat, during the time when national expression reached its height in his music. The concerto came into being for the most part while he was staying with his friend Alois Göbl, secretary to Prince Rohan of Sychrov castle, near Turnov, and it occupied him from July 5th to the middle of September 1879. At the end of July he paid a private visit to Joseph Joachim in Berlin, and no doubt discussed the new work with him and awakened his interest. Dvořák dedicated the concerto to the great violinist, and posted the manuscript score to him at the end of November. In a letter dated January 15th, 1880, he told Ludevít Procházka that Joachim had promised to play the concerto as soon as it was published.

---

[1] It is instructive to compare the recordings of Maxian/Czech Philharmonic/ Talich and Wührer/Vienna Symphony/Moralt in this concerto. Maxian playing Kurz's version and Wührer Dvořák's. In the former much is made of tempo variations in both the first and the last movements, and the gain is enormous. In the latter the tempi are rather slow and the playing is heavy and turgid.

Once Joachim was able to try the work through, he found it necessary to suggest that a thorough revision of the score should be made. On May 9th, 1880, Dvořák wrote to Simrock as follows:

According to Mr. Joachim's wish I worked most carefully over the whole concerto, without missing a single bar. He will certainly be pleased by that. I put the greatest effort into it. The whole concerto has been transformed. Besides retaining themes I wrote several new ones. The whole conception of the work, however, is different. The harmonization, the instrumentation, the rhythm, the whole course of the work is new. I shall get it ready as soon as possible and give it immediately to Mr. Joachim in Berlin.[1]

Joachim kept the concerto for two years, and then in the summer vacation of 1882 made a number of revisions himself to the solo part. He recognized 'the very genuine beauty' of the work, but advised Dvořák to lighten the instrumentation, after which he hoped the composer would visit Berlin to hear his concerto tried out at the Hochschule. Dvořák did as he suggested, and the rehearsal took place in mid-November.

Robert Keller, who was Simrock's adviser, criticized Dvořák for joining the first and second movements together, and wanted this changed, but the composer was adamant and would make no concession. On December 16th, 1882, he wrote to Simrock: 'You know that I esteem that man (Keller) and can appreciate him, but this time he went rather far ... I am therefore fully of your and Sarasate's opinion that the first two movements can—or must— remain as they are.' The score was published as op. 53 by Simrock in 1883, and the first performance was given in Prague by Ondříček on October 14th. Joachim never performed the concerto,[2] which may seem strange considering he praised the work and took so much trouble to improve it. But it should be remembered that Joachim, the man who had championed Dvořák's sextet and E flat string quartet with such enthusiasm, and helped greatly to make this rising Czech musician better known in Germany and England, was a staunch supporter of the classical stream of composition, an

[1] It is not possible to determine the extent of the changes made by the composer, for he appears to have destroyed most of the pages that he was unable to use again in the new score.

[2] *The Musical World* of 15. III. 84 published information that is corrobated by Dvořák's letter to Ondříček of 9. IV. 84. They stated that Joachim, who was playing a Mozart concerto at the Crystal Palace during Dvořák's first visit to London, was prepared to play the Czech composer's concerto in addition. Manns is said to have insisted that in that case Dvořák himself should conduct the work, but the Philharmonic Society objected as they had invited him over, and besides, their own concert, at which Dvořák would appear on the rostrum, was to take place after the Crystal Palace concert. See also Henry Hersee's letter in *The Musical World* of 29. III. 84. The concerto was first played in London by Ondříček two years later.

admirer of Schumann and an opponent of Liszt and his followers. As Tovey
has stated,[1] 'He evidently did not trust himself to take Beethoven's later
works as models: indeed to the end of his life he always had a smile of pity
for the inexperienced composer who will not learn from any Beethoven
earlier than the last quartets.' In his *Hungarian Concerto* for his own instrument he adhered strictly at the outset to the Beethovenian symphonic tutti,
and to the traditional alternation of tuttis and solos later. He must have had
serious misgivings about Dvořák's foreshortened first movement to have
kept the work in his possession for two years unperformed. It seems probable, after making improvements and further suggestions, trying the composition through and pondering over it, that this ultra-conservative musician
could not conscientiously allow himself to appear in public as the concerto's
advocate.

Briefly, Dvořák dispensed with an introductory symphonic tutti, he
provided no tutti to mark the change from exposition to development, and
it is astonishing to find that he cut the recapitulation short after only thirty-
six bars, and wrote at that point a short linking passage that leads directly
into the Adagio ma non troppo. The exposition of the first movement
starts on broad lines with an all-important bipartite principal theme in A
minor, shared by the orchestra and the soloist:

Ex. 5.

Two subsidiary ideas follow, one in B flat, and the other suggesting D minor
at first, and so appealing that it is unfortunate that it does not reappear
(Ex. 6).

[1] Essays in Musical Analysis, III, p. 107.

The second subject, commencing at bar 148, continues for only twenty-one bars, which is too few. Dvořák knew his own mind, but he made serious structural miscalculations. Fortunately this only applies to the first movement, and in any case the music is most attractive.

The F major Adagio has a ternary basis, with a stormy interlude in the tonic minor. The free recapitulation begins in A flat. Almost as soon as the main key is re-established the orchestra, with an unexpected twist of harmony, entices the soloist into A major, but a rather similar harmonic progression serves to restore the tonality. The Finale starts as a typical *furiant* in A major, and has another theme highly characteristic of this dance for wind instruments alone when the tonality shifts away from the tonic:

This theme has obvious affinities with the well-known folk-song, 'Sedlák, sedlák' (see p. 149). The movement is a sonata rondo, with the important central section a *dumka* in $\frac{2}{4}$ time and in D minor. Each time the Rondo theme returns after an interval it is scored differently, and on the first of these reappearances the imitation of the sound of Czech *dudy*, or bagpipes, is delightful. In this exceptionally national movement even the E major waltz theme becomes naturalized, thanks to its three-fold Slavonic dancers' stamp at the end:

THE CONCERTOS

VIOLONCELLO CONCERTO

The violoncello concerto in B minor, op. 104, was the only new work completed by Dvořák during his third year in the United States. From its content it is clear that his thoughts were turning homewards, and for the first time in an important work composed in America we find American colouring reduced to a bare minimum. It is rather surprising that Dvořák should have chosen to write a concerto for the 'cello, because, according to Josef Michl, he considered it to be a beautiful instrument but only in orchestral and chamber music. He admired the fine middle register, but complained about the nasal quality of the high notes and the mumbling of the bass. He himself, as he said in a letter to Alois Göbl,[1] was the person who was most surprised at his decision to compose such a concerto.

The immediate stimulus to composition is believed to have been Victor Herbert's performance of his own second 'cello concerto at Brooklyn in the spring of 1894. In the slow movement Dvořák was particularly intrigued to observe the composer's cunning in accompanying the solo instrument with three trombones, and it put ideas into his head. Hitherto Dvořák had used the classical orchestra in concertos, but in his B minor concerto he added a piccolo, three trombones, a tuba and triangle. Another reason for composing this work may well have been because Hanuš Wihan, his close friend, a member of the Bohemian String Quartet, and the leading exponent and teacher of the 'cello in his own country, suggested at some time that he should do so. It is clear that he wrote it with Wihan in mind. The sketch and the score were prepared simultaneously. The first movement was begun on November 8th, 1894, and the finale on 'New Year's Day, 1895', but there is no date at the end of the sketch. The full score occupied him between November 18th and February 9th.

While he was at work on the concerto he heard of the serious illness of his sister-in-law, Josefina Kaunitzová, with whom he had been in love in 1865 when she was his pupil and a budding actress. This caused him to use the melody of a song of his which was a favourite of Josefina's, 'Leave me alone' (op. 82, no. 1), in the middle section of the second movement, transforming it, however, from $\frac{4}{4}$ to $\frac{3}{4}$ time. Josefina's death on May 27th, a month after his return to his homeland, affected him deeply, and impelled him to remove four bars just before the end of the work, and substitute sixty new bars. This addition, commencing at bar 449, includes another version of the song Josefina loved, and was intended as a memorial to her.

During August that year when on a visit to Lužany castle, where a few years earlier his Mass in D had had its first performance, Wihan played the concerto through with the composer at the piano. Dvořák had already dedicated the work to him. Wihan suggested some alterations to the solo part in

[1] 10. XII. 1894.

103

the first movement, several of which were adopted, but he also wrote a 59-bar cadenza for the Finale. Dvořák's views on this were made clear in a letter he wrote to Simrock on October 3rd:

I have had some differences of opinion with Friend Wihan over a number of places. I don't like some of the passages—and I must insist on my work being printed as I wrote it. The passages in question can be printed in two versions, an *easier* and a *more difficult* version. I shall only give you the work if you promise not to allow *anybody* to make changes— Friend Wihan not excepted—without my *knowledge* and *consent*—and also not the cadenza that Wihan has added to the last movement. There is no cadenza in the last movement either in the score or in the piano arrangement. I told Wihan straight away when he showed it to me that it was impossible to stick such a bit on. The Finale closes gradually diminuendo, like a sigh, with reminiscences of the 1st and 2nd movements—the solo dies down to *pp*, then swells again, and the last bars are taken up by the orchestra and the whole concludes in a stormy mood. That is my idea and I cannot depart from it.

Dvořák was annoyed with Wihan, because a cadenza would have ruined his conception of a farewell tribute to his sister-in-law. It was not unreasonable to suggest that he may have been sufficiently piqued to have changed his plans, prevented Wihan from giving the first performance, and allowed another 'cellist to have that honour instead. In fact Leo Stern played the concerto first at a Philharmonic Society concert in London. Correspondence has recently come to light, however, which refutes this theory.

Dvořák informed Francesco Berger, the Philharmonic Society's secretary, in a letter dated December 25th, 1895, that Wihan was prepared to play the concerto in London preferably in April; in any case, owing to other commitments, March 19th would be unsuitable for him. On hearing the Society's plans for the forthcoming concert, Dvořák wrote this short note on February 14th, 1896:

My dear friend Berger,

I am sorry to announce you that I cannot conduct the performance of the celo conzerto, the reason is I have promised to my friend Wihan—*he will play it*. If you put the conzerto into the programme I could not come at all, and will be glad to come another time.

With kindly regards
Sincerely yours
Ant. Dvořák

On the back of the letter Berger drafted his reply, dated February 17th, which begins as follows:

104

My dear friend and honoured master!

We should have been most happy to have had Mr. Wihan to play your concerto. But as you told me he could not come on the 19 March we thought to please you by including the work, and have engaged Mr. Leo Stern who says he knows the work. Now when all this is done you write to say you cannot come if we include the concerto. It is very embarrassing for us, but as you wish it we will take the concerto out.

In the end Dvořák decided to fall in with the Society's arrangements, and by the beginning of March he was rehearsing daily in Prague with Leo Stern in preparation for the concert in London on March 19th.[1] Wihan did not play the concerto until January 25th, 1899, when he performed it under Mengelberg's direction at The Hague. He repeated it on December 20th that year in Budapest with Dvořák conducting.

In the first bars of the concerto our attention is immediately held by the lapidary main theme announced in sombre tones by the clarinet:

Ex. 9.

It has sometimes been assumed that the flattened seventh in the second bar shows yet another instance of the influence of Negro spirituals, but this assumption may be incorrect. The mood of the opening is not altogether dissimilar to the beginning of the seventh symphony (1884), where flattened sevenths occur, and furthermore Dvořák originally sketched the first thirty-five bars of the concerto in D minor, the same key as the symphony. The tutti is written on the lines of a symphonic exposition, and Dvořák seemed unaware of the danger of presenting his second subject there in the relative major key, which Beethoven just avoided doing in his third pianoforte concerto. But he does manage to conjure up an air of expectancy and

---

[1] The author discovered these letters after Šourek's death, and too late for them to be taken into account when the violoncello concerto was published in the Complete Edition. The correspondence appears more fully in *Music and Letters* (April 1958) and *Hudební rozhledy*, X, 7 (1957).

mystery just before the soloist enters *Quasi improvisando*. The second subject begins with a lovely melody first given to the horn:

Ex. 10.

and then passed to a clarinet; and oboe joins in with imitations while the return to D major is delightfully delayed, and finally the whole is enriched by the addition of more instruments and a soaring counter-melody for violins. Dvořák told Göbl in the letter already referred to that he had given much thought to this theme before he was satisfied with it. Whenever he played it over he became excited. Tovey has described the quoted bars as 'one of the most beautiful passages ever written for the horn.' With the exception of a passing note it is pentatonic in D and A majors, and only later are additional notes used.

When the solo 'cello enters the material is treated in the expansive and decorative manner so fitting in a work of this kind, and before long the principal theme is played in diminution by the soloist (Ex. 11a), and in the striking manner shown below when chords of B minor and G minor with an added sixth are juxtaposed (Ex. 11b).

Ex. 11a.

In one of the several new themes the 'cellist plays arpeggios against an ambiguous harmonic background. (For other ambiguous passages see pp. 70 and 41–42.) Dvořák thought it worth while to copy out this passage for Göbl to see. Out of this mist the rich key of F sharp major is made to shine.

After the climax at the end of the exposition gloom casts its shadow over the scene, but before long there is a brief passionate outburst by the violins on the dominant of A flat minor. From this point the development ceases,

Ex. 11b.

and instead the 'cellist enters over tremolando strings with a wonderful meditative version of the main theme in augmentation in the newly established key, while a flute makes delightfully discreet comments in the higher octave. This is one of Dvořák's most inspired moments. Florid writing for the soloist leads on to a climax in the tonic key, but it is the second subject that appears here in full glory, the whole of the first subject and the transition having been short-circuited. This is a brilliantly successful dramatic stroke. The remainder of the recapitulation is regular, and a short coda brings the movement to an end.

The Adagio ma non troppo in G major opens in a calm lyrical mood, passes through a tonally ambiguous passage to a momentary climax, and then becomes hushed. A rude awakening follows as the whole orchestra bursts forth in the key of G minor, and at this point Dvořák tenderly recalls his song 'Leave me alone', suggested to him by the news of Josefina's illness. The melody of the original song on its second appearance, and the two versions adopted in this concerto, in the slow movement and the coda of the finale, are shown here:

Ex. 12a.

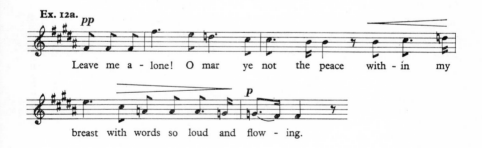

Leave me a - lone! O mar ye not the peace with - in my

breast with words so loud and flow - ing.

Ex. 12b.

[mp] molto espressivo

Ex. 12c.

Out of this melody fresh ideas flow and other keys are reached, until the opening section returns, but this undergoes much alteration and expansion as if Dvořák were reluctant to bring the movement to a close.

The Rondo unfolds with such an abundance of ideas and in such leisurely fashion that Dvořák wisely foreshortens the latter part of the movement. The first episode never returns. To our great surprise the second episode reappears in the tonic major, with the theme played by a solo violin, only thirty-two bars after its first full statement. The extended coda in B major follows, and gradually becomes more dreamy. The clarinets remind us of the opening bars of the concerto, 'Leave me alone' is heard once more, in the major key this time as at the beginning of the song, there are ghostly echoes of the first movement theme, and finally come the stormy closing bars.

When Brahms first saw Dvořák's concerto he was deeply impressed by it, and although he had published his own double concerto a few years earlier, he grumbled to Hausmann: 'Why on earth didn't I know one could write a violoncello concerto like this? If I had only known I would have written one long ago!' Far too few outstanding 'cello concertos have been composed, which is a pity. To write such a concerto poses special problems, and notably that of balance, but even though Dvořák did not appear to trouble himself as greatly over this in the present work as Joachim had troubled him over his violin concerto, or as Elgar did with his own 'cello concerto, he had enough experience and natural instinct to write what would sound well. He could write sufficiently effectively for the soloist to dominate the orchestra when necessary, by both tone and technique, and was also able to surround the solo instrument with a glorious aura of orchestra colour. Noble, yet not without tenderness, humour and many other qualities, this work is not only one of Dvořák's finest achievements, but is also the greatest concerto ever composed for the violoncello.

Programme Music and Overtures

Dvořák was first and foremost a composer of absolute music, and turned readily to the creation of symphonies, concertos and chamber music. At first when he wrote works which involved the setting of words he showed a lack of aptitude, but in time he increased his skill, yet without ever attaining as high a level in these branches of music as when there was no poetry to direct his paths. He first composed songs because he was in love, and operas for a variety of reasons. He had a great admiration for Wagner, and by playing regularly in a theatre he was gaining useful practical experience of compositions for the stage. He was ambitious without realizing fully the implications of what he was about to embark upon, and what qualities were required for the task. He knew opera to be a most desirable world to conquer. Perhaps, too, national pride was a contributory factor, as it undoubtedly was when he wrote his first cantata. Experience gained through the association of music with poetry helped him to extend the boundaries of expression in his music.

Although a staunch nationalist, he refused to identify himself closely with either the 'staročeši', the ardently nationalist and pan-Slavonic conservative group, or the 'mladočeši', the liberal group that tended to favour neo-romanticism and which was also nationalist. Unlike Smetana he had no strong links with Liszt. As a life-long worshipper of Beethoven, however, he could hardly hesitate over the composition of quasi-programmatic overtures, even if, as seems likely, he needed to weigh the pros and cons more closely before following the example of his friend Tchaikovsky by venturing to compose symphonic poems. Dvořák was open-minded, and ready, perhaps too ready, to follow new paths, even though this might mean in the present instance disappointing those of his admirers who regarded him as an upholder of classical traditions. Had he wished to show that he could rival Smetana in this new field he would have composed symphonic poems far sooner, and not waited until nearly a dozen years after his predecessor's death. This type of composition was practically the only one then current which Dvořák had not made use of, and perhaps he had the satisfaction of thinking that this new departure of his would demonstrate once more his adaptability and versatility. Possibly his conversations with Seidl, the keen Wagnerian who was his close friend in New York, helped him to come to a decision.

In his manuscript book entitled 'New York 1893. Jottings' he sketched a theme for a composition based on Erben's *Golden Spinning Wheel*. His correspondence of that time suggests that the work would have been a cantata, and in any case the theme was never used. But it is perhaps significant that at that time he was being drawn again towards Erben's world of fantasy, and it was not long before this magnetic attraction proved to be irresistible and he used four of these ballads as subjects for symphonic poems.[1]

OVERTURES

The overture that Dvořák wrote between January 21st and 23rd in 1882 for Šamberk's play *Josef Kajetán Tyl* was rarely heard serving its intended function, and almost immediately became in effect a concert overture called *My Home*. However, the title *My Country* conveys the meaning better. Very naturally it is a nationalist work, and practically the whole of the musical material is derived from two melodies, the folk-song 'Na tom našem dvoře', and Škroup's 'Kde domov můj?' which is familiar as the Czech national anthem. Both of these melodies are used with some freedom. After the Introduction is over the folk-song, which was heard in the opening bars, becomes the basis of the first subject, but with the speed so greatly increased that it takes on the spirit of a vivacious Slavonic dance. The lyrical second subject is formed out of Škroup's theme. The whole is worked out most effectively on sonata form lines. The least satisfactory feature of the work, however, is the coda, which is somewhat naïve and pretentious, and for a brief moment suggests that the composer was attempting unsuccessfully to create the same kind of impression that Brahms did by means of the broadening of note values at the end of his first symphony. Nevertheless the work is attractively scored, and is characteristic of Dvořák for this period. A patriotic work that succeeds in all respects is a rarity.

Dvořák's next concert overture, as it must inevitably be called, was written between August 9th and September 9th, 1883, after the F minor trio and the *Scherzo capriccioso*. Unquestionably the work belongs to one of Dvořák's finest periods, and the composition of so national a work at a time when he was being tempted to write operas in German for Vienna and Dresden has some significance. F. A. Šubert, director of the Prague National

[1] The allegedly autobiographical string quartet in F minor is not mentioned here, and will be found discussed in another chapter.

Theatre, had asked Dvořák to compose music for a trilogy he intended to write on the subject of the Hussite period. The composer became so interested in the project, that he lost no time in completing his *Hussite* overture, op. 67, while Šubert never progressed any further than his first act. The overture was first performed on November 18th that year, when, two years after the disastrous fire, the opening of the newly-built National Theatre was celebrated.

The Hussite wars, one of the blackest periods in the history of Bohemia, were caused by the spontaneous Protestant and Puritan revolt after John Hus had been treacherously burnt at the stake. They were in the first place a protest against corruption within the Church, secondly they were a rebellion against the powerful landowning Church and Germans, and thirdly they were an assertion of Slavonic national pride. For a dozen years the extremist Taborites swept all before them, but later they were totally defeated by the moderate Utraquists at Lipan. Finally at Iglau in 1436 the Church was forced to concede recognition to the Utraquists.

It is important to recognize that the Hussite movement represents for the Czechs a powerful demand for national rights, and that Hus himself is remembered primarily as a national hero rather than as a religious reformer. It will be recalled that in 1620 the last of the gains of the Hussite period were lost, when Bohemia came under the heel of the Hapsburgs, and once again the traditional Czech hatred of Teutonic overlordism was intensified. The mutual Teutonic-Slavonic zenophobia caused Hans von Bülow to be sharply criticized by his own countrymen for repeatedly performing Dvořák's overture in various parts of Germany. He replied to Hermann Wolff, the impresario, in 1887: 'I will answer for everything I conduct. Next to Brahms the most important composer is Dvořák.'

The overture, following Šubert's plan for his trilogy, seems to express 'the origin of the Hussite movement' in the introduction, 'the Hussite wars' in the exposition and development, and 'the restoration of peace after the wars' in the recapitulation and coda. Dvořák made use of two melodies sung by the Hussite warriors as they marched into battle bearing aloft the sacred chalice. The first of these is the Hussite chorale, 'Ye who are warriors of God.' The Mladá Boleslav version of this melody, which Dvořák used, is quoted below, transposed down a tone. The chorale is hinted at in the Introduction, and Dvořák's fuller version is heard immediately after the complete statement of the first subject in the Allegro con brio (Exx. 1a and 1b).

Ex. 1a.

III

Ex. 1b.

The composer also drew upon the thirteenth-century St. Wenceslas plain-chant, the first half of which is quoted here in its modern version. Dvořák omitted the first and third phrases and used the rest to form the second important theme of his Introduction:[1]

Ex. 2a.

Ex. 2b.

Dvořák's second subject is directly derived from the second phrase of the plainchant, repeated sequentially. The processional opening theme of the Introduction is the composer's own, but we notice a resemblance between bars 5–6 and the equivalent bars of ex. 2b. This plainchant fragment is quoted deliberately from bar 9 onwards, and after two bars is combined with the first half of the Hussite theme. The main theme of the Allegro, which helps to give the latter part of the development its drive, and which served as a study for the more powerful main theme of the Finale of the seventh symphony, besides anticipating a subsidiary theme in the first

[1] It is most surprising that Šourek apparently was unaware that Dvořák used more than a single fragment of this plainchant. Smetana quoted from the Hussite chorale in *Tábor* and *Blaník*, and Suk used it in *Prague*. The second melody appears in Suk's *Meditation on the old chorale 'St. Wenceslas'* and in Novák's *St. Wenceslas Triptych*, and one of its phrases occurs at the beginning of Martinů's violin concerto.

movement, has diminutions of the Hussite theme in its third and fourth bars:

Ex. 3.

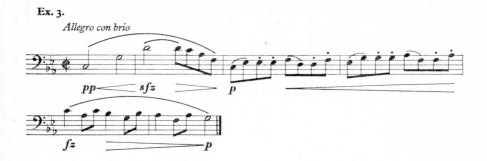

Thus every theme in the overture has either a direct or an indirect relationship with the two historic themes.

The Introduction is in C major, and the exposition in C minor and E flat major, but the recapitulation is in C major, with the exception of a brief change of mode. This unique choice of keys for Dvořák was obviously suggested by the underlying programme. He considered starting the recapitulation of the first movement of the *New World* symphony in the tonic major, but decided not to. He was fully aware of the power of the Hussite theme. However its most impressive appearance comes immediately before the recapitulation, when it is played by muted horns in the remote key of B major, as if it were a faint signal from far away. This noble work deserves to be much more frequently performed.

Dvořák returned to music of the quasi-programmatic type when, at the age of fifty, he contemplated life in its various aspects, and attempted to synthesize his views in his triple overture, *Nature, Life and Love*. Later he renamed the three separate overtures *In Nature's Realm*, op. 91, *Carnival*, op. 92, and *Othello*, op. 93, but he had considered naming the first both 'Summer Night' and 'In Solitude', and after composing the third wondered whether he should re-name it 'Tragic' or 'Eroica'! Šourek explains the composer's attitude as follows: 'Deeply religious in feeling, above all he saw in Nature the unfathomable work of a Divine Will, but in a certain pantheistic sense he also saw it as the giver of Life, which is both beautiful and ugly.' Dvořák's theme representing Nature:

Ex. 4.

links the overtures together, in the first of which it is the main theme, in the second only briefly referred to, while in the third it becomes rather more ominous. The theme has a curious resemblance to another nature theme, the melody of 'Morning Mood' in the incidental music to *Peer Gynt*.

In Nature's Realm was composed between March 31st and July 8th, 1891, and dedicated to Cambridge University, which had honoured him with a doctorate on June 16th that year. *Carnival* was written between July 28th and September 12th, and dedicated to the University of Prague, which had made him a Doctor of Philosophy on March 17th. *Othello* bears no dedication, and was begun during November and completed on January 18th, 1892.

In Nature's Realm, far from being a nocturne, seems to show how Man gradually becomes aware of the hidden springs of the forces of Life when day has drawn to a close. The overture is in sonata form with a few introductory bars and a quiet epilogue. The second subject is in the mediant major, a key rarely used in this way by Dvořák, and starts with a lively dance of a type not encountered elsewhere in his music. A chorale-like motif heard at the beginning of the epilogue, pentatonic like the Nature theme, anticipates a cadence in the Finale of the sonatina of the American period. This overture with its bird songs epitomizes the composers' delight in natural surroundings, and especially his love for his home in the spruce forest of Vysoká, where this work was written. It has been overshadowed by the brilliance of *Carnival*, and deserves to be heard more frequently.

The second overture compares rather unfavourably with Berlioz's *Le carnaval romain*. It has plenty of *élan* and vitality, but very little attempt has been made to hold anything in reserve for the crown of the work. The reflective section in the key on the flattened seventh, G major, which comes between the exposition and the development, and is framed by passages rather too reminiscent of *Tannhäuser*, is, however, a most beautiful inspiration, imaginatively conceived and exquisitely scored. In this passage Man withdraws for a while from the wild enjoyment of life, and recognizes that the origin of it all lies in Nature.

Dvořák made some of his intentions clear regarding *Othello* by indicating in the full score at what points certain events occurred. From these hints it is clear that he had no intention of keeping strictly to Shakespeare's drama, but instead wished to treat the subject of the Moor's jealousy in his own way. With so dramatic a subject it was impossible for him to keep within the bounds of sonata form, and consequently the form of the recapitulation, if it can be called that, is dictated by the composer's programme.[1]

---

[1] Roger Fiske in his essay in P. Hartnoll's *Shakespeare in Music* (London 1964) tentatively puts forward the interesting theory that Dvořák was more influenced by Verdi's opera than by Shakespeare's play. Naturally it was never Dvořák's intention to present a comprehensive musical picture of this dramatic subject or of its hero.

The Introduction opens with a passage in the Lydian mode, which towards the end of the work represents Othello praying after he had strangled Desdemona. Before it is repeated the jealousy motif raises its head. A few bars later the Nature theme is heard, chromatically altered to suggest its dark side, and this is followed soon after by the jealousy motif given out in full:

Ex. 5.

The Allegro con brio in F sharp minor starts with the jealousy and Nature themes, and a lyrical derivative of the former, the meaning of which is not clear. During the transition a theme is heard which steadily soars up an octave before coming to rest, seeming to suggest Othello's and Desdemona's love.

The second subject group, as one would expect, is more directly connected with Desdemona, and starts with one of Dvořák's swayings between one discord and another, suggesting the distressed heroine pleading that she is innocent, while a fragment of the jealousy motif, modified by the influence of Nature, appears in the accompaniment (Ex. 6). A concise, chromatically rising, yearning theme, associated with their mutual love, follows on and broadens out diatonically. At the end of the exposition Wagner's eternal sleep motif is hinted at, which is curious, but it can only be intended to portray a delicious but ephemeral moment of time.

The course of the drama can be followed without much difficulty. Othello eventually becomes goaded by the repeated whispering of evil thoughts, a self-quotation of the four-note motif of Dvořák's *Requiem*

Ex. 6.

Mass foreshadows the tragedy, and the Nature theme is heard in a new guise, accompanied by wailing flutes, and becoming more and more insistent.

Ex. 7.

Gradually we are led on to the great catastrophe, which is heralded by a chromatic descent of diminished sevenths, perhaps suggested by Berlioz's 'Witches Sabbath'. At cue 18 Dvořák wrote: 'Othello murders her at the height of his anger'. Once again Desdemona declares her innocence, and then dies peacefully to the sound of the chromatic love motif, while the strings accompany tremolando *sul ponticello* to send shivers down the spine. Othello begins to repent, prays, kisses Desdemona for the last time, contemplates his terrible deed, resolves to take his own life, and (cue 22) stabs himself.

This overture is without question Dvořák's finest, and also his most successful piece of programme music. Possibly it is neglected because people prefer Dvořák to be gay, contented or melancholy, but not tragic. The reminiscence of Wagner would seem to be a miscalculation, but it is evident that success lay more easily within the composer's grasp when he was composing *Othello* than when at work on the *Hussite* overture. He had eight more years of experience and the symphony in D minor, op. 70, behind him, and, without the need to use pre-existing musical material, he could provide his own to meet his exact requirements. Shakespeare, however, must take a good deal of the credit.

Symphonic Poems

Dvořák, for the first time since *The Spectre's Bride*, returned again to K. J. Erben's celebrated *Bouquet of Folk Tales* for the romantic ballads which served as his inspiration for the first four of his symphonic poems. The fifth, *Heroic Song*, is not connected in any way with literature. *The Water Goblin*, op. 107, *The Noon Witch*, op. 108, and *The Golden Spinning Wheel*, op. 109, were all sketched in rapid succession, and then scored for orchestra in the first months of 1896. The first was sketched between January 6th and 10th, the second between the 11th and 13th and the third between the 15th and 22nd, while the scoring took from January 24th to February 11th, from February 14th to 27th and from March 4th to April 25th respectively. These three works were given a public rehearsal by the orchestra of the Prague Conservatory on June 3rd that year, but their first public performances took place in London. Hans Richter conducted *The Golden Spinning Wheel* on October 26th, and Henry J. Wood performed *The Water Goblin* on November 14th and *The Noon Witch* on the 21st. *The Wild Dove*, op. 110, was sketched and orchestrated between October 22nd and November 18th the same year, whereas *Heroic Song*, op. 111, was sketched between August 4th and 23rd, and scored between August 24th and October 25th, 1897. Janáček conducted the first performance of *The Wild Dove* at Brno on March 20th the following year, and Mahler gave the *première* of *Heroic Song* in Vienna on December 4th.

Possibly the most interesting and original feature of the four works based on Erben is that many of the themes were arrived at by setting the poet's lines to music.[1] In the first work no fewer than seven themes were conceived

---

[1] It would be interesting to know whether the composer was aware that Brahms composed the theme of his Ballad op. 10, no. 1, in a similar way.

in this way, including the main and some subsidiary motifs of the three characters. A consequence of this was that most of Dvořák's themes have regular four-bar phrases, but our attention is often drawn away from this weakness by the abundant invention of the accompanying figures and the strong rhythmic propulsion. Squareness of phrase is avoided in *The Golden Spinning Wheel*, where there are more settings of Erben's words, but the rhythm is freer. This unusual method of composition was less used in the second and fourth symphonic poems.

While Dvořák composed themes to which Erben's words could be sung, Janáček later developed a system of composition based on themes embodying the natural melodic rise and fall of spoken words. It will be realized that in forming his musical material in association with lines which are typically Czech both in their metre and thought content, Dvořák was bound to create works which were fundamentally national. Janáček admired them greatly, and described them as the most completely Czech of all his friend's compositions.

In *The Water Goblin* we first encounter the king of the underwater regions sitting on a poplar over the lake in the moonlight, sewing the red boots he will wear at his wedding on the following day. Next morning in a cottage not far away a maiden rises early to take her washing down to the lake, but her mother, having had a presentiment, warns her not to go. The girl insists, however, but when dipping the first garment in the water, the little bridge on which she stands collapses. She is now in the power of the water goblin, and becomes his wife, as he had originally planned. While sadly nursing her dear little goblin baby she sings a lullaby, which makes her husband angry. She demands to be allowed to return to her mother, and after much heated argument her husband agrees on two conditions: that she returns to him before vespers, and that he has charge of the baby. When back at home her mother will not allow her to return to the lake. The water goblin, impatient with waiting beyond the appointed time, knocks loudly at the door and then raises a storm, during which a thud is heard on the doorstep of the cottage. On opening the door the baby is seen with its head severed.

The music is divided into eight sections:

The water goblin alone. Allegro vivo, B minor.
The maiden and her mother. Andante sostenuto, B major and minor.
The maiden falls into the clutches of the water goblin. Allegro vivo, mainly B minor.
Misery of life under the lake, and lullaby. Andante mesto, B minor; Un poco più lento, B major, B flat and A.
The quarrel. Andante, various keys.
The maiden at home. Lento assai, B major.

The final tragedy. Allegro vivace, various keys.

Coda, not suggested by the poem. Andante sostenuto, B minor.

In the third scene the maiden sinks into the water to the favourite Russian device of a descending whole tone scale. In the sixth we must assume that the scene opens in the evening.

The water goblin's principal theme resembles that given to the chorus near the beginning of *The Jacobin*, and it is also the C minor theme of the Finale of the G major symphony inverted:

Ex. 8.

Like most of the other themes in this work, it starts with repeated notes. It dominates the greater part of the music. It is heard as a rhythm on the timpani when the girl decides to go to the lake, contrary to her mother's advice, it provides the triple knocks on the door, and in many places it is used to emphasize this creature's sinister power. In fact one is inclined to think that a theme of this kind, so characteristically regular in shape, will not bear all the repetition that it is given here.

Since the work is in simple rondo form, it is curious to find that all three episodes are in the tonic major or minor. Not until halfway through the score do we lose sight altogether of the original tonality, so as a whole the work is very strangely proportioned, and rather unsatisfactory. Also Dvořák in three places repeats his material, newly arrayed in delightfully attractive orchestral colouring, it must be admitted, instead of allowing it to grow naturally. On the positive side it will be agreed that the composer brings the tale vividly before us, and many of his ideas are very beautiful.

The poem on which *The Noon Witch* is based is so terse, that Dvořák found it necessary to enlarge on it. His scheme is as follows: a child when playing with its toys becomes fretful, so its mother first chides it good-naturedly, then scolds it crossly and threatens to call the noon witch; the child quietens down, but again becomes fractious, and the mother becomes angry once more; the tiny brown witch appears with a sheet over her head, demands the child and performs a weird dance, while the mother, with the child in her arms, beseeches her to have mercy; at noon the witch disappears and the mother faints; her husband returns home, but when his wife revives, the child is found to have been suffocated. Probably to some extent unconsciously, Dvořák practised a notable economy of themes in the present work. The child's theme, ex. 9a is later transformed into the mother's threat of the witch, and is then used for the latter's grotesque dance, ex. 9b:

Ex. 9a.

Allegretto

Ex. 9b.

Allegro

while the mother's scolding theme, ex. 10a, becomes the witch's demand for the child, ex. 10b, and another of its derivatives, ex. 10c, turns out to be an inversion of the witch's dance:

Ex. 10a.

Allegretto

Ex. 10b.

Andante sostenuto

Ex. 10c.

Maestoso

The entry of the witch, scored for violins, violas and bass clarinet, is most effective (ex. 11), and when, according to Janáček, she stretches out her long skeletal fingers, we hear wood-wind and horns play a stridently chromatic passage after the manner of Liszt (ex. 12):

Ex. 11.

Andante sostenuto

Ex. 12.

This is a well-written and successful composition. Possibly the mother's scolding becomes too much like a spirited Slavonic dance, but her agonized chromatic supplications are true enough, and, unlike the case of the water goblin, the influence and presence of the witch are felt strongly enough during her relatively short scene and through hints of her theme at the beginning and end of the work.

The next symphonic poem suffers from an utterly fantastic tale, when compared with some of the wilder flights of fancy on the part of the romantic poets. A king while out hunting calls at a cottage to ask for a drink of water, and immediately falls in love with Dornička, who opens the door to him (bars 1–214). Next day he returns, but is greeted by the girl's stepmother, an old hag, whom he orders to bring the beautiful maiden to his castle (bars 215–327). Dornička is taken through the forest by the hag and the hag's own daughter, who closely resembles the king's bride; she is murdered by them, and her hands, feet and eyes are taken to the castle (bars 328–541). The king greets the two arrivals, and being deceived about the girl, their wedding is celebrated festively; a love scene follows, and then, telling the queen to spin diligently, the king departs for the wars (bars 542–685). A mysterious old man, having found Dornička's mutilated body, sends his boy three times to the castle to exchange first a golden spinning wheel for a pair of feet, then a golden distaff for two hands, and finally a golden spindle for a pair of eyes; with the aid of living water he restores the maiden to life (bars 686–773). The king returns victorious, and the queen proudly shows him her magnificent spinning wheel, but when she begins to use it, it creaks out the secret of the crime (bars 774–931). The king searches for his true love in the forest, finds her, and takes her back to the castle, where there is great rejoicing (bars 932–1080). In Erben's poem the two criminals are torn to pieces by wolves.

The principal motif of the king is transformed to personify the evil stepmother, and later the mysterious, kindly old man, as shown here:

Ex. 13a.

Ex. 13b.

Ex. 13c.

(Get up, my lad, hurry, it is urgent; take that golden spinning wheel:)

Dornička has a beautiful motif in which the triplet galloping figure of the king is heard on the cor anglais in a legato form. This motif is also used without modification to represent the king's false bride, who has no personal motif of her own. The spinning motif either derives from the galloping motif, or suggested it, for they are similar in shape, except that the second and third notes of one are reversed in the other. Dvořák appears to have used this motif for musical rather than programmatic reasons, when the stepmother and her daughter are on their way to the castle. He goes further than in *The Water Goblin* in setting Erben's lines to music, and when the wicked queen is asked to exchange the limbs, he writes in genuinely declamatory style, which brings him momentarily much closer to Janáček:

Ex. 14.

„Kup-te, pan-ič-ko! dra-hý ne-ní, můj o-tec pří-liš ne-vy-ce-ní, za dvě nohy jest."

(Have it, lady, it isn't expensive; my father doesn't value it particularly; it costs two feet.)

As the work is long, cuts suggested by Josef Suk are generally made, but these spoil the proportions of the composition. If the first appearance of the stepmother (bars 276ff) is omitted, the crime in the forest loses much of its significance, and if cuts are made in the old man's scene, it follows that the unfortunate girl is brought to life with some of her limbs missing. A cut might well be made from cue 20 to cue 21, as this section is uninspired. The wedding love music is too opulent, and the 'declaration of love' music is rather mannered when it returns in the final scene. Most of the king's music is attractive, and the stepmother's theme is tellingly used in her important scene. Dornička's music is delightful, and the old man's scene provides us with probably the most imaginative and certainly the most ravishing scoring in any of Dvořák's music.

The Wild Dove is divided into five clear-cut sections. An attractive young widow follows her husband's coffin to the churchyard lamenting bitterly (Andante, marcia funebre). Although Erben reserves the revelation that she had poisoned him until later, Dvořák presents here what he described as a fate motif, but which is more satisfactorily thought of as representing her guilt. A handsome young man very soon drives away all thoughts of her husband, and she thinks again of marriage (Allegro-Andante). After a very short time there is feasting and dancing to celebrate her second wedding (Molto vivace—Allegretto grazioso). Her conscience is smitten when she hears a dove cooing in an oak tree above her husband's grave, and, overcome with remorse, she drowns herself (Andante). Finally there is an epilogue based on the opening funeral march, but gradually the sharp edge of the guilt motif is softened, as if to suggest that she had expiated her crime (Andante).

Insofar as the widow's, the guilt, and the young man's themes rise scale-wise and then gradually descend, they are variants on a single musical thought, but they are readily distinguishable from one another:

Each gives rise to its own mutations, such as the coy triplet diminution of the widow's theme. Dvořák appropriately suggested the union of the couple at the beginning of their nuptials by combining the widow's theme in $\frac{3}{4}$ with the man's in $\frac{2}{4}$. He then introduced a bagpipe tune with a Lydian fourth, which starts on the mediant like the man's theme, but by the fourth bar it follows the contour of the widow's theme:

In the richly scored love music that follows new forms of these themes are combined.

The widow's feigned grief is vividly suggested by means of flutes and violins playing consecutive semitones descending chromatically, immediately after the trumpet has first announced the guilt motif. The dove, represented by flute shakes and high reiterated harp notes, linked together by an oboe, may be presumed to be a turtle dove.[1]

The last of the symphonic poems, *Heroic Song*,[2] has no detailed programme, but Šourek believed it represented Dvořák's own artistic destiny, a view that has been questioned recently.[3] The hero's early show of determination and confidence is quickly followed by disappointment and sorrow, but this is ameliorated by hope. Thanks to renewed determination obstacles are overcome, and ultimately there is an unqualified triumph. Since the work's three main sections are Poco adagio, lacrimoso, then Allegretto grazioso, and finally Più mosso, it resembles another 'through darkness to light' composition, Liszt's *Tasso, Lamento e Trionfo*.

Unlike Liszt, however, Dvořák starts with an introductory Allegro con fuoco, which contains the musical germ of the work, from which various metamorphoses emerge:

Ex. 17.

Internal evidence makes it plain that the *lacrimoso* melody grows out of an inversion of this fundamental germ:

Ex. 18.

[1] The German title of this work, *Die Waldtaube*, is sometimes absurdly mistranslated as *The Wood Pigeon*, which Dvořák's bird couldn't possibly be.

[2] Composed a year before Strauss' *Ein Heldenleben*.

[3] See Jiří Berkovec's Introduction to the Complete Edition score, in which he points out Dvořák has in mind a kind of 'spiritual hero'. The title of the work appears to have been suggested by Vítězslav Novák.

Only the consoling theme in A flat major has no connection with it, but here we detect a passing reference to Liszt's Adagio mesto theme. Dvořák's opening pages are close in spirit to sonata form ideals, and give expectations of something finer than the rather trivial Allegro grazioso and the occasional bombast elsewhere.

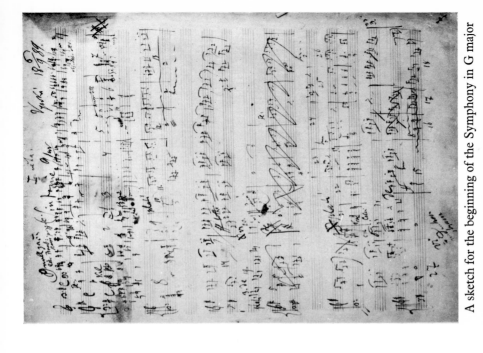

A sketch for the beginning of the Symphony in G major

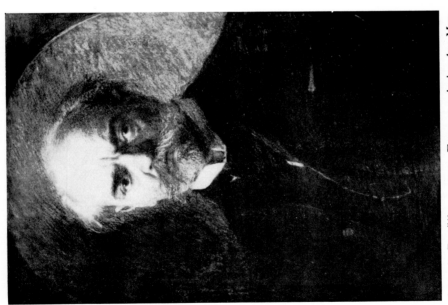

Antonín Dvořák, c. 1901. From a painting by Max
Švabinský

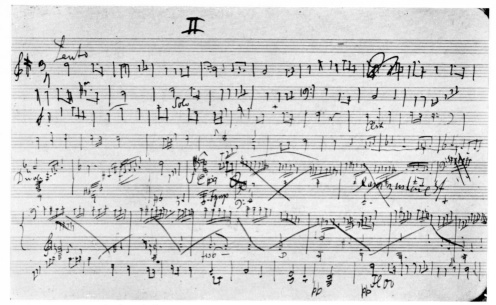

A sketch for the slow movement of the 'Cello Concerto

The first page of the autograph full score of the 7th Symphony. The translation of the words at the foot of the page is: "This main theme occurred to me when the festival train from Pest arrived at the State station in 1884."

VI

Miscellaneous Orchestral Works

During Dvořák's years of poverty as he himself is said to have stated, he always had plenty of paper to build a fire with. Much later, in 1887, he made a note of the 'Compositions which I have torn up and burnt', and this list of eighteen works includes two overtures in E minor and F minor, a *Romeo and Juliet* overture and three *Nocturnes* for orchestra, in addition to a quantity of chamber music and a mass. That his memory was not always reliable is shown by the inclusion of the first two symphonies on the list, so that it is possible there may have been other errors, works included by mistake or inaccurately described. Besides, there may be some works that he omitted to mention. There are scarcely any compositions extant which we know to have been written during the years 1862–1864 and 1866–1869, yet in 1865 and 1870 Dvořák's output was considerable, so that it is not unreasonable to suppose that he may well have completed an average of at least two substantial works in each of those sparsely represented years.

During January and the beginning of February, 1867, he composed seven Intermezzi for single woodwind, two horns, two trumpets, timpani and strings, the first being entitled 'Capriccio' and the sixth 'Serenade'. Šourek suggests that the 'overtures in E minor and F minor' may in reality be found among the Intermezzi, the composer's description being incorrect. This would mean that Dvořák was wrong in calling them overtures and also in stating the keys, for none of these pieces is in either of the keys he mentioned. The mistakes we know Dvořák to have made in compiling his list were not caused by inaccurate recollection of works he had composed, but by faulty remembrance of the fate of his compositions. Within a short time of preparing the list he found the score of the symphony in B flat, and in 1923 *The Bells of Zlonice* was brought to light. The overtures in question are described in much more precise terms than some other items ('Two trios', 'Two quartets', 'Two more quartets'). Although we cannot be certain that he wrote two overtures, is it not more likely that he did so than that he should have confused them with some slight orchestral pieces? The date of composition of the overtures cannot be determined.

Dvořák's incomplete numbering of the Intermezzi does not correspond with the order in which he wrote them, and two lack specific directions of tempo or character. The rhythmic momentum of the Allegro con brio in A major succeeds in holding the attention, even though the material is light and inconsequential. The Capriccio is well organized, which cannot be said of the two remaining square and repetitive quick movements. The slow movements show the composer in the most favourable light for that time, and most notably the Serenade, in which his still favourite instrument the oboe, helped out by the other treble woodwind instruments, sings a long sustained melody against a persistent patterned background for horns and violins in alternation:

Ex. 1.

Dvořák keeps the interest alive by means of judicious harmonic changes, modulations and the avoidance of perfect cadences. We wonder how much that might have been worth preserving was lost in that holocaust of his compositions.

The overture in F major composed at the end of 1871 was written for the earlier, Wagnerian setting of *King and Charcoal Burner*. The opera was not performed during the composer's lifetime, but Smetana conducted the overture at a Philharmonic concert on April 14th, 1872. The *Romeo and Juliet* overture was composed in July 1873, but was never performed.

There seems to have been a misconception regarding the three Nocturnes composed not later than October 1872. The manuscript is not known, but some string parts of the second piece have survived from the performance on March 30th, 1873. It is unlikely that either the first or the third of these pieces is connected in any way with the *Nocturne* in B major for strings, op. 40, which originated as the Andante religioso of the E minor string quartet, subsequently became the first of the two slow movements of the G major string quintet, and which was detached later, revised and published independently. The second of the three Nocturnes, an Andantino in ⅜ time in F major, bears the title 'May Night' and anticipates the fourth *Humoresque*. The *Nocturne* in B major was lengthened when it was rewritten for string orchestra, and this may have been done shortly before the performance on January 6th, 1883. The influence of Wagner is apparent in the first part. Over a very prolonged dominant pedal a fervent melody unfolds, at first diatonically and then chromatically, the scoring being particularly rich. Two further ideas are presented, but the opening melody never returns in any other than a most fragmentary form. This work should be much better known than it is.

RHAPSODIES

A few months after Dvořák had decided to follow in the footsteps of the Viennese classical masters and turn his back on Wagner, we find him looking over his shoulder in the direction of Liszt. A notice in the new musical periodical *Dalibor* (19. IX. 1874) reported that the composer had just finished a Rhapsody for full orchestra, and added that he intended to start on a larger cycle of Slavonic rhapsodies similar in style to Liszt's *Hungarian Rhapsodies*. He did not carry out this intention, however, until four years later. His *Rhapsody* in A minor, op. 14,[1] was composed between August and September 12th, 1874, but at some unknown later date the composer decided to alter the title to *Symphonic Poem*. As in the case of the much later *Heroic*

[1] Dvořák also allotted the opus numbers 18 and 19 to this work. Šourek seems to have called it op. 15 in error. The manuscript bears the number 14, an earlier numbering having been scratched out.

Song, the Rhapsody has no programme, and there is no indication even that it suggested any specific non-musical theme or concept to the composer.

Dvořák composed his Rhapsody in a far more symphonic style than the Liszt rhapsodies. It centres around two concise motifs, presented in alternation as in the second *Slavonic Rhapsody*, and a third lyrical theme appears later in two different forms. The declamatory first motif has a little in common with the first theme of Berlioz's *King Lear* overture, but is much more concentrated. Initially Dvořák does not establish his key clearly, and after only fourteen bars presents his second theme in the extremely remote key of D flat major. Later this theme reappears in martial style, rhythmically and melodically changed. The composer appears to have been dissatisfied with his Rhapsody, which remained unperformed and unpublished until after his death. The plan of the work is deficient, for it lacks a sufficiently strong tonal centre, and the changing moods seem to have been assembled without a clear enough aim in view. Diminished seventh harmony is used rather frequently. Yet the music itself is sufficiently attractive to warrant an occasional performance. The work was published posthumously by Simrock in 1912, but it is uncertain what score was used for the preparation of this edition, which differs substantially from the autograph score. It seems most unlikely that Dvořák prepared a revised score at any time: had he done so it would almost certainly have been referred to in the Dvořák-Simrock correspondence. The new Complete Edition score conforms to Dvořák's manuscript.

During the period between the *Rhapsody* in A minor and the *Slavonic Rhapsodies* national characteristics became increasingly conspicuous in Dvořák's music. These characteristics are seen in the *Moravian Duets*, the D minor string quartet, and more especially in the *Symphonic Variations* of 1877, but they reached a climax in the following year in the first set of *Slavonic Dances* and the sextet for strings, the year in which the Rhapsodies were written. Possibly Dvořák used the word 'Slavonic' in order to give the Rhapsodies a wider appeal than they would be likely to have if labelled simply 'Czech'. They are of course Slavonic, but the composer seems to have avoided seeking inspiration from outside the national frontiers of his country, which places the music in a rather different category from that of the *Slavonic Dances*. Furthermore, whereas in several instances the Czech composer adapted national melodies in his Dances, in the Rhapsodies all the themes appear to be original, with the possible exception of a hint of the Czech national anthem in the G minor *Rhapsody*. The first *Slavonic Rhapsody*, op. 45, no. 1, in D major, was composed immediately before the Dances, from February 13th to March 17th, 1878, while the other two works, op. 45, no. 2, in G minor and op. 45, no. 3, in A flat major were written between August 20th and December 3rd that year after several more compositions had been completed.

The first two Rhapsodies received their first performance with the composer conducting at the first concert ever to be devoted entirely to Dvořák's music. This took place in the concert hall on Sophia Island, situated in the River Vltava in Prague, on November 17th, 1878. Hallé presented the first *Rhapsody* in Manchester two years later, and repeated it in London in May 1882. The second *Rhapsody* was heard in Vienna under Gericke's direction in November 1881, and in London in June 1883 with Richter conducting. The third *Rhapsody* was immediately much more successful than either of the other two works. The first performance took place in Berlin on September 24th, 1879, when it was conducted by Wilhelm Taubert. Dvořák went to Vienna for the performance given by Richter on November 16th that year, and so was present on the first occasion that one of his orchestral compositions was performed in the Austrian capital. On his return to Prague he wrote enthusiastically to his friend Göbl:

Quite briefly I should like to tell you that I have just been to Vienna after receiving a telegram from Richter; I set out last Friday and was present at the performance of my third Rhapsody, which was liked very much and I had to show myself to the audience. I sat close to Brahms by the organ in the orchestra, and Richter drew me out. I had to appear. I must tell you that I immediately won the sympathy of the whole orchestra, and that out of all the new works they tried over, and Richter said there were sixty of them, they liked my Rhapsody best of all. Richter embraced me on the spot, and told me he was very glad to know me, and promised that the Rhapsody will be repeated at an extra concert in the Opera House.

I promised to go for the performance of the Serenade and had to tell the Philharmonic I would send them a new symphony for the next season. On the day after the concert Richter gave a banquet at his house, in my honour so to say, and invited all the Czech members of the orchestra. It was a splendid evening that I shall not easily forget for the rest of my life. It was something like the one in the summer at Joachim's. The criticisms in the Viennese papers were good except for one or two. I have kept them for you. Dr. Hanslick has not written yet, but I went to see him and he told me he liked the work very much and was also at the general rehearsal with the score, so it must have interested him greatly. He is going to write a longer article about me, and so wrote to Prague for some biographical facts which Debrnov sent him. Something else interesting. This third Rhapsody is being played most of all: it has already been given in Berlin, Dresden, Budapest, Vienna, Karlsruhe, Münster, Wiesbaden, etc., and will be performed very soon in London.

Hanslick's article in the *Neue Freie Presse* included these comments on the *Slavonic Rhapsody*:[1]

> Dvořák's orchestral effects, moreover, by no means belong to the artificial flowers sewn at will on a piece of tapestry; they are natural blossoms, or rather, something blossoming brightly out of the musical thought and not to be regarded apart from it. Everything in the work denotes an extraordinary feeling for genuine orchestral effect.

Dvořák adopted a different design for each of the *Slavonic Rhapsodies*. The first has a large ternary structure with a coda, and is like a solemn procession with a vigorous march for a middle section. The long melody in $\frac{6}{4}$ time, with which the work opens and which comes round more than once, is in six-bar phrases at first, and when the tonality changes from D major to F sharp major there are quaint angularities in the melodic line, including some sevenths with dominant harmony that persist in rising. To counterbalance the upward shift of a major third in the opening section, the march takes us to the key of B flat, a major third lower. The new theme, like a great many of Dvořák's melodies, turns to the relative minor, but in this instance a tonic pedal continues without interruption, and the contrast provided by the sustained melodic line for the horn lends an added fascination to this passage:

Ex. 2.

The march is enlivened by sudden Slavonic bursts of speed, and the spirit becomes like that of a gay Slavonic dance. When the processional theme returns it is treated freely, and even appears in diminution within $\frac{2}{4}$ bars, but the climax comes when the main theme and the march are heard together. It will be noted that, like the principal theme, the march is in six-bar phrases; the two themes must have been designed for this marriage, and only one slight modification was necessary in the first phrase of the opening melody to

---

[1] The article appears in translation in *The Musical Standard*, 24. I. 1880.

allow it to move with the march theme to the relative minor. After a quickening of tempo Dvořák gives us one of his most poetic codas as the procession gently fades away into the distance.[1]

The second *Slavonic Rhapsody* is an irregular species of rondo, with, as the first 'episode', a waltz that starts in the tonic key and which is based on the theme quoted below as well as on a little new material. The second episode breaks fresh ground. Like the *Rhapsody* in A minor, op. 14, the G minor *Rhapsody* opens with a pair of alternating and sharply contrasted themes, in this case in quadruple and triple time, moderato and allegro. Having learnt from his earlier mistake Dvořák presents them both in the same key, thereby establishing the tonality very strongly and cancelling the ambiguity of the introductory bars. The moderato theme clings particularly firmly to the keynote, whatever the harmony may be. It includes the first four notes of 'Kde domov můj?', the Czech national anthem (see p. 110), and it reappears later stripped of all decoration to form the main material of the ternary second episode, but the change is so great that the derivation may be overlooked. The middle section of the episode has the character of a rustic dance. The allegro theme strives upwards heroically by semitones, somewhat after the manner of Brahms' first symphony (Ex. 3). Early in the coda the moderato theme is combined with a presto version of the waltz theme. This work, which owes a little of its forcefulness to Beethoven, comes to a brilliant conclusion.

To Šourek the changing moods of the third *Slavonic Rhapsody* call to mind tournaments, royal hunts, chivalrous love, carnivals and dances in medieval times. The opening bars for harp solo help to conjure up thoughts of glorious times of old, partly because they remind us of the prelude for two harps in Smetana's *Vyšehrad* (1874); furthermore there is a resemblance between Smetana's motif and Dvořák's theme, although one moves between dominant and upper tonic and the other between tonic and subdominant (Exx. 4a and 4b).

The form of the work cannot be neatly labelled and has some curious features. It is best shown in tabulated form:

Intro.	A	B	A	B	Intro.	A	B	C	Coda
A♭	A♭	A♭ and F	A♭	E and F		A♭	B	A♭	A♭ and F	A♭

The use of the two sharp keys before and after the introduction when it returns, and the general symmetry of the scheme should be noted. Theme A

---

[1] Šourek suggests the work may be interpreted as representing the period of Czech pre-history when Grandfather Čech surveyed the land of Bohemia from the hemispherical-shaped hill Říp, that lies a few miles north of Prague, and chose it for his people, and when the legendary queen Libuše founded the first Bohemian dynasty.

Ex. 3.

is a version in quick duple time of the harp theme quoted above, with its first note placed at the beginning of a bar. B, a light-hearted theme announced *grandioso* by full orchestra, and C, a gentle melody given first to

Ex. 4a.

Ex. 4b.

a clarinet, contravene a common rule by appearing first in the tonic key. It was surely a mistake to postpone the arrival of C until so late in the work. Although there is clearly an over-emphasis of the tonic key, this is allayed to some extent by numerous modulations within each section which cannot be indicated above. In spite of these criticisms the third *Rhapsody* surpasses the other two. The second is much more ambitious than the first, but Dvořák was not equal to the task he set himself. In the third he shows more imagination than in either of the earlier works and succeeds in saying what he wished to say.

DANCES

Immediately after Brahms had suggested to Simrock that he should publish Dvořák's *Moravian Duets*, the Berlin publisher asked the Czech composer to write a set of *Slavonic Dances* for him similar in style to the *Hungarian Dances* of Brahms. As soon as Dvořák had completed his first *Slavonic Rhapsody* he composed the first set of eight dances for pianoforte duet. He began them on March 18th and they were finished by May 7th, 1878. In April he started to arrange them for full orchestra and completed the task on August 2nd. This was rather more than just orchestration, for modifications were made at the same time. The first, third[1] and fourth dances were performed in Prague, with Adolf Čech conducting, at a concert of the Association of Czech Journalists on May 16th in the same year.

Louis Ehlert, the German critic of *Die Neue Musikzeitung*, performed a wonderful service to Dvořák when reviewing the duet version of the dances and the *Moravian Duets* in the Berlin *Nationalzeitung* (15. XI. 1878), and in doing so succeeded in making the Czech composer famous in Germany overnight. Ehlert's article appears in Šourek's *Antonín Dvořák: Letters and Reminiscences*, from which the following extracts are taken:

> Here at last is a one hundred per cent talent, and what is more a completely natural talent. I consider the Slavonic Dances to be a work which will make its triumphant way through the world in the same way as Brahms's Hungarian Dances. There is no question here of some sort of imitation: his dances are not in the least Brahmsian. A heavenly naturalness flows through this music and that is why it is so popular. Not a trace of artificiality or constraint . . . Whoever finds a jewel on the public highway is under obligation to report his find. I beg the reader to look upon these lines from that point of view . . .

[1] In Simrock's edition of the piano duets nos. 3 and 6 were interchanged. The numbering in the orchestral version agreed with the composer's manuscript. In the Complete Edition Dvořák's numbering has been restored in the version for four hands.

The following February August Manns performed three of the dances at the Crystal Palace, thus introducing Dvořák's name to Britain for the first time, and before very long his fame began to spread there rapidly.

After the success of the first set of *Slavonic Dances*, which were bringing huge profits to Simrock, the publisher lost little time in asking the composer to write a second set of dances. In February 1880 Dvořák told Simrock that he wished to wait until the autumn before starting the dances as he felt more inclined to write something serious just them. Dvořák postponed work on the dances for a very long time, and when Simrock asked him once again more than five years later he was still unprepared for the task. Simrock's pestering provoked Dvořák to make a sharp reply on January 1st, 1886:

> You will forgive me but I simply haven't the slightest inclination to think of such light music now. I must tell you that it won't by any means be as simple a matter with the Slavonic Dances as it was the first time. To do the same thing twice is devilishly difficult. As long as I am not in the right mood for it I can't do anything. It's something that can't be forced . . .

Three days later he reminded Simrock that he had promised to send him the dances in the summer. '*You imagine composition to be much easier than it actually is*', he wrote, 'it is only possible to start when one feels *enthusiasm*.' He kept his word and sent this letter to his publisher on June 11th:

> Dear friend,
>
> I have been here at Vysoká for six weeks, and as the weather is favourable and the country so lovely I am better off than Bismarck at Varzin, yet at the same time I am far from being idle. It spend most of the day in my garden, which I keep in beautiful order and love as I do 'the art divine', and I go rambling through the forest. There is not much time for composing but now it is going ahead briskly. I am enjoying doing the Slavonic Dances immensely and am sure that this (the second series) will be quite different (no joking and no irony!). They are not however, likely to be finished by July 1st, but certainly will be by the 15th, and then there will be time enough as they won't be coming out before September in any case?

Simrock was delighted with the dances for piano duet, as he told Dvořák as soon as they were published. He wanted them orchestrated as soon as possible, and when this had been done the composer sent a note with the score saying, 'As I have already said several times—their instrumentation was so successful that I can say—it sounds like the devil . . .' The dances were composed between June 9th and July 9th, 1886, and the orchestration took the composer from the second half of November until January 5th, 1887. The character of the dances is quite different from the spirit of the first set, composed on the crest of the wave of national feeling. Dvořák was eight years older, and had some of his greatest compositions behind him, so that we could hardly expect him to return again to quite the same easy, gay, vivacious and melodious style of the earlier dances. He omitted trumpets and trombones in the tenth and twelfth dances, and dispensed with trombones and timpani in the last. Less common phrase lengths occur from time to time, and in the ninth, fifteenth and sixteenth dances there are more themes than usual. Dvořák tends to make his melody and harmony more chromatic, which gives additional depth of feeling and greater pathos to the music. All in all they represent a greater artistic achievement than the earlier set of dances, and stand high in the world's dance music.

The classification of Dvořák's dances is not a simple matter. Šourek and others have identified them with various dances of Czechoslovakia and elsewhere, without, however, making it clear that some of them merge characteristics of more than one dance. It is worth recalling that Dvořák had played in the Nelahozeves village band when a youngster, and that he later played in the Komzák Dance Band in Prague. He had a good knowledge of the dances of his country, and was drawn naturally towards folk art, but he could not be described as a folk-lorist. Nevertheless he was sufficiently well-informed to be able to include characteristics of dances of other Slavonic countries in his two sets of *Slavonic Dances*, and at the same time avoid Hungarian elements. Against this may be set a suggestion of imprecise knowledge in certain directions, which is illustrated by the question he once asked Ludvík Kuba.[1] He did not feel under the same kind of compulsion to concentrate on the idealization of a single dance at a time, as Smetana and Janáček had in their Czech and Lachian Dances, and hardly a single instance occurs where he had a particular dance in mind to the exclusion of all others. On Dvořák's idealization of his dances Antonín Sychra has made the following comments:

> Consciously and intentionally Dvořák tends towards giving folk music a monumental and often a heroic semblance. The Jugoslav *kolo* in the 15th dance can be a telling example. Without a trace of elementary repetition of one and the same little motif, and mounting rapidly to ecstasy, there is not much here of the individual melodic colouring of Jugoslav folk music. Instead the heroic spirit is intensified, it is self-confident, free, hard in places, elsewhere highly sensitive. It is the same in the two *furiants* . . . Even in the poetization Dvořák goes beyond Janáček; he is not afraid of stylization, he satisfies himself with the credible and convincing nature of the basic mood.[2]

[1] See chapter 8, p. 206.
[2] *Estetika Dvořákovy symfonické tvorby.*

Dvořák's first dance starts as a *furiant*, or swaggerers' dance. This Bohemian dance is in quick triple time, with strong accents on the first third and second beats of the first two bars, giving the impression of a bar of $\frac{3}{2}$ time followed by two of $\frac{3}{4}$ time. The classic example is the traditional 'Sedlák, sedlák', the first part of which was used by Smetana in *The Bartered Bride*. The *kolovrat* has similar cross accents, but as is seen in 'Šel sedlák' the metre of the first bars is the reverse of that found in the *furiant*. Treating the dance with some freedom, Dvořák maintains the impression of $\frac{3}{2}$ for some time, before reverting to the more rapid movement. The A major section has no suggestion of *furiant* rhythm. Phrases end on second beats as in the *mazur*, but the tempo is too fast for this Polish dance. Dvořák used this theme again for the sake of national colouring in the second act of *Dimitrij*, but was careful then to reduce its speed.

The second piece consists of melancholy sections in E minor and gay interludes in major keys. František Bonuš[1] sees in the lively sections hints of leaping dances for men only, such as the Brno *vovčácká*, the Slovak *odzemek*, the Ukrainian *gopak* and *kozáček* (Cossack dance) and the Polish *krakowiak*, but it unlikely that the composer drew his inspiration from so many possible sources. The G major theme bears a strong resemblance to the following *vovčácká*:

Ex. 5a.

Ex. 5b.

Allegro vivo

---

[1] I am deeply indebted to F. Bonuš and Jarmil Burghauser for the very generous assistance they have given me towards this section of my book.

It is necessary, however, to emphasize that the whole piece is a very characteristic Dvořákian *dumka*,[1] which is not a dance.

The next dance is based on the first part of 'Sluníčko je nade mlejnem', a dance song of the *mateník* group that comes from Střítež in eastern Bohemia and which Zemánek has classified as a *klatovák*. All *mateník* dances have alternations of duple and triple time. Since Dvořák avoids writing $\frac{3}{4}$ sections his dance resembles a *polka*.

Ex. 6a.

'Sluníčko je nade mlejnen'

Moderato

Allegro   Moderato

Allegro

Ex. 6b.

Poco allegro

p

In the più mosso the character changes to that of a *skočná*. The most familiar example of this Bohemian leaping couple dance occurs in *The Bartered Bride*.

The fourth dance reminds Bonuš of a Silesian *mazur* of the Nový Jičín district, but it is untypical of the *mazur* in general, and in certain respects resembles a *polonaise*. It has some of the characteristics of a *sousedská* (neighbours' dance), which was introduced for the elderly people of Bohemia at a time when the popular dances were too rapid for them. Nevertheless Dvořák's dance as a whole cannot be described as a *sousedská*. In the fifth dance there are suggestions of both a *skočná* and a *vrták*, which is rather similar in style. The main theme partly resembles the *vrták* 'Hop, holka, svlíkej kabát', but lacks the three-bar phrase structure of the first bars of the

[1] The *dumka* is discussed more fully on pp. 205–6.

139

dance song. Bonuš thinks the first section of the sixth dance resembles a *minet*, the rustic equivalent of the minuet of high society, but even if the rhythm of the melody suggests this, the accompaniment points strongly towards the *sousedská*. Characteristics of the *minet* and *mazur* are merged in the G major section.

The seventh dance springs from a variety of sources, but Dvořák appears to have taken as his starting point a Moravian *tetka*. This dance in duple time starts at a moderate pace, but includes sections at double speed in the style of a *kvapík* (gallop). It is always in a major key. By chosing the key of C minor Dvořák demonstrates clearly that he does not wish to be bound strictly by the limitations of one particular dance, but the relationship remains between what he wrote and the *tetka*. After a few bars of canon at a bar's distance for oboe and bassoon in simple crotchet and quaver rhythm, rushing semiquavers suggest the excitement of a *kvapík* section, but here elements of *skočná* and *vrták* may also be detected. When he wrote the first four bars the composer probably had either the *tetka* 'Hop škrk Helena'[1] or 'Tetka kam dete' in mind, but instead of starting with a leap from tonic to dominant he did the reverse. This opening gambit, I suggest, reminded him of the Moravian folk-song 'U Jamolic na rohu',[2] where a similar leap is taken in the opposite direction in a minor key. This song provided him with his fifth and sixth bars, which are almost identical with the fourth and fifth bars of the folk-song and bring about a Moravian modulation. The canon, we observe, is brought closer at this point (Ex. 7a, 7b and 7c).

Ex. 7a.

<hr>

[1] Quoted in my paper in Proceedings of the Royal Musical Association, Vol. 89, 1963. The first eight bars are identical with those in 'Tetka kam dete'.

[2] The Moravian 'Na tom našém nátoní' and Slovak 'Pri Nádaši v tom poli' are very similar to this song.

Ex. 7b.

Moderato   'U Jamolic na rohu'

Ex. 7c.

Allegro assai

These same two bars seem to have helped to remind Dvořák of the student song 'Měl sem tě holka rád', which became the basis for the section that starts in A flat major and continues in F major (Exx. 8a and 8b).

Ex. 8a.

Moderato   'Měl sem tě holka rád'

The last dance of the first set is a splendid example of a *furiant*, and here the normal metrical pattern of this dance is presented at the outset, with characteristic Dvořákian alternations of minor and major. The dance is rich in invention. In the peaceful middle portion and the equivalent part of the coda the dance is temporarily put aside.

It is very probable that when V. J. Novotný stated in 1886 that the ninth dance, the first of the second and finer set, was an *odzemek*, he had obtained

Ex. 8b.

the information from the composer himself. Bonuš sees in it characteristics of several of the leaping dances of Slovakia and eastern Moravia, and prefers to say that it is of the *skoky* type.[1] It is wilder than any of the dances of the first set, and this mood serves to emphasize the tenderness and feminine charm of the interlude in D major and B minor. This is founded on two themes taken from the composer's fourth *Eclogue* for piano of 1880. The B minor theme foreshadows the principal theme of the *American* quartet, and the syncopated rhythm seems to suggest folk-song influence.

It is easy to recognize *mazurka* characteristics in the E major and C major sections of the tenth dance, but the beginning is more difficult to classify. Because of its plaintive mood Šourek considered it to be a *dumka*, but it does not resemble other *dumkas* of the composer's. It has a waltz-type accompaniment and so could perhaps be regarded as a *sousedská*. The resignation and seriousness of tone of this dance would have been unthinkable in the earlier cycle. The eleventh dance is a mixture of styles. The opening bars strongly suggest a type of *skočná*, but the three-bar phrases are untypical of this dance. In the second of the two slower sections a few bars are borrowed from the folk-song 'Pod dubem, za dubem' and transformed in a remarkable way. The original major fragment of melody appears much depressed in B flat minor with an accompaniment in the major key, arranged rather like *tierces de Picardy* in reverse. In this section Bonuš sees some elements of a Lachian *kozácká*. The intensely nostalgic and very fascinating piece that follows has no brighter or lively contrasting sections as one would expect to find in Dvořák's *dumkas*, but its melancholy character tends to confirm that this is how it should be classed. It includes suggestions of the *starodávný*, a walking dance of Moravia, Silesia, Poland and Lusatia closely related to the *polonaise*, and known in Poland as the *polski*. It is probable that

[1] This is Bonuš's term for the leaping dances for men, some of which have been mentioned above in discussing No. 2 of the cycle. The Slovakian and east Moravian *hajduch* and *verbuňk* and the Ukrainian *kolomajka* are of this class.

18 th/2 96

Dvořák's irate letter to the secretary of the Philharmonic Society, London, regarding the projected first performance of the 'Cello Concerto; also showing Berger's draft reply on the back page

Sophia Island, Prague, where *May Night* (1873), the Serenade in E (1876) and the *Symphonic Variations* (1877) received their first performances

the composer may have had the folk-song 'Já tu nebudu!'[1] in mind when he wrote it, because the deliberate, rhythmically patterned turns of his first two bars are an exact inversion of the beginning of the song. The delay over establishing the key of D flat major through lingering on an added 6th on the supertonic and the intentional repetitions help to give it its unique character.

In the *špacírka* at first the men and girls strut along holding hands, and then they dance round wildly in a circle. For his thirteenth dance Dvořák made use of the variant of this dance found at Vysoká, the small village south of Prague where he spent so much of this time. He changed the melody from major to minor, gave the whole far more character, and curiously enough ended in the relative major. It is possible to divide a composite dance of this sort into separate elements, seeing a *chorovod*[2] in the poco adagio and a *kvapík* in the vivace sections, but as a whole the dance can only be a *špacírka*. A comparison between the two versions reveals the transformation that Dvořák made (Exx. 9a, 9b and 9c).

Ex. 9a.

Moderato

Allegro

etc.

Ex. 9b.

Poco adagio

ff

5

fz

etc.

The fourteenth dance gives the impression of being a *polonaise*, but the presence of syncopation in the accompaniment suggests some *starodávný*

[1] See ex. 16, p. 46.

[2] This slow walking dance of Russia, Ukraine, Poland and Slovakia has no set rhythmic scheme, and can have 2, 3, 4, 5, and even 7 beats in a bar.

Ex. 9c.

influence. The dance that follows is a wild *kolo*,[1] a rapid round dance in duple time found in various parts of Jugoslavia and also in Bulgaria, where it is called *choro*. Although dotted rhythms do not appear to be a normal feature of this dance in Jugoslavia, the following extract from a *choro* point to a possible origin for Dvořák's rhythm in bar 33:

Ex. 10.

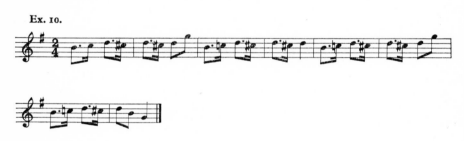

Judging by the general mood of the last dance, which may be described as a *sousedská* that includes some elements of a *mazurka*, Dvořák was somewhat reluctant to bid farewell to this second set of dances, the composition of which must have given him untold joy, and which revealed very clearly one aspect of his genius. It was as if he felt obliged to tear himself away unwillingly in order to prepare once more for work on larger projects, such as the revision of *King and Charcoal Burner*, and composition of his Mass in D and the piano quintet.

Dvořák's remaining dances probably belong to the period 1879–81, with the exception of a polka, *The Woman Harpist*, written during the time when he was a member of the Komzák Dance Band.[2] This manuscript is lost.

---

[1] A dance that was much favoured by Haydn. Perhaps his most striking example is to be seen in the Finale of the string quartet, op. 33, no. 3 ('The Bird'), based on a traditional melody from Bosnia and Dalmatia.

[2] He had composed dances when a boy at Zlonice. In an interview with *The Sunday Times* (10. V. 1885) he described how he copied out Liehmann's band parts without

In commemoration of the silver wedding of Franz Josef I and Elisabeth of Austria he wrote a *Festival March* for full orchestra with harp *ad lib*. This was probably written early in 1879; it was published that year by Starý of Prague. It is a cheerful piece in C major with a Trio in F. The principal theme is strongly syncopated. Like many another *pièce d'occasion* it does nothing to enhance its composer's reputation.

The *Prague Waltzes* and the *Polonaise* in E flat were composed during December in the same year. The waltzes were written at the request of the Ball Committee of the Národní beseda (National Club) of Prague, when Smetana, Fibich, Šebor, Rozkošný and others were invited to enrich the dance repertory. Dvořák's contribution was a 'Viennese style' cycle of five waltzes preceded by an Introduction and concluded with a coda that recalls the first, third and fifth dances. The *Polonaise* seems to show the composer's obvious delight in the rhythm of this attactive Polish dance. Earlier in 1879 he had written a polonaise for 'cello and pianoforte, and another occurs in *Rusalka*. The *Polonaise* in E flat was published in a version for piano duet arranged by Zubatý and revised by the composer himself, but it has only recently been issued in its original form. The *Polka for Prague Students* in B flat of December 1880 was written on conventional lines for an orchestra composed of piccolo, flute and clarinet (one of each), four horns, two trumpets, one trombone, timpani and strings. It is difficult to determine when precisely the *Gallop* in E major was written, but Burghauser assigns it to the same period or possibly a little later than the *Polka*. Once again syncopation is a prominent feature.

It is not as well known as it should be that Simrock commissioned Dvořák to orchestrate nos. 17–23 of the Brahms *Hungarian Dances*, and it may be said that he could hardly have put this work into better hands. This occupied Dvořák from October 29th to November 6th, 1880.

S<small>ERENADES AND</small> S<small>UITES</small>

The Serenade in E major, op. 22, for string orchestra, was composed very quickly from May 3rd to 14th, 1875, during a period when Dvořák wrote three chamber works and was about to start on his fifth symphony. In the following autumn preparations were made for a performance of the Serenade later on in Vienna under Richter's baton, but this did not materialize. The first performance was given by Adolf Čech in Prague on December 10th the

understanding anything about transposition. 'Once', he relates, 'I determined to try my hand at a score myself. I wrote a polka for strings, 2 clarinets, 1 cornet, 2 horns and 1 trombone. With great pride I carried it home to Nelahozeves and had it tried out by our band there. How anxiously I waited for the opening chord! It was all right, bar the cornet part, which I had got in quite the wrong key. The mistake was soon remedied by transposition, but I leave you to guess the effect.'

145

following year, and the work was not heard in Vienna until Kretschmann conducted it there on February 24th, 1884. Starý of Prague published the composer's own arrangement for pianoforte duet in 1877, and the orchestral version was brought out in 1879 by Bote & Bock.

This romantic work is in five movements. Both the light-hearted Scherzo (no. 3) and the Finale start canonically, and the Trio of the Waltz (no. 2) and the Larghetto (no. 4) are both enriched when their melodic themes are repeated canonically. The first movement, Moderato, is simple and child-like, but the subdivision of violas and 'cellos gives it richness and the expressive interjections of the violins during the main theme are telling. The Waltz and Trio have decided charm, and are linked together by a rhythmic motif coming from the twelfth bar. When the melody of the beautiful Larghetto is compared with the Trio theme in the second movement they are found to be two versions of the same basic musical thought, a motif descending from the upper tonic through the leading note to the mediant and then repeating a third lower:

Ex. 11a.

Ex. 11b.
Larghetto

It is no surprise to find that the Finale begins in F sharp minor instead of E major, for during the years 1875–1876 Dvořák composed five works with finales that commence in foreign keys. The form of the movement, however, is curious. After prolonged preparations the tonic key is established briefly by the second theme, which then moves towards the dominant. In the place where there might have been a development the Larghetto theme returns. A recapitulation follows, after which the last portion of the first movement reappears.

In his next serenade Dvořák wrote for a group of wind instruments and began with a March, and so approached much more closely to the traditional type of cassation, but there are only four movements and one Minuet. The Serenade in D minor, op. 44, is scored for two oboes, two clarinets, two bassoons and double bassoon, three horns, violoncello and double bass. Like the earlier serenade it was composed very rapidly, between January 4th and

18th, 1878. It was dedicated to Louis Ehlert, the critic who made Dvořák famous in Germany, and it was performed first in Prague on November 17th, 1878, by members of the orchestra of the Provisional Theatre with the composer conducting. This serenade has several unifying features. A rising fourth occurs at the beginning of all except two of the themes or is found in them later. Secondly, except for the reversing of the stresses, the main theme of the last movement is very similar to that of the March. Thirdly, the March returns near the end of the Finale. The somewhat pompous opening movement has a middle section that includes some wistful harmony, a shortened and altered repetition of the first section, and a coda that recalls themes from both parts. The charming Minuet has many subtleties and above all an intensely Czech feeling, reminding us occasionally of Smetana. The tempo increases to Presto for the Trio, which is vitalized by *furiant* cross accentuation. The gem of the whole work is the remarkably original Andante con moto in which a most appealing and tenderly expressive melodic line, shared between clarinet and oboe, is accompanied by a moving bass line for the two stringed instruments and a highly syncopated rhythm for horns:

Ex. 12.

Out of this material grows almost the whole of the movement. Just as Tovey could readily forgive Dvořák for taking so long to bring the second and third movements of his 'cello concerto to a close, so in this Andante we cannot help expressing out delight that in the guise of the true lover he postpones the moment of parting for as long as possible, while treating us to such lovely romantic regrets as these:

Ex. 13.

After this movement the Finale may seem rather frivolous but it is not without wit. This is a unique work that is rewarding to both audiences and performers.

Intending to follow up the Serenade in D minor with a third serenade, Dvořák began to sketch a March and Minuet, both of which he left unfinished. Shortly afterwards, possibly in April 1879, he composed the *Czech Suite* (Suite in D major), op. 39. This work should have borne a higher opus number, but as Dvořák had promised to offer all his future compositions to Simrock, and Schlesinger, also of Berlin, made demands on him as well, he passed it off as an earlier work so that the latter could publish it. Adolf Čech who conducted almost as many first performances of Dvořák's music as the composer himself, presented the *Czech Suite* in Prague on May 16th, 1879. It reached England in the year following publication, when it was heard at Bristol on May 8th, 1882 with Riseley conducting.

At the time of the first performance Dvořák gave the suite its title, no doubt because three of the movements were given the names of Czech dances. The third movement, however, which is entitled 'Sousedská (Minuetto)', appears to be misnamed, and is strongly influenced by the *mazurka*. It developed out of the sketch for the Minuet mentioned above, where it was the theme for the Trio (Exx. 14a and 14b). The small

Ex. 14a.
Trio

orchestra of oboes, bassoons, horns and strings in the first two movements is used to suggest bagpipes or *dudy* in the Preludium (Pastorale),

Ex. 14b.

Allegro giusto

without, however, confining the music to one key. Apart from the second movement, Dvořák wrote two other polkas in D minor, in the sextet and the D minor string quartet, which suggests that he was attracted by polkas that are tinged with melancholy. The Trio bubbles over with cheerfulness. In the *mazur* flutes and clarinets replace the oboes and horns. One theme suffices, and after a few bars this is heard in canon. The fourth movement, a Romance, is scored for flutes, oboes, cor anglais, bassoons, horns and strings. Here the lovely flute phrases that include Lydian fourths are echoed two octaves lower by the cor anglais:

Ex. 15.

Andante con moto

One of the secrets of Dvořák's success in a romantic movement such as this is that his imagination prevents him from repeating himself exactly. A rather larger orchestra is utilized for the fine spirited Finale, which is conceived on much more symphonic lines than any of the earlier movements. In the short interlude in the middle of the movement the characteristic rhythm of the *furiant* is found, and not elsewhere, although the Finale is subtitled 'Furiant'. Two themes occur here, the first having a fairly obvious connection with the folk-song 'Sedlák, sedlák'. The other theme is remarkably similar in general shape to the Romance theme quoted above:

Ex. 16.

(Presto)

The Suite in A major for pianoforte was composed between February 19th and March 1st, 1894, and was the fifth work to be completed in America. Almost a year later while engaged on the finale of the 'cello concerto Dvořák scored this Suite for orchestra, just as he had already done in the cases of the *Slavonic Dances* and *Legends* for piano duet. Although the pieces are among the composer's slighter compositions he made use of a large orchestra in three out of the five movements, requiring piccolo and double bassoon in addition to the normal woodwind in pairs, full brass and percussion. The themes are characteristic of the American period, several having an obvious pentatonic basis, while some include flattened sevenths and 'Scotch snap' syncopations. Their treatment tends to be artless, unpretentious and often charming in its own way, but occasionally we are caught off our guard by an unexpected modulation, when a customary sequence of notes is deliberately avoided, or when unexpected phrase lengths are encountered. In the second piece, for instance, an answering phrase of four bars is used with confidence to round off the abrupt and twice heard initial one-bar motif. The movements are Andante con moto, Allegro, Moderato (alla Polacca), Andante, and finally an Allegro in which the theme of the first movement reappears.

VARIATIONS, LEGENDS AND SCHERZO

Dvořák did not often write variations. Besides the *Symphonic Variations* and the set for pianoforte they occur in two of his symphonies and in his chamber music. Five sets were written within a period of four and a half years, and among these is the only long series, consisting of a theme, twenty-seven variations and a finale. The manuscript is inscribed '*Symphonic Variations* (op. 28)[1] for full orchestra on an original theme from the partsong "I am a fiddler" composed and entangled by Antonín Dvořák'. They were composed between August 6th and September 28th, 1877. Ludevít Procházka conducted the first performance in Prague on December 2nd that year. When publishers first took an interest in Dvořák's music they only wanted his smaller works, and consequently this did not suit them. Curiously enough at that time no second performance of the *Variations* took place, and it was not until almost a decade later that anything more was heard of them.

Knowing that Richter was going to London to conduct another series of concerts there, Dvořák wrote to him in Vienna on March 28th, 1887, as follows: 'If you would like to have something new, then I would suggest a work that has not yet been published, but which will not remain so for long if you launch it. It is a large work for orchestra . . .' Richter replied at once:

> Your letter made the general rehearsal of such a piece of rubbish as 'Harold' (by our choirmaster Pfeffer) slightly less painful, and I am glad to come into contact with a musician by Divine grace. Before fixing my London programme I had intended in any case to enquire

[1] This number was incorrect; 39 would have been more suitable, or 40, the number used at one concert. Simrock published the work as op. 78.

whether you had something new for me. Now your Symphonic Variations come as a splendid embellishment to my programme: and so they are *definitely* accepted with my warmest thanks. Please send me the score as soon as possible . . .

When replying to his friend, Dvořák told Richter that his kind letter had brought tears to his eyes. 'I am fully aware', he wrote in English, 'that you are the only man and musician (among so many others) who understands me quite well and to whom I must always be obliged, having done so much for me.' On May 13th Richter wrote from London:

Dearly esteemed friend,

I have just returned entranced from the first rehearsal for the third concert at which we are playing your Symphonic Variations. It is a magnificent work! I am happy to be the first to perform it in London, but why did you hold it back for so long? These Variations can take their place among the best of your compositions. I shall send you news of the performance.

With kindest regards,
Yours,
Hans Richter

They will be in the programme of the next Philharmonic Concerts in Vienna.

After the concert on May 16th at St. James's Hall[1] Richter told Dvořák: 'Your Symphonic Variations had an enormous success, and at the several hundred concerts which I have conducted during my life no *new work* has ever had such a success as yours.'

The male-voice part-song 'Já jsem huslař' composed early in 1877 provided Dvořák with his theme, but a little modification was necessary in bars 10–13 to give it a ternary structure. In view of the composer's close friendship with Brahms and his probable acquaintance with the *Variations on a Theme of Josef Haydn*, published three years earlier, it may not be a coincidence that both themes are ternary, and that there is a remarkable resemblance between the stepwise ascent bar by bar and the rhythmic pattern of each in the middle portion. Perhaps recollection of the St. Antoni Chorale may have helped Dvořák to decide to use this rather curious $7+6+7$ bar theme in which the Lydian fourth figures so prominently, but his choice was fully

---

[1] Šourek was seriously misinformed about the first London performance of this work. It did not take place on May 15th at the Crystal Palace, August Manns' orchestra did not play on that occasion, and neither, as is stated in *Antonin Dvořák: Letters and Reminiscences* was it a Philharmonic concert! Richter had his own series of concerts and an *ad hoc* orchestra of 100 players in 1887.

justified. The theme is announced in the simplest possible manner and no attempt at full harmonization is made until the opening phrase returns:

Ex. 17.

Lento e molto tranquillo

In the first variations counterpoints are added to the melody, and in the fourth a partial inversion of the melody is used as a bass. Several harmonic variations follow, and almost at once the phrase structure becomes more flexible without the basic form and the derivation of the variations from the theme becoming obscured. The variations tend to flow into one another without a break, and several times a rhythmic germ is carried over from one to the next. Diminution of bars 3–4 of the theme run through Variation 8, and in the next two variations the rhythm common to both the Brahms and

Dvořák themes is the most prominent feature.[1] From this point onwards the speed varies greatly. Variation 13 would appear to stem from the theme's third and fourth bars, but this does not become evident until the ninth bar. The hushed fourteenth variation is one of Dvořák's loveliest inspirations, and deserves quotation from the fifth bar onwards:

Ex. 18.

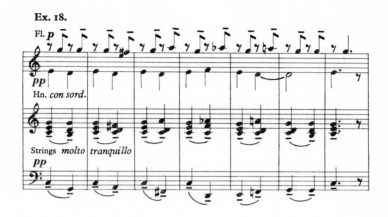

After the delicacy and restraint of this exquisite study in pastel shades the peace is shattered by the full weight of the trombones and basses in pompous declamation, to which the woodwind respond wittily in gentle treble tones. Following a Scherzo in $\frac{3}{4}$ time there is a shift to D major (Variation 18), a key that may be said to have been suggested by the implied harmony of the second bar of the theme. The subtlety of the transformed melody played by a horn and the filigree decorations first of the violins and then of a solo flute are entrancing. The next six variations are centred a tone below C major. The first of these, a waltz, hovers between B flat major and minor, whereas the remainder are unquestionably minor. Variation 22 begins with a striking horn solo, and the twenty-fourth foreshadows some of the mystery of Marbuel's description of the splendour of his red mansion in *Kate and the Devil*. The next two variations, which are a pair, return to the original key through G flat and D majors, and are followed by an echo variation, the last of the set. The Finale presents the theme as a fugue, works up to a climax, resumes in gay polka style and then ends with a jubilant peal of bells over an ostinato.

Tovey classes Dvořák as one of those variation composers who 'knows his theme'. It is also true that he chose extremely well when he selected this

---

[1] I am not alone in my conviction that the words 'Schlaf', Kindchen, schlaf'' written in the manuscript against Variation 9 are not in Dvořák's handwriting. There is only a very slight resemblance to the *Volkslied*.

theme, and in consequence his lively imagination had the opportunity of blossoming freely. Having reached maturity two years earlier, in this work he was able to demonstrate much more clearly than before his growing skill and resourcefulness in the use of orchestral colour. This is one of his most significant works.

It is not clear why the ten pieces for piano duet that Dvořák later orchestrated at Simrock's request should be entitled *Legends*. This might be thought to imply a programmatic content, as it does in the case of the Largo of the *New World* symphony, and yet this does not seem to be the case here. They are rather more in the style of romantic mood pictures, idylls and dances of the people, free flights of the composer's imagination on a limited time scale; and only by internal evidence is it possible to guess at Dvořák's thoughts while he was in the act of creation. The pieces were composed spontaneously and not to order soon after completion of the D major symphony, and were written for the most part between February 11th or 12th and March 22nd, 1881, but the first version of the tenth *Legend* bears the date December 30th, 1880. They were orchestrated during the following November and December. Dvořák dedicated them to Hanslick, who remarked, 'Perhaps this is the most beautiful of all the ten Legends, perhaps another one is; about that there will be different opinions, within the general verdict that they are all beautiful!' In a letter to Simrock (8. VIII. 1881) Brahms said, 'Tell Dvořák how his Legends continue to charm me. That is a delightful work and one envies the fresh, cheerful and rich resourcefulness of that man.' Bennewitz gave the first performance of the first, third and fourth *Legends* in their orchestral colouring at a Prague Conservatory concert on May 7th, 1882.

The *Legends* seem to have been overshadowed to some extent by the *Slavonic Dances*, yet in numerous respects they are equally attractive, and it seems clear that Dvořák's heart was in his work when he composed them. He infused them with a thoroughly Czech spirit. In the sixth *Legend* there is a direct quotation from his symphony in E flat of 1873, which now appears as one of the subsidiary themes, and alongside his countermelodies and rich harmony there are some echoes of Smetana's first quartet. Although the general description ternary may be applied to the majority of the pieces, the design of each is quite individual. The first and third have a dance character and the eighth hints at *furiant* rhythm. The fourth is a solemn march with lively interludes. The ninth is written throughout on a tonic pedal, except when chromatic harmony drives Dvořák to abandon it temporarily. Whereas at times the music seems to be quite close in spirit to Czech folk-song and dance, elsewhere a romantic emotion is apparent; we see this in the fourth *Legend* when anxiety or fear is suggested by falling major sevenths accompanied by pulsating triplets, early in the fifth piece when the melody undulates in a charmingly restrained yet expressive manner, and in the second where the following passage occurs:

Ex. 19.

The tenth piece is particularly rich in texture, in countermelodies and modulation, and possesses a real sense of organic growth. These miniatures gave Dvořák excellent opportunities to show his skill in felicitous scoring, the imaginative use of harmony and modulation, together with brief passages in canon, and the chance of expressing contrasting and changing moods. When performing the *Legends* it is generally preferable to select a small number of them rather than to play the whole set at one time.

It was in the period of indecision of the years 1883–85 that the *Scherzo capriccioso* was written. Dvořák saw before him the glittering prize that awaited him if he conquered the operatic stage in Germany and Austria, while at the same time he had a deep-rooted conviction that if he made a bid for such glory he would be betraying the cause of Czech nationalism. He began work on the *Scherzo* on April 4th, 1883, almost as soon as the F minor trio was completed, and finished it by May 2nd. Adolf Čech conducted it first at a concert of the Society of Czech Journalists on May 16th, and on March 22nd in the following year Dvořák conducted it himself at the Crystal Palace when on his first visit to London. It was later taken up by Richter and Nikisch.

Capriciousness is suggested in this rather larger than average Scherzo by the strong suggestion of the key of B flat major at the outset in place of the principal key of D flat major, by the choice of the totally unrelated key of G major for the second subject, which is a waltz, by the extremely wide range of mood between the various themes, and also by certain somewhat vague and unpredictable passages. The truculent main theme:

is used to interrupt the feminine grace of the waltz just after it has become more alluring, and the D major episode that starts so peacefully, coloured with the dark tones of cor anglais, clarinets and bassoons, ends menacingly with powerful syncopations. The mood of defiance is never far away and consequently the lyricism is thrown into greater relief. A delightful touch occurs when in the development the bass clarinet takes up the main theme and is responded to gently by a flowing flute melody that grows out of the theme's fourth bar. There is nothing complex about the form of the Scherzo. An Introduction headed by the principal theme leads to the first and second subjects, and then all that has already been heard is repeated with a few modifications. The D major episode occurs next, followed by development of the opening bars of the main theme with the second portion of the episode, and with a hint of the waltz later on. The first and second subjects return in the same keys as formerly without the Introduction, and a long coda, at first contemplative and then building up to a huge climax, brings this splendid work to a close. Twice we notice a foretaste of *Rusalka*: in the harp cadenza in the coda, and in the exquisite restatement of the cor anglais melody by flute and clarinet in unison accompanied above by broken octaves on the violins, which seems to evoke the supernatural world of Bohemian folk-lore.

VII

Chamber Music for Strings

It was not until two years after graduation from the Organ School in Prague that Dvořák composed any music of importance, but when he did so he indicated clearly his interest in chamber music. His first two opus numbers were given to a string quintet and a string quartet. He wrote thirteen more string quartets and two other string quintets at irregular intervals over a period of about twenty-six years. As is the case in other types of music, Dvořák was slow to learn his craft, but having done so he turned out a succession of works which take their place among the finest chamber music of the last quarter of the nineteenth century.

The beautifully neat manuscript of the quintet in A minor was begun on June 6th, 1861, but no date is given at the end of the work. Slight alterations were made considerably later, very probably in 1887, but the quintet was not performed during the composer's lifetime. The work is in three movements without a Scherzo. Dvořák's lack of experience in the use of sonata form is evident. In the first movement seventeen bars of the second subject and by far the greater part of the development section are in the tonic key, and the second subject is recapitulated in F major and D minor. The Finale, which at first is reminiscent of Mozart's G minor piano quartet and the second subject of which may be derived from the Andante of Schubert's G major quartet, again settles down in F major in the recapitulation. A subsidiary theme from the second movement reappears in this section. The Lento is much the most promising movement, for it is pleasing melodically and constructed with some skill. It was a happy thought to bring back the main theme more richly scored in A major instead of in F and to follow it with a much shortened recapitulation of the opening bars.

The string quartet in A major of March 1862 shows progress in some directions. We notice in particular an enrichment of the texture, especially in the Andante affettuoso ed appassionato, and a slightly better understanding of what is expected in a development section. We also find here what is most probably Dvořák's first Scherzo. The influence of other composers still remains strong, and a serious fault that was to recur in Dvořák's music for another nine years rears its head for the first time. This is the inability to prevent his movements from growing to unjustifiable lengths. In this particular case there is unnecessary repetition and some padding. When the composer returned to this quartet twenty-five years later he made cuts amounting to a hundred bars or so in both the first and last movements, he reduced the Andante by the same means to less than two-thirds of its original length, and only left the Scherzo and Trio untouched. Drastically pruned in this way the quartet was performed for the first time by the Ondříček Quartet in Prague on January 6th, 1888.

The three movements in A major all start with themes that proceed from E to F sharp and on, directly or indirectly, to C sharp, except in the case of the Scherzo where the first two notes are reversed. This may not be due to a conscious attempt at unification. In the coda of the Finale there is a brief intentional reminder of the introduction to the first movement. The syncopated Schumannesque beginning of the Scherzo is attractive:

Ex. I.

but it loses its charm and subtlety when it returns with the bar lines placed a beat earlier. The characteristically Czech theme that follows it in the first place makes a curiously incongruous companion theme. A combination of rhythms in $\frac{3}{4}$ and $\frac{3}{2}$ time, so typical of the *furiant*, occurs in the Trio for what is very probably the first time in Dvořák's music.[1]

It may be asserted with some hope of accuracy that Dvořák composed a clarinet quintet in B flat minor, although the only information we have of it derives from the composer's not wholly reliable list of compositions that he destroyed. As Burghauser states, the unusual combination of instruments and the key are strong pointers in this direction. The quintet may be presumed to have been written between 1865 and 1869, a period when Dvořák wrote several other works that were destroyed later.

Next we encounter a group of three string quartets strongly influenced by Wagner, which the composer was doubtless thinking about when in 1887 he listed 'Two Quartets' and '2 other Quartets' among the composition that he had torn up and burnt. Fortunately all the string parts have survived. In the D major quartet only the Scherzo is in Dvořák's handwriting, but he himself made a considerable number of corrections to the other movements. The first violin part is inscribed 'Quartetto II', but no dates are given. The parts of the E minor quartet were copied out by Dvořák, but as there are very many mistakes that have not been corrected it is unlikely that they have been used. The first violin part was finished on December 22nd, 1870, the viola part on December 30th and the 'cello part one day earlier. The work is described as 'Quartetto III'. The remaining quartet in B flat major has not come down to us in Dvořák's handwriting, but the composer made corrections to the parts without noticing all the mistakes, which suggests that he played it through with friends and then laid it aside unperformed.

Šourek came to the conclusion that the D major quartet was written towards the end of 1869 or during 1870, before or almost immediately after composing *Alfred* (May 26th to October 19th, 1870). Since it is extremely probable that Dvořák copied out the parts of the E minor quartet immediately he had finished composing it, and in the absence of conflicting evidence, we may assume that no other string quartet intervened between these two works. We cannot be quite so certain about the B flat quartet. When allotting numbers to the other two works, did the composer recollect that he had written a quartet in 1862, and regard it as sufficiently worth while counting? Šourek assumed that he did, and so placed the B flat quartet fourth, but Burghauser, partly on stylistic grounds, places it second in his *Thematic Catalogue* and follows it with the quartets in D and E minor.[2] It is conceivable that the work with the most advanced chromatic harmony came

---

[1] This quartet has already been recorded by Vox Productions, Inc., who are at present issuing records of all Dvořák's chamber music, including the hitherto unpublished quartets.

[2] It must not be assumed that since Dvořák was sufficiently interested in his first quartet in 1887 to make improvements to it, he would have thought much of it when at the height of his strongly Wagnerian phase.

third, and also possible that the quartet that is rather more orthodox in form than the other two may have been the middle one. That the E minor quartet is different from the others emphasizes the fact that the B flat and D major quartets make a reasonably good pair.

Under the sway of Wagner, Dvořák rejected the idea of writing any movement in sonata form in his string quartet in B flat. The first movement is amorphous and monothematic. Although there is contrast within the initial bars of the work, there is no suggestion of a second subject of any kind. The movement is like a rich and varied improvization on a fourteen-bar theme, with the apex centrally placed at bar 273, just before one of the repetitions in the tonic key of the opening bars. Wagner's influence is seen in the chromatic melody and harmony, and yet the movement has an underlying precision of rhythm and even a diatonic foundation that appear to owe something to Haydn. The second movement, the highlight of the quartet, is again monothematic, but it is possible to discern a ternary structure with a coda added. In the florid middle section the theme is used in dimunition in a variety of keys. The recapitulation, if it can be called that, is extremely free. The theme, treated as *unendliche Melodie,* has a nobility that reminds us of Beethoven. It is interesting to note that with only slight alterations it became the theme of the slow movement of the D major symphony about ten years later:

Ex. 2a.

Ex. 2b.

There is no Trio to the Scherzo, which is constructed on one basic theme that sometimes appears extended or varied. The first four notes are taken from the beginning of the theme of the first movement, but Dvořák was much more intent on unification when he reached the Finale. Here Allegro giusto sections in $\frac{2}{4}$ time, taken directly from the first movement, alternate with Allegro con fuoco sections in $\frac{4}{4}$ that continue the dotted rhythms of the Allegro giusto. The first bar of the Finale's distinctive introduction theme reappears several times, sometimes modified. The Introduction, opening with an unaccompanied solo for 'cello, includes in the third and fourth bars the germ of the much more enigmatic passage for solo 'cello that comes at the beginning of the Finale of the quartet in A flat, op. 105:

Ex. 3a.

Andante   Quartet in B♭

Ex. 3b.

Allegro, non tanto
poco sostenuto   Op. 105

The quartet in D major has a first movement in sonata form with contrasted first and second subjects, a Scherzo with a Trio, and a Finale that approximates to a rondo. But in the first and last movements Dvořák was far from happy in his choice of these traditional forms. In the opening movement the 31-bar principal theme is heard three times, and partially even a fourth time, before making way for the second subject. The long development section makes no very significant contribution to the scheme, and in the recapitulation after the second subject has returned the composer launches into a further 140 bars or so of similar development of his material. The whole movement is not far short of 700 bars in length.[1] The two middle movements are much more successful. The first part of the flowing Andantino has two themes, the first being in B minor and the second modulating freely around G major. For the Scherzo the main material is taken from the well-known Slavonic patriotic folk-song 'Hej, Slované!' of Polish origin

Ex. 4.

Allegretto

[1] Allegro con brio, C time. The first movement of the symphony in B flat (Allegro con moto, $\frac{2}{4}$) has 729 bars.

('Jeszcze Polska nie zginęła'), which provides a firm and vigorous basis for the movement. Dvořák introduced dotted rhythms and additional phrases, and in general elaborated the melody and avoided the simple phrase structure of the original in order to provide greater vitality and more variety. The main theme of the Finale shows a type of chromaticism that appears elsewhere in this quartet (Ex. 4). The melody seems like a strange inverted form of the familiar *Fledermaus* theme, which is either pure coincidence, or alternatively suggests there might have been a common origin for both themes.[1]

If in the long melodic lines, the yearning upward leaps decorated with *gruppetti*, and the chromatic harmony of these two quartets we can see the influence of Wagner's operas prior to *The Ring*, the quartet in E minor suggests instead the impact on Dvořák of *Tristan und Isolde* and of Liszt. As Šourek has pointed out this quartet is the first long non-programmatic Czech composition to be written in one continuous movement. The work begins as a sonata form movement designed on generous lines and marked 'Very quick and energetic'. Having reached the middle of the development section it breaks off to make way for a peaceful Andante religioso in B major. This is short-lived, and the fast section resumes from where it was interrupted. Once more the slow section returns and the work is concluded with a coda based on the stormy first part. Perhaps the most striking example of Wagnerianism is to be found in the passionate second subject:

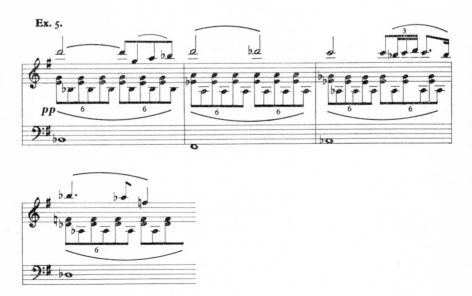

Ex. 5.

---

[1] *Fledermaus* was first performed in Berlin in 1874, some four years after the quartet was written.

Dvořák realized before long that this quartet was a failure, that in all these three works he had not paid sufficient attention to clarity of form and had allowed himself to be carried away by the fertility of his invention. It was not that his musical ideas were necessarily bad, but that they had been misconceived for the exacting medium for which he was writing. Wagner, after all, was hardly the ideal model for a composer of chamber music. Out of the wreck, however, he salvaged the Andante religioso, revised it and added a double bass part, making it form the first of two slow movements in his string quintet in G major; later, however, he withdrew it. Eventually, after expanding it and making further revisions, he published it in 1883 as *Nocturne* in B major for string orchestra.

Dvořák's fifth and sixth quartets were composed towards the end of 1873, during a momentous period of his life. After years of struggle and lack of success his *Patriotic Hymn* had brought him public recognition for the first time, and it was largely due to this that he was able to marry Anna Čermáková on November 17th, even though his troubles had not come to an end. It must have been a bitter blow to him when in September his second opera *Král a uhlíř* was rejected by the directors of the Provisional Theatre after it had been put into rehearsal. The string quartet in F minor, op. 9, was composed during that fatal month and finished on October 4th. Šourek was of the opinion that Dvořák sought to express in this work the contrast between the tragedy of his former existence, with its poverty, artistic failures and the unsatisfactory outcome of his deep love for Josefina Čermáková on the one hand, and on the other his optimism for the future, in which he foresaw the successes that were coming to him and the happiness that married life would bring. There may be some truth in this, but it is unwise to attempt to see an analogy here with Smetana's first autobiographical string quartet (of 1876) because Dvořák's work is not planned with any such clear cut scheme in mind. If it were, one would expect the Finale to be in F major instead of F minor, or at least to have a more cheerful principal theme. We have no record of any utterance made by the composer concerning the content of his quartet, so it is preferable to suggest that the themes do no more than reflect the conflicting thoughts of the composer at the time of composition.

As in other works of this period we notice that the composer tends to give his themes a stronger individuality, coupled with greater clarity and brevity, but in his first movement of well over six hundred bars he is still unable to avoid prolixity. Unfortunately the manuscript of this quartet has disappeared, and all we have at present is Günter Raphael's version, published posthumously, which may not correspond strictly to the composer's intentions.[1] Four pages from the beginning of the Scherzo were lost

[1] Šourek points out that the cuts Raphael advocates for the first and last movements interfere seriously with their basic structure.

many years ago, so that it is impossible to know how the Chopinesque waltz that forms the repeat of the Scherzo should be expanded in order to reconstruct the first part of the movement. There is much more national colouring to be seen than in any earlier work, and the theme in A flat major and minor in the Finale anticipates by several years the animated spirit of the *Slavonic Dances*:

Ex. 6.

Four years later Dvořák rewrote the Andantino for violin and piano, or small orchestra, and published it as *Romance*, op. 11.

The manuscript of the quartet in A minor, op. 12 (later altered by the composer to op. 10), is one of the most fascinating and tantalizing of the Dvořák documents that we possess. Although it is now incomplete it reveals in no uncertain terms the musical dilemma in which the Czech composer found himself at the time of his marriage, and his final struggle to free himself from the clutches of that Klingsor of the theatre, Wagner, so that he could breathe instead the pure air of Viennese classicism. Between November and December 5th, 1873, he wrote this work in five continuous sections, consisting of an Allegro in A minor in truncated sonata form, lacking a recapitulation, a ternary Adagio in E major, a Scherzo and Trio in F major, an Andante appassionato with variations, rather free as regards key but starting from E major, and finally a sonata form Allegro in A major. The first two sections have themes that start with a scale that ascends through a fifth; the melody of the fourth section grows out of the third bar of the Trio, which in turn was derived from the waltz of the F minor quartet; also the introduction to the fifth section has a link with the first part. We note, too, that the second subject of the first section reminds us of Brahms, and an important rhythmic motif in that section seems to have been suggested by bars 13–16 of the same composer's piano quintet.

Dvořák's attempts to reshape the quartet on more orthodox lines took place in two stages, and may have occurred immediately after he had first completed his work, and during the interval between finishing the fourth symphony and starting to compose *Král a uhlíř* for the second time. It is obvious that substantial changes were necessary to convert this pentamerous composition into a quartet in four separate movements. Dvořák added to the first section to make it suitable as a first movement, wrote a new Scherzo and Trio based on the Poco allegro variation of the original fourth part, placed a greatly revised version of his earlier Poco adagio third, and utilized his final section with emendations for the Finale. The greatest loss is the rather Wagnerian Andante appassionato, which one would have expected Dvořák to have salvaged, for he was not averse to rescuing the Andante religioso of his E minor quartet at a later date. However, he did not do so, and consequently it remains unknown today. The opening bars show some of its potentialities and its inherent beauty (Ex. 7).

Without an attempt at reconstruction the work as a whole can neither be performed in the original version nor in its revised form. The urge to compose a *Král a uhlíř* quite free of Wagnerian influence may have seized the composer before he had quite finished reshaping his quartet; in any case he appears to have lost interest in it from that time. Dvořák, however, had crossed his rubicon.[1]

The second string quartet in A minor, op. 16, only took from September 14th to 24th, 1874, to complete. This was Dvořák's first chamber work to be published, Starý of Prague issuing the parts in March 1875. Subsequently Bote & Bock of Berlin published both score and parts in 1893. Some of the alterations shown in the manuscript are not even included in the German edition, which suggests that Dvořák made them after that appeared.[2] The work is written on the normal four-movement plan with the Andante coming second. At first Dvořák conceived his third movement as a minuet, but it appears to have been more closely related to the *mazur* than to that dance. However, he changed his Allegretto marking to Allegro scherzando, and altered the time signature from $\frac{3}{4}$ to $\frac{3}{8}$.

The first movement is not only the composer's most successful sonata form allegro at that time, but is also an appealing if unpretentious movement, and is in good chamber music style, which the Finale cannot possibly claim to be. The lengthening of the first subject in the recapitulation, to include a beautiful change of key from A minor to A flat major by treating the former leading note enharmonically as the new tonic is as delightful as it is unexpected. In the Andante cantabile we find two pointers to the future: a cadence in which the bass and another part move chromatically in contrary

[1] This quartet is discussed by me in greater detail in 'Dvořák at the Crossroads', *Music Review*, XXIII, 1 (1962), and in 'Šestý kvartet Antonína Dvořáka', *Hudební rozhledy* XI, 6 (1958).

[2] The Complete Edition score incorporates these alterations.

Ex. 7.

motion, as in the Lento of the composer's last string quartet, and secondly a foreshadowing of the poignant falling diminished seventh passage that occurs in the Poco adagio of the seventh symphony (see p. 80). The two movements are in identical keys, and the vital notes C, D flat, and E natural repeated, are the same. The first two bars of the movement show the resemblance clearly, but later even the *acciaccatura* of the symphony appears (Exx. 8a and 8b):

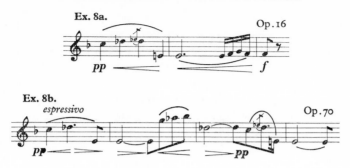

The group of four semiquavers is a feature common to four themes in this work. In contrast with his original intention to have a straightforward repetition of the first part of this movement, Dvořák shows this in quite a new light when it returns. The middle section is much too repetitive. The last movement, the first of Dvořák's finales to commence in a foreign key, is unorthodox in form. The two main themes and a variant derived from the first, like the main theme of the first movement, commence with three adjacent rising notes. A figure taken from the Scherzo of Beethoven's op. 74 is worked to death, and the work ends much too orchestrally. This quartet, however, despite its faults, represents a decisive step in the right direction.

Having just polished off his comic opera, *The Stubborn Lovers*, Dvořák transported the spirit of the theatre into the first and last movements of his next work, the quintet in G for string quartet and double bass. Composed early in 1875 at the time that he was first awarded the Austrian State Prize, it was expressly written for a chamber music competition sponsored by the Umělecká beseda (Artistic Circle). The jury of three, Antonín Bennewitz, Fibich and Ludevít Procházka, unanimously awarded the prize of five ducats to Dvořák because of the quintet's 'distinction of theme, the technical skill in polyphonic composition, the mastery of form and . . . the knowledge of the instruments' displayed, which seems to us to be rather generous praise. The first performance took place at an Umělecká beseda concert on March 18th, 1876, with Ondříček among the performers. At that time the quintet had five movements, the second being a thirty-seven bar Intermezzo (Nocturno)[1] borrowed from the Andante religioso of the E minor string quartet, and later to become the *Nocturne* for strings, op. 40. Ignoring Dvořák's protests, Simrock published the four-movement work in 1888 as op. 77, although it should have been op. 18.

This cheerful and lighthearted quintet, in which the double bass provides a new tone colour and frees the 'cellist from the bass line, reaches its highest level in the buoyant Scherzo in E minor and the meditative Poco andante in

[1] This is published as a supplement to the quintet in the Complete Edition.

C major. By transformation of theme, precisely the same five notes form the basis of both the Scherzo and Finale, even though the keys are different. In the first movement it is surprising to find F major (the key on the flattened seventh of G major) chosen for the naïve second subject. An early show of contrapuntal dexterity in the development unfortunately leaves Dvořák with no further important cards to play in this section. The subordinate theme of the Scherzo offers a notable instance of a 'Moravian modulation':

Ex. 9.

The Trio suggests the influence of Schumann. One of Dvořák's expressive and beautifully flowing slow movements follows, and has some richly soaring passages for the first violin in the middle section.

MATURE COMPOSITIONS

A year later between January 20th and February 4th, 1876, shortly before starting to sketch the *Stabat Mater*, Dvořák wrote his string quartet in E major, originally op. 27, but published by Simrock twelve years later as op. 80! Some of the composer's sorrow due to the death of his first daughter Josefa during the previous September, two days after her birth, is reflected in this work, for although it is in a bright tonality it is often plaintive and melancholy, and the A minor slow movement has the mood of a *dumka*. As far as can be ascertained at present the earliest performance does not appear to have taken place until April 4th, 1889, when the quartet was played at the Princes' Hall, London, at Harvey Löhr's annual concert by Szczepanowski, Grimson, Richardson and Whitehouse.[1]

In contrast with the G major quintet, the E major quartet keeps well within the bounds of genuine chamber music style, in fact the first movement, with its wistful beginning, its chromaticisms, it shifting tonalities and its restraint, is Dvořák's most intimate movement up to that time. Characteristically, the theme of the second subject, a rhythmic variation on the subsidiary theme of the slow movement of Beethoven's op. 18, no. 1, is foreshadowed in D flat major long before it makes its official entry in C sharp minor. Early in the recapitulation this theme returns delightfully transformed into an irresistible dance, after which the remainder of the exposition is created anew.

In the Andante con moto the simple second theme is capable of providing more drama than is immediately apparent. After the brief return of the movement's opening bars this theme is given to the first violin while the 'cello has the main theme (at letter G), and a few bars later the instruments reverse their roles, while unrelated keys pass by in rapid succession. The wayward Schumannesque Scherzo is accompanied by an unduly perfunctory Trio. In the sonata form Finale Dvořák again returns to the problem of writing a movement in which the principal key is approached obliquely. A long declamatory theme for the viola, that starts in G sharp minor and modulates freely, leads after thirty-one bars to an emphatic chordal theme that first establishes the key of E major and then immediately shifts to the relative minor. Since the viola theme is heard in the development it is subsequently kept in reserve until the coda. In this work Dvořák made no deliberate attempt at linking his themes or movements in any way, and only by a stretch of the imagination may the Finale's attractive second subject be associated with the main theme of the first movement.

This is the first of the seven string quartets of Dvořák's maturity. Not all are works of outstanding genius, but professional quartets are depriving their public of some of Dvořák's finest music if they limit themselves in their performances to the inevitable F major quartet, with possibly the E flat quartet as an alternative. Amateur quartets will find unique pleasures in store for them in all these works.

It is possible that Dvořák may have composed his string quartet in D minor, op. 34, especially for Brahms as a token of gratitude, because the older man had been kind enough to offer to recommend his friend Simrock

---

[1] It was repeated at Charles Hallé's chamber concert on June 21st. Both these performances were decidedly earlier than the Joachim Quartet's playing of the work in Berlin, which was tentatively suggested as the first performance in the recently published *Antonín Dvořák Thematic Catalogue*.

to publish the Czech composer's *Moravian Duets*. The quartet was begun on December 7th, 1877, some four days after this welcome news had arrived, and it was completed on December 18th. Dvořák asked if he might dedicate the quartet to the German musician, and he received the following reply during March 1878:

> I regret very much that I was away from home when you were here. The more so as I have such an aversion for letter writing that I cannot hope in the least to make up for it by correspondence. And today I shall merely say that to occupy myself with your things gives me the greatest pleasure, and that I should give a good deal to discuss individual points personally with you. You write rather hurriedly. When you are adding the numerous missing sharps, flats and naturals, then it would be advisable to look a little more closely at the notes themselves, and at the part-writing, etc.
>
> Forgive me, but it is very desirable to point out such things. I consider myself honoured by the dedication of the quartet . . .
>
> Warm greetings from
Your entirely devoted,
J. Brahms

Finding that Simrock was not interested in the quartet at that time, Brahms, it seems almost certain, turned to Schlesinger who published it instead.

Despite his good fortune and brightening prospects this was a very unhappy time for Dvořák; his second daughter Růžena (Rose) had died on August 13th at the age of barely eleven months, and his three and a half-year-old son Otakar passed away on September 8th. He was therefore left childless. It was these events that spurred him on to finish his *Stabat Mater*, and the wound was still unhealed when he turned to his next important work, this quartet. Evidence of this may be observed in the plaintive tone of the first movement, and by the way the Alla polka in B flat and the D major Adagio are continually drawn towards their relative minors. He was at that time on the fringe of his nationalist phase. He already had the *Symphonic Variations* behind him, and after only three more months he started work on the *Slavonic Dances*.

The first movement is slightly Schubertian, and begins with continuous undulating quavers for second violin and viola that are reminiscent of the opening of the Viennese master's A minor quartet. Dvořák, rather originally, lets the third and fourth bars of his main theme serve as the beginning of his second subject, which makes their combination in the development perfectly natural. The magical opening of the development in B major was a stroke of genius. A stormy passage from the exposition is omitted from the recapitulation, but returns in the coda, which ends defiantly. The whimsical Polka is followed by a Trio in rapid ⅜ time which has been described by Šourek and others as a stylized *sousedská*. This is very misleading, because a *sousedská* has three beats in a bar, not one. The Adagio's first bars and haunting subsidiary theme are quoted here to show how for the second time in this work one theme gives birth to another:

When the main theme returns on the viola it is accompanied by a soaring violin countermelody, plucked rhythms for the second violin and a tremolando bass. By a fine piece of craftsmanship the second subject theme from the first movement returns in the coda, from which we observe that the groups of semiquavers in the above quotations are in effect diminutions of the first movement's third bar. Sonata form is again used for the tight-rhythmed finale.

The string sextet in A major, op. 48, composed shortly after the *Slavonic Dances*, occupied Dvořák from May 14th to 27th, 1878. On July 29th in the following year Joachim, who must have heard of Dvořák through his friend Brahms, held a soirée at his Berlin home in the Czech composer's honour, and during the evening the sextet and the string quartet in E flat, op. 51, were performed. Dvořák was astonished to find himself being fêted in the presence of such distinguished people, which was quite a new experience for him. Hellmesberger introduced the same two works to Vienna in mid-October, and Joachim brought the sextet to St. James's Hall, London, on February 23rd, 1880. Both works were immediately successful, and they did much to spread the composer's fame outside his own country. Dvořák's nationalism is most apparent in the sextet's two middle movements, a Dumka in the rhythm of a polka, and a so-called Furiant that includes brief quotations from the first *Slavonic Dance*. Although he was not tempted to compose another sextet Dvořák must have enjoyed writing this one, and as was customary with him he shared the interest in it between the players in an exemplary fashion.

The first movement has a rich lyrical main theme, a pithy second subject in the mediant minor and a closing section in the major. The first bar of the second subject is heard very early in the movement, which in this case is an unfortunate anticipation, owing to the conspicuous rhythmic character of the theme. A harmonic foreshadowing of the opening bars of the C major quartet occurs when the closing theme takes a nostalgic turn. The development is extremely short, a mere 56 bars out of a total of 339. The newly conceived second subject and closing section reappear in the recapitulation in F sharp minor and major instead of in the tonic. The steady march of the rhythm, the crescendos up to second beats, the unexpected $\frac{6}{4}$ in the second bar, the falling leading note in the fifth, and the five-bar phrase structure help to make the Dumka one of Dvořák's most original movements:

Ex. 11.

Poco allegretto

An equally attractive double interlude follows in F sharp minor and major. It is curious that after composing two most typical *furiants* in his *Slavonic Dances* Dvořák should have called his vivacious Scherzo by that name.

Since it has none of the essential cross accents the description is misleading. Finally comes a fine set of five variations and stretta on a theme that is clearly in B minor, and which, except for transitory modulations, does not reach A major (the tonic key) until the final cadence when the second half has been repeated. This movement gives opportunities for colour contrasts: the theme is announced in sombre fashion by violas and 'cellos alone, and in the third variation, while the first 'cello transforms the melody to make it conform to a rigid rhythmic pattern, the remaining instruments sustain widely spaced *pp* chords. The next variation's undulating quavers and repeated triplets in the bass are obviously modelled on Variation VI of Beethoven's op. 74. The conclusion of the work is unfortunately excessively boisterous.

Dvořák's sudden rise to fame led to numerous requests for new works. Jean Becker, the leader of the celebrated Florentine Quartet, asked for a Slavonic work, and got just what he wanted. The composer, after beginning to sketch a quartet in B flat major, wrote instead the string quartet in E flat, op. 51, which he then dedicated to Becker. During composition he broke off to attend to other works, and consequently the quartet was not finished until March 28th, 1879, although it was begun on the previous Christmas Day. The private performance at Joachim's house and the Hellmesberger Quartet's performance in Vienna during October are referred to above.[1] The quartet was first heard in London on December 18th, 1880, when Madame Norman-Néruda (later Lady Hallé), Ries, Zerbini and Piatti played it at a Saturday Popular Concert.

The beautiful arpeggiated opening of this quartet shows Dvořák's originality, his subtle sense of harmonic colouring, and his insight into the secrets of writing for a quartet of strings (Ex. 12). After this broad theme has run its course rhythmic elements come to the fore, and then the second subject follows in polka rhythm. During the development the main theme stalks in mysteriously in augmentation while the polka theme humorously appears in the bass. As the much shortened recapitulation begins with the second subject, the coda is mainly derived from the principal theme. The ending, in which the first violin has the arpeggios alone, is particularly lovely.

The two middle movements, Dumka and Romanza are both slow, but for contrast the Dumka contains lively scherzo-like *furiant* sections. Both movements are in fact quite different in character. The second theme in the

---

[1] According to *Schweizerische Musikzeitung* for 1879 and 1880 and contemporary Swiss newspapers this quartet was not included in the repertory of the Florentine Quartet during their Swiss tour in the autumn of 1879, probably because it was not published in time for them to prepare it. Šourek incorrectly assumed that they performed it.

Ex. 12.

(*Allegro, ma non troppo*)

Dumka (bar 39) is almost identical with the main theme of the projected quartet in B flat, but is now much slower in pace. For the G major *furiant* Dvořák borrowed the first few notes of the elegiac G minor melody, given to violin and viola alternately over *pizzicato* chords for the 'cello at the beginning of the movement. The aptly-named Romanza in B flat is based for the most part on one theme, but this begets a new thought in G major that is immediately repeated in the minor mode. The first bars eventually return in the subdominant, but the tonic key is restored four bars later. A partly chromatic descending scale for the viola adds greatly to the peaceful

Copy of the letter from Brahms to Dvořák in which he accepts the dedication of the String Quartet in D minor. The greater part of the letter appears in translation on p. 170

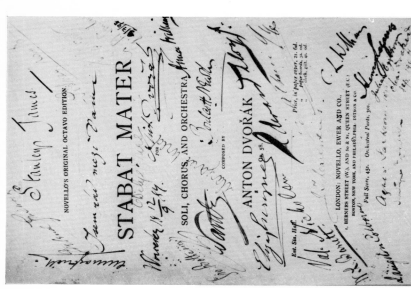

Copy of the title page of the full score of the Stabat Mater autographed at Worcester in 1884 by Albani, Edward Lloyd and Charles Santley (soloists in the performance), by members of the orchestra and others, and by Dvořák who conducted. The composer added above the title: "I am happy among you."

Hanuš Wihan, Antonín Dvořák and Ferdinand Lachner, who in the first months of 1892 played the Dumky Trio in many towns of Bohemia and Moravia

conclusion. The vivacious Finale, which is in sonata form with slight rondo influence, has a main theme that would appear to be of the *skoky* type, that is, it seems to suggest a leaping dance for men only rather than a *skočná*. The development is more contrapuntal than is customary with Dvořák. When the slower second subject reappears the theme is transferred to the 'cello, and in place of this the second violin has a new countermelody.

The next compositions for string quartet, the Two Waltzes, op. 54, nos. 1 and 4, were arranged by the composer in that form from the original piano versions either at the end of 1879 or early the following year, and they were particular favourites with amateur string quartets. To make them suitable for performance by a string orchestra a double bass part was added, but not, apparently, by Dvořák.

On a postcard dated November 5th, 1881, Dvořák wrote to his friend Göbl at Sychrov:

> When are you coming, for I am already becoming impatient? I am very busy. I had to postpone work on the opera [*Dimitrij*]. I read in the newspaper that on December 15th Hellmesberger will play my new quartet, which still doesn't exist! What could I do but leave the opera and write the quartet. I already have three movements prepared and am working on the Finale. I must also orchestrate the *Legends*. As you see I am very busy—very . . .

Between October 7th and 9th Dvořák composed the first movement of a quartet in F major for Hellmesberger, with a few bars not completely filled in, but he abandoned this. On October 25th, about the time that he saw the newspaper report, he started preparing the score of his quartet in C, op. 61, finishing it on November 10th. The Quartet Movement was found by Šourek after the composer's death. Burghauser has suggested to me that Dvořák might have laid it aside because the beginning is so similar to Agathe's recitative in the second act of *Der Freischütz*. This may have been a sufficiently weighty reason for rejecting the movement, because Dvořák seems to have been at pains to write a work that was sufficiently worthy of being performed for the first time in Vienna, which more than any other city had a right to be regarded as the home of the string quartet, and where comparisons would be made with the quartets of the Viennese masters. This Allegro vivace is characteristic of its composer, but it is not the equal of the movement that replaced it.

The C major quartet shows a lessening of obvious national traits, which give way before the influence of Beethoven. Nevertheless Dvořák could not help remaining himself and being thoroughly Czech in each of the movements, and most of all in the Finale, where the rhythm of the main theme reminds us of the *skočná*, although the customary accents are missing. Two themes from the Polonaise in A for 'cello and piano of 1879 became the principal themes of the Scherzo and Finale after some rhythmic changes were made. The beginning of the Poco adagio is taken from an unused sketch Dvořák made for his violin sonata, op. 57. Even though two extra bars were added in the quartet, a few harmonic modifications were made, and the simple chord accompaniment was changed into a more highly organized and fluid series of triplets passing to and fro between viola and 'cello, fundamentally the opening bars of each remain the same.[1] The echoes of the sustained violin melody, which would sound ineffective on the piano, are admirably suited for the second violin. A curious point is that Dvořák could have contemplated writing the slow movement of the sonata in F major, when that is the key of the first movement.

The striking opening bars of the quartet, for which no apology to Handel is needed:

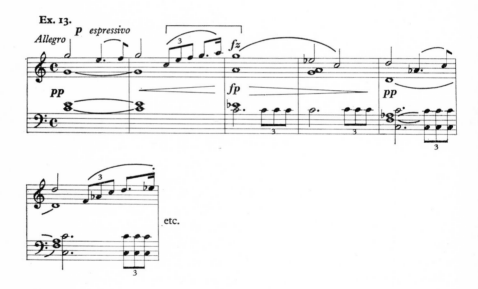

Ex. 13.

etc.

open the doors of tonality wide, so that it is perfectly natural for the second subject to start in the unusual key of E flat major, even though it does conform to convention by veering round to the dominant key soon afterwards. By making the development lead directly to a subsidiary theme Dvořák most successfully short circuits the recapitulation, and then, in order to allow the second subject to reappear in the tonic, he gives us a delightful glimpse of the viola re-statement of the principal theme in a new key, A

[1] 12 bars of the sketch are printed in the Annotations to the sonata in the Complete Edition.

major. Normal transposition of the remainder of the exposition a third down leads to E major, to which Dvořák has no objection. Even in the coda he is in no hurry to re-establish the key of C, and in fact when he had almost arrived there he obscures the tonality with one of those passages that would have puzzled Hadow, and continues at his own pace. Another audacious and wholly unexpected harmonic passage occurs in the Poco adagio.[1]

This is another of Dvořák's romantic movements, and here the yearning, upward striving melody with which it begins only finds solace in the serenity of the contrasting theme. The transition (letter D to letter E) is a flaw in Dvořák's scheme, because, beautiful as it is, it has no thematic connection with the rest of the movement. The theme of the Scherzo, apart from its origin in the 'cello Polonaise and its remarkable resemblance to a figure in the second act of Smetana's *The Secret* (1878), which Dvořák of course knew, is very closely related melodically and rhythmically with the bracketed portion of the main theme of the first movement. Dvořák is in the gayest of moods in the Trio, and also in the Finale, which is a sonata rondo. For this movement the Polonaise theme was completely transformed from a flowing melody in triple time into a skittish Slavonic tune in $\frac{2}{4}$:

Ex. 14a.

Ex. 14b.

Vivace

[1] The chords are: dominant minor ninth on C with appoggiatura minor thirteenth; diminished seventh on A with appoggiatura D flat; dominant minor ninth on B flat with appoggiatura minor thirteenth, resolving as an interrupted cadence on to the triad of C flat major.

At the beginning of 1887 Dvořák decided to write a string trio that he, as a violist, could play with Josef Kruis, a chemistry student who lodged at the same address, and Jan Pelikán of the National Theatre orchestra, who taught Kruis the violin. He wrote his *Terzetto*, op. 74, between January 7th and 14th, but on trying the work through with his friends he discovered that Kruis was not equal to playing the first violin part. He therefore immediately wrote another easier work entitled *Maličkosti* (Bagatelles), and then made a new version of this second work for violin and piano by January 25th, publishing it as *Romantic Pieces*, op. 75. The second string trio remained unpublished in its original form until 1945, when it appeared as op. 75a with the title changed to *Drobnosti* (still meaning Bagatelles or Trifles), in order to distinguish it from the *Maličkosti*, op. 46, for two violins, 'cello and harmonium. Simrock was always most interested in Dvořák's small compositions, whereas the Czech master naturally preferred to spend most of his time writing much more important works. Occasionally, however, he welcomed an opportunity to relax, just as he did when he wrote the violin sonatina for his two children. On January 18th, 1887, he wrote to his publisher:

> I am now writing some small Bagatelles for two violins and viola, and this work gives me just as much pleasure as if I were composing a great symphony; what do you say to that? They are, of course, intended for amateurs, but didn't Beethoven and Schumann also write with quite insignificant material, and how?

It is most unusual to find a string trio written for this combination of instruments. We notice that the viola player does his utmost to make up for the absence of a 'cellist in the Scherzo of the *Terzetto*, and in the Finale it would have been an advantage to have a firmer and deeper bass line on occasions. But when due allowance is made for the limitations and possibilities of an ensemble of this kind it will be seen that Dvořák acquitted himself well. The Introduzione in C major and Larghetto in E are simple in structure and intimate in tone. The Scherzo is a spirited *furiant* with a charming and beautifully coloured waltz for a Trio. Finally comes the Tema con variazioni, which, unlike the first movement, is in C minor. The theme itself is of particular interest because the tonality is uncertain until D flat major is reached, and only in the last bars does the ultimate goal become clear (Ex. 15).

It offered Dvořák plenty of scope for variations of diverse kinds: melodic, rhythmic, imitative, recitative, and so on. It also shows how his great resource, imagination and experience enabled him to demonstrate many different ways of combining these three instruments. As chamber music the *Drobnosti* are much less interesting. The four movements—Cavatina, Capriccio,

Romance and Elegie—are more satisfactory in their later form for violin and piano.

During April and May of the same year (1887) Dvořák arranged for string quartet twelve of the songs from his cycle *Cypresses* of 1865, calling them first *Echoes of Songs* and then *Evening Songs*. Just as he revised these early songs when he prepared them for publication as *Four Songs*, op. 2 (1882), and *Love Songs*, op. 83 (1888), so here he improved on his first drafts. None of the *Four Songs* is found in this set, but all of the later collection, together with nos. 7, 12, 16 and 18 of the early cycle are included. Josef Suk revised ten of the pieces and published them in 1921 with the original title *Cypresses*. Recently all twelve have been published just as Dvořák wrote them, and it will be seen that he gave the vocal line either to the first violin or to the viola, and adapted the accompanying parts suitably for the other instruments.

American Works

Dvořák spent his first long vacation in the United States at the Czech settlement of Spillville in north-east Iowa, surrounded by his children, for they had crossed the Atlantic to spend the summer with him. In this happy atmosphere he started work immediately, first on the string quartet in F, op. 96, the 'American', and then on the string quintet in E flat, op. 97, also nicknamed 'American'. The sketch for the quartet only took from June 8th to 10th, 1893, which pleased Dvořák so much that he wrote at the end of it,

'Thanks be to the Lord God. I am satisfied. It went quickly.' Two days later he began to prepare the score, and finished it on June 23rd. The Kneisel Quartet gave the first performance at Boston, Mass., on January 1st, 1894. Each of the movements contains at least one theme or motif that uses the major or minor form of pentatonic scale, and melodies in minor keys have flattened sevenths. None of these themes bears any strong resemblance to Negro spirituals or plantation songs, but owing to the limitations of the scales adopted it is hardly surprising that turns of phrase that occur in Negro song should also appear in the quartet. The syncopation and 'Scotch snaps' in the main theme of the first movement may quite possibly be due to Negro influence, but these are common enough in Slovak folk-song, and both the general shape and rhythm of the theme were foreshadowed seven years earlier in the B minor melody of the ninth *Slavonic Dance*.

The opening of the quartet is modelled on the beginning of Smetana's E minor quartet, *From my Life*, viola melody, violin tremolandos and sustained pedal note on the 'cello included, but Dvořák's conception is more adroit, and in contrast with Smetana's prolonged declamation his theme is pithy, but square. The second subject starts in A minor and continues with a second theme in A major. Towards the end of the developments notes 4–8 of the main theme give rise to a fugato—in F minor, an unfortunate choice of key. Early in the recapitulation of this concise movement the 'cello is given a new expressive melodic passage in D flat major, the key from which the composer needs to approach his second subject. The mood of the Lento, the crowning movement of the work, strongly suggests that Dvořák's thoughts were turning towards his homeland with those feelings of nostalgia which came upon him so frequently when he was in America. The whole movement grows out of the beautiful melody that the 'cellist takes over from the first violinist.[1] It is felicitously accompanied with discreet syncopations and rocking semiquavers deriving from the melody itself, and reaches its climax in the third paragraph. The semiquavers continue ceaselessly, until finally the last tragic version of the melody is heard on the 'cello, bleakly accompanied by *pizzicato* chords and a telling tremolando in the bass.

The Scherzo is in *ababa* form, in which (*b*) is an augmented version of (*a*) in the tonic minor. The scoring is varied, but the movement halts too frequently at the end of its eight- and sixteen-bar phrases. A subsidiary idea came into being in an unusual way. When strolling in the woods near Spillville Dvořák noticed a red bird with black wings that sang a rapid song incessantly. He noted this down and then adapted it for his scherzo:

---

[1] 'Cellists should be on their guard against playing the fifth note in bar 17 as E instead of D; cf. Violin I in bar 9. The misprint in the Simrock edition has resulted in practically all the leading quartets being at fault here.

The bird could hardly be any other than the scarlet tanager, which frequents that district, and besides having black wings has a black tail. Through the kindness of Eric Simms I was able to listen to a recording of this and other American birds. The recorded song resembled Dvořák's sketch in general style, with some differences, notably that there were five brief melodic fragments, not four, and that the descending third did not occur at the beginning of the phrase. However, no doubt there are some variations in this bird's notes. The song is extremely rapid and might well have provoked Dvořák to describe the scarlet tanager as a 'damned bird'. The rondo Finale is extremely vivacious, but, unlike the finales of the two previous quartets, is essentially homophonic. We can perhaps imagine Dvořák improvising for mass on the little organ of the St. Wenceslas church at Spillville in the chorale-like central episode.

The quintet in E flat followed immediately after the quartet, the sketch and score occupying Dvořák from June 26th to August 1st. Again the Kneisel Quartet gave the first performance, on January 12th, 1894, at the Carnegie Hall, New York, with M. Zach as second viola. While Dvořák was at Spillville a band of perhaps as many as twenty North American Indians went there to sell medicinal herbs, and remained for several days. The party was led by Big Moon, and included his wife Large Head, and their legal adviser John Fox. They were said to belong to the Kickapoo tribe. Dvořák and his family came in contact with them daily, and on two or three occasions the whole band assembled at the inn at his request to perform Indian songs and dances.[1] Kovařík recollected that one of the melodies he heard the

---

[1] I am indebted to the late Otakar Dvořák for some of this information. Kickapoos are Central Algonquins, and not Iroquois as Kovařík stated. Frances Densmore informed me that the Kickapoos, being a small unimportant tribe, would not have found it easy to make up an adequate party by themselves for singing and dancing, and that they would very probably have been mixed with Indians of other tribes. The Kickapoos were most closely associated with the Fox and Sauk Indians, but it does not necessarily follow that there were any members of these tribes at Spillville. On the evidence of a photograph in the possession of Dvořák's heirs, John Fox was a Yankton, that is to say, a member of one of the Siouxan tribes.

Indians sing at that time bore a resemblance to the second subject of the quintet's first movement. Both themes are shown here:

Ex. 17a.

Ex. 17b.

The almost continuous dotted rhythm associated with Dvořák's theme might have been suggested by an Algonquin drum rhythm, although it was in any case a favourite rhythm of the composer's. The so-called 'Indian drum rhythm' that runs through the Scherzo is far too complex to be Indian; in fact the remainder of the work appears to be virtually untouched by any Indian influence. The Larghetto is free from the primitive elements embodied in the movements that encompass it: pentatonic themes and minor sevenths, emphasis on pure rhythm, counterpoint at a minimum (not to the exclusion of attractive countermelodies), short phrases that are immediately repeated, and, in the case of the Finale, rudimentary structure.

The extra player, the second viola, starts alone in the Introduction with a melody soon to be heard in diminution as the beginning of the main theme. The development is primarily concerned with the second subject (quoted above), but a mournful melody in B minor shared by the two violas, set against a figured background and second subject interjections, provides a very individual episode. The first bars of the exposition are missing from the shortened recapitulation, but they become the basis of the coda. In this section the exotic lower *appoggiaturas* first heard in bars 47–50 are given particular emphasis. A two-bar rhythm on one note and a primitive theme mainly in crotchets are the mainstay of the Scherzo. In the Trio the viola is again chosen for another melancholy B minor melody.[1]

On page one of Dvořák's first American sketch book, dated December 19th, 1892, we find the original draft of the melody used for variations in the Larghetto of the quintet. The composer contemplated using the second half of the melody:

[1] The theme for variations in the sextet has a rather similar character, it also is in B minor, and once more viola colouring is used.

Ex. 18.

for a new setting of S. F. Smith's National Anthem, which was sung at that
time to the tune of *God Save the Queen*:

> *My country,'tis of thee,*
> *Sweet land of liberty,*
> *Of thee I sing.*
> *Land where my fathers died,*
> *Land of the pilgrims' pride,*
> *From every mountain-side*
> *Let freedom ring!*[1]

He also hinted in a letter to Simrock (13. X. 1893) that he was thinking
seriously of expanding it into an independent work for, it is believed,
baritone, chorus and orchestra, but nothing came of this idea. The two-fold
melody, half in G minor and half G major, needed touching up a little for the
quintet. It was raised a semitone in pitch and given a key signature of seven
flats. In its new form the second part took on a strong resemblance to
Beethoven, and not only to his sonata op. 26, which is in the same key. The
same types of figuration are used for both halves of the theme in each of the
variations, and sometimes the distinctive rhythm with which the theme
opens is carried over from one part to the other. The fifth variation, which
quietens down after opening wrathfully, may possibly have acquired its
five-note descending scales from the Finale of Mozart's E flat symphony,
K.543. In the sketch book Dvořák experimented with the major part of his
melody, changing it into quick $\frac{2}{4}$ time and giving it a new ending, instead of
repeating the previous eight bars. When at the end of the Larghetto he
returns to his unadorned theme, it is interesting to find that he provides just
the right finishing touch by adopting the additional melody of this sketch
and changing it into steady triple time. The G minor repeated note theme in
the Finale is closely related to the cimbalom theme in the Finale of Schubert's trio in E flat, op. 100, and also to a similar theme in the Presto of
Smetana's trio in G minor, where we again notice that the keys are the same.

LAST QUARTETS

Dvořák began work on a new quartet in A flat shortly before finally leaving
America in April, 1895, but he then put it aside. Forgetting that he revised

[1] His melody makes no provision for lines 4-7.

the end of the 'cello concerto in June, he wrote to the 'cellist, Wihan, saying (30. VII. 1895): 'Since I came back from America I haven't put pen to paper, and so the new quartet begun in New York is still not finished. The first movement incomplete and not even the beginnings of the others! Here at Vysoká I grudge the time and prefer to enjoy the beauties of the countryside.'

He was content and very relieved to be home again after so long a period away. During September he made a piano arrangement of the concerto, but he wrote nothing new until November, when he started on the string quartet in G, op. 106. Having completed the score between November 11th and December 9th he returned to the A flat quartet, and finished that as well. The Bohemian Quartet (Hoffmann, Suk, Nedbal and Wihan) gave the first performance of the G major quartet on October 9th the following year in Prague. The Gompertz Quartet played it in London on November 25th, and the Bohemian Quartet repeated it in Vienna on December 4th. Slight traces of American influence remain in this work: the E flat major theme of the Adagio is almost pentatonic for eight bars, and, as Gerald Abraham has pointed out, the beginning of this melody is referred to again, perhaps subconsciously, in bars 95–102 of the Scherzo. Of much greater significance is the fact that Dvořák had rejected the somewhat facile manner that is rather too apparent in the two previous works. He may have shown lack of judgment in his Finale, but his first two movements are unquestionably among the greatest in any of his chamber music.

The very unusual opening theme seems to express Dvořák's unbounded joy:

Ex. 19.

A second theme appears hesitatingly in E minor, which is not an anticipation of the second subject, for it soon returns confidently in its complete form in the tonic key. After a short period of strife, a foretaste of what is still to come, slight hints of the second subject begin to be heard. But the key of G major is so firmly established that we are taken by surprise when the new theme springs upon us in B flat major. For added colour we are transported into B major, but only briefly. A mysterious interrupted cadence leads to the exceptionally powerful development section, in which first of all sections of the first subject themes are combined and then the second subject is thrown into the melting pot as well. When the recapitulation is reached the main theme returns delightfully transformed, the second theme is missing and the second subject is considerably changed.

Like Schubert, Dvořák was fascinated by changes from major to minor and *vice versa*. In the Adagio ma non troppo we have in reality some rather free variations on a theme in E flat with two facets, or, more accurately, two related themes, one of them minor and the other major, but perhaps the most remarkable feature is the way Dvořák moulds this movement into a dynamic and deeply moving whole. Those who imagine that deep emotion is not found in Dvořák's music would do well to get to know better the D minor symphony (op. 70), the F minor trio and this movement. It is the composition of a fifty-four year old man who had experienced bitterness, sorrow and failure as well as peace, happiness and success, a man who knew what life had to offer, and who valued more greatly the simple joys of family life, and of communion with God and with nature, than being lionized in a foreign country. The first bars of the Adagio's themes are shown here, together with the accompaniment figure associated with the first of these:

Ex. 20a.

Ex. 20b.

Ex. 20c.

Later the falling sixth in (a) becomes a diminished seventh, similar to those in ex. 8 above. This becomes the heart of the passionate climax that develops out of the section in F sharp minor, and which culminates after the crisis in a splendid affirmation of (b) in C major,[1] succeeded by a dreary *pp* echo of it in the minor over a dominant pedal. There follows a brief recapitulation of (b) restored to its original key, and a coda, which ends peacefully in the major.

The Scherzo in B minor has real character and some surprises. The dog fight between viola and 'cello that accompanies the canonic section is comical, and the whispering staccato background to the theme when it is heard for the last time is a delight. The Finale is an irregular rondo, with a pair of quite distinct themes, major and minor, in the tonic key, and a second subject in E flat major. Halfway through the movement the triplet second subject melody from the first movement returns, and in its train the main theme follows as well. A temporary slackening of the movement's impetus does no harm, but when shortly before the coda the same triplet theme returns, and in alternation with a fragment of the Finale's second subject is repeated three times over, raised a semitone higher each time, it is necessary to protest.

The score of the quartet in A flat, op. 105, dates from March 26th, 1895, but at that time Dvořák progressed hardly any further than the end of the exposition.[2] When the G major quartet was finished he resumed work on the earlier composition. A letter to Göbl (23. XII. 1895) gives a vivid picture of the composer at the time:

> Praise God we are all well, and we rejoice that after three years we can again spend a delightful and happy Christmas in Bohemia! It was so different last year in America, where we were so far away in a foreign land and separated from all the children and friends! However, the Lord has granted us this blissful moment, and therefore we are all inexpressibly happy.
>
> Now I am very industrious. I work so easily that I couldn't wish for anything better. I have just finished a new quartet in G major and now I am already coming to the end of a second in A flat; I have completely finished two movements already, I am just writing the Andante, and I think I shall finish the work after the festival.

He did—on December 30th in fact. It is probable that this work was given its first public performance by the Rosé Quartet in Vienna on November

---

[1] Dvořák may well have been influenced by a rather similar passage in the same key in the Largo sostenuto of Smetana's quartet, *From my Life*.

[2] The sketch in the Library of Congress shows that it was the composer's intention to repeat the exposition, and suggests that he had started thinking about the development. Later the repetition was eliminated.

10th, 1896,[1] where the Bohemian Quartet repeated it on January 15th, 1897. The Dannreuther Quartet played it in New York on December 20th, 1896, and Gompertz presented it in London on January 27th of the year following.

The groping introduction to the first movement throws the relative brightness of the Allegro appassionato into relief, but this too has its darker aspects. The first subject is composed of separate extrovert and introvert limbs, the first springing directly from the introduction, and the second having expressive drooping sevenths and some sombre five-note chords that remind us of the end of the slow movement of Smetana's first quartet. In the similar endings of each neither the quintuplet of semiquavers nor the detached quavers should be overlooked, for in Dvořák's music tags are often significant. The second of these immediately becomes the bass of the second part of the theme, and then takes over other important functions. Shorn of its first note the quintuplet is much used in the development while the first theme is combined with the formerly genial but now earnest theme of the second subject. In the latter part of the development the falling melody reappears in G major and F sharp minor at a slower tempo, after which the bars that follow lead directly to the middle of the transition, so that once again Dvořák has successfully telescoped his recapitulation.

The Scherzo is a superb *furiant*:

Ex. 21.

We notice that the cadence bars of the theme become the basis of the next section in combination with a slightly different version of the above quotation. Later their inversion blossoms out into the glorious melodious singing of the Trio. In this movement there are recollections of *The Jacobin*. First of all Julie's lullaby is quoted from, and then at the end of the Trio the latter part of the Count's aria, 'Ten úsměv děcka' (That little child's smile), is start- lingly conspicuous, and the keys are identical in each instance with those in

[1] Mr. Burghauser has kindly brought this new fact to my notice, and informed me that the Hellmesberger Quartet did not play this work in Vienna until after the Bohemian Quartet's performance. The last-mentioned ensemble gave a private performance of the work in Prague on April 16th, 1896.

the opera. As the Lento e molto cantabile gradually unfolds, each repeated section is made to sound quite different from the previous bars by means of changes of scoring and the addition of countermelodies. In the middle section the diminished seventh chords, heavily disguised with pedals and chromatically descending appoggiaturas, show the composer reaching out into new harmonic depths, after which the original melody, returning embellished like a variation, is truly enchanting. The Finale presents a novel variation on sonata form. Besides the normal second subject, there is also a 'third subject' that first appears in G flat major, and is subsequently recapitulated in the subdominant key.[1]

These two quartets stand high among Dvořák's compositions, the G major especially so. When good recordings of them appear in the gramophone catalogues, they are unfortunately apt to disappear again very soon because of lack of demand. It is a pity that less fine chamber works by Dvořák have achieved such popularity that the public is only comparatively rarely given the opportunity of discovering what it is missing.

[1] Can the march from *Carmen*, an opera Dvořák admired greatly, have been at the back of his mind when he began this movement ? There are some rhythmic similarities, and in each there is a corresponding shift to the subdominant after four bars.

VIII

Chamber Music with Pianoforte

There is a slight possibility that Dvořák may have written a pianoforte trio during early manhood, judging by the list of his compositions that he handed to V. J. Novotný towards the end of 1887. It may be presumed that the other two trios mentioned in the same list, and described by the composer as 'no good', are the pair from which an Adagio was selected for performance by Ludevít Procházka and the Hřímalý brothers for the 'sixth free musical entertainment' in Prague on July 5th, 1872.[1] These works have disappeared. Dvořák also finished a sonata in F minor for 'cello and piano (op. 10) on January 4th, 1871, the piano part of which was probably destroyed. This work is akin to the E minor string quartet, for the three sections are joined together, and the third part returns to the themes of the beginning. The Andante maestoso melody foreshadows the allegretto grazioso theme for clarinets in *Heroic Song* of twenty-five years later.

Dvořák's piano quintet in A, op. 5, which must not be confused with the famous quintet, op. 81, in the same key, was probably composed during the late summer of 1872, and was performed on November 22nd that year at a concert in Prague organized by Procházka. According to the composer's testimony he destroyed the score, but when he was revising early works in 1887 with a view to having them published, he asked Procházka for his copy, and then made a number of sweeping changes in the work, cutting out two-fifths of the first movement and modifying both of the others. The main theme of the first movement returned at the end of the Finale in the earlier version, but not in the later draft. Dvořák seemed dissatisfied with his patching up, for he apparently made no attempt to offer the work to Simrock, and almost immediately he began work on the op. 81 quintet. The earlier work has recently been published for the first time. It is a transitional work, showing the composer's progress in the direction of classicism, especially in the

---

[1] Dvořák indicated that the trios were written in 1865 and 1866, but his memory for facts was unreliable, and these dates were no doubt the result of some guesswork. The trios may not have been composed before 1871 or 1872.

use of clearly defined and concise themes. If on the one hand we begin to see Dvořák's musical personality gradually emerging, on the other we notice that he still had much to learn regarding musical form. Several sheets of the earlier version were cut out of the score and have not been traced.

Except for a curious over-emphasis of the bass note in first inversions of the tonic triad, the principal theme of the first movement, complete with Czech repetitions of the opening figure, is promising enough. The naïve theme of the second subject, rhythmically related to the first theme, seems to be inhibited by the strong magnetism of the keynote every time it makes an effort to move away. At times the harmony associated with both these themes is rather static, but this is not found elsewhere. The development shows inexperience, and to our surprise the second subject is now omitted from the recapitulation. In the Andante sostenuto Dvořák roams freely but always melodiously with some extreme modulations and in a great many keys. Perhaps here more than anywhere else in the work he makes really imaginative use of the five instruments. In the strongly rhythmic Finale in $\frac{6}{8}$ time he avoids establishing the tonic key for almost forty bars, chiefly by the use of elaborated augmented sixth and dominant minor ninth chords. He foolishly presents his second subject theme in the tonic key, and the protracted treatment of this in a variety of keys, including the tonic, merely emphasizes the mistake. Without the provision of a development the material is recapitulated with some modifications.

The next two works, a violin sonata in A minor (op. 19) written in January 1873, and an octet (op. 22), subtitled 'Serenade', completed in September of the same year, have both been lost. The sonata was in three movements, and as in the piano quartet, op. 23, the third movement was a combination of Scherzo and Finale. The octet was written for pianoforte, two violins, viola, double bass, clarinet, bassoon and horn. It is not known if it was performed. The sonata was played at an Umělecká beseda (Artistic Circle) concert in January 1875 by Josef Marcus and Josef Jiránek.

Within a year of hearing the good news that he had been awarded the Austrian State Prize, Dvořák composed two trios and a piano quartet. He had some difficulty in discovering how to write sympathetically for a keyboard instrument, because although he was a capable pianist and organist he was first and foremost a string player. In all these works we notice at times that he tended to write for the piano in a rather superficial manner, exploiting its upper and middle registers and neglecting the potentialities of the bass, or clinging to meaningless figurations. In consequence of this deficiency the effect of the music is somewhat diminished. At the same time he was a rapidly maturing artist, one who was not only gaining in self-confidence, but also in skill, craftsmanship, personality and power of musical expression. It was during this time that he wrote his F major symphony, the work which

The New Czech Theatre, Prague, where in 1881 *The Stubborn Lovers* was first performed, and, in the following year, *Dimitrij*

The original staging of *Dimitrij*

Title page of the vocal score of *The Jacobin*, designed
by Mikoláš Aleš

The National Theatre, Prague, during the period when Dvořák's last four operas were
presented there for the first time. The former bridge over the Vltava is shown

shows more clearly than any other what an outstanding composer he already was in 1875.

The piano trio in B flat, op. 21, was probably written during March and the first half of April of that year, if, as seems likely, the date on the manuscript is inaccurate. It was performed in Prague on February 17th, 1877, by Karel ze Slavkovských, Ondříček and Sládek, and was published by Schlesinger of Berlin three years later. Some time before publication, and perhaps even before the performance, Dvořák wrote a new Trio for the Scherzo and made some cuts in the Finale. Sometimes the first movement reminds us of Schubert and Schumann, but the swaying between two conflicting dominant sevenths just before the second subject, the modulations in the development, and many other features, are fingerprints of Dvořák himself. Starting calmly and spaciously, the moment the main theme is heard in diminution the movement suddenly springs to life. The second subject is overlong and repetitive, but there is no monotony of key. Although the development concentrates on the first theme, it shows sound workmanship and a quite surprising range of mood. In the recapitulation we are treated to changes in the order of themes and other modifications, but not the condensation that the first bars suggest. It is possible that the theme of the second subject may have been derived subconsciously from the principal theme, and so may the melody of the Adagio molto e mesto. This movement is in *ababa* form, with the second statement of (*a*) lowered by a semitone, and with (*b*) transformed when it returns. A delightful polka follows, but the Trio is lacking in character. Finally comes an Allegro vivace with a sonata form basis that starts in G minor and reaches the tonic key after twenty-four bars, at which point a jubilant canonic theme is announced. During the development, which is better described as an outcrop of the second subject, the slow movement theme returns.

The composition that followed, the piano quartet in D major, op. 23, is a rather more unassuming work. It is the first of Dvořák's two compositions for this combination of instruments, and both Scherzo and Finale are merged in the third movement. Only eighteen days were needed for its completion, from May 24th to June 10th, 1875. It was slightly revised before Schlesinger published it in 1880, and it had to wait until December 16th that year for its first performance, which was given by Kopta, Mareš, A. Neruda and Slavkovský at an Umělecká beseda concert in Prague. It was a charmingly romantic idea to waft the first movement's main theme into B major as early as the tenth bar. The material unfolds gradually, but just as the repetitions of the second subject theme begin to be tiresome the exposition takes on a new lease of life. The development, which is weak in any case, is further marred by the transposition *en bloc* of a score of bars, without any significant changes being made. The principal and second subject themes are combined grandioso in the coda. The short set of variations on an attractive theme in B minor:

Ex. 1.

is charming and sometimes naïve, and it does not give very much indication of Dvořák's amazing mastery of this form as shown in the *Symphonic Variations* of only two years later. In the third variation the melody is inverted, and in the fourth the tonality swings between E flat major and B minor. The chromatically-tinged harmony gives the coda a fittingly plaintive valedictory character. In the Finale a flowing Allegretto scherzando in ⅔ time alternates with an Allegro agitato in ¼. We are treated to one of Dvořák's earlier instances of *furiant* rhythm in the first part for a few bars only, and notably in the section in C sharp minor. The allegro unfortunately compares unfavourably with the scherzando.

The third work of this group, the piano trio in G minor, op. 26, is the first of Dvořák's compositions to express the composer's sorrow at the death of his two-day-old daughter Josefa during the previous September. It was again written quickly, between January 4th and 20th, 1876. Bote & Bock of Berlin published it in 1879, and it is believed to have had its first performance on June 29th that year at Turnov, when the composer played it with Ferdinand Lachner and Alois Neruda. In this trio Dvořák made a valiant attempt to limit the number of themes he employed. The Finale has three, and the first movement two, the first of which is compounded of three or four interrelated elements; the Largo has only one theme. It must be confessed that in the present instance the task was greater than Dvořák could successfully accomplish at that time with the themes that he had chosen.

The slow movement presented no real problem to him, and the Scherzo, whose 5-bar theme opened up various canonic possibilities, practically wrote itself. The arresting main theme of the first movement possesses great possibilities, but in Dvořák's hands it fails to grow and develop adequately, while the second theme is too trivial in so sombre and passionate a context. The Finale is the weakest movement, and here the composer seems to lose grip at times in unsatisfactory modulations and bad joins. To make his principal theme face both ways, that is, to have a minor and a major form, does not seem to be the happiest of solutions.

The origin of the *Maličkosti* (Bagatelles), op. 47, is slightly similar to that of the *Terzetto*. From 1878 onwards some musical friends of Josef Srb-Debrnov, the enthusiastic writer on music and organizer of concerts, used to meet at his flat to play string quartets. They even played Smetana's first quartet *From My Life* before it had been publicly performed.[1] The players, some of whom were professional executants, were V. J. Novotný (later replaced by Ferdinand Lachner), Váša Laub, Tomáš Kovařovic, and their host, who was the 'cellist. Dvořák wrote these pieces for a rare combination of instruments, two violins, 'cello and harmonium, because Srb-Debrnov possessed a harmonium. They were composed between May 1st and 12th, 1878, just as Dvořák was completing his first set of *Slavonic Dances*, and were played by Lachner, Vorel, Neruda and the composer at an Umělecká beseda concert on February 2nd, 1879. Srb-Debrnov received the dedication.

The five pieces, clearly the work of an imaginative nationalist composer, are unpretentious but polished trifles in simple forms. The first and third borrow two bars from the well-known folk-song 'Hrály dudy u Pobudy' (The Bagpipes were playing at Pobuda), turn them from major to minor, and make them the core of the music. There is even an indirect reference to the same two bars in the last piece. The second piece, which is marked Tempo di minuetto, serves as a peaceful interlude. The fourth, Dvořák's only music written practically throughout in canon, includes a brief section of canon three in one at the distance of a quaver, but the remainder of the time it is two in one at the octave at a bar's distance. The composer's genius, however, seems to shine most in the third piece, a delightfully fresh and spontaneous Allegretto scherzando. The keyboard part should not be played on a piano, but on a harmonium, for which it is much better suited.

The sonata in F major for violin and piano, op. 57, was composed between March 3rd and 17th, 1880, shortly after Dvořák had completed the second version of his violin concerto, a work which did not reach its final form until two years later. He began writing a Poco adagio in F major as the second

[1] At the first private performance of Smetana's quartet, Dvořák was the viola player.

movement, and then laid this aside, writing instead a Poco sostenuto in A major in ⁶₄ time. Clearly it would not have been satisfactory if all three movements had been in the same key. The rejected sketch came in useful shortly afterwards for the C major string quartet. Writing to Göbl from Berlin, Dvořák reported (1. IV. 1880): 'I played the sonata with Joachim yesterday, and he liked it very much.' It is probable that Josef Klimeš and Zdenka Havelková-Hlávková were the first to perform this work in public at their concert at Chrudim on September 23rd that year, presumably immediately after it had been published by Simrock.

This sonata marks Dvořák's first success in writing satisfactorily for the piano in a chamber music work, although as the *Theme and Variations* show he had reached this stage a few years earlier in solo piano music. One cannot help noticing that the influence of Brahms has not only assisted him over this hurdle, but has also helped to direct his thoughts during composition, for example in the melody of the slow movement and in the rhythmic treatment of themes in the first movement. The sonata, or, more precisely, the first pair of movements, represents Dvořák at his most intimate, and indeed it seems appropriate to describe the first bars as fragile and sensitive:

Ex. 2.

The questioning opening phrase and the positive, but restrained, response provide Dvořák with sufficient contrasting material for most of his needs. As in the sixth symphony, the second subject is centred in the submediant major; that is, it begins and ends in D major, but between times it modulates freely, and even returns to the tonic key for eleven bars. The first subject is considerably changed in the recapitulation, but not the second subject, which is what one normally expects to find in Dvořák's music. The gay nationally coloured Finale is freely modelled on sonata form. It has two subordinate themes (cf. string quartet in A flat, op. 105), in F minor and E flat major, and a working out section developing a new theme that appears to have grown out of both the E flat motif and the principal theme.

TRIO IN F MINOR

The next work, the pianoforte trio in F minor, op. 65, is a product of the highly critical period in Dvořák's life, which is discussed in greater detail on pp. 10-11. It suffices here to say that Dvořák was being torn in two directions, and that eventually his national consciousness and pride overcame the temptation to try to become internationally famous in the field of opera. The trio was written before his mind was made up. The spiritual suffering he was undergoing accounts for his choice of the unusual key, and can be seen in the content of the work as a whole, for, like the symphony in D minor op. 70, it is composed in epic style. Dvořák's dilemma is also reflected in the difficulties he encountered in moulding his themes and shaping his work, in fact in the seriousness with which he approached his problem and in the unprecedentedly critical frame of mind in which he worked in order to strive to satisfy his lofty ideals.

Instead of taking between two and three weeks to compose the trio, as in the case of other chamber works, we may assume that he was engaged on it for rather more than two months. The first sketches are not now extant. The only manuscript score available now was begun on February 4th and finished on March 31st, 1883. Although this shows the work completed, there are a great many revisions and corrections to be seen, some of which were almost certainly made after the date given at the end of the score. Some of these alterations are far-reaching, and in the development of the first movement alone only fifteen of the seventy-one bars remained unchanged.[1] This score, however, still differs in detail from the printed version in numerous ways, and is so untidy and disorderly that Dvořák was compelled to prepare a new score, probably during May, between the composition of the *Scherzo capriccioso* and the opera *Vanda*. The second score has been lost. Although Dvořák composed the slow movement before the

[1] For a description of the manuscript, see *Musica*, XIII, 10, Kassel 1959.

Scherzo, and intended it to come second, as the manuscript shows, he later reversed the order of these two movements.

Simrock published the trio during the autumn of 1873. It was performed for the first time by Lachner, Neruda and Dvořák at Mladá Boleslav on October 27th, and they repeated it on November 13th at an Umělecká beseda concert in Prague. J. C. Fuller-Maitland and two others played it at a charity concert at Kensington on January 11th in the following year.

In this work once again the influence of Brahms is felt, and this is wholly beneficial. It need hardly be said that the trio cannot be otherwise than highly characteristic of Dvořák. Its spirit, however, is very different from that found in so many of his works. When writing in a major key Dvořák was often in the habit of flattening the sixth degree of the scale, and to a lesser extent the second degree as well—probably for reasons not dissimilar to Mozart's when he used Neapolitan sixth chords—but in this trio the depressions occur in every movement, and are much more frequent than in any other of Dvořák's works. The anguish and poignancy of the D minor symphony is achieved by quite different means, during the parts of the work that are in minor tonality, whereas the major portions are much more calm and serene, with, however, touches of sadness here and there; and in that work the Finale's second subject is positively cheerful. If in the symphony Dvořák's aim was to make a powerful impact through the deep contrast between turbulence and composure, in the trio, on the contrary, he preferred to sustain the note of

Ex. 3.

tragedy, and to exploit the many shades of expression that lie within its orbit. Again, in the symphony, the calamitous final bars pass from D minor through G minor to reach their catharsis in the *tierces de Picardie* of the last chords, but in the trio the tonic major is reached and infinite peace reigns thirty-one bars before the work ends.

The tremendous passion inherent in the first movement's principal theme becomes immediately apparent (Ex. 3).

A supplementary theme is given out at once by the strings, headed by three strong chords, and another soon follows on the strings which is taken up by the piano.[1] In the transition a quieter version of the second theme is combined with elements of the main theme. The 'cello opens the second subject group with a broad nine-bar melody in the submediant major, starting with an augmentation of the first portion of the main theme, but the themes sound entirely different and it seems unlikely that the composer was aware of these connections. At first Dvořák placed a much weaker theme here in the remote key of C sharp minor, which he took without alteration from the beginning of the ill-fated string quartet in A minor, op. 12, but finding it was unsuitable at this point he reversed his themes, using this one as the basis for the resolute pendant to the 'cello melody:

Ex. 4a.

Ex. 4b.

The development concentrates entirely upon the first two themes of the first subject. When the second of these appears dreamily in augmentation on the 'cello in G flat major, we are reminded of a similar transformation in the first movement of the 'cello concerto (Molto sostenuto, fig. 10). The first part of the recapitulation is composed entirely anew. Almost immediately the music reaches the depths of despair as the strings repeat figure (x) from the main theme interrogatively, descending by semitones. The first supplementary theme is omitted. The transition material returns at the expected time, but leads back to the missing chord theme before the second subject reappears. At the end of the coda, which is longer than usual, Dvořák makes the main theme sound particularly poignant by flattening the fourth and seventh notes (C flat, G flat).

C sharp minor had a hold on Dvořák while he wrote this trio, for, apart from considering using it prominently in the first movement, it became the key of the second subject in the rondo Finale, and is also the key of the

[1] This theme had its origin in Dvořák's song, 'The Cuckoo', op. 7, no. 3.

Scherzo. To a large extent it is the combination of a $\frac{2}{4}$ melody[1] with a continuous accompaniment of triplet quavers that gives this movement its fascination. The extremely syncopated accompaniment of the Meno mosso springs directly from the type of part played by the second and third violins in a lively Slovak dance. The ternary Poco adagio has two themes to each part. The finely expressive 'cello melody with which this movement opens is later heard somewhat varied, but it is omitted at first when the opening section returns. In the middle section Dvořák temporarily loses his inspiration, regaining it when an eloquent melody for the violin appears in B major. In the coda this returns in a particularly poignant form:

Ex. 5.

and at this moment it anticipates in a remarkable way the principal theme of the Finale of the D minor symphony.[2] The breadth of thought combined with the influence of the dance, in which *furiant* rhythm is mixed, helps to make the trio's Finale a movement of tremendous verve. The final change to the major mode, which has been referred to above, is magnificently brought about by means of a rhythmically changed version of the first movement's principal theme.

PIANO QUINTET

On August 16th, 1887, Dvořák wrote to Göbl,[3] 'I'm doing nothing new now, only improving several old works a little and sending them to Simrock.' Two days later he started composing his piano quintet in A major, op. 81,

---

[1] Cf. its ♫ ♩ | ♩ ♫ rhythm with the Czech folk-song 'Kdybys byl, Honzíčku' in Erben's *Prostonárodní české písně a říkadla: Nápěvy*, No. 259.

[2] See p. 82, ex. 28.

[3] Not to Simrock, as is sometimes stated.

and it was finished on October 3rd. It is probable that the idea of writing this work gradually crystallized in his mind after having revised his early piano quintet in the previous spring, and having found that he was unable to transform it into a worth-while composition. By starting from the very beginning again his chances of succeeding were tremendously increased. With the serious crisis of the years 1883–85 resolved, Dvořák entered his second nationalist phase, which lasted for six years, until the beginning of the American period. The first fruits of that time were the second set of *Slavonic Dances* and the *Terzetto*, and works that followed later included the E flat piano quartet, the *Dumky* Trio, the opera *The Jacobin*, the G symphony and the triptych of overtures. This was a period of contentment, when for the most part the Czech master was able to work in a happy environment. During the summer months he could spend long periods at his house on the edge of the forest land of Vysoká, where he was happier than anywhere else. It was here that he wrote his delightfully fresh and unique quintet, one of the three finest piano quintets ever written. He dedicated it to Dr. B. Neureutter, who was a professor of medicine and a generous patron of music. It was first played by Karel Kovařovic, Karel Ondříček, Pelikán, Mareš and Alois Neruda at an Umělecká beseda concert on January 6th, 1888. In London it was performed on May 11th by Charles Hallé, Wilma Norman-Néruda (Lady Hallé), Ries, Straus, and Franz Neruda.

This work probably epitomizes more completely the genuine Dvořák style in most of its facets than any other work of his. Laughter and tears, sorrow and gaiety, are found side by side, as well as many moods that lie between these two extremes. All are presented with consummate mastery, they are decked in a wide range of instrumental colouring, and through the whole sweeps the life-blood of vital rhythm. In the first few bars the lovely 'cello melody turns characteristically towards the minor mode, and in fact the second theme and the earlier part of the transition theme are firmly rooted in A minor. The second subject, in which the viola leads the way, is in another minor key, the mediant. Since Dvořák, following a sudden change of tonality, goes directly from the development to the second statement of the main theme, retaining hardly any of the first subject, and as in his sextet, bringing back his minor second subject in a new key (F sharp minor), there results here a curious minimization of the tonic key that is unparalleled in the remainder of his music. The coda helps to restore the balance, naturally, but in the recapitulation and coda combined scarcely more than a third of the bars are in the tonic.

The Andante con moto is a particularly beautiful *dumka*, the melancholy spirit of which is relieved by a cheerful melodic section in D major[1] which returns again later, and a vivace whose theme is derived from the opening

[1] The melody is sadly misquoted in Robertson's *Dvořák*.

bars of the movement. These bars recur before and after the phrases of the main melody like a kind of frame, and in addition they influence the countermelody. At first the viola has the melody on its dark C string while the piano sparkles high in the treble (Ex. 6).

When the *dumka* returns the 'cello plays the melody and the violins take over the countermelody. After the vivace the scoring is again changed, the piano being given a continuous series of descending arpeggios that combine dotted and triplet rhythms. Although Dvořák added in parenthesis the word 'Furiant' to his Scherzo, the movement is not a genuine example of this

Ex. 6.

Andante con moto

dance.[1] During the Poco tranquillo section the main Scherzo theme reappears as a pathetic shadow of its former exuberant self. In the gay Rondo which concludes the work the restatements of the principal theme are singularly incomplete. Usually Dvořák could be relied upon to provide a Finale that was perfectly fitting in its context, even if occasionally there are a few signs of lack of taste in the codas. Here he has fortunately solved the problem of bringing his work to a satisfactory culmination extremely well, and much better than in, for example, his otherwise superb G major string quartet.

PIANO QUARTET IN E FLAT

On August 10th, 1889, Dvořák reported to Göbl: 'I've now already finished three movements of a new piano quartet and the Finale will be ready in a few days. As I expected it came easily and the melodies just surged upon me. Thank God!' Simrock, as it happens, had urged Dvořák to write such a work four years earlier. He reminded him repeatedly of his promise to do so, and could not understand why he did not make a start, but the composer waited until the time was ripe. He had actually made a brief sketch for the beginning of a piano quartet in October 1887, but made no further progress on it. Simultaneously sketching and preparing the score of the quartet, op. 87, occupied the composer from July 10th to August 19th, 1889. Yet again the Umělecká beseda claimed the first performance, when the work

[1] Burghauser suggests to me that the subtitle may perhaps have been added because of a verbal association with the folk-song 'Když jsi ty, sedláčku, pán', the melody of which has some similarity with Dvořák's theme in bars 60 ff.

was played at their Popular Concert on November 23rd, 1890, by H. Trneček, F. Lachner, Mareš and Wihan. It was played in London at Dannreuther's Musical Evening on January 5th, 1892.

This quartet has unfortunately been overshadowed by the piano quintet. It may not have quite the same immediate appeal as the earlier work, and its spirit may be a little less relaxed, but it has many excellent qualities and the two works are in fact complementary. Dvořák's handling of the strings and piano in opposition to each other should be noted. In the first bars the sententious statement of the strings provokes the piano to give a capricious response, which is an opening gambit with great possibilities (Ex. 7).

Quiet restatements of the first bar by the strings receive brusque replies

Ex. 7.

from the piano. With the addition of the flowing second subject melody in the mediant major, Dvořák has practically all the material he needs, for his transition theme in dotted rhythm (bar 33) is a playful variant of the first bar of the above quotation. The development only uses the main and transition themes. At letter K the principal theme is heard in B flat minor. Fourteen bars later the second subject appears in B major, but after eight bars this slips into E flat major. In this manner Dvořák has once again brilliantly foreshortened his recapitulation. In the coda the 'cello plays the first bar of the main theme linked to the beginning of the second subject in a mysterious tremolando, while violin and viola transform the above-mentioned brusque replies into the gentlest of comments.

In the Lento in G flat major the melodies, lovely as they are, seem to have surged upon Dvořák a little too freely, for there are five of them, and he was not able to conceal some of the joins with his customary skill. The movement is binary with a coda, the last three themes being transposed into the tonic when they return. It opens calmly with a conversation between 'cello and piano. When the fourth theme is reached in the dominant minor the mood is agitated and stormy. This section is succeeded by the extremely effective fifth theme, which is related to the third. Although it is in the major mode the violin's syncopated appoggiaturas help to give it a particularly plaintive character (Ex. 8).

The Scherzo, Allegro moderato, grazioso, is a delightful movement. Sometimes we hear the cimbalom playing, especially when the fifteen-bar opening melody comes round for the third time. The alternative theme, composed around four notes, provides a fascinating interlude, and leads to some unforeseen happenings. The codetta is connected with both these themes. Canon and lively rhythms are combined in the Trio. The Finale, which

Ex. 8.

abounds with energy and good humour, is in the key of E flat minor.[1] The second subject, following the pattern of Dvořák's other sonata form finales, consists of a series of fresh thoughts, together with an imitative variant on the main theme. The last of these to appear is particularly rewarding for the viola. Thanks to the second subject E flat major is firmly established in the recapitulation.

DUMKAS

Dvořák entitled his next work 'Dumkas, op. 90, for piano, violin and 'cello.' The word *dumka*, pl. *dumky*, is a diminutive of the noun *duma*, which in turn derives from the verbs *dumat'*, *dumać*, etc., in Slavonic languages, with the meaning 'to meditate, ponder or brood' as well as 'to think'. In Ukraine the words *duma* and *dumka* came to be used with reference to the peasant's recollections or narrations in verse or song of deeds of heroism in bygone days, and one of these ballads, 'Oh, the Czar was in Merenovya', is included in Kuba's collection of Ukrainian folk-songs.[2] The melody is limited to the first four notes of a minor scale and is marked 'Rather quickly',

[1] Among the very few works in major keys that have finales in the tonic minor are Haydn's symphony No. 70 and quartets op. 76, nos. 1 and 3, Mendelssohn's *Italian* symphony, Brahms's G major violin sonata, B major trio and third symphony, and also Dvořák's *Terzetto*. Tovey overlooked Dvořák altogether when he stated categorically that Haydn was 'imitated only by Mendelssohn . . . and Brahms', in referring to this unusual feature in his article on Haydn in Cobbett's *Cyclopedic Survey of Chamber Music*.

[2] L. Kuba, *Slovanstvo ve svých zpěvech*, Vol. VI, Part I, pp. 122–124.

so that it has no direct relationship with any of Dvořák's *dumkas*. For melodies that express brooding it is instructive to turn to two Serbian songs in H. Möller's *Das Lied der Völker*,[1] and in each of these we notice a significant increase of speed, adagio to allegretto, in one case, and andante quasi recitativo to allegretto in the other. It is in songs such as these that we perceive the musical prototypes of the characteristic Dvořákian *dumka*, but it is much more probable that the Czech composer was influenced by Ukrainian, Russian or Polish examples than by those of the southern Slavs.

According to C. R. Halski[2] the word *dumka* may have first acquired its musical connotation when it was used for a composition published in 1821 by the Polish operatic composer, Kurpiński, with the title 'Dumka of the Jabłonna Peasants'. Moniuszko first published his celebrated song 'Kozak' (The Cossack) in 1850, and subtitled it 'dumka'. It is quite probable that Dvořák was familiar with this. Although it has no change of tempo or mood, it could have influenced him in one respect. It has a marked rhythm not unlike that of a *polka*, and consequently has a slight link with the second movement of his sextet, op. 48.

It is perhaps hardly surprising that, faced with various types of *dumka*, Dvořák should have had some doubt as to its exact nature. It has been reported that after he had already composed several *dumkas* he met Ludvík Kuba, the painter and collector of Slavonic folk-songs, in a coffee house, and that he asked him 'What is a dumka?' It is a pity that this encounter cannot be dated, and also that Kuba's reply has not been recorded. It is clear, however, that Dvořák's conception of a *dumka* gradually crystallized into a musical form, the basic mood of which is pensive and melancholy, but which has sections interpolated that are serene, cheerful and even sometimes exceptionally ebullient, among the most typical examples being the second *Slavonic Dance*, the second movement of the string quartet in E flat and the slow movement of the piano quintet. Nevertheless it is possible to find other movements that do not correspond with this type and which may justifiably be called *dumkas*; one of these is the twelfth *Slavonic Dance*.

Dvořák's *Dumkas*, or *Dumky* Trio, stands quite apart from traditional chamber music forms. The movements, six in all, are in E minor, C sharp minor, A major, D minor, E flat major and C minor, so there is no unity of key, and neither is there any important thematic connection between them. The first three *dumkas* succeed one another without a break; four are in binary form, and the other two are in ternary and simple rondo forms. In a rather restricted sense the *dumkas* may be described as variations on a theme, but the connecting thread is a non-musical one, a state of mind. When

[1] Vol. II, pp. 211–12.
[2] *Grove's Dictionary of Music and Musicians*, 5th Ed., Supplementary Vol., article 'Dumka'.

Lassus wrote his *Penitential Psalms* he was confronted with the task of composing a series of works that resemble one another in emotional feeling, and that centre, as Van den Borren has pointed out, around only two basic emotional states: despair and hope. Yet he succeeded in conveying similar emotions in a variety of subtly different ways.[1] It was less difficult for Dvořák when composing his trio, for he was able to rely on dance and other elements to provide vivid contrast, a factor which he could seldom do without. Even though he was far less restricted technically than Lassus was three centuries earlier, it is necessary to acknowledge that in the slower sections of his trio alone he was able to suggest pensive states of mind that are very varied in character.

The trio was composed between some time in November 1890 and February 12th in the following year. It was played for the first time by Ferdinand Lachner, Hanuš Wihan and Dvořák himself in Prague at a Civic Circle concert on April 11th, held in celebration of the conferment of the honorary degree of Doctor of Philosophy on the composer by the Charles University, Prague. During the first five months of 1892 the same three players performed the work in some forty towns of Bohemia and Moravia, prior to Dvořák's departure for the United States. Because of the composer's quarrel with Simrock, the trio was not published until 1894, and consequently it was not heard abroad until more than three years after it had been composed. Isidor Cohn, Lady Hallé and W. E. Whitehouse presented it at the St. James's Hall, London, on June 13th in that year.

The first of the *dumkas* opens with a bold declamatory theme over added sixth harmony, and soon gives way to a doleful melody ascending and descending in sixths. The second theme becomes the basis of the light-hearted quick section. In the majority of the *dumkas* a minor first section implies that there will be a major contrasting section, and *vice versa*. The pathos of the second *dumka* is realized largely by means of a deliberately monotonous accompaniment, coupled with changes from minor to major and back again (Ex. 9).

In the third *dumka* the vivace springs from the first section, part of an ascending scale being taken over for the melody, and bars 13–14 becoming the accompanying figure. The next movement has a fascinating beginning. We are kept in suspense while first the piano starts with a stereotyped pattern of accompaniment and then the violin begins a monotonous figure; to these the 'cello melody is finally added. Out of a diminution of this melody Dvořák shapes his *scherzando* theme. A plaintive chromatic melody and a wildly gay theme provide the diametrically opposed material for a later episode. There

[1] Van den Borren: *Orlande de Lassus*, 1930, p. 112. 'Ces états d'âme ne sont point nombreux et pivotent, en fait, autour de deux sentiments essentiels: désespoir et espoir. Mais que de nuances dans l'exécution!'

Ex. 9.

is so little that is meditative about the fifth movement that it scarcely deserves the name *dumka*. The link here is a four-note rising (and falling) scale which appears in three different forms, the second decorated with brilliant roulades of semi-quavers, and the third being a lively canon. The last *dumka* has such a beautiful beginning that we long to hear more of it, as we do in the coda, and earlier also when it blossoms out into a lovely melody on the violin's G string, strikingly reminiscent at first of the Ukrainian folk-song 'I go out on the hillock':[1]

[1] L. Kuba op. cit., p. 25.

Ex. 10a.

'выйду я на гóроньку'

Ex. 10b.

Lento   sul G

mp   molto espress.   f   più f

Although the *vivace* theme, foreshadowed earlier, is somewhat common-place, its treatment is not without subtlety.

Writing from New York to her 'dear old godfather' Alois Göbl, Dvořák's daughter Otilie said (9. XII. 1893): 'And now he [Daddy] has written a Sonata [*sic*] for piano and violin in an easy style and dedicated it to me and Tony.[1] Of course we're playing it too. It is delightful and he wrote it maybe in under a fortnight.' It occupied Dvořák from November 19th to December 3rd. It was a charming idea of the composer's to make his op. 100, this sona-tina in G, a work for his own children. He told Simrock, however, that adults ought to be able to enjoy it as well. At the beginning of the previous September when on a visit to St. Paul, Minnesota, Dvořák was taken to see the Minnehaha Falls, and he was overwhelmed by their beauty. While he stood there a melody came to him, which he jotted down on his starched cuff, and later this became the main theme of the sonatina's slow movement. Judging by the form the melody took when he wrote it down in a sketch book a month later, it needed several finishing touches, for only bars 1–2 and 5–6 are the same there as in the final version.[2] It is not known when the first performance of the sonatina took place.

Coming as it did immediately after the *New World* symphony, the F major quartet and the E flat quintet, the sonatina is, as one would expect, a work wholly characteristic of Dvořák's American period. Several of the themes are pentatonic, flattened sevenths take the place of leading notes in minor keys, syncopations occur, and the thrumming of a mandolin is suggested by the simple tune accompanied by spread chords in the Lar-ghetto. The first movement's second subject, on the other hand, may have been modified, perhaps unconsciously, during composition to make it

[1] Their names appear on the sketch. The manuscript score is dedicated to Otilka, Tony, Annie, Mařenka (Magdalena), Otakar and Zinda (Aloisie), in fact to all of his children, although the last four names were added later. Otilie was fifteen and Antonín ten at the time.

[2] The names 'Indian Lament', 'Indian Canzonetta' and 'Indian Lullaby' were not given to this movement by the composer.

correspond more closely with the well-known Moravian folk-song, 'Dolina, dolina, níže Nových Zámků' (The valley below Nové Zámky). Despite the limitations that Dvořák imposed on himself, the sonatina has real musical value. The first and last movements are in unabridged sonata form. The Larghetto is outstanding because of its flow of melody charged with meaning. The Scherzo fulfils its purpose excellently, and the Finale contains one of Dvořák's loveliest melodies:

Ex. 11.

The last phrase quoted was echoed later in the Finale of the A flat string quartet (bars 153–160).

IX

Pianoforte Music

With the exception of the *Theme and Variations* all of Dvořák's keyboard music consists of either short pieces or sets of pieces. In two instances, the *Poetic Tone Pictures* for two hands and *From the Bohemian Forest* for four hands, the composer has given us delightfully varied collections of pieces that appear to reflect his impressions of parts of the countryside that he loved, even if, as seems probable, the titles were added afterwards. Possibly the *Legends*, also for piano duet, might be grouped with these two works, but it is perhaps unwise to do so because Dvořák has given us no hint of their content. The remainder of the piano music consists mostly of dances, including the two famous sets of *Slavonic Dances*. The composer did not entirely rule out the possibility of writing a piano sonata, and in fact while in America he sketched a theme which he thought might be suitable in a work of this kind, but he then dismissed the idea from his mind. He was not at all strongly tempted to write large scale piano compositions, and evidently considered it was preferable in his case to write sonatas for more than one instrument.

Dvořák's first surviving composition is the *Forget-me-not Polka* for which his teacher Liehmann wrote a Trio. This was composed at Zlonice when he was fourteen or fifteen years of age. Early in 1860, when on a visit to Zlonice, he wrote another polka with a trio, which is in a spirited Bohemian style with slight Viennese echoes.

During his period of study at the Organ School, Prague, he wrote five preludes, a fugato and two fugues in D major and G minor for organ, which are now in the State Conservatory of Music, Prague. The fifth prelude, written on a given theme, and the second fugue, with a subject of the traditional 'And with his stripes'—Mozart *Requiem* 'Kyrie' type, were performed at Dvořák's public final examination on July 30th, 1859. It may be noted that in the G minor fugue Dvořák avoids using a regular counter-subject, he misses the opportunity for a *stretto*, and asserts his independence by changing the rhythmic emphasis of the subject on its last appearance. The group of middle entries that is associated with a prolonged pedal on B flat has the undesirable effect of detracting from what should be felt as the culmination of the fugue, the reassertion of the tonic key. However, it is apparent that Dvořák was proficient in contrapuntal writing and in the use of sequences and decorative figuration, and that he could also maintain the style of a given fragment with ease, a valuable discipline that led to the economy of material to be seen in later works.

Apart from pot-pourris from each of the two versions of the opera *King and Charcoal Burner,* no further piano music is known until we come to the Two Minuets, op. 28, which may have been composed in February 1876. Indications of instrumentation in the first published edition suggest that they may have been written originally for orchestra. As in Viennese waltzes each of the minuets is composed as a series of dances in different keys and ends with a return to the initial idea.

Working on the piano concerto apparently awakened Dvořák's interest in music for this instrument, for his *Dumka,* op. 35, and the *Theme and Variations,* op. 36, followed very shortly afterwards, both being composed in December 1876. He dedicated the *Dumka* to Mrs. Olga Hoppe, the sister of his friend Dr. Emil Kozánek. It is the first of his compositions to bear such a title. Neither this nor the similarly named piano piece of eight years later is a typical example of Dvořák's conception of this Ukrainian art form, yet in the earlier of the two pieces we can already see the embryo of the Dvořákian *dumka.* The prevailing melancholy mood is relieved from time to time, and at one point becomes decidedly gay and dance-like. This piece has a simple romantic appeal.

It seems probable that when writing the *Theme and Variations,* Dvořák took some hints from the first movement of Beethoven's sonata, op. 26, which is a set of variations on a theme which has the same time signature and which is in the same key. It cannot be claimed with certainty that Dvořák's plaintive, chromatically descending figure stems from Beethoven's fifth and sixth bars. It might well be a coincidence that the two themes, despite different modulation schemes, have some similarity of form, for the pattern is extremely common. What is much more likely is that the rhythm of Dvořák's first variation was suggested by the older musician's first variation, and it can hardly be fortuitous that the third variation of each set is in the tonic minor and that both start with similar syncopations (Exx. 1a, 1b). It will be remembered that Dvořák was a great admirer of Beethoven. Dvořák's conception, however, is totally at variance with that of Beethoven. He has invented a theme that lends itself well to those expressive flattenings which appealed to him so strongly, and to avoid repetition he extended the variation principle delightfully to subsections of variations. Furthermore, instead of feeling obliged to make them conform closely to the shape of the original, he was wise enough to allow them to grow freely and imaginatively.

This is particularly striking in the beautiful third variation, and again in the peaceful sixth variation, in which the tonality is found to have shifted to G flat major. It is evident that Dvořák's pleasure in writing his set of eight variations must have been coupled with the feeling that he knew what he wanted to say, and was at last confident that he had sufficient mastery of pianoforte style to say it effectively, as indeed he does. This is much more than a valuable study for the *Symphonic Variations* of a few months later; it is Dvořák's finest composition for the pianoforte.

The so-called *Scottish Dances*, op. 41, written a year later, are of the Ecossaise type, which suggests a link with Schubert rather than a Celtic origin. As in the earlier minuets they incorporate the cyclic principle in an elementary form. The first of the two *Furiants*, op. 42, was written at the end of May 1878, and the second one added almost four months later. In the meantime Dvořák had orchestrated his first set of *Slavonic Dances* and composed the *Three Modern Greek Poems*. Like the Scherzo of the sextet these are not typical examples of *furiants* such as are to be found among the *Slavonic Dances* and in the *Dumka and Furiant* of a few years later.

No sooner had the success of the *Slavonic Dances* and *Moravian Duets* made Dvořák leap into fame, than numerous German publishers urged him to let them have similar compositions. Simrock had secured the option to publish if he wished all Dvořák's new works, but the composer, finding himself in a buyers' market, decided that the opportunity that this offered was too good to be missed. Having insufficient old works with which to satisfy the new demands made on him, he practised a little deception and passed off new works as old. Perhaps he eased his conscience a little with the thought that he had started to write his piano *Silhouettes* some five or more years earlier, even though towards the end of 1879 he revised them thoroughly and added some newly composed pieces. He could certainly claim that some of the themes were old, for they came from his first two symphonies and the *Cypresses* song cycle of 1865. Hofmeister published the twelve pieces as op. 8, which may have been a number the composer had set aside for the earlier drafts.

The *Silhouettes* in reality form a cycle of unpretentious pieces bound together by themes that reminded Dvořák of his unavailing courtship of Josefina Čermáková. With a little imagination the first piece could be thought of as representing the dejected lover, for it uses the opening phrase of his song 'In deepest forest glade I stand', within a frame possibly suggesting the inexorable hand of fate, the theme here being the main one from the first movement of *The Bells of Zlonice*. The same two themes form the basis of the fifth *Silhouette*, and the theme from the symphony again figures prominently in the last piece. In the early drafts it also occurred at the end of the second and third pieces. The Scherzo and Finale themes from the same work were utilized in the eighth and ninth *Silhouettes*, and the second symphony's Scherzo and Finale themes were re-worked in the eleventh and sixth pieces respectively. The pieces are in simple style and sometimes a trifle repetitive, but even when inspired by polka rhythms, as in the third piece, the composer avoids the danger of making his phrases uniform in length. In the tenth piece, which is written in Dvořák's romantic vein, there is a notable breadth in the melody, and to our surprise the apparently transitory modulations lead to a conclusion in the key of the relative minor.

During the months following the completion of the *Silhouettes* Dvořák composed several more sets of pianoforte pieces. First came eight *Waltzes*, written between December 1st, 1879, and January 17th, 1880, which are marked op. 53 on the manuscript, but which Simrock published as op. 54.[1] Four *Eclogues*, op. 56, occupied him from January 24th to February 7th, and after an interval, during which he wrote some of the *Gipsy Melodies* and the violin sonata as well as revising his violin concerto, he composed four *Album Leaves*, half a dozen *Piano Pieces*, op. 52, and six *Mazurkas*, op. 56. The *Album Leaves* were begun on May 27th and it is presumed that all three sets of pieces were finished less than a month later. Four of the *Piano Pieces* were published by Hofmeister, and Bote & Bock issued the *Mazurkas*, but the rest of the pieces remained in manuscript until after the composer's death.[2]

[1] Dvořák evidently forgot that he had already allotted op. 53 to his violin concerto.
[2] The second and third of the *Album Leaves*, together with a *Moderato in A major*, composed in February 1881, were published in 1921. The fourth *Album Leaf* was published in the same year coupled with the fifth of the *Piano Pieces* (Allegro molto)

Nevertheless the first *Eclogue* was transformed into the fifth of the *Mazurkas*, and six years later when composing the ninth *Slavonic Dance* Dvořák found in the fourth *Eclogue* the two themes he was needing for the D major and B minor episode.[1] It will be recognized that the composer was sufficiently self-critical to realize that some of the pieces he produced during this period were below the standard that he set for himself, and furthermore that in the case of the *Piano Pieces* he selected for publication the Impromptu (Presto, G minor), Intermezzo (Larghetto, E flat), Gigue (B flat) and Eclogue (Poco allegro, G minor) because they formed a suitable integrated whole.

Dvořák became interested in composing waltzes when the Ball Committee of the Národní Beseda (National Society) asked leading Czech composers to write dances for them, but the dances that he actually wrote are intended for the drawing room and concert hall, and not for the ballroom. He would not agree to Simrock's suggestion that they should be called *Czech Waltzes* or *Slavonic Waltzes* because, as he pointed out, this dance is of German origin. Viennese elements appear in some of Dvořák's pieces, but so also do Czech characteristics: the sixth might be called a *sousedská*, the seventh is strongly Slavonic and so is the second. Several of the *Waltzes* have unusually imaginative codas. Within a short time the composer made effective adaptations of the first and fourth of the set for either string quartet or string orchestra. In the *Eclogues* and *Album Leaves* Dvořák was not aiming high, but some of the pieces have a simple charm, as for instance the first eclogue. The fourth of the *Album Leaves* (Allegretto) is much the most significant of any of these pieces. Although it starts in G major the principal key is revealed as E major. The middle section is a sustained despairing cry in the tonic minor. The *Piano Pieces*, op. 52, deserve to be much better known than they are, and it is strange that Dvořák did not make an effort to have the fifth piece published, for it is one of the best of the set. Despite Schumannesque touches these pieces have decided character and are typically Dvořákian. It was Dvořák's intention to write a second set of *Ecossaises*, but as far as we know only one of these dances was completed, and six weeks later this was converted into a mazurka. This, however, was not included among the published *Mazurkas*, its place having been taken by the transformed eclogue, which is one of the most attractive of the set. The spirit of the mazurka is felt particularly strongly in the second dance, and rather less so in some of the more intimate pieces.

under the title of *Two Impromptus*. The first *Album Leaf* and the hitherto unpublished *Piano Piece* (Tempo di marcia) are appearing for the first time in the *Complete Edition of Dvořák's Works*.

[1] The beautiful countermelody in the D major section, which is given to the violins in the orchestral version, is missing in the *Eclogue*.

After the sudden demand for piano music was over Dvořák only occasionally returned to this medium. He wrote the *Impromptu in D minor* on January 16th, 1883, at the request of V. J. Novotný, who published it in the Musical Supplement of *Humoristicky listy*. The *Dumka and Furiant*, which the composer misleadingly called op. 12, were written the following year during the time of his second visit to England. It is probable that when the *Dumka* was published F. A. Urbánek's fee was sent to a Catholic charity, for the manuscript bears the inscription 'presented for charitable purposes in Paris'. The *Furiant* was offered to J. W. Coates, editor of *The Magazine of Music*, and published in the Christmas Supplement, 1884. Both of these pieces were dedicated to Mařenka Rusová, the daughter of Dvořák's friend Antonín Rus, the Písek judge. The *Humoresque in F sharp major* was written for a collection of pieces published that same year by Urbánek, and was included in the first volume. After an interval of three years Dvořák wrote a couple of dances, *Two Little Pearls*, for 'The Young Czech Pianist', another of Urbánek's collections, and an *Album Leaf* (in E flat major) was written a few months later in an autograph album for 'K. H.' at Písek.

Pianists are recommended to turn their attention to the neglected *Impromptu*, in which Dvořák adopts a richer harmonic palette than was usual for him. The *Dumka*, once again, is not a typical Dvořákian example of this form, but it makes a splendid foil for the highly characteristic and fiery *Furiant*. In the *Two Little Pearls* Dvořák has written a lively dance in $\frac{2}{4}$ time with the title 'Do kola' (In a Ring),[1] and a *sousedská* which he appropriately calls 'Grandpa dances with Grandma'.

The *Poetic Tone Pictures* came into being between April 16th and June 6th, 1889, after a four-month lull in creative work, an unusually long period for Dvořák, but during part of that time he was attending rehearsals of his new opera *The Jacobin*. On May 19th he informed Simrock about his new work. 'I imagine the pieces will be sure to please you', he wrote, 'because I took great pains when working on them ... Every piece will have a title and will express something, in some respects like programme music, but in the Schumann sense; still I must point out at once that they don't sound Schumannesque.' Several of the thirteen pieces are rather more virtuosic than hitherto, and Lisztian textures and rhetoric appear. Sometimes also there are direct suggestions of other composers, 'Reverie' for instance obviously stemming in certain ways directly from Chopin, and 'Serenade' very probably from Bellini. 'In the old castle' not only recalls the melody of 'Watchman's song', but also adopts the figuration that Grieg marked 'Geister der Nacht', thus strongly suggesting that the castle the composer

---

[1] *Do kola* is the name of a Slovak couple dance in duple time which begins quietly and works up to a pitch of excitement, but since Dvořák begins *vivace* it is clear that he is not thinking of this dance.

had in mind, like Macbeth's, was haunted. The mood pieces 'Toying' and 'Tittle-tattle' represent an interesting and successful new aspect of Dvořák's compositional art. 'On the holy mount', which ends with the chime of a church bell, is notable for its simplicity and sincerity, but perhaps the most immediately appealing pieces are the charming 'Goblin's dance' and the 'Furiant', a dance that almost invariably inspired the Czech composer.

The Suite in A, op. 98, originally written for solo piano, is preferable in its orchestral version and is therefore discussed in Chapter VI.

Dvořák decided to write another set of ecossaises, or *New Scottish Dances* as he called them, while on holiday at Vysoká during the latter part of July and in August 1894, and he made use of several of the themes he had jotted down in his American sketch books. It soon became clear that the title he had chosen would not do, because although the pieces were all in duple time their character varied far too much; so he changed the name to *Humoresques*. The regular eight-bar periods betray their dance origin, just as the frequency of pentatonic themes, the lack of leading notes in minor keys and some syncopated rhythms point to their American origin. A theme from one of the sketch books labelled 'Marš funebre' (*sic*) was transformed into the main theme (*vivace*) of the first humoresque. The fourth piece is based on a theme intended to represent Hiawatha as a child in the projected opera on that subject,[1] and the last of the set is derived from a theme that was to be used in the Scherzo of a symphony in B minor, a work on which no progress was made. The seventh Humoresque in known the world over. Another similar set of *Humoresques* was begun immediately the first set was finished, but only a Lullaby and Capriccio were completed. The *Humoresques* were published at once as op. 101, but the last two pieces remained unpublished until after the composer's death.

PIANOFORTE DUETS

Like the Suite in A major, the two cycles of *Slavonic Dances* and the *Legends* were orchestrated immediately after they had been completed. Since the Dances and Legends are much better known and more attractive in this form than as piano duets, it has been thought best to discuss them with the orchestral music. Despite the unpopularity of piano duet playing today, there is much pleasure to be gained by playing the pieces in their original versions. In his orchestral and chamber music Dvořák invariably shared the

---

[1] The answering phrase in the humoresque differs from that in the Hiawatha sketch, and is a metrically changed version of the beginning of 'May Night', the second of the three *Nocturnes* for string orchestra written in 1872. It may be inferred from what is stated in the introduction to the Humoresques in the Complete Edition that the first phrase rising through the Lydian fourth is found in 'May Night', but this is incorrect.

musical interest freely among the players, which is a factor that undoubtedly helps to lead towards performances that are convincing, and that also, for a variety of reasons, results in a more immediate response to his music by audiences. In a similar manner the second player in the piano duets is always found to be most generously treated by the composer, a point that should not be overlooked by potential duettists.

The suite of duets *From the Bohemian Forest*, op. 68, was not orchestrated, although one of the pieces, 'Silent Woods', has become well known in the composer's version for 'cello and piano, and he later provided this with an orchestral accompaniment. Written towards the end of 1883 and completed on January 12th the following year, during one of his greatest periods, this set of pieces was inspired by a part of the country not far distant from Vysoká, through which Dvořák took particular pleasure in tramping on foot.[1] When planning the work he was far more concerned over the titles of the pieces than about writing the music, as his librettist Marie Červinková-Riegrová related, for he complained to her that Schumann had used up most of the suitable titles. His visit to the traditional folk carnival at Maleč is recalled in the nationally coloured 'Walpurgis Night', a spirited dance in which there seems to be no intention to suggest the powers of darkness lurking nearby. On the other hand a sinister atmosphere is vividly conjured up in 'By the Black Lake'. The imaginative fourth piece is aptly named 'In Wait', and the fifth, 'Silent Woods', or more literally 'Repose' or 'Peace', is another of Dvořák's romantically lyrical slow movements. The suite begins blithely with 'In the Spinning Room', and ends tempestuously with 'From Troublous Times', in which a melodious theme from the Scherzo of the earlier of the two symphonies in D minor makes an unexpected appearance.

[1] In the July previous to the composition of these duets Dvořák invited Janaček to accompany him on one of these jaunts, but it is not known whether the invitation was accepted. They had accompanied one another on similar trips before this.

X

Compositions for Violin
and Violoncello

Dvořák was much more strongly attracted by big compositions than by small ones, as may be seen from his correspondence with Simrock. Even though our knowledge is incomplete regarding the works of his period of musical apprenticeship, it is clear nevertheless that his attitude was similar then. Apart from a couple of polkas and a similar number of opera pot-pourris, we have no piano pieces dating earlier than the two Minuets of 1876, no 'cello piece before the *Polonaise* of 1879, and no violin piece until the *Romance*, which, although it cannot be dated exactly, may quite possibly have been written at approximately the same time as the Minuets. At this time, owing very largely to increasing recognition, he was beginning to feel impelled to produce a few minor compositions. The earliest compositions for violin and 'cello appear to have been the sonata in F minor for 'cello and piano of 1871 and the sonata in A minor for violin and piano of two years later. The same tendency is to be seen in the choral music. Two Masses and the *Hymnus* were composed between the late 1850s and 1872, but none of the part-songs he is known to have written is any earlier than 1876. We can detect a similar reluctance on Dvořák's part to write songs, for, apart from the *Cypresses*, which were composed for strongly personal reasons, these did not begin to stream from his pen until 1875.

After it became clear to the composer that his unperformed string quartet in F minor, op. 9, of 1873 was not a success, he reworked the Andante con moto for violin solo, providing it with both piano and orchestral accompaniment. The *Romance* is in fact a new composition, for although the principal theme is the same as in the quartet, the two subsidiary themes are new. It was performed by Josef Marcus with orchestral accompaniment in December 1877 and published as op. 11 within two years. Originally it was dedicated to Ondříček, as the manuscript of the pianoforte version shows, but for some reason that cannot be fully explained the dedication was withdrawn before the work appeared in print. Since the manuscript of the B major *Nocturne*, op. 40, for violin and piano cannot be traced at present, it is difficult to decide whether or not it antedates the string orchestra version. Its origin has been discussed in another chapter.

The *Capriccio*, a concert rondo, is believed to have been composed in June 1878 and later given the opus number 24. There is good reason to think that Dvořák made an orchestral version of the piano accompaniment at the time of composition, even though no score or orchestral parts have yet come to light. This virtuoso piece is improvisational and meditative in the andante sections and dance-like in the allegros, and its main theme is adapted to both speeds. It is unfortunate that no authentic edition has appeared at the time of writing. It is true that Günter Raphael took it upon himself to revise it and to publish it posthumously, but as we would expect his version shows little respect for the composer's intentions.

A more immediately successful work, the *Mazurek*,[1] op. 49, was written during the following February, and orchestrated on the 15th of that month. This piece may not possess the more incisive rhythmic characteristics of a Chopin mazurka, but it is a welcome addition to the violinist's repertory, and there are unexpected delights in the coda. The first half dozen notes strongly remind us of Silcher's familiar 'Freut euch des Lebens', though a delightfully Dvořákian touch follows immediately. But the composer may not have been thinking of Silcher's tune, for the opening notes also resemble those of the Czech song 'Paňmámo! sládek jde k nam'. The piece is dedicated to Sarasate. On March 29th, 1879, Ferdinand Lachner and the composer Fibich gave the first performance at the same Umělecká beseda concert at which Smetana's first string quartet was given its *première*.

Šourek has suggested that the *Ballad* in D minor, op. 15, was a new working-up of a discarded sketch for the slow movement of the seventh symphony, even though Dvořák invariably chose a new major key for this movement in his symphonies in minor keys. The *Ballad* was almost certainly despatched to J. W. Coates for publication in the Christmas Supplement of his *Magazine of Music* no later than the end of October 1884, and so was in all probability composed during that month, although it could have been written earlier.[2] The symphony was not begun until December 13th. In view of their period it is quite natural that both this and the *Ballad* are tragic in mood, but there does not appear to be any evidence to support the view that the two movements might have been connected, or even that Dvořák began making preliminary sketches for the symphony at a time when he was fully occupied with *The Spectre's Bride*. The mood of melancholy prevails in this piece, except for an outburst of passion that gives a hint of the stormy main theme of the symphony's Finale.

[1] There are three distinct types of mazurka; the *mazur*, the *kujawiak* and the rather faster *obertas*. *Mazurek* is a name given to the first of these, especially in Silesia.

[2] Šourek was unaware that Coates, in a personal interview with Dvořák early in September, had commissioned six small compositions, and had asked for a song, a waltz (pianoforte) and a piece for violin and piano first. This is confirmed by his letter of 19. IX. 1884.

COMPOSITIONS FOR VIOLIN AND VIOLONCELLO

The set of four *Romantic Pieces*, op. 75, which were first conceived as a string trio,[1] are among the most successful of Dvořák's slighter compositions. The titles Cavatina, Capriccio, Romance and Elegy suit the music so well, that it is curious that the composer withdrew them when preparing the new version of the pieces. If they are played in succession there is justification for reversing the order of the last two, so that the prolonged and persistent lachrymose mood of the one is succeeded by the serenity of the other. Incidentally this change makes the keys of the first and last pieces correspond. The work was composed towards the end of January 1887 and performed at an Umělecká beseda concert on March 30th, by Karel Ondříček, the brother of the famous violinist, and the composer.

Besides the violin and piano pieces Dvořák composed a Gavotte for three violins without accompaniment in 1890. This is written for violinists of modest attainment, and each player is given an interesting part.

During the summer of 1879 Dvořák wrote his *Polonaise* in A for 'cello and piano, a virtuoso piece that makes effective use of the rhythms of this dance in its principal section whenever this prevails, although elsewhere the composer prefers to suggest a different spirit. In the C major trio we find an anticipation of the Finale theme of the C major quartet, written two years later. A comparison between the two shows the eventual epigrammatic crystallization of his original thought.[2] The *Polonaise* was published posthumously in 1925.

Shortly before setting off with F. Lachner and H. Wihan at the beginning of January 1892 on his farewell concert tour prior to leaving for America, Dvořák realized the need to provide Wihan with some solos. On December 25th and 26th he wrote a 'Rondo for Professor Wihan', op. 94, which he orchestrated two years later, and on the 27th and 28th he arranged for 'cello and piano the eighth *Slavonic Dance* and 'Silent Woods', the fifth piece of the piano duet cycle *From the Bohemian Forest*. At about the same time he arranged the second *Slavonic Dance* similarly for Lachner. Wihan played the *Rondo* first at Kladno on January 6th. If the *Rondo*, with its rather repetitive subject, its regularly balanced phrases, its initially insistent full closes and its superficial bravura, gives the impression at first of being an unworthy example of Dvořák's fine craftsmanship, this is dispelled later when the composer's imagination comes into play. It then becomes impossible to predict with any certainty what path the music will be likely to take, and we experience some really delightful moments. However, it must be admitted that the much more modest piece, 'Silent Woods', is better suited to the innate character of the instrument than the *Rondo*.

[1] See p. 178.
[2] See exx. 14 a and b on p. 177.

Part Three

VOCAL MUSIC

XI

The Songs

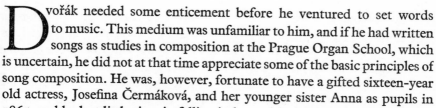

Dvořák needed some enticement before he ventured to set words to music. This medium was unfamiliar to him, and if he had written songs as studies in composition at the Prague Organ School, which is uncertain, he did not at that time appreciate some of the basic principles of song composition. He was, however, fortunate to have a gifted sixteen-year old actress, Josefina Čermáková, and her younger sister Anna as pupils in 1865, and he lost little time in falling in love with the elder of the two girls. His failure to win her love caused him to turn to a recently published book of romantic poems by the Moravian writer Gustav Pfleger-Moravský, and to set a cycle of eighteen of them with the title *Cypresses*. Twelve years later Josefina became the wife of Count Kaunitz, but in the meantime Dvořák had married Anna.

Each of the Cypress songs was probably copied out neatly immediately after being sketched. All except one of the neat copies are dated. The first fifteen songs were copied from the 10th to the 20th of July, 1865, and the last three on the 26th and 27th of that month. The early 'cello concerto had been completed shortly before, and at the beginning of August the composer was at work on his second symphony. Inexperience stares us in the face in these songs. At times the accompaniments are no more than rudimentary harmony exercises, but elsewhere Dvořák shows genuine feeling for keyboard style. Most of the songs appear to have been conceived instrumentally, and show a preference for a ternary structure or a reminder of the opening phrases as the song draws to a close, whether or not this suits the poem. Sometimes the mood of the verses is caught, and at other times it is missing altogether. Only two of the songs seem to be free of declamation faults. Dvořák's friend Karel Bendl drew his attention to this weakness, which led the composer to add a note at the end of the score of his song cycle in September 1866, admitting that the criticism was justified. However, it is important to appreciate the fact that at that time the rules of Czech prosody had not been established, the older group of poets favouring the *časomíra* system, in which alternations of long and short syllables often conflict with the normal stresses of the language. The nature poet Hálek reflects in his work the vacillations of the time. Smetana at first adopted the older system, but was then persuaded by Krásnohorská to abandon it. Dvořák had little difficulty in stressing syllables satisfactorily in later works,[1] although he was inclined to vary his rhythmic patterns when words were repeated, which occasionally led to unsatisfactory accentuation.

He seems to have had a particular affection for his first songs. Parts of the sixth and tenth songs reappeared in the first version of his opera *King and Charcoal Burner*, and the second of these was used again later in *Vanda*; the seventeenth provided material for the first and fifth of the piano *Silhouettes*, op. 8. Four of the songs were revised in 1881 and published the following year as *Four Songs*, op. 2. Twelve others were chosen and adapted for string quartet in 1887 and given the title *Echoes of Songs*, which was later changed to *Evening Songs*, although no attempt was made to alter the original conception of the songs to any great extent; ten of these were published posthumously with the title changed back to *Cypresses* after Josef Suk had made a number of important alterations. A year after Dvořák had made the quartet versions he selected eight of the original songs, all of which had been included in the chamber music group, and revised these, publishing them in 1889 as *Love Songs*, op. 83.

When revising the songs Dvořák made sure that the declamation was greatly improved. Changes of key were made in two cases, and in the second song (op. 83, no. 7) it was altered from G major to G minor. The eleventh song (op. 2, no. 3) was changed from $\frac{2}{4}$ to $\frac{3}{4}$, and the thirteen and seventeenth songs (op. 2, no. 4 and op. 83, no. 5) from common time to $\frac{3}{8}$. The accompaniment of the fifth song was so good that it was retained practically without alteration for the later version (op. 2, no. 2), but substantial changes had to be made in the voice part in two of the verses. The sixth song (op. 83, no. 4) needed very little revision.

It is surprising that Dvořák made no attempt to revise the sixteenth song, 'There stands an ancient rock', for he succeeded much better than in most of the other songs of that time in penetrating to the heart of the poem. This is progressive (*durchkomponiert*) in form, and the composer presses forward well from verse to verse and on to the final climax. These last bars show an example of sequence a minor third higher, in this instance leading from the relative minor key to the tonic *minor*, and thus providing poignancy where it is most needed:

---

[1] In the Czech language the first syllable of a word is stressed unless it is preceded by a preposition which takes the stress instead. Some one-syllable words are stressed and others are not.

Ex. 1.

(There all my sorrow will sleep for eternity.)

Perhaps the most revealing changes were made to the eleventh song. The earlier version is in E flat minor, whereas the revised song appears to be in G flat major, but frequently veers towards and ends on the chord of E flat major. Comparison of a few bars from the beginning of each song will show how Dvořák retained the germ of his earlier commonplace song, but transformed it into something far more imaginative (Exx. 2a and 2b). Since the revised songs belong more properly to the period of maturity in song composition, it will be convenient to defer fuller discussion of them until later in this chapter.

Dvořák wrote a pair of love songs for baritone voice on October 24th, 1865, using verses by Heyduk, the poet of the *Gipsy Melodies*. Although it is not made clear in the poems that the love is unrequited, the composer evidently interpreted them in that way. His first song, in A minor, begins and

Ex. 2a.

Ex. 2b.

(My heart, often in pain, is plunged in sadness.)

ends with an imperfect cadence (augmented sixth, followed by dominant, subdominant, tonic and dominant); the second, which starts in F major, veers round to A minor and finishes inconclusively with the same two bars as in the first song. Dvořák ignores the imagery of the verses, but creates a feeling of romantic yearning.

During 1871, after an interval of more than five years in song writing, Dvořák set five poems by Eliška Krásnohorská, the librettist of Smetana's last four operas, and two of these were published later as op. 9, nos. 1 and 2. At about the same time he composed two ballads *The Orphan* and *Rosemarine*, to words by Erben. The following year he wrote *Four Songs on Serbian Folk Poems* (op. 6) to the translations of S. Kapper, but when published they were given German and English translations and the Czech text was omitted. A further set of *Six Songs from the Queen's Court Manuscript*, op. 7, was written that year. One song of this set, 'The Lark', appeared in 1873 as a supplement to the Czech musical periodical *Dalibor*, and had the distinction of being Dvořák's first published composition. The composer was 31 years of age at that time. The whole set of songs was published by Starý (as op. 17) later in the same year.

The songs of this group are a decided improvement on *Cypresses*. Declamation is satisfactory, and the accompaniments have more character. We also notice a decided tendency to favour strophic form, a tendency which is naturally most pronounced in the settings of Serbian poems. This marks the beginning of a predilection which remained with him for the rest of his life, the desire to set a poem strophically or to use some modification of strophic form whenever the opportunity presented itself. He even applied the same principle on a broad scale to both ballads. In *The Orphan* the first 42 bars are repeated in their entirety, and are then followed by a further repetition of material already heard together with some that is new. With so rigid a design, the music fails to follow the poem very closely. *Rosemarine* is even more rigid, for the melody is heard twice over and there are no additions; there is very little variety of rhythm and an unending succession of two-bar phrases.

In 'Meditation', the third of the Krásnohorská songs (op. 9, no. 2), the music of the first two verses is almost identical, but after that the remaining verses are differently set. In the last verse: 'Such love divine we only knew from holy pictures that in church we view . . .', the composer's strong religious faith emerges strikingly. In the Serbian song 'Warning' the persistent use of a dominant seventh chord in its last inversion emphasizes the central theme of the poem effectively. In this instance the irony of the verses spurred on Dvořák to write one of the best songs of this period. The remaining songs of this set are lighter in character, and in all of them the piano unnecessarily doubles the vocal line.

For many years it has been thought that the Queen's Court (*Dvůr Králové*) manuscript was a forgery, like Macpherson's *Ossian* and the writings of Iolo Morganwg, Václav Hanka, the discoverer, having been responsible for the lyrical parts, which Dvořák drew upon for his set of songs. New archeological and chemical evidence has recently been produced to refute this view, and this, coupled with the doubt whether any other early nineteenth century Czech poet apart from Mácha would have been capable of writing anything of equal artistic value, reopens a problem that was believed to have been finally resolved.

The *Queen's Court* songs are as unpretentious as the poems themselves. If the monotonous quaver rhythm in 'The Strawberries' is intended to suggest the jog-trot of the pony, why, one wonders, is it heard long before the homeward journey has begun? 'The Flowery Message' is progressive in form, but a conventional cadence is heard three times at points in the narrative which seem to demand different treatment. In some other songs of this set Dvořák is too inclined to take refuge in a well-worn cadential formula, when he might well have written something more telling. Although he fails to capture the mood of 'The Rose', he succeeds well in 'The Forsaken', even if we might wish for a stronger climax. In this song he uses the same music twice over, making slight modifications in some places. The key F minor and the Neapolitan depressions help to create the right image, but it is not quite clear why the song ends on a dominant chord. Is it because the maiden has no-one to turn to?

Next Vítězslav Hálek's collection of poems, *Evening Songs*, claimed Dvořák's attention, as they did that of Smetana three years later. Dvořák set twelve of the poems, presumably in the summer of 1876, although only one of the songs is dated. They were probably written shortly after the *Moravian Duets* and the first sketch of the *Stabat Mater*, at a time when the composer's reputation was rising rapidly. Two of the songs were published with the Krásnohorská pair as nos. 3 and 4 of op. 9, four appeared as op. 3, five others, with their accompaniments touched up at a later date, were published as op. 31, and the remaining song, 'Thus as the moon in heaven's dome', was considered by Dvořák to be too weak for publication.

The songs are very varied, and range from light comedy to profound seriousness. 'I dreamed last night that you were dead' owes a good deal to the *Moonlight* sonata, and part of 'When God was in a happy mood' has been drawn from Mozart's K. 475. Knowledge of Brahms's music undoubtedly helped with 'All ye who are oppressed', but the weight of affliction has been overstressed, and the implications ignored of the promise: 'Here are remedies for all troubles, here the heart is eternally young . . .' A great opportunity was missed. A change is made from minor to major towards the end of 'When God was in a happy mood', and the conclusion is peaceful, although the final words are: 'And often when a teardrop falls the heart must break with sadness.' Another song ends on a dominant chord, without a hint as to the reason, and the fascinating modulations from E minor to F minor and E flat major in 'All through the night that bird sings' were included solely for musical reasons. It is difficult to escape the conclusion that on rather too many occasions Dvořák forgot the significance of the words he was setting, and that the poem became a peg upon which he could hang the musical ideas that were uppermost in his mind.

He was in his element in 'Spring came flying from afar', and wrote spontaneously and with great verve, while in 'I am that knight of fairy tale' he conjured up a suitably light-hearted mood for such a subject. 'Like a linden tree' is basically strophic, with the accompaniment varied each time, and the vocal line blossoming out in the third verse. It is repetitive in its fourth and fifth phrases, and has scarcely any variation in phrase lengths, but it has its attractions as a sentimental romantic song.

During the years 1887–89 Dvořák composed four sacred songs with organ accompaniment, *Ave Maria* and *Ave maris stella* for alto or baritone, *Hymnus ad Laudes in festo Ss. Trinitatis* for medium voice, and *O sanctissima* for alto and baritone duet. These are simple and reverent settings, but lack distinction. The *Ave Maria*, however, stands apart from the rest of these songs, for our interest is held when unexpected horizons come within our vision after an interrupted cadence.

Dvořák wrote his *Three Modern Greek Poems* for performance at the first concert consisting entirely of his own compositions. This took place on November 17th, 1878, and the songs, with orchestral accompaniment, were sung by Josef Lev, baritone singer at the National Theatre, Prague. The piano score bears the same date as that at the end of the full score of the first set of *Slavonic Dances*.[1] Two of the songs are ballads and the third is an elegy. The first, 'Kolja', describes a rather improbable and presumably the last episode in the career of a rebel who fought against the Turks. The composer succeeds in giving this a slightly exotic and primitive character, which is acceptable but not genuinely Turkish, and the accompaniment reflects the changing moods of the poem. The second song, 'Nixies', draws attention to Dvořák's interest in supernatural beings rather more significantly than the witch scene had done in his opera *Vanda*. Perhaps he may even at this time have had a passing thought of writing some more ambitious work centred around a subject of this kind at a later date. The beginning of the song tends to halt at regular intervals, but it becomes much more integrated later. The music of the naiads is attractive. We also notice that the engaging folk-song-like basic theme of the song, with its first two bars descending

---

[1] The recent discovery of the oboe part from the orchestral version seems to point to the fact that the piano version may have come second.

through a minor triad, is changed to express the yearning of the shepherd boy when he is about to speak of his desire for the loveliest singer among the spirits:

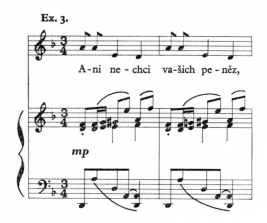

Ex. 3.

A - ni ne - chci va-šich pe - něz,

mp

'The Lament of Parga', subtitled 'Heroic Song', tells of an Albanian city which was betrayed into the hands of the Turks. The warriors are called upon to dig up the bones of their fathers, so that the Turks might never trample on those they have failed to conquer. At climaxes Dvořák relies too much on the diminished seventh, but in general, without an attempt being made to reflect line by line changes, the musical treatment is fitting in relation to the trends of the words. In these three songs the accompaniment has a rather more important role than was normal for Dvořák, and in the keyboard transcription it tends to be unpianistic.

The song cycle, *Gipsy Melodies*, was written for and dedicated to an admirer of the composer's songs, Gustav Walter, tenor singer of the Vienna Court Opera. As a compliment to Walter, Dvořák set the German translations especially prepared for him by the poet himself, instead of using Adolf Heyduk's Czech verses. The composer's dating of the songs appears to be inaccurate, but it is assumed they were written between February 18th and 23rd, 1880.

The songs display far more assurance than any Dvořák has written previously, and the natural way he made modifications in his melodies and modest departures from strict strophic form is readily apparent. It should, however, be pointed out that if Amalia Joachim, the wife of the violinist, had not suggested, after seeing the published songs, that an extra verse should be added to the first one, this would have been much more regular in form, and the second verse in the tonic major would have been missing. The accompaniments add greatly to the songs, several providing a vital or racy dance character, or the suggestion of a cimbalom, and one, in 'Songs my mother taught me', offering the fascinating pull of $\frac{6}{8}$ rhythm against the voice's $\frac{2}{4}$. Dvořák's skill in using the voice is much greater than before, as for instance in the quiet, telling and unforgettable rise to a long E flat in the third song, 'All round about the woods are still':

Ex. 4.

The music may not be similar to the gipsy music with which we are most familiar, but it embodies gipsy elements, and is at the same time pure Dvořák. How he must have enjoyed composing these songs!

The first revision of songs from the *Cypresses* cycle took place at the end of 1881. Dvořák made a mistake when he retained the original ternary structure in the song which became the first of the op. 2 set, for by doing so he ignored the threat inherent in the last two lines of the poem. In the fourth song the nature of the words does not justify rising to as big a climax as in the earlier version, yet once again a legacy of the past is allowed to mar his new conception of the song. There are dangers in attempting to improve imperfect compositions unless these are treated in a more ruthless manner. The third song of the set came through the ordeal splendidly, and emerged as one of Dvořák's best songs. It has been quoted from already in this chapter (see p. 228, ex. 2a), and the unusual final bars for piano are shown elsewhere in this volume (p. 44, ex. 13). Alec Robertson has rightly drawn attention in his biography to the beautiful vocal line in the last verse.

During Dvořák's second visit to England, to conduct his *Stabat Mater* at the Worcester Festival in September 1884, he was asked by John W. Coates to write six compositions for the sum of £90 for publication in *The Magazine of Music*. Later, Dvořák sent Coates a song, *The Wild Duck*, which proved unsuitable, and the song has subsequently been lost.[1] In the following year he set German translations of two Czech folk poems, 'Sleep, my child

---

[1] Coates wrote as follows to Dvořák on November 3rd 1884: 'With regard to Song the "Wild Duck", it has much character, and would be most interesting to musicians. It is, however, hardly suitable for popular purposes, and a song such as the "Princess of Thule" would be far better for making your music widely known among the people. If agreeable to yourself, I should be pleased if you would compose music to the words of song "Princess of Thule", sent herewith, in exchange for the "Wild Duck". I await your kind reply before returning M.S. of the "Wild Duck".' The composer did not respond to Coates's suggestion. The only works by Dvořák to appear in the supplement of the periodical were the *Ballad*, op. 15, for violin and piano, and the *Furiant*, op. 12, for piano.

sleep,' and 'When I see thee, my sweetheart'. These were published posthumously without opus number. The simple yet original lullaby has considerable charm.

Further settings of folk poems followed in the early part of September 1886, with the title *In Folk Tone*, op. 73. Three of these have Slovak words and the remaining one Czech. They were composed soon after the second set of *Slavonic Dances*, at a time when Simrock was anxious to have more small works to publish, because he found they were profitable. The tenderness of 'Good night' is its main charm, while 'When a maiden was a-mowing' has a deftness and gaiety which are delightful. For a folk-song setting, the song in G flat major, 'Nothing can change for me', is exceptional, on account of the poignancy of its chromatic vocal line and harmony.

The *Four Songs*, op. 82, were written by Dvořák between December 30th, 1887, and January 5th the next year, in order to pacify Simrock, when, through a misunderstanding, the *Queen's Court Manuscript* songs were re-published by Novello in London, after four of them had been issued by the German publishing house. For these new songs the composer selected from Otilie Malybrok-Stieler's collection of German translations of Czech art and folk poems, which had been published in that language in Prague. The songs were dedicated to Frau Sophie Hanslick, wife of the Vienna critic. Mrs. John P. Morgan of New York made the English translations of these, and also of the previous and next sets, but when the composer stated that Mrs. Morgan's translations were the only ones authorized by him, he showed himself to be a rather imperfect judge of sensible English.

These songs are among Dvořák's best, so that it is a pity that in three out of the four the accompaniment doubles the voice line most of the time. The accompaniments of op. 73 are much more independent. The first song, 'Leave me alone', was the favourite of Josefina Kaunitzová, née Čermáková, who had inspired him to compose *Cypresses*, and it may have reminded her of one of these early songs.[1] Phrases from this song were used in remembrance of her in the slow movement and the finale of the 'cello concerto. (See pp. 107-8, exx. 12a, b and c). The song is composed in one of Dvořák's large scale 'strophic' designs, the whole of the progressively composed music of the first three verses being used again for the fourth stanza and the fifth verse, which is sung twice. This is one of Dvořák's most beautiful songs. 'Over her embroidery' is unique among his eighty or so songs, for it is in C major for the first verse and in B major for the last, this latter being a direct transposition of the first part of the song. It is evident that Dvořák considered the second of these keys more suitable for suggesting peace of mind than C major. He chose the key for 'Nothing can change for me', referred to

[1] 'In deepest forest glade I stand', op. 83, no. 6.

above, for similar reasons of key colour, so singers need to be cautious over transposition of his songs in some instances.

The *Love Songs*, op. 83, the second batch of songs from the *Cypresses* cycle to be revised, were rewritten in early December 1888, shortly after the opera *The Jacobin* was completed. Dvořák was reluctant to make substantial changes in the fourth and eighth songs of this set, apart from writing a much better accompaniment for the latter, and only the end of the sixth song was much altered. These may be taken to be additional symptoms of his affectionate regard for his early songs. He was aware of the advisability of emphasizing the final words of the fourth and fifth songs, he rewrote a considerable portion of the first song, altered considerably the third and seventh, and transformed the fifth rhythmically. If these songs, despite their many good points, do not quite stand up to the best of this composer's vocal writing, it is probably because he retained in them too much of his original conceptions. There is individuality and character certainly, but in two of them the

Ex. 5a.

Ex. 5b.

accompaniments are deficient, and they tend to be slightly reminiscent of romantic song of an earlier period.

It is too much to expect the genius of Schubert to blaze forth, but perhaps in the third song, 'I wander oft past yonder house', he can be seen to make an approach towards Schubertian style, while remaining true to himself. It is illuminating to compare the opening bars of the original song and those of the new version (Exx. 5a and 5b).

The sixth song, 'In deepest forest glade I stand', one of the very few dramatic songs he wrote, is among the best of the set, yet much is taken bodily from the original song. However, Dvořák used up the words more quickly than formerly, in order to allow the first climax in the poem to catch up with the musical climax, and thus avoid the mistake of making it come five bars too soon. From this point he discarded the rest of his early song.

The *Biblical Songs*, op. 99, were composed between March 5th and 26th, 1894, during Dvořák's second year in the United States. Gounod had died the previous October, his friends Tchaikovsky and Hans von Bülow had died during November and February, and his own father was suffering from his last illness at Velvary, a few miles from Prague. Dvořák was by no means entirely happy cut off from his homeland, and so, with this series of sorrows to bear, it was natural that so earnest a Catholic should wish to commune with God and reaffirm his strong faith in his Creator. The expression of religious belief in musical terms led to some very varied results in the nineteenth century, which ranged from the worldly *Stabat Mater* of Rossini and the sentimental oratorios of Gounod to the exalted spirit of Beethoven's *Missa solemnis*. Dvořák was not as much at ease in composing the Christian music for *St. Ludmila* as he was in writing the pagan music, which suggests that he found it more difficult to compose religious music, unless he had really good cause to do so, and entirely suitable words to set. The *Biblical Songs*, like the *Stabat Mater* and *Requiem Mass*, were composed because Dvořák felt compelled to proclaim his religious faith at that particular time.[1]

He chose the words of these ten songs from the *Book of Psalms*, but occasionally made slight modifications to the text. The verses he selected were as follows:

1. Psalm 97: 2–6.
2. Psalm 119: 114–115, 117, 120.
3. Psalm 55: 1–2, 4–8.
4. Psalm 23: 1–4.
5. Psalm 144: 9; Psalm 145: 2–3, 5–6.
6. Psalm 61: 1, 3–4; Psalm 63: 1, 4.
7. Psalm 137: 1–5.
8. Psalm 25: 16–18, 20.
9. Psalm 121: 1–4.
10. Psalm 98: 1, 4, 7–8; Psalm 96: 12.

Three of the songs are partially strophic, but the rest are progressive and tend to be freer than was normal with Dvořák. The keynote seems to be simplicity of expression, and in several of the songs an almost child-like faith in the Creator is expressed. The pentatonic basis of the tenth song and certain turns of phrase in the second and fourth songs remind us of Negro spirituals and the composer's American style. Here and there there are traces of commonplace and conventional progressions, due perhaps to the influence of certain kinds of music associated with the church in Dvořák's time. Of much greater significance, however, is the reverence and sincerity of the settings. Most of the songs are marked Andante, and if this is made to be rather spacious much is gained. It is an advantage if the songs can be

[1] Warning is necessary about the numerous changes made in the vocal line to accommodate English and German translations. The Artia Complete Edition score is recommended.

performed with organ in church, even though this means the accompaniments lose some of their definition. The composer scored the first five songs for voice and orchestra, and no doubt this manner of performance would be particularly effective in a consecrated building.

The first song opens impressively with a vivid expression of awe and fear of the Lord, a mood that gives way to confidence and trust in the last two verses. One would not expect Dvořák to be particularly venturesome in these songs, but in 'Hear my prayer', which is outstanding, the anguish of the extreme modulations is particularly striking. Perhaps the finest of the set is 'By the waters of Babylon', which inspired Dvořák much more than 'The Lord is my shepherd'. It starts simply as if in C minor, gravitating towards E flat major, then restarts in C major, finally settling in E flat after an unforgettably heartfelt cry that Jerusalem must not be forgotten. 'I will lift up mine eyes' is yet another instance of a song starting in one key and ending in another. In reality, there is what amounts to a long-drawn-out modulation from F major to A flat major, which may perhaps be intended to suggest complete confidence in the Lord. The earlier change to the tonic minor does not seem to have been prompted by the words that accompany it, 'He will not suffer thy foot to be moved', and neither do the words 'he that keepeth thee will not slumber' suggest that there should have been an extreme modulation, so that caution is advisable in attempting to discover Dvořák's motives. The purely laudatory songs are placed halfway through and at the end of the cycle, the most jubilant of these being the last, 'O sing unto the Lord a new song', in which pentatonicism and dance elements are merged.

Two more songs remain to be mentioned briefly, a *Lullaby* to words by F. L. Jelínek, written at the end of 1895, and *The Smith of Lešetín* of August 1901 on a text from Svatopluk Čech. The *Lullaby* is a strophic song, simply and tastefully set. The second song is treated as a ballad, although there is little story to unfold; it merely contrasts the vigorous forge music and episodes of the blacksmith's love. By the repetitions of large sections the song is given a sense of balance, but without an obvious attempt having been made to fuse it into a continuous whole. It was to have been part of a larger composition, either a cantata or a song cycle that did not materialize. Josef Suk edited it and published it posthumously.

Dvořák learned the craft of song composition and at times produced exceptionally good work, but writing songs never came completely naturally to him. Literature did not have a sufficiently powerful attraction for him *per se*, and only occasionally did he have sufficient imagination when setting a poem to rise above an average level and create something really memorable and individual. Like Brahms he was an instrumental composer turned song writer, but he found it difficult to scale the heights that the German composer reached, and besides he was to some extent handicapped by lack of fluency in keyboard writing, especially in earlier years. Acute sensitivity to poetic lines, such as Grieg possessed, was unknown to him, and consequently he was quite incapable of creating anything which could approach the *Haugtussa* cycle. He succeeded best when he avoided attempting to express deep emotions and dramatic situations, and when re-creating the spirit of folk-song. He maintained a more consistently high level in the *Gipsy Melodies* than in any other of his works for solo voice, but there are gems to be found elsewhere among his collections.

VOCAL DUETS

Dvořák wrote twenty-five vocal duets, all except two of which are settings of Moravian folk poems, although only thirteen of these, the ones published as op. 32, are usually referred to as the *Moravian Duets*. The two which stand apart are *O sanctissima*, already mentioned earlier in this chapter, and *Child's Song* for two unaccompanied voices, which was published posthumously.

All the duets with Moravian words were composed during the years 1875–77, with the exception of *On our roof*, which was written in the spring of 1881. First Dvořák wrote three soprano and tenor duets in March 1875 for Jan and Marie Neff, a wholesale merchant and his wife, in whose home he gave piano lessons at that time. He followed these with five duets for two sopranos composed between May 17th and 21st, 1876, which he described as Cycle II, adding the provisional number op. 29. From June 26th to July 13th that same year he composed another ten duets, Cycle III, op. 32, one of which, 'The Ploughboy', was for soprano and tenor, while the others were for female voices. Thirteen duets from the second and third cycles, all now intended for soprano and contralto, were published in Prague at the end of 1876 with some financial assistance from Neff, and given the definitive number op. 32. These were among the compositions Dvořák submitted the following year when he hoped for and succeeded in gaining the Austrian State Prize for the third year in succession. Brahms, as one of the judges, was so impressed by them that he wrote to his publisher Simrock recommending that he should publish the duets, and this advice was quickly acted upon. From that time onwards Simrock published most of Dvořák's compositions, and consequently his music spread to a much wider public than he could have expected to reach with any works of his published in provincial Prague. Louis Ehlert, reviewing the duets in the Berlin *Nationalzeitung*, said: 'When I re-read them I was convinced that I should see lovely maidens casting blossoms about them on which dew would glitter.'

Dvořák composed four more duets for soprano and contralto during the autumn of 1877, which were published two years later as *Four Duets*, op. 38, and dedicated to Neff. That same year Simrock issued the four earlier duets for soprano and tenor as op. 20, and these were dedicated to Marie Neffová. The op. 32 set had been dedicated jointly to Mr. and Mrs. Neff. The poems for these duets had been taken from František Sušil's big collection, *Moravian National Songs*, but the original melodies were not used by Dvořák.

The melodic freshness, the charm and the simplicity of the duets account for their immediate success. The majority are gay, but some are plaintive and a few merge mirth and melancholy. Although some are conversational, only two of these allot the upper and lower voices strictly to the two characters of the poems. The forms are simple, and especially those of op. 38, where three out of the four duets are strophic.

Although the op. 20 group are less well known than the set of thirteen duets that followed, there is no reason why they should be. The third from this set, 'Poverty', is a beautifully worked miniature in F sharp minor, basically ternary, but with no exact repetition anywhere. The fourth, 'The Last Wish', starts very gaily but becomes solemn and subdued to match the moods of the verses, while the voices sink lower and lower in pitch, until finally they rise as if in an uncontrollable sob.

Turning to the op. 32 duets, we notice 'Fly sweet songster' dwells a great deal on the dominant seventh chord in its last inversion to express longing, and recalls Smetana's rather different use of the same chord in the first bars of *Dalibor*. This is one of the most appealing duets of the collection. The next fails to express bitterness, but at the Meno mosso gives us one of Dvořák's delightfully ambiguous passages, which swings chromatically between a G minor inversion and an unresolved dominant seventh in F. As the lovers part for the night in the fifth duet, 'The little field of Slavíkov', the voices descend in pitch and drop to a whisper, and the duet ends in the dominant key. The sixth duet does not follow the moods of the poem very closely, but the music is attractive. The next one, 'Water and tears', makes amends for the previous one by contrasting the music for the stranger and the maiden most effectively: the modulations to the mediant major showing how timorous the girl is.

In the ninth duet the bride does not seem greatly upset that she has forgotten to bring with her her garland and her ring. We are carried away, however, by the strong rhythmic impulse of the music. 'Grass, be green!' is partly in a dashing allegro molto in C major and at other times in a lilting quasi andante con moto in F sharp major. 'Captured', the eleventh duet, has a winning folk-song-like simplicity, while the last of the set, 'The wild rose', is again simple and appealing, and includes some Schumannesque touches.

The first of the op. 38 duets modulates from E major to G major to suggest a ray of hope, when the lassie is told by her lover that he will make her his bride if the cuckoo calls at Christmas. Dvořák used a similar key relationship —B major to D major—for an *anticlimax* in op. 2, no. 2, to suggest the dawning of day bringing an end to a dream of perfect love. The second and third of these duets seem rather over-repetitive in their short phrases. The fourth expresses the unbearable sorrow of a jilted girl by wandering hopelessly from key to key.

XII

Cantata, Mass and Oratorio

There appears to be considerable doubt as to whether Dvořák wrote a Mass in F minor in addition to the Mass in B flat major that he composed some time during the years 1857–59. The second of these two works, although it was most probably destroyed by Dvořák, was, according to him, seen by Josef Foerster, father of J. B. Foerster the composer, and furthermore the first two bars were written down from memory by Dvořák's fellow student at the Organ School in Prague, Václav Urban.

Much later, Dvořák made a setting of the patriotic hymn, *The Heirs of the White Mountain*, using only the latter part of Vítězslav Hálek's poem. Hálek (1835–74) was an outstanding nature poet and the editor of *Máj*, the foremost Czech literary almanac of his time. Among his poems are *Evening Songs*, several of which were utilized by Dvořák for his opp. 3, 9 and 31, and *In Nature's Realm* which he set as part songs. The *Hymnus* was completed on June 3rd, 1872, and dedicated to the poet. A little later Dvořák eliminated some Wagnerian influences from the orchestration. This short cantata was very successfully performed on March 9th the following year under the direction of Karel Bendl, another of the composer's former colleagues at the Organ School. It is significant that this was the first time that Dvořák had tasted success. As a result of this encouraging sign the composer was able to marry Anna Čermáková before the year was out. He also began to gain rapidly in confidence, and within a little more than two years, at the age of thirty-four, he reached maturity as a composer.

During the first half of January 1880 he revised his cantata, and the new version was conducted by Knittl in Prague two months later. He informed Janáček on a postcard dated February 9th, 1884, that he was obliged to make a copy of the score quickly which he could take with him to London a month later, as Novello was going to publish it. It is probable that when he began the task of copying further changes became inevitable, and these delayed him. The third version of the score was not finished until May 3rd, five weeks after he had returned to Prague. As far as is known the final form of the *Hymnus* was first performed by Mr. Geaussent's Choir at St. James's Hall,

London, on May 13th, 1885, with the composer conducting. In the same year Novello published the score as op. 30 with the inscription 'dedicated with feelings of deep gratitude to the English people'.

The six verses that Dvořák set fall into two sections, the first expressing the lamentations of the Czech people for the independence they lost in 1620 at the battle of the White Mountain,[1] and the second being a call for loyalty and valour in the fight for freedom at the time of the rebirth of national consciousness. The first part, although in E flat major, is despondent in character. At the beginning of the second part the key changes to C major and the speed increases to Allegro non tanto, quasi maestoso. A heroic theme, slightly reminiscent of the Hussite chorale,[2] leads the way here:

Ex. 1.

In this part there is some effective choral writing including some rather unorthodox fugato entries. The work ends triumphantly in the original key.

STABAT MATER

A few months after his two-day-old daughter Josefa had died Dvořák began composing his first important religious work, the *Stabat Mater*. He completed the sketch between February 19th and May 7th, 1876, and then laid it aside for seventeen months while writing the *Moravian Duets*, the piano concerto, *The Cunning Peasant*, the *Symphonic Variations* and some smaller works. During 1877, while he was occupied with the *Variations*, misfortune struck the Dvořák family. First their eleven-month-old daughter Růžena, during a brief time when she was not being watched, drank a solution of phosphorus intended for making matches, and died on August 13th. Secondly, their first-born son Otakar, who was three-and-a-half years of age at the time, caught smallpox and died on Dvořák's birthday, September 8th. This was indeed a bitter blow, for the parents were left childless. At the first suitable moment Dvořák brought his sketch to light, and between sometime in October and November 13th he prepared the full score of his choral composition.

[1] The hill *Bílá hora* on the outskirts of Prague.
[2] See p. 111.

If the *Patriotic Hymn* was to help to make the composer's name at home, this new work was to do far more. It was performed first in Prague on a rather curious date, December 23rd, 1880, with Adolf Čech conducting, and after Simrock had published it it was given by Janáček at Brno (2. IV. 1882) and by Hruška at Mladá Boleslav (29, V. 1882). The first foreign performance took place under Imre Bellowicz in Budapest (5. IV. 1882), and the following year Joseph Barnby presented the work in London (10. III. 1883). Many more performances followed: at Birmingham (27. III. 1884), Pittsburg (24. VI. 1884), Worcester (11. IX. 1884), New York (13. XI. 1884), Hereford (1885), Gloucester and Vienna (1886), Norwich (1887), besides performances at Zagreb, Mannheim and elsewhere. But perhaps the most important of all was that conducted by the composer himself on March 13th, 1884, when on his first visit to London. This was unquestionably a great personal triumph, and marked the beginning of Dvořák's extremely cordial relationship with English music lovers.

Dvořák's *Stabat Mater* is the work of a sincere and pious Catholic working in the second half of the nineteenth century. Just as it is apparent in *Fidelio* that Beethoven was primarily an instrumental composer, so here the same thing may be said of Dvořák. Words are frequently repeated. Sometimes, when the final line of a particular number has been reached, Dvořák will return to the first line and work through most of them again; and in the case of the 'Eja, Mater' only three lines of verse are needed for the 111 bars of music. In consequence he is able to impart to the separate numbers a shapeliness that does not spring directly from the text. He also makes use of well-controlled and consistent rhythmic elements, with, in certain cases, strong propulsive qualities.

The writing for the four soloists and chorus is perfectly fitting for Dvořák's conception of the work, even though here and there one can take exception to his setting of verses or individual words[1] of this Latin sequence. In the 'Eja, Mater', fine as it is as an independent piece of music, Dvořák starts in such a strongly rhythmic manner that he seems to have forgotten the spirit of the words until letter A is reached. 'Tui Nati vulnerati' is very lovely music, but rather more serene than one might wish it to be. Could it have been chance that the 'Quis est homo?' phrase is similar to one in the 'Lacrymosa' of Berlioz' *Grande Messe des Morts*? The tenor solo with chorus, 'Fac me vere', which anticipates the first bars of the theme for variations in

---

[1] At the beginning of 'Fac, ut ardeat cor meum' the important word 'cor' is sung to the shortest of notes at the weakest point of the bar. In the 'Inflammatus' Dvořák has been misled by the poetic metre, and in consequence the second syllable of 'judicii' is always stressed and prolonged, whereas, in opposition to the trochaic metre of the lines, he has sometimes accented the second syllable of 'virginum' in 'Virgo virginum praeclara', although elsewhere this is sung on an inconspicuous semiquaver. Dvořák's knowledge of Latin was very slight.

the *Terzetto*, is one of the least interesting numbers. Elsewhere Dvořák achieves greater things, and some of these will be mentioned presently. Here, however, it should be remarked that Dvořák could not be expected to sustain moods of solemnity and lamentation indefinitely, for that was contrary to his nature. Neither could he be expected to break away completely from the worldly and even cheerful spirit of much of the devotional music of Mozart, Haydn and Schubert, for it was to that tradition that he belonged. He was a simple man who did not question the faith in which he was nurtured, and consequently he did not probe deeply into the reality of God, the mystery of death and resurrection, and the nature of man's sin. He knew all it was necessary for him to know, and he worshipped the Lord with a cheerful heart. While making no attempt to dramatize his subject, Dvořák makes it plain that he was conscious of the exceptional sorrow and profound reverence expressed in Jacopone da Todi's poem. Four of the ten numbers may indeed be written in major keys, but it need not be inferred from this that their mood is contrary to that of the text.

Dvořák's serious approach to his task becomes immediately apparent at the beginning of the work when rising octave F sharps lead the eye upwards to the figure of Christ on the Cross, and when poignant chromatic descending figures disclose to us the sight of Mary weeping beneath. Expressively chromatic part-writing, climaxes that culminate on dark diminished seventh chords, and the felicitous combination of clarinets and flutes with the solo tenor voice are a few of the ingredients that contribute to the success of this fine long opening number. The coda of the bass solo with chorus, 'Fac, ut ardeat', has some particularly lovely transformations of its basic theme. The 'Inflammatus' for contralto solo surpasses all the other solo numbers. There is a Handelian quality in its steady marching bass, but the vocal line is very characteristic of Dvořák. The thematic material of the first number returns in the last, 'Quando corpus morietur', but when the climax is reached the expected diminished seventh is replaced by a chord of G major, which throws a blaze of light on to the choral ejaculation 'paradisi gloria'. It must be admitted that the chromatic writing that precedes this is much better suited to the first lines of the poem. The end of the work is handled with the greatest confidence, and here the key of D major replaces B minor.

During the first two months of 1879 Dvořák made a setting for male voice choir and orchestra of *Psalm 149* for the celebrated Hlahol Choral Society of Prague, taking the text from the Králíky Bible. The Choir performed the work on March 16th that year with Knittl conducting. Eight years later the composer re-wrote his *Psalm* for mixed choir, and it was published in this form by Simrock as op. 79, although it had originally borne the number 52. The work is an effectively written paean of praise in C major expressing the general mood of the verses without attempting to follow them in detail. In several ways it is rather uncharacteristic of the Czech master, especially when it is remembered that it was written while he was at work on the string quartet in E flat, op. 51. Nationalism seems to have been temporarily forgotten, and instead there are modal tendencies and modulations that may possibly have been suggested by the *Missa Solemnis*, brief reminders of *Die Walküre* and *Die Meistersinger*, powerful Handelian choral interjections, and a curiously timorous orchestral introduction that combines suspensions with chromatic part-writing, and seems to have a baroque or Gluckian ancestry. All the themes are presented in the tonic key, but the brief and sudden shifts to B flat major and A major provide sufficient variety.[1]

THE SPECTRE'S BRIDE

The success of the *Stabat Mater* in London made Dvořák think of writing an oratorio for England. In September 1883 he told Marie Červinková-Riegrová, the librettist of *Dimitrij*, that he was considering writing one on St. Wenceslas, John Hus, or a similar subject. During his first visit to London in March 1884, Henry Littleton of Novello & Co. offered him the very attractive sum of £2,000 for an oratorio to be performed at the Leeds Festival, and the Birmingham Musical Festival also asked him to write a work for their 1885 season. As he could not find a suitable text for an oratorio he turned to K. J. Erben's collection of twelve ballads, *A Bouquet of Folk Tales* (1853), and selected 'Svatební Košile' (The Wedding Shifts), based on a legend that is current in many parts of Europe, telling of a long absent lover returning to his bride, or a soldier to his sister, and who eventually reveals himself to be a corpse leading her to her grave. The legend appears in numerous varied forms, but the most celebrated version, *Lenore* by G. A. Bürger, has so many points of resemblance to Erben's poem, that it was undoubtedly an important influence. In Erben, however, the unfortunate girl is taken through the night on a fearful journey on foot, instead of on horseback, and, a most unusual feature and one that would have appealed very strongly to Dvořák, she is ultimately saved through confession and prayer.[2]

[1] Mrs. J. P. Morgan's English translation (Simrock edition), presumably made from the German version, which is longer than the original Czech, is not recommended.

[2] Bürger's poem was translated by Sir Walter Scott among others, and given the title 'William and Helen'. There is a fine Breton version of the legend, *Ar breur mager* ('Le frère de lait' in Villemarqué), in Denmark there is *Aage og Else* ('Sir Ogey and Lady Elsey' in Prior), and in Britain *Sweet William's Ghost* (Scottish), *The Demon Lover* (Irish), *Alonzo the Brave and Fair Imogine* and *The Suffolk Miracle*. In Eastern Europe similar Slavonic legends were used by Zhukovsky in *Svyetlana* and Mickiewicz in *Romanticism*. The version in *Des Knaben Wunderhorn*, although published some forty years after Bürger's poem was written, is much older.

It is highly significant that Dvořák chose this subject, for it was the first time that he showed how strongly he was attracted by the fantastic folk-lore of his country. Later he toyed with the idea of composing a cantata on Erben's *The Golden Spinning Wheel*, and after returning from America he not only wrote symphonic poems on four of Erben's ballads, but also composed *Kate and the Devil* and *Rusalka* to fairy tale libretti. Finally he turned to an Italian source for yet another kind of enchantment for his last opera *Armida*. This love of romantic supernaturalism was an important element in Dvořák's character. The subject that he had chosen includes in Erben's version some important Czech characteristics, the brides' traditional spinning, bleaching and sewing of her wedding garments and preparation of the nuptial wreath during the girls' long period of waiting. Although Dvořák's cantata was immensely popular during and after the composer's lifetime, today it seems to us to be longer than is tolerable for such a subject, the periodic repetition of lines of verse, which can be such a valuable element in story telling, results in similar ground being covered twice over, with a consequent weakening of the dramatic impact, and it is difficult for us to take the strange happenings in the charnel house seriously.

The sketch for *The Spectre's Bride* was begun on May 26th, 1884. On July 8th Dvořák wrote to Göbl as follows:

I feel so happy here that the new work is turning out so well; this week I intend to finish off the sketch, and the rest will then work out satisfactorily. Thank God that my guardian angel didn't desert me this time, but how could it be otherwise for I love him so much. I think (and you'll see that I'm not deceiving myself) that this composition is in every respect the best of all my works, not excepting the *Stabat*. Only I beg you not to mention that to anyone; it would sound like self-praise, which as you of course know is distasteful to me. As for people who can neither sense, nor smell, nor hear, to them I should never say anything of the kind; to you, however, I can tell everything, just as my feeling and reason dictates.

The full score was begun on July 24th, eight days after the sketch had been completed, and by November 27th, six months after starting work, the task was accomplished. Novello published the cantata with the opus number 69 in the following year.

The first performance took place at Pilsen on March 28th, 1885, under the composer's direction, and performances followed at Olomouc and Prague during May. In August Dvořák travelled to Birmingham to conduct the first English performance on the 27th, an event that was one of the greatest successes of his life. After this the cantata was seized on by choral societies in various parts of the English-speaking world. Hallé conducted it at Manchester (26. XI. 1885), W. L. Tomkins gave it at Milwaukee (2. XII. 1885), and Mackenzie performed it in London (2. II. 1886). Within one fortnight August Manns presented it at Edinburgh (1. II. 1886), Glasgow (11. II. 1886) and at the Crystal Palace (13. II. 1886). A few months later it reached Melbourne (October 26th), and Richter conducted it at Nottingham (November 9th). It was heard in Budapest in the following year and in 1892 it was sung in Leeds and Cardiff.

In both Erben's and Bürger's versions of the legend the girl's despair at her lover's failure to return leads her to wish herself dead. Šourek has suggested that this sin of hers, and also the calamity with which she is threatened can be associated with the basic motif that runs through the cantata:

Ex. 2.
(*Allegro commodo*)

It seems unrealistic, however, to link this theme closely with her guilt because it is announced immediately before the chorus sings of her piety and purity, some time before her despair gets the better of her, and it is not used at all in her confession in the third part. It may possibly be connected with the imminent catastrophe, but the *pp* theme in the chorus's first bars suggests this more strongly:

Ex. 3.

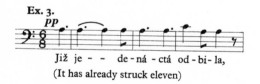

Již je - - de-ná - ctá od-bi-la,
(It has already struck eleven)

Furthermore this interpretation is borne out by the ultimate reappearance of the second theme when the dancing skeletons chant 'The body belongs to the grave; woe to you who have been heedless of your soul!' A fragment of the main theme, the falling fifth, is in fact used in two quite different situations: during the girl's vigil shortly before the bridegroom appears, and secondly to suggest the tolling of the church bells in the last part. This is a sharp reminder that Dvořák made no effort to work consistently with representational motifs in this work. Instead he appears to have used these two recurring themes primarily for unification, but also adapted them to the needs of a given moment without concerning himself as to whether the context was closely related to earlier portions of the work where the same theme is heard.

The cantata is divided into three sections: the vigil and arrival of the dead man; the wild nocturnal journey; and the final scene in the charnel-house and graveyard. It is made up of a series of closed forms, although these follow one another without breaks, and, as in the *Stabat Mater*, balance of form is achieved with the aid of word repetition. A solo baritone and the chorus are allotted the narrative portions, and a soprano and a tenor take the parts of the girl and the bridegroom. In the marathon journey by night Dvořák effectively conveys the sense of speed, and then the slow progress made first in rocky country and later when impeded by bog. The girl's fatigue, too, is well suggested by baritone and chorus in combination in laboured chromatic harmony over a significantly rhythmic pedal bass, but Dvořák missed a chance for really telling dramatic expression when eventually the girl is horrified to see that the appearance of her companion is changing, and she says: 'mad and terrible is your appearance, your poisonous breath is like venom and your heart like solid ice.'

Each time the words 'Fair is the night' are set, the impression is given that the travellers have come to a halt, but it is extremely unlikely that Erben visualized it in that way. Dvořák was obviously in a dilemma here, for having decided to make his setting of the ballad into a reasonably full evening's entertainment, he felt the urgent need to offer the same kind of contrast in the second part that 'My sweetheart made me sorrowful' and 'Hail Virgin Mary!' provide in the first and third. Although there are macabre touches in the score from time to time, Dvořák lacked the instinct for this type of thing, to be found in such good measure in Berlioz, Liszt and Mahler, and consequently we find the most gruesome section of the poem is set as a stirring song for baritone with choral sections following each verse. The recitative 'Where art thou, Father dear?' and the aria that follows, 'My sweetheart...', are probably the most outstanding pages of the score, but there are plenty of other rewarding sections, due to Dvořák's fine lyrical gifts, coupled with his splendid sense of rhythmic movement.

Writing half a century ago Sir Frederick Cowen said that 'the weird and novel music at once produced an effect on the audience that is still felt whenever the work is performed.'[1] Even if the cantata had remained in the repertory it would inevitably have lost its power to astonish today, but not to charm, for Dvořák's genius is displayed in numerous entrancing ways. Although it is not possible to agree with the Czech composer that *The Spectre's Bride* is his finest work up to the time that he wrote it, it is clear that he was fully conscious of his growing mastery, and that he took particular delight in the subject and the enlarged possibilities that it opened up to him.

[1] *My Art and My Friends*, 1913.

The harmonic colouring is richer than usual, if perhaps momentarily a trifle too lush, and the scoring for an orchestra that includes cor anglais, bass clarinet and harp shows unusual skill and imagination. Some of the choral writing has a vigour and power without parallel in any of his earlier music except *Dimitrij*. The cantata is, in fact, a vital link in the chain leading from Dvořák's Russian opera to *The Jacobin*, not so much on account of the masterly use of the chorus, but because in the work as a whole, the composer seems to find wings to soar as he wishes without let or hindrance. There seems to have been no heart-searching, no striving to produce a monumental work, as in the case of the D minor symphony that followed it—his inspiration flowed naturally and spontaneously. One sincerely hopes that, at the least, well chosen extracts will make their appearance from time to time in concert programmes so that the cantata will not be completely forgotten.

St. Ludmila

Just after Dvořák left home on March 5th, 1884, to travel for the first time to London, a letter reached Prague inviting him to compose a choral work for the Leeds Musical Festival. After some delay he sent a reply on March 19th through Oscar Beringer, saying that he would be prepared to write an oratorio for the 1886 festival. Fred. R. Spark, the honorary secretary, said in his reply (24. III. 1884) that 'the orthodox oratorio form is not the most attractive to the present generation', and suggested instead 'a sacred cantata not exceeding an hour and a half in performance'. The following day Dvořák replied to say that he wished to compose either a cantata or oratorio that would occupy a whole morning or evening, and added, 'I am particularly anxious to write an important work for you.' The committee accepted this, but later expressed some doubts about the subject of the oratorio. After the composer's appearance at Birmingham to conduct *The Spectre's Bride*, Henry Littleton, who acted as intermediary in the negotiations, reported as follows: 'I find he is determined to carry out his own idea as to subject, and, as he is distinctly proving himself to be one of the greatest musical geniuses we have ever had, he must be allowed to decide for himself. The oratorio will therefore consist of a considerable portion of the life of the Bohemian saint, the holy Ludmila.'[1] The subject, as it happens, is not of narrow national interest, but is universal in appeal, for it centres around the arrival of Christianity in Bohemia c. A.D. 873.

The libretto has excellent dramatic possibilities, but the celebrated Czech poet, Jaroslav Vrchlický, can be criticized for certain aspects of his poem. The character of Ivan is unsympathetically drawn, in fact in Part I he is

[1] Spark, F. R. and Bennett, J.: *History of the Leeds Music Festivals 1858–1889*, 2nd edn. Leeds 1892.

caricatured as an aggressive Christian fanatic, and later it strikes us that his ideals are lower than they should be when he hastily promises that Bořivoj shall marry Ludmila if he accepts the new faith. It would be a decided advantage if the libretto could be re-written and condensed, so that the best music of the oratorio, which was written during one of the composer's greatest periods, may not be forgotten.

Šourek suggests that Dvořák was not completely satisfied with the text. Once he began work, however, he toiled at it almost without interruption, and even cancelled engagements to conduct his own compositions in Bremen and Frankfurt and refused invitations to visit friends, in order to ensure that the work was ready well in advance of the date of performance. The whole composition occupied him from September 17th, 1885 to May 30th, 1886. Part I was sketched between September 17th and November 23rd, being 'completed during the time when The Cunning Peasant was murdered in Vienna' (19. XI. 1885), as the manuscript informs us. Before proceeding further, the composer prepared the full score of this part, a task he completed on January 18th. He sketched Part II between January 19th and February 26th, beginning the full score on the same day that he began the sketch and finishing it on April 3rd. He was engaged on the sketch of Part III from April 6th to May 5th, and the full score from May 8th to 30th.

Dvořák conducted the first performance at Leeds on October 15th, 1886, with Albani, Patey, Edward Lloyd and Santley as the soloists. He also directed performances at the St. James's Hall, London, on October 29th, and at the Crystal Palace on November 6th, but by the second of these the audience for this big work had dwindled considerably. Manchester heard it on November 25th, and between February 25th and March 25th, 1887, Dvořák conducted it four times in Prague. St. Ludmila was published that year by Novello as op. 71. It was dedicated to the Žerotin Music and Choral Society of Olomouc.

The composer obviously worked on his oratorio with Handel in mind, for, apart from dividing his work into as many as forty-five separate numbers, there is a noticeable emphasis on choral writing, two of the choruses are for double choir, there is more contrapuntal texture than was usual with Dvořák, and sometimes the music is distinctly Handelian. Since this was the composer's first, as well as his last, oratorio, and he was aware of the English delight in Handel, it was a natural step to emulate the greatest master of this form. In point of fact St. Ludmila also has much in common with the Czech master's opera Dimitrij (1881–82). An important link between these two works, a link that also connects St. Ludmila with several of his operas, is Dvořák's use of representative themes, although here, as elsewhere, he did not use these themes consistently. It is therefore unwise to attach indelible labels to them.

The noble theme announced at letter D in the first chorus:

Ex. 4.
Andante

seems to be associated with light. At this point it is heard in the context of sunlight shining on the pagan people, but it assumes a new and much greater significance before long, when it appears to represent the light of Christian truth. A brief 'tumult motive' accompanies the entry of Ivan among the heathen Czechs, and this signifies agitation of one kind or another at later points of the drama. When Ivan mentions the Cross a new theme is heard, which recurs at significant points, but sometimes the Cross is mentioned without reference to this theme. Šourek suggests that a fourth theme:

Ex. 5.
Andante moderato

is obviously connected with the love of Prince Bořivoj and Princess Ludmila, but since it is first heard when Ludmila and her attendant Svatava are struggling through the gloomy forest to find Ivan, before Bořivoj has seen her and fallen in love with her, it would be more reasonable to regard it as representing the princess herself, and in particular, perhaps, the enlightened and consequently more radiantly beautiful Ludmila. She has no theme of her own in Part I.

It is perhaps surprising to find Dvořák more at ease in writing the pagan than the Christian music in the first part, but this may be due to the defects in the libretto. The second chorus is a delightful spring-like song of devotion to the goddess Baba. The simple charm of Ludmila's first aria is suggested by the words, in which she recalls her childhood's days. This point is not made clear in Troutbeck's English translation, which here, as elsewhere, is rather too free. At this stage, however, it would have been better to establish her personality more definitely in musical terms. Her second aria has much more distinction and far greater depth of feeling. The dramatic chorus 'What man is this?' is powerful and restrained by turns, whilst the last chorus in this part, although at times conventional and somewhat Handelian, culminates in a splendidly impressive peroration. Dvořák gives a good impression of journeying into the unknown at the beginning of Part II, but when Svatava sings, 'I wrongly put my trust in you when you led me to chasms so dark' (letter D), the mood temporarily eludes Dvořák. Orchestral colour is effectively used, trombones and cor anglais, for instance, in Ivan's proclamation in recitative, bass clarinet in Bořivoj's aria with chorus, and flute in nos. 19 and 20. An angelic choir is heard in the concluding chorus.

In Part III the baptism of Ludmila and Bořivoj takes place, the drama itself being over. Svatava's aria is charming and is imaginatively accompanied, but the chief glories here are the opening and closing choruses. The first of these is a supremely confident hymn in Russian style, based on the oldest known Czech liturgical melody, 'Hospdine, pomiluj ny' (Lord, have mercy on us). Dvořák seems to have taken what he needed from the second phrase of the plainchant:

Ex. 6a.

Ex. 6b.

Allegro commodo

ƒ Hos - po - di - ne, po - mi - luj ny!

The last quartet and chorus begins similarly, but later vigorous fugal passages alternate with impressive sections in harmonic style.

MASS IN D

Dvořák wrote his next choral work in response to a request from Josef Hlávka, a distinguished philanthropic architect who founded and became the first president of the Czech Academy of Sciences and Arts. He needed a

Mass for performance at the consecration of his private chapel at Lužany. The ceremony took place on September 11th, 1887. The Hlahol Choir of Pilsen sang the work with the composer conducting, and Hlávka's wife Zdeňka and Dvořák's wife Anna were the soprano and contralto soloists in the sections intended either for solo voices or semi-chorus. The first public performance took place at Pilsen on April 15th in the following year. The Mass in D was composed with organ accompaniment, but five years later it was rewritten with orchestral accompaniment, and in this new form it was performed first by August Manns on March 11th, 1893, at the Crystal Palace. Considering that it is not a big work, it is surprising that it took from March 26th to June 17th, 1887, to complete it in its original form.

This Mass is a mixture of the idyllic and the conventional. It seems reasonable to suppose that Dvořák might have composed a more compelling work if it had been intended originally for an important public occasion, and one that demanded orchestral accompaniment. He seems to have been unconcerned about being unliturgical, and as a composer who was much more experienced in instrumental forms than in choral composition, he applied some of their principles to this work. In the 'Kyrie' there is a coda recalling the 'Christe' section. Formal balance is secured in the 'Credo' by a repetition of the first fifty-six bars for the setting of 'Et in Spiritum Sanctum . . .' and the words that follow, and the same material is used for the coda-like conclusion. The words 'Credo in unum Deum' are allotted to the choir. When 'Passus, et sepultus est' is reached Dvořák was reminded of *Tristan*. The loveliest music of the Mass is to be found in the 'Agnus Dei', the first half of which unfolds as a leisurely accompanied fugal exposition on an eight-bar theme (Ex. 7). As we might expect, Dvořák draws on this to make a telling conclusion to the work.

REQUIEM MASS

Before Dvořák left Birmingham after the triumphal success there of his *Spectre's Bride*, he was asked by Harding Milward on behalf of the Birmingham Musical Festival if he would be prepared to compose a 'great oratorio' for their 1888 festival.[1] During his visit he was given a German translation of *The Dream of Gerontius* by a Father of the Birmingham Oratory. It is almost certain that he failed to give a definite answer to the proposal from Birmingham in the months that followed for several reasons. At that time his attention was wholly taken up with the composition of *St. Ludmila*; furthermore he had received other requests for compositions, he had his own ideas

[1] Letter from R. H. Milward to Dvořák, 22. I. 1886.

Ex. 7.

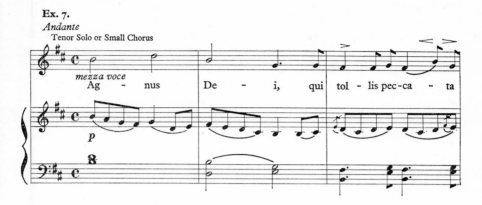

as to what he should work on next, and besides it was not easy to find an entirely suitable subject for a second oratorio. At the end of 1886 it was rumoured in London that Dvořák had decided to set Newman's poem. This proved to be incorrect, but it is possible that although the Cardinal's symbolical and psychological mysticism was not likely to appeal readily to a man of simple and direct beliefs like Dvořák, *Gerontius* may have assisted the composer indirectly in his eventual decision to write a Mass for the Dead. Although Birmingham failed to get the work they wanted for 1888, they continued to press for a choral composition, and at the beginning of 1890 received the long-awaited reply saying that the composer was prepared to write a Requiem for them for the 1891 festival.[1] Later the Festival Committee became anxious because Henry Littleton of Novello & Co. had been unable to agree with Dvořák over the terms under which his firm would be allowed to publish the *Requiem*,[2] but this obstacle was overcome and

[1] Letter from Charles G. Beale, Chairman of the Musical Sub-Committee, to Dvořák, 10. I. 1890.
[2] Ibid. 25. II. 1891.

publication took place at the end of 1891, too early, however, to include several of the composer's last-minute revisions.[1]

Dvořák's *Requiem* was neither composed as the direct result of the loss of any personal friend or relative, nor because his thoughts were turning towards his own ultimate departure from this earth. He was still extremely active and in the best of health as he approached the age of fifty, and his fame and success were still increasing. It is probable that as a sincere and devout Catholic he felt called upon to testify to his faith in God, the supreme Judge, through his art, just as in his *Stabat Mater* and Mass he had given musical expression to his belief in Christ the Redeemer and in God the omnipotent and omniscient Creator of heaven and earth. Before long he was to add yet another affirmation of his unshakable faith in the shape of a *Te Deum*. The *Requiem* was sketched between January 1st and July 11th, 1890, and the full score prepared between August 2nd and October 31st. It was Dvořák's op. 89. The Birmingham performance, conducted by the composer, took place on October 9th 1891. Hallé performed it at Manchester on March 3rd and at Liverpool on March 21st, 1892, and two days later Barnby presented it at the Royal Albert Hall. The first Czech performances took place at Olomouc on March 12th and 13th, with the composer conducting, and he gave two further performances at Kroměříž on April 23rd and 24th. Adolf Čech directed it in Prague on the 25th, and on November 30th the composer again gave an important first performance of it, at Boston, Massachusetts.

This *Requiem* is another of the Czech master's works that is not strictly liturgical, but there is musical justification for his licence. The work is divided quite naturally into two halves, the first consisting of the 'Introit', 'Gradual' and 'Dies Irae', the last of which is subdivided into six parts, and the second comprising the 'Offertory', 'Hostias', 'Sanctus' and 'Agnus Dei' (together with 'Lux aeterna'), but including a repetition of the last two lines of the 'Dies Irae' ('Pie Jesu') interpolated as a separate number immediately before the 'Agnus'. This provides for a first part expressing sorrow, confession and supplication, and a second part carrying the message of spiritual consolation. The contrast of atmosphere between the two parts is very marked.

The work is unified by a four-note chromatic motif, or motto, which may perhaps symbolize grief, although other interpretations are possible; among these, the view put forward by Burghauser in correspondence with the author, that it may represent a woeful questioning regarding the import of life and death, is worthy of special consideration. Alec Robertson points out that Dvořák's initial theme, which starts with this motif, might have been

---

[1] The Complete Edition score (1961) is the first published version of the work to incorporate these corrections.

suggested by the plainchant 'Introit' in the *Missa pro Defunctis,* which in view of the contour of the two melodies may well be the case. If so the transformation is a particularly interesting one:[1]

Ex. 8a.

Re - qui-em ae - ter - - nam

Ex. 8b.

The basic motif occurs in various ways in almost all sections of the work, but it is normally used as a binding element, rather than as the main musical material of any section of the work. The entire theme, as quoted above, is only utilized in the 'Introit' and 'Agnus Dei'. The 'Tuba Mirum' begins with a four-fold repetition of the motif rising by semitones each time, punctuated by ominous strokes on the *tam-tam,* and culminating in a Tristanesque version of the same theme. There are also other occasional suggestions of plainchant in this work. The most notable of these is seen in the first melody for voices in the 'Offertory', and due very likely to Dvořák's familiarity with the Gregorian 'Lux aeterna' melody (Exx. 9a and 9b).

Ex. 9a.

Lux ae - ter - na lu-ce-at e-is, Do-mi-ne:

The Czech composer's natural gift for lyricism, fertilized here and there by liturgical melody, helps to make the *Requiem* essentially a melodious work.

---

[1] Robertson: *Dvořák,* p. 119. Dvořák's motif is obviously related to the familiar B, A, C, H theme, but it is unusual in rising initially, against the natural gravitational pull, so to say, without gathering strength before striving upwards. The motto theme of Vaughan Williams' F minor symphony, the inversion of Dvořák's motif, is less striking. The Requiem motif, which may also be traced to bar 11 of the Brahms Requiem, reappears in Dvořák's *Othello,* and in Suk's *Asrael* symphony, written in memory of Dvořák and his daughter Otilie, Suk's wife. A later instance is found in Martinů's *Fantasies Symphoniques* (1953).

Ex. 9b.

Do - - mi-ne Je - su Chri - ste, Rex glo - ri-ae, Rex

glo - ri-ae

Whereas the motto theme serves as a point of focus in the work as a whole, other themes are used to bind individual numbers together. Each time Dvořák adds the words 'Domine Jesu . . .' to the 'Hostias' he returns to ex. 9b. These two sections are linked further by the fugue 'Quam olim Abrahae', the subject of which may have been suggested by the Czech hymn 'Vesele zpívejme'. This may not be an outstanding example of fugal style, but when given a good performance it carries conviction, and the climax is certainly impressive. The three opening notes of the 'Sanctus' are used again in the 'Pie Jesu', but the motif that dominates the accompaniment of the 'Dies Irae' has much more significance. Like Verdi, Dvořák repeats almost the whole of this number after the 'Tuba Mirum', and at the end of the 'Lacrymosa' he introduces a reminder of this particular motif. The 'Rex tremendae' theme is reminiscent of Verdi's, and it is possible that the beautiful ending of the 'Gradual', where Dvořák modulates from B flat major, the tonic key, and closes in G major, may also have been prompted by the Italian master's magical, but rather different use of the same two keys or chords at the end of his 'Dies Irae'.

Dvořák is careful to secure formal balance in the individual numbers. Often when there is musical repetition the parts given to the orchestra are taken over by the voices, and *vice versa*, or those presented by solo voices are transferred to the choir, and sometimes the score is enriched with added parts. The brass is most effectively used and never abused. The bass clarinet and cor anglais are of great importance in providing a sombre element in the 'Lacrimosa' and 'Hostias'. Soloists and choir interchange freely and informally, and only three of the numbers do not call upon both groups.

The work has many lovely moments, among which may be mentioned the soprano solo in the 'Gradual', the touching prayer 'Voca me cum benedictis' that follow the furious opening of the 'Confutatis', and also the 'Recordare' for solo quartet. The *Requiem* stands on a higher level than the *Stabat Mater*, partly because Dvořák's stature as a composer had greatly increased, but chiefly because here he penetrated much more deeply into the spirit of the text he was setting. Worldly elements are wholly absent and the sincerity of Dvořák's conception carries great conviction. This work deserves to be placed high among settings of the *Missa pro Defunctis*, for it takes its place as one of the most lofty, eloquent and distinguished choral compositions of the nineteenth century.

Te Deum

As the Fourth Centennial Celebrations of the discovery of America by Columbus were due to begin on October 12th, 1892, a fortnight after Dvořák's arrival in the United States, Mrs. Thurber requested the composer to write a choral work for the occasion, the words of which she promised to send him. Joseph Rodman Drake's poem, *The American Flag*, had not arrived towards the end of June, so Dvořák set to work instead on a *Te Deum*, in order to ensure that he would have a new work ready for performance during the festivities. This occupied him from June 25th to July 28th, and hardly had he completed it than the long-awaited poem arrived. The *Te Deum*, op. 103, for soprano, bass, chorus and orchestra, was performed in New York on October 21st, with the composer conducting, and the Triple Overture was included in the same programme.

Instead of subdividing the canticle into three parts according to the natural divisions of the text, Dvořák preferred to unite the last verse of the second part ('Aeterna fac cum sanctis . . .') with the first two verses of the third in a separate choral number, and to use the remaining verses beginning with 'Dignare Domine' for a fourth section. His aim appears to have been to produce a work whose four parts, Allegro moderato maestoso (C), Lento maestoso (C), Vivace ($\frac{3}{4}$), and Lento—Poco più mosso—Ancora più mosso (C), would have the same kind of tempo relationship as the movements of a symphony. It must be admitted, however, that this arrangement of the text is not altogether satisfactory as far as the 'scherzo' movement is concerned.

In the middle section of the first part, which expresses awe in face of the majesty of God, the initial orchestral motif, slightly modified, is used responsorially in conjunction with choral repetitions of 'Sanctus Dominus Deus Sabaoth' between the verses sung by the solo soprano. The jubilant opening material returns at the conclusion of this part. A bass solo follows in which sections of the choir sing the prayer 'Te ergo quaesumus . . .' unliturgically but very effectively both before and after the words 'Tu ad dexteram . . .'. A quaver motif given to the violas early in the third part would serve well to suggest wood nymphs in the Bohemian forests; it gradually makes itself felt more and more strongly, and seems to provide the work with a pantheistic element. At the beginning of the fourth part the solo soprano is given a most expressive melody line:

Ex. 10.

Lento

Di-gna-re Do-mi-ne, di-gna-re Do-mi-ne, di-e   i - sto   si - ne pec-ca - ta

nos cu-sto-di - - - ri

to which the choral contraltos respond with reminders of the first part's theme to the words 'Miserere nostri, Domine'. A telling passage for double basses *pizzicato* accompanies their second petition, after which the entire section is repeated a minor third higher. This cyclic work ends even more jubilantly than it began, with unliturgical Alleluias.

It is curious that in this composition, written on the eve of his departure for the United States, Dvořák should have anticipated to some extent the change of style that is seen in the first work he composed when on American soil, for in the *Te Deum* we find several themes formed from four notes of the major and minor pentatonic scales. A possible explanation is that Dvořák conceived the spirit of praise in terms of the common chord and the added sixth chord, and from the second of these he was able to fashion all but one of those themes. It seems more probable, however, that he may already have known a little about the characteristics of American folk music, and that he wished to embody these in his canticle as a compliment to America. V. J. Novotný, who had published an article entitled 'Songs of the American Indians',[1] may have discussed the subject with him personally, but only one of the songs he quotes in his article is pentatonic, and to anyone who is familiar with songs of the Iroquois and the Comanches his transcriptions must be regarded as suspect.[2] The Fisk Jubilee Singers, on the other hand, toured Europe during the same period. Even supposing they did not sing in Prague, undoubtedly news of them would have reached that city. Although Dvořák's themes are unlike Negro melodies, it is natural that they should be closer to them than to the much more primitive Indian songs.

THE AMERICAN FLAG

With his *Te Deum* ready for performance at the forthcoming Columbus quadricentennial celebrations, it was no longer urgent for Dvořák to make

[1] In *Dalibor*, Aug. 20 and Sept. 1, 1879.
[2] If Dvořák happened to come across Th. Baker's *Über die Musik der Nordamerikanischen Wilden* (1882) he would have received a rather more authentic yet still far from adequate impression of the nature of the music of the Iroquois and Plains Indians.

the setting of J. R. Drake's poem, *The American Flag*, asked for by Mrs. Thurber. He sketched the cantata at Vysoká between August 3rd and the early part of September, 1892, and then postponed preparation of the full score until after reaching New York. The score occupied him from November 1st until January 8th, 1893, during which period he began to work on his *New World* symphony. His patriotic cantata then appears to have been forgotten for a while. The work is written for alto, tenor and bass soloists, mixed chorus and orchestra. The New York Musical Society gave the first performance on May 4th, 1895, after the composer had left America for the second time, never to return. He sold the work to Schirmer, who published it as op. 102, but only in vocal score.

The cantata is less characteristic of the Czech master than his previous composition, and shows the influence of both Wagner and Liszt. Whereas in the *Te Deum* there is a brief and inexplicable passage of Wagnerian harmony near the end of the third part, here the spirit of Wagner prevails far more conspicuously in the first chorus ('Colours of the Flag') and also in the Finale ('Prophetic'). In particular the alto solo early in the first number, and which returns at the beginning of the Finale, has close affinities with the so-called Love Feast motive in *Parsifal*. In all sections of the cantata except the two Apostrophes to the Eagle another theme, unquestionably symbolizing the flag and first played by the cor anglais, is heard in a number of Lisztian metamorphoses, and furthermore, at the mention of death in the Third Apostrophe to the Flag ('The Sailor'), the music effectively takes on a semblance to that of the Hungarian composer. Dvořák is at his liveliest and most himself in the brilliant march for orchestra in the middle of the work.

FESTIVAL SONG

Dvořák's last choral work was written by request in 1900, to commemorate the seventieth birthday of the Vice-President of the Prague Conservatory, Dr. Josef Tragy. The composer was given a poem by Vrchlický to set. Although Dvořák respected and admired Tragy, he was angry at having to undertake the commission, as Jindřich Káan related, because no musical ideas had occurred to him during the previous fortnight. Later he said he had tried to write the work three times, but he was obliged to throw all three sketches into the stove. After re-hearing the hymn 'Tisíckrát pozdravujem Tebe' in church, however, and noticing how the rhythm of the music corresponded exactly with the metre of Vrchlický's poem, he speedily finished his ode after shaping his principal choral theme out of the melody he had heard. The full score was completed between April 7th and 17th, and the composition was privately performed at the Conservatory on May 29th, five days after the anniversary. It was written for mixed choir and full orchestra, and was published by M. Urbánek as op. 113.

The *Festival Song*, an invocation to the spirit of music, is a cheerful but not very distinguished work, and one that is much less enterprising as regards key than was customary with Dvořák.[1] It divides into three sections, in which the same material is presented differently each time. In writing the work Dvořák seems to have been somewhat self-conscious over musical technique, because, apart from concluding his ode with close imitations in the choral writing, he marked against an orchestral interlude the words, 'Yearning for the musical art (Studie contrapunktické)'.

---

[1] Dvořák's enthusiasm in the peroration to his *Te Deum* resulted in modulations from G major to E minor, F minor, A flat major, and back to G major in less than three bars.

XIII

Part-Songs

Dvořák's earlier sets of short choral songs have strong links with the *Moravian Duets* and were composed during the same period. At that time the composer showed a strong interest in folk poetry and especially that which originated in Moravia, and it was from these sources that he took most of the texts he required. The *Four Part-Songs for Mixed Voices*, op. 29, which antedate the *Duets* by three months, are settings of two Moravian poems and two poems of Heyduk, a poet to whom he was soon to turn for the texts of his *Gipsy Melodies*. In the last of the set, 'Forsaken', Dvořák took the seven stanzas from two different south Moravian versions of this folk-song, both of which are found in F. Sušil's *Moravian National Songs*.[1] The three *Choral Songs for Male Voices*, which lack an opus number and were written in January 1877, are again settings of Moravian and Heyduk poems. The *Bouquet of Czech Folk-Songs*, op. 41, for male voice choir, from the end of the same year, derives textually from Czech and Moravian folklore. These last two sets were published together posthumously, but omitting 'The Czech Diogenes', the fourth chorus from the Bouquet. Very shortly afterwards Dvořák wrote *From a Bouquet of Slavonic Folk-Songs*, op. 43, the first and third of which are Slovak and the second Moravian, and at the end of 1878 after having completed his third *Slavonic Rhapsody* he turned to Čelakovský's translations of Lithuanian folk-songs for his *Five Choruses for Male Voices*, op. 27.

Dvořák was not only influenced by the simple and naïve poems but also by the songs collectively. His part-songs reflect to some extent the spirit and character of the folk tunes, their rhythm and simple phrase structure, their modulations and their melodic shapes. Nevertheless, even though in 'The Guelder Rose' (op. 41, no. 3) the initial phrase appears to bear a direct relationship to the folk-song melody, and in 'Forsaken' (op. 29, no. 4) an identical 'Three Blind Mice' cadence occurs at the end of the first stanza, Dvořák's conception is totally different in each case and the few similarities

---

[1] *Moravské národní písně*, 3rd edition, Brno 1860. The texts of several of Dvořák's part songs and all except one of his *Moravian Duets* appear in this source.

that may be detected are unimportant. These choruses are in fact original compositions. All are *a cappella* with the exception of op. 43, which has a pianoforte accompaniment, but all the existing published versions adopt Dr. Zubatý's arrangement of this for four hands.

In the second of the part-songs for mixed voices, a charming lullaby, the folk-song style is enhanced by some unexpected key changes. The most attractive of the set is 'Forsaken', in which Dvořák's predilection for varied repetitions is shown to advantage, and the recapitulation of the first part is unusually free.

Sometimes one gains the impression that Dvořák felt himself restricted when writing for a male voice choir, which may perhaps help to account for the faulty progressions in 'The Sweetheart's Resolve' (op. 41, no. 2). Most of the posthumous part-songs are simple in character, and pleasing without being in any way exceptional, but in two cases the composer produced choruses that rise well above the average level and show him in full command of his medium. His imagination appears to have been fired by the laconic folk-song 'The Beloved as Poisoner', a topic that he pursued further twenty years later when he composed his symphonic poem *The Wild Dove*. The part-song is delightful. The next chorus, a setting of Heyduk's 'I am a Fiddler' (Já jsem huslař), is the source of the original theme used by the composer for his *Symphonic Variations*. As may be seen by the fertility of his imagination in making use of the theme here, he already foresaw that it possessed great potentialities, and he allowed little more than six months to pass before converting it into one of his outstanding orchestral compositions. The part-song possesses an intrinsic interest of its own and ought to be much better known.

The next group of part-songs, op. 43, retains a folkloristic character, but the accompaniments afforded the composer new opportunities for a much richer texture, and in particular for figuration and decoration, counter melodies and interludes, things which he seized upon and put to excellent use in 'Miraculous Water', in which we notice there is even a hint of the beginning of the last section of the *Dumky* Trio (see page 265). This is a particularly beautiful chorus, and probably it was due to the religious element in the words that Dvořák lavished on it exceptionally loving care.

The Lithuanian part-songs make an attractive set, but 'The Lost Lamb' and 'Dwellers by the Sea', which tells of a girl's drowned brother, drew from the composer the most imaginative response. In Dvořák's only humorous part-song, 'The Sparrow's Party', the host gets into trouble through becoming too merry on his home-brewed beer.

In addition to these settings of folk poems, Dvořák composed first of all *The Song of a Czech* for unaccompanied male-voice chorus. This was probably written towards the end of 1877. At the change of time signature

the opening phrase of the Hussite chorale is introduced, but only three out of the five patriotic stanzas by Kamenický were set, and the work remained incomplete. It was published posthumously.

For *In Nature's Realm*, op. 63, Dvořák turned for the third time to poems of Vítězslav Hálek, and between January 24th and 27th, 1882, made settings of five of them for mixed voices unaccompanied. Even though the seasons do not follow in any normal sequence, the title and choice of keys show that it was intended as a short cycle of choral songs in praise of nature. Since he was by that time a more experienced composer who was also a keen nature-lover, and no doubt welcoming an opportunity to write a light composition in which he was able to relax and refresh himself while at work on his grand opera *Dimitrij*, we are not at all surprised to find a charming plasticity, freshness and spontaneity in each of the choruses. In the third, for instance, we imagine we hear the ripening rye rustling in the breeze. Dvořák reserves the most joyful chorus for the end, and even makes effective use of imitation to strengthen it. Because of its general character and fluctuating speeds this is perhaps the most typically Slavonic of all his part-songs.

The last of these compositions, a setting for mixed chorus of K. Pippich's *Hymn of the Czech Peasants*, gives the impression of having been tossed off in a hurry. It is disappointing to find that when the music of the first verse comes round for the third time there is no attempt to vary it or extend it in order to attain a bigger climax than before. As in the case of other compositions included in this chapter the opus number that it was given, 28, is misleading. The only published version available has a four-hand piano accompaniment, but the work was written with orchestra, and according to the manuscript the score was completed in one day, on August 13th, 1885.

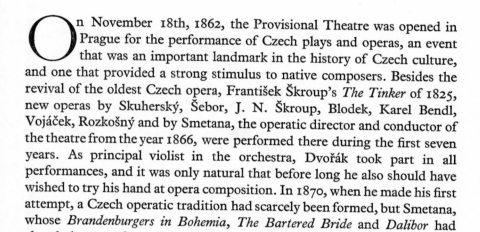

XIV

The Operas

On November 18th, 1862, the Provisional Theatre was opened in Prague for the performance of Czech plays and operas, an event that was an important landmark in the history of Czech culture, and one that provided a strong stimulus to native composers. Besides the revival of the oldest Czech opera, František Škroup's *The Tinker* of 1825, new operas by Skuherský, Šebor, J. N. Škroup, Blodek, Karel Bendl, Vojáček, Rozkošný and by Smetana, the operatic director and conductor of the theatre from the year 1866, were performed there during the first seven years. As principal violist in the orchestra, Dvořák took part in all performances, and it was only natural that before long he also should have wished to try his hand at opera composition. In 1870, when he made his first attempt, a Czech operatic tradition had scarcely been formed, but Smetana, whose *Brandenburgers in Bohemia*, *The Bartered Bride* and *Dalibor* had already been performed, had laid the necessary foundations.

During his student days Dvořák had developed a profound admiration for Wagner's music, and on February 8th, 1863, he had the unique experience of playing in a programme consisting of *A Faust Overture*, the Prelude and two excerpts from *Die Meistersinger*, the Prelude to *Tristan*, Siegmund's declaration of love, and the Overture to *Tannhäuser*, with the great composer himself conducting. Although Dvořák's love for Wagner began to show itself in his chamber and orchestral music of the 60s, it was not until the end of the decade that the flood-tide of Wagnerianism seized the struggling Czech musician, leaving an indelible mark on three string quartets and his first two operas.

ALFRED

For his first essay Dvořák chose a German libretto by Karl Theodor Körner which he came across in an old almanac.[1] He was obviously attracted

---

[1] Körner was a prolific romantic poet born at Dresden in 1791 and killed in the Napoleonic wars at Schwerin at the age of twenty-two. Schubert wrote an operetta, *Der vierjährige Posten*, to a libretto of his, and Weber set three of his patriotic songs.

by a subject that centred around the struggle between the Saxons and the Danes, which would be certain to remind Czechs of the history of their own country, although it is strange that at a time when national feelings were running high he should have used a text in the language of the Czechs' over-lords. The opera occupied him from May 26th to October 19th, 1870. Having completed the work, Dvořák took no step towards having it per-formed, and even concealed the fact that he had written an opera from his closest friends.

In *Alfred* we find representative themes used for the chief characters and the two main groups of people, a tendency for the vocal parts to be declama-tory while the orchestra provides the main musical interest, long melodic lines, Wagnerian chromaticism and harmony, and prominent use of the cor anglais. The motif of Alfred's troops[1] might be taken to be genuine Wagner. To a lesser extent we notice the influence of Czech folk-song in the ballet for the jubilant Danes, Verdi in the handling of the crowd scenes, Liszt in one of the themes of the overture, and Smetana's fondness for swinging between dominant seventh and tonic (but in a Wagnerian setting) in the prelude to Act II, Scene 2:

Ex. 1.

Much of *Alfred* is rather colourless and characterless, partly because there is insufficient action, and Dvořák must have realized that there were many

[1] Quoted in Šourek: *The Orchestral Works of A.D.*, p. 278, ex. 3.

weaknesses. He made no attempt to make alterations and revisions, but five years later he made use of the duet for Alvina and Harold in Act I in *Vanda*, another of his ill-fated operas. There was a prospect of a performance of the overture to *Alfred* in May 1881 at the Academy of Czech Journalists, when it was to be played under the title *Tragic Overture* in order to conceal its origin, but the composer's third *Slavonic Rhapsody* was performed in its place. The overture was published posthumously by Simrock with the title changed to *Dramatic Overture*.

KING AND CHARCOAL BURNER

Dvořák wrote his first Czech opera a year after *Alfred*, probably between April and December 20th, 1871. *King and Charcoal Burner* shows less dependence on Wagner, but representative themes are again used for certain aspects or ideas associated with the four chief characters. The charcoal burner's theme appears in two different forms, in order to express disapproval of the courtship of the young couple and to suggest cordiality when unwittingly he entertains the king. Frequently non-recurring themes are used to replace the principal motives when it is necessary for the characters to be shown in a fresh light or in a changed situation. There are obvious signs of the influence of *Die Meistersinger* in a chorus of peasants and a dance at court, but it is more interesting to be able to observe occasionally a stronger sense of individuality and of national feeling than was usual in Dvořák's music at that time. This is clearly seen in a portion of the bagpipe tune heard in Act I (Ex. 2). Dvořák utilized the tenth and sixth of his *Cypresses* song cycle for Liduška's air and her duet with the king in Act II. Later he borrowed a portion of Act I for a chorus in *The Cunning Peasant* and took the principal theme of the E flat symphony's Finale from the big ensemble in Act III.

The opera was eventually put into rehearsal at the Provisional Theatre in the autumn of 1873, but there were numerous complaints from the singers and orchestral players. Smetana declared, 'It is a serious work, full of ideas and genius, but I don't believe it can be performed.' His opinion was endorsed by Adolf Čech, who said, 'And he was right. When we had studied the work hard for about four weeks, Dvořák, who helped the soloists, came round to the opinion that the whole work was too complicated, some points presenting insurmountable difficulties to the singers.'

It appears that the composer was not aware of the weaknesses of the libretto. Bernard Guldener, using the pseudonym B. J. Lobeský, had taken his plot from an old successful comedy for a puppet theatre, originally written by Prokop Konopásek, and already used for operas by F. Škroup and others under the title *Oldřich a Božena*. But Guldener was a poor poet, and

Ex. 2.

he introduced an absurd love tangle between the burgrave, a lady of the court, the king and the queen in the last act.

Dvořák's severe setback over his second opera, and the slowness with which he was managing to achieve recognition, left in their train fits of depression, even after his first success in 1873 with his cantata *The Heirs of the White Mountain*. It is possible that his happiness at the birth of his first child, Otakar, on April 4th, 1874, together with the further progress of Smetana, whose fifth opera and second comedy, *The Two Widows*, had been performed on March 27th, may have provided Dvořák with the necessary stimulus to turn once again to Guldener's libretto, the story of which appealed to him because it was thoroughly Czech. But he had no intention of repeating the mistakes of his first version, and therefore, in making this second setting of the same text, he rejected the whole of his earlier opera and created an entirely new work, a task that occupied him from April 17th to November 3rd.

The second version of *King and Charcoal Burner* contrasts very greatly with the earlier one. Dvořák was at this time making a rapid retreat from his early love, Wagner, and he took as his models instead the comic operas of Weber and Lortzing, together with some suggestions from the works of Smetana for good measure. He replaced the complex polyphonic and harmonic texture of the two earlier operas with a decidedly simpler and more direct manner of writing, and made less effort to express situations and words musically. He used three themes that recur for occasional reminiscences, but without making any attempt to treat them in the manner of Wagnerian *leitmotive*. To some extent these new features foreshadow methods adopted by Dvořák in his next five operas, in which the trend away from Wagner was to continue.

The plaintive aria sung by Liduška in Act II is one of the most attractive parts of the new score. The words are poor, and Dvořák's shapely but somewhat conventional closing bars fail to suggest strongly enough her continued feeling of uncertainty, but there are several charming and imaginative touches. The cabaletta-like ballad for the king in Act I, in which extreme modulations are used to suggest his fears when lost in the forest, is not only dramatic but also extremely effective, and is Dvořák's best piece of writing for the stage at that time.

The opera was presented at the Provisional Theatre on November 24th, 1874, and given four performances. In course of time, however, it became imperative to improve the libretto, and especially Act III, a task that was entrusted to V. J. Novotný, who had already revised Smetana's *Dalibor*. When the revision was complete Dvorak re-composed the last act early in 1887, but as with *Tannhäuser*, there are inconsistencies of style in this final version of the work.

THE STUBBORN LOVERS

The prospect of public performances of his comic opera persuaded Dvořák to lose no time in commencing another, *The Stubborn Lovers*, a one-act village comedy with a libretto by Josef Štolba, which had been written expressly for him four years earlier. At that time it had fallen on stony ground, as the composer was passing through his Wagnerian phase, but now it was just what he needed. The libretto was not dramatic, but it was witty. Dvořák probably began work on it during September 1874, and he finished it on Christmas Eve. Although the opera divides into separate, symmetrically arranged numbers the music is practically continuous. It might be described as a monothematic work, for the theme associated with Řeřicha's scheming dominates the opera. Dvořák can usually be counted upon to give us something worthwhile when a pathetic aria occurs in a comic opera, but Toník's aria is of interest in other ways too; it presents a preliminary sketch for the languid opening of the twelfth *Slavonic Dance*, and in its middle portion is found an early form of the Trio melody of the G major symphony. This little work has the distinction of being the first Czech comic opera to dispense with spoken dialogue.

The opera remained unperformed until October 2nd, 1881, when a very poor performance was given at the New Czech Theatre, after which it was withdrawn from the repertory, a fate which it did not deserve.

Vanda

In the second half of 1875, immediately after composing his symphony in F major, Dvořák set to work on a grand opera in five acts, which only took him from August 9th to December 22nd to complete. The subject of *Vanda* is concerned with the legend of the pagan Polish princess who swore to sacrifice her life if her people were successful in defeating a German invasion. The heroine is supposed to have been a cousin of Libuše, the heroine of Smetana's opera of that name. It was well known when Dvořák wrote his opera that Smetana had composed *Libuše* some three years earlier, and the younger man's choice of a subject may have been influenced by that knowledge. The libretto of *Vanda* was written by František Zakrejs and Václav Beneš-Šumavský, and is one of the worst that Dvořák used. As Šourek points out, the versification is trite, verging on parody, and it was a mistake to spread the subject over as many as five acts—three would have been sufficient. Dvořák's opera may have been adversely affected by his sorrow at the death of his two-day-old daughter Josefa, but no excuse can be offered for Vanda's inordinately long leave-taking before throwing herself into the Vistula.

The orchestral texture suggests a partial return to the manner of Wagner, but once again representative themes are not used with any consistency. It is worth noting that Prince Roderick, who acts treacherously in the face of Vanda's magnanimity, is given music that fails to suggest villainy. Vanda's vow, the dramatic climax of the fourth act, is conceived with a real sense of dignity, and whereas the singing of her people at that time does not betray the emotion that they are trying to hide, this is suggested by the *tremolando* accompaniment for the strings. Besides the re-appearance of the duet from *Alfred*, the tenth of the *Cypresses* songs is made use of once more. In Act I, when expressing the idea of the supposed intervention of the gods, Dvořák invented a theme which after modification at a later date became the theme associated with the Noon Witch in the symphonic poem of that name. Originally *Vanda* began with a short introduction, but four years afterwards for a revival of the work Dvořák substituted an overture, the only part of the work to be published during his lifetime. This uses the themes of Homena, the sorceress, and Slavoj, Vanda's lover, but the heroine's theme is no longer used, and, rather inappropriately, prominence is given to a new theme suggestive of a Slavonic dance that lacks Polish affinities.

The opera was a failure when it was first produced at the Provisional Theatre on April 17th, 1876, but it received four performances. It gave the composer some valuable experience in painting on a huge canvas, which bore some fruit in his next grand opera, *Dimitrij*, and probably it made him more cautious in the future about accepting any libretto that lay to hand. Dvořák's hopes for his opera were raised later when at the end of 1879 Jauner, to whom Brahms had been speaking about Dvořák, contemplated producing

Vanda at the Vienna Court Opera;[1] the performance, however, did not materialize.

THE CUNNING PEASANT
(THE SCHEMING FARMER)

During the first half of 1877, after an interval of just over a year, Dvořák composed the opera *Šelma sedlák* to a libretto by a medical student, J. O. Veselý, who was convinced that he had the power to be the saviour of the 'wretched literature' of his country. The Czech title is not easy to translate. The rich peasant Martin is a trickster; he is roguish, yet not a rogue in the knavish sense. Since his cunning proves insufficient to force his daughter to wed Václav, the most satisfactory title for the work would be *The Scheming Farmer*. The plot is not very original, for the imbroglio of the disguises is remarkably similar to that in *The Marriage of Figaro*, and the marriage plans have an affinity with those in *The Bartered Bride*, but without the prospective bridegroom being a fool. The work is in two acts, but is sometimes given in three with much alteration in the order of the music, which seems an unnecessary interference with the intentions of the composer.

Once again use is made of representative themes. There is a majestic one for the peasants' homage to the Prince and Princess. Another motif is associated with Martin's scheming. A third is closely linked with Bětuška's love for Jeník, but it also occurs when Martin tries to enlist the Prince's aid for the match between his daughter and Václav. Šourek has labelled a fourth motif 'princely seduction', but if this is a correct assumption it is curious that it is not used when the Prince mistakes his disguised wife for the girl he plans to seduce. His romantic nature is revealed in two melodies which form the basis of his two arias, and one is strongly reminiscent of Mozart's 'Se vuol ballare'. A three-note motif is effectively used to portray the Chamberlain as a vain peacock. Bětuška's touching lament has melodic resemblances with Vendulka's air in the same key in Smetana's *The Kiss*, which was given its first performance the previous November. The charming love duet in the second act has delightful changes from major to minor and back, and also reminds us at one point of a well-known French lullaby. Buffo elements are present in Martin's music, and when the women conspire together, and national characteristics are most obvious in the music of the peasant lovers, in the choral music, and in the striking polka at the beginning of the second act. If Dvořák found it difficult to create music that would fit each of his principal characters like a glove, and that would, for instance, distinguish Bětuška clearly from Jeník, he could on occasions match his music well to a given situation. He was particularly successful where the

[1] Letter from Dvořák to Göbl, 23. XI. 1879.

unfortunate Václav discovers he has been bamboozled by the over-zealous Martin, and storms off in a huff to the village where there are plenty of girls to choose from:

Ex. 3.

Aj,   va - še dce - ra   ne-ní je - di - na,   jet' ho-lek pl - ná   dě - di - na;
(Why,   your   daughter   isn't the only one,   isn't   the village full of girls!)

Outstanding features of the work are the richness of detail in the orchestral texture, and the melodiousness that abounds everywhere.

When Adolf Čech conducted the first performance of this opera at the Provisional Theatre on January 27th, 1878, it was given a warm welcome. Simrock published it, together with *The Stubborn Lovers*, in 1882, and performances then took place at Dresden (24. X. 1882), Hamburg (3. I. 1883) and Vienna (19. XI. 1885). Ernst von Schuch's production at Dresden was highly successful, and has especial significance as the first performance of an opera by Dvořák outside his own country. In Vienna the work was staged at a time when there was exceptionally bitter feeling between Austrians and Czechs, demonstrating students had to be disciplined, and the work was performed with so little enthusiasm that the inevitable result was a fiasco.

The Scheming Farmer demonstrates decisively that Dvořák has passed out of his prentice stage as an operatic composer. He was not a natural dramatist, and found word-setting less easy than composing unfettered by a text. As yet he had not been able to show that he could express deep emotions in a work for the stage, and this libretto did not give him much opportunity for this, but the moods are well contrasted: there is wit and humour, tenderness and pathos, expressions of loyalty to the Prince and uninhibited displays of high spirits. Dvořák's fertile musical imagination flowed freely, and it is clear that his growing success in other fields of his art gave him an ever increasing self-confidence. The work contains much that cannot fail to delight.

Shortly before his first success abroad with the *Slavonic Dances*, Dvořák had asked Julius Zeyer to write a libretto for him, and he received the three-act drama *Šárka*.[1] Although he was not satisfied with this he began making preliminary sketches. When three years later the libretto of *Dimitrij* came into his hands he dismissed Šárka from his mind. In 1889 his interest was

---

[1] Fibich's opera on the same subject uses a different version of the legend. Janáček set Zeyer's text without asking permission, to the annoyance of the author.

again aroused, in fact, as J. V. Sládek reported to the librettist,[1] he had become very enthusiastic. But again he lost interest in the subject. When writing *Kate and the Devil* he adapted the motif he had sketched for Ctirad to suit Jirka.

During December and January 1881/82 Dvořák composed incidental music for F. F. Šamberk's play, *Josef Kajetán Tyl*,[2] consisting of an overture (better known as *My Home*, and discussed elsewhere in this volume), two entractes and music for seven scenes. In practically all the music some reference is made to Tyl's and F. Škroup's 'Kde domov můj?' (Where is my home ?), which was to become the official Czech national anthem in 1918, and the folk-song 'Na tom našem dvoře'. Most of the music takes the form of melodrama, a branch of music in which Fibich was to take such interest a few years later.

DIMITRIJ

For the subject of his next opera Dvořák used a historical account of the false Demetrius, who, having claimed to be the son of Ivan IV (The Terrible) succeeded Boris Godunov and was in turn overthrown by the boyars. Marie Červinková-Riegrová, a gifted woman who inherited an acute political perception from her father, based her libretto on Schiller's dramatic fragment and on Ferdinand Mikovec's drama, which had been performed in Prague in 1855, taking additional hints from Khomyakov and Ostrovsky.[3] Whilst endeavouring to keep as close as possible to historical fact, she makes Dimitrij convinced that he is the rightful heir, even though she herself considered him in reality to have been an imposter. The libretto had been written in answer to a request from Šebor, but when Červinková heard his setting of another libretto of hers, *The Frustrated Wedding*, she realized that he would be unable to do sufficient justice to *Dimitrij*, and so offered it instead to Dvořák. The Czech master was fortunate to have a libretto as good as this, one that possessed such possibilities for lyrical and dramatic expression, but because it has some resemblances to Scribe's librettos he was later charged with having composed an opera on out-moded Meyerbeerian lines. Musically the work owes nothing to Meyerbeer or to Mussorgsky, whose *Boris Godunov* was unknown to him, but Wagner's influence is occasionally felt. Sometimes there are slight anticipations of Dvořák's own D minor symphony, which might be expected in a work written on the eve of his greatest period.

[1] Letter to Zeyer, 15. IV. 1889.
[2] J. K. Tyl, 1808–1856, Czech playwright.
[3] *Dimitri Samozvanetz* by Khomyakov and *Dimitri Samozvanetz and Vasily Shuisky* by Ostrovsky; viz. J. Burghauser's critical edition of Červinková's libretto (Prague, 1961).

Dvořák began the sketch for *Dimitrij* on May 8th, 1881, completing it in less than five months. He did not start work on the full score until December 11th, and owing to further interruptions it was not finished until September 23rd, 1882. The first performance took place most successfully at the New Czech Theatre, Prague, on October 8th of that year, with Moric Anger conducting. Hanslick declared the opera to be 'rich in beautiful and original music, the production of genuine and eminent talent', and he was particularly impressed by the grand concerted pieces and choruses, by the tender charm of the song sung by Xenie after her rescue and of Dimitrij's duet with her in Act IV. However, he was not satisfied with the libretto. He drew attention to the 'continual psychological wavering of the three principal personages', and in particular objected very strongly to the callous murder of Xenie by hired assassins without there being any justifiable motive. This compelled Dvořák, early in 1883, to persuade Červinková to provide an alternative solution, against her better judgment.[1] He later replaced the overture with a prelude, and added some brilliant ballet music for the Polish scene.

The opera was presented in this revised form on November 28th, 1885, at the National Theatre, Prague. *Dimitrij* was performed for the fiftieth time on February 24th, 1892, and on June 2nd that year it was given in Czech by the National Theatre company at the International Exhibition, Vienna. Earlier attempts to have the work performed abroad were unsuccessful.[2]

During 1894, as an indirect result of the conversations he had with Seidl, Dvořák made further revisions to the first, third and fourth acts, which occupy fifty-eight pages of one of his American sketch books. His aim then was to convert the opera into a Wagnerian music drama, but when he heard the new version he was sorry that it lacked the lyricism of the earlier one.[3]

Representative themes, which undergo some transformations, are used for four of the characters. Two of these themes are associated with Dimitrij, one symbolizing his nobility and the other his tragic destiny. They are generally held in reserve for suitable dramatic moments, while Xenie's

[1] She rewrote almost the whole of the fourth act. According to Schiller Xenie was poisoned by Marina, who was the instigator of the crime in her libretto, but in Mikovec's version she stabs herself. The three versions are compared scene by scene in Burghauser, op. cit.

[2] On 17. VI. 1884 Dvořák wrote to Dr. F. L. Rieger, the librettist's father, saying that Gye, the conductor of the Italian Opera at Covent Garden, wanted to present *Dimitrij* under his personal direction during the next winter season. It was not performed there.

[3] The Umělecká beseda vocal score (1912), which is largely based on the earlier versions of the opera, also incorporates a few of the revisions of 1894, but gives no indication of the extent of these changes. Publication of the score in the critical edition is awaited.

theme, which epitomizes her sweet nature, is much more often made the life blood of the musical texture. A brief melodic fragment suggests Marina's love for Dimitrij, but at other times she is given music with virile mazurka rhythms to represent the other side of her character, the proud and jealous Polish princess. It is unfortunate that, when she overhears Dimitrij tell Xenie that he will make her his czarina after dissolving his marriage with Marina, she sings phrases that are identical with theirs. Neither Marfa, Ivan

Ex. 4.

the Terrible's widow, nor the Patriarch are allotted special themes, but Shuisky has one that is brief and telling.

The libretto offered Dvořák excellent opportunities in the big choral scenes, and he rose to the occasion. A Russian atmosphere is immediately suggested by the crowd in the first act, but the climax for the chorus comes in the huge fresco in Act II, when the Poles and Russians are at loggerheads. It is surprising to find here the two halves of the theme of the composer's first *Slavonic Dance* adapted to make an effective mazurka.

Dvořák tended to sacrifice speed of action to the demands of musical form, which sets serious problems for those producers who are fully aware of the dangers of cutting. From the composer's angle it enabled him to concentrate on lyricism, to make this a more melodious work than any of his other operas. It has some particularly lovely moments, in some of which unexpected harmonic touches and characteristically Dvořákian orchestral colouring play an important part. The scene in which Marfa is about to take her oath is impressive, and the long duet between Dimitrij and Marina in Act III is notable for its sustained dramatic interest. A delightful episode occurs when Xenie, seeking refuge from some drunken Poles in the vault of the czars, sings a folk-like song which is interrupted by an off-stage chorus and is combined with comments from the love-sick Dimitrij, who sees her for the first time from his place of concealment. Xenie's theme is woven into the particularly beautiful ending of their duet in the last act (Ex. 4).

THE JACOBIN

Dvořák had asked Štolba to collaborate with him in a comic opera in two or three acts, and after completing *Dimitrij* he invited Červinková to do the same, but she thought that comedy was not her *métier*. However, the idea of having a schoolmaster *Musikant* as a central figure occurred to her by chance. She then evolved the scenario of *The Jacobin*, secured Dvořák's provisional approval, and wrote the libretto. At that time Dvořák was being severely tempted to make a bid for success in the opera houses of Vienna and Germany, for which her libretto was unsuited. He thought *The Jacobin* was in some respects reminiscent of other Czech operas, and he would have preferred a subject with greater contrasts, 'something like *Carmen*' as he said.[1] Hanslick was convinced that Dvořák would succeed with a German text and subject, and consequently Baron Hoffmann, the *Generalintendant* of the Vienna Court Opera, sent him two librettos. He also considered setting an adaptation of Kleist's *The Broken Pitcher*, as well as *Count Frederick* and some Czech subjects, and in January 1886 he asked Červinková to prepare a libretto of *The Dragon's Coronet*, but she refused. Writing to her on August 31st, he said, 'Regarding *The Jacobin*, we shall still have to give it more and more thought. It will be necessary to cut parts, to add others, etc., etc., of course with your agreement.' Later, in a letter of August 1st, 1887, she showed how annoyed she was that he had dilly-dallied so long over her libretto:

[1] The first Prague performance of *Carmen* took place on January 3rd, 1884. According to Bráfová's 'Rieger, Smetana, Dvořák', he knew the score some two years earlier. It was obviously the dramatic and lyrical characteristics of this opera that appealed to Dvořák, yet that type of subject seems quite foreign to his nature.

If you don't fancy and aren't enthusiastic about *The Jacobin* . . . please don't be afraid and return the libretto to me. If those who dissuade you about *The Jacobin* provide you with a libretto that would satisfy you better, I should cordially wish you well. You ask for another libretto, romantic and fantastic. However, I have other work ahead . . . all the same I have such great respect for the art of music and for your art especially that I should have been ready to attempt something that would inspire you to bring honour to Czech art and the Czech name—if there is not another who would satisfy you better than I . . . Why should I write a new libretto ? That would give me trouble for several months, perhaps with you over what I should have written . . . and then there will be criticisms again . . . and instead of one libretto I shall have two lying idle . . .

This letter appears to have done much towards making Dvořák take action at last, after a period of five years without composing any new opera. By that time the spiritual crisis, which brought in its train such splendid works as the F minor trio, the *Husitská* overture and the symphony in D minor, had been resolved, and once again he was satisfied with a characteristically Czech subject.

He commenced work on November 10th, 1887, and brought it to a conclusion on November 18th a year later. Adolf Čech conducted the first performance at the National Theatre, Prague, on February 12th, 1889, and within five years the opera had been given thirty-four times. There were some criticisms of both the libretto and the music. When Dvořák asked Červinková to make revisions she responded readily, transferring the conversation with the old Count from the second act to the third, deleting the arrest of Jiří and adding Bohuš's pronouncement that he is the Count's son. She did this in 1894, a year before her death, and between February 17th and December 7th, 1897, shortly before composing *Kate and the Devil*, Dvořák rewrote the last two acts. The new version was presented at the National Theatre on June 19th, 1898, with Čech again conducting.

Červinková borrowed some of the chief characters of *The Jacobin* from Jirásek's *At the Ducal Court*. These are: the kindly schoolmaster *Musikant* (Benda), his pretty musical daughter (Terinka) who loves a youth (Jiří), who in turn is jealous because the girl's father encourages the attentions of a supposed Italian singer (who becomes Filip, the burgrave, in Dvořák's opera). The plot, however, is her own. When composing this work Dvořák thought with affection of his former teacher at Zlonice, Liehmann, who also had a daughter Terinka.[1] He must have particularly enjoyed setting the

[1] An autograph dated September 7th, 1858, that Dvořák wrote for Terinka, is preserved in the Dvořák Museum at Zlonice. Written in copper plate handwriting, it is a stanza of formal verse asking her to remember her faithful friend if at some future time she should be overcome with grief.

charming singing-class scene. He informed Simrock that he was composing the opera for his own pleasure.

Dvořák's attempt to portray his characters musically is very closely linked with his use of recurring themes, of which there are several. Most important of all is the motif that symbolizes Bohuš's filial love and his eventual return to favour. This is used in the highly original and most effective lullaby which his wife, Julie, sings in order to remind the old Count of his deceased wife and melt his hard heart. It is first heard played by the flute when Bohuš and his wife appear incognito in the town at the beginning of the opera, and it begins with the rising and falling fourths that are discussed elsewhere as a Dvořákian fingerprint. Jiří's attitude to the burgrave is vividly shown in the mocking tune he sings, which returns whenever the two are on the stage together, and with which the burgrave turns the tables on Jiří, when he converts it from $\frac{2}{4}$ to $\frac{3}{4}$ time. The character of the schoolmaster is somewhat sentimentalized, his theme being that of the serenade which he composed as a welcome for the Count. A chromatic descent of chords or a descending chromatic scale is heard when the dread Jacobins are mentioned. There are two themes associated with the Count. One of these suggests his nobility, and the second, a chromatically rising motif, symbolizes his remembrance of his son's childhood. When this second theme is used the Count emerges musically as a vividly human character whose emotions conflict with what he believes to be his duty. Dvořák had recently passed through a situation in which he was somewhat similarly placed, and but for this he would no doubt have been incapable of setting this scene so convincingly.

Problems of movement and transition are satisfactorily solved, and in the first act the spirit of the dance is never far away. The subject of the opera suited Dvořák admirably, and he showed himself equal to the task of setting it. In this work he was truer to himself than in any other of his operas.

Shortly after his arrival in New York, Mrs. Jeannette Thurber interested Dvořák in the idea of composing an opera based on Longfellow's *Song of Hiawatha*. She had difficulty in securing an adequate libretto, and eventually was obliged to apply to Vienna for one. During the composer's second autumn or winter in America he made sketches of themes for Minnehaha, Hiawatha's childhood, Gitche Manito's fanfare for the assembly of warriors, a dance for the wedding (in the style of a *skočná*!), and the twitterings of birds. Later on, during the period of the 'cello concerto, he made further sketches, including the following draft of 'Onaway! awake, beloved!' in which it is seen that he was not quite at ease in setting English words (Ex. 5). By the time the libretto arrived from Vienna and a translation had been made, Dvořák was deciding to leave America, and consequently he abandoned the idea of writing an opera on this subject.

Ex. 5.

Reconstruction of possible intended version

On - a - way! a-wake, be - lo - ved! Thou the wild-flo - wer of the

First draft

for - est! [Thou the wild-bird of the] prai - rie! Thou with eyes so soft [and]

fawn-like! If thou on - ly look-est at me, I am hap-py, I am hap-py,

As the li-lies of the prai-rie When they feel the dew up-on them!

Two years later *The Athenaeum* stated (14. VIII. 1897): 'It is reported that Dr. Dvořák has for some time past been engaged upon the composition of an operatic version of *Uncle Tom's Cabin*. He formed the idea to write an opera on this subject while he was still residing in the United States.' There appears to be no more substance in musical gossip of this kind than in the information given earlier by *Dalibor*, *The Athenaeum* and other periodicals that the composer had nearly completed *Hiawatha*, and the rumour spread by *The Musical Standard* (25 .VII. 1885; 22. VIII. 1885) that he intended to set two operatic libretti by Mrs. Aimée Beringer, wife of the pianist, firstly *Samson and Delilah* and then *Twelfth Night*.

KATE AND THE DEVIL

Dvořák's last three operas show him turning once again towards the methods of Wagner. This phase was probably initiated as a direct result of his friendship with Anton Seidl, the enthusiastic Wagnerian conductor who gave the first performance of the *New World* symphony. These works also show the delight he took in the realm of phantasy during his last years, a delight which became evident at the time of the symphonic poems based on subjects from Erben's *Bouquet of Folk Tales* (1853), but which had already been foreshadowed twelve years earlier when he composed *The Spectre's Bride*. The story of *Kate and the Devil*, which makes an excellent subject for a comic opera, comes from a well-known folk tale that was included in Božena Němcová's *Fairy Tales* (1845) and was the subject of a three-act play by J. K. Tyl (1850). Adolf Wenig, a young schoolmaster who was a nephew of F. A. Šubert, the director of the Prague National Theatre, prepared the libretto.

Dvořák started sketching his opera on May 5th, 1898, and began to prepare the full score twelve days later. His daughter Otilie's marriage to Josef Suk on November 17th, the same day that Dvořák and his wife celebrated their silver wedding, was a temporary but enjoyable interruption to his work. By February 27th the opera was finished. The first performance took place

Ex. 6a.

Tempo di Marcia

Ex. 6b.

Andante maestoso

very successfully on November 23rd, 1899, under the direction of Adolf Čech at the National Theatre, Prague. In December of the following year Dvořák was awarded a first prize of 2,000 Kronen for *Kate and the Devil* by the Czech Academy of Sciences and Arts. The first foreign performance took place in April 1909 at Bremen, and early the following year the Brno Opera Company took it to Vienna. When the work was produced at Oxford on November 22nd, 1932, it was the first of the composer's operas to be performed in Britain.

In all his previous operas representative themes had been used, but generally rather unsystematically. In *Kate and the Devil* Dvořák shows himself to be by no means wholehearted in adopting Wagnerian methods, but there is a more conspicuous use of the *leitmotiv* principle, without the symphonic interweaving of themes, and at times there is a much more deliberate utilization of declamatory vocal writing than hitherto. This latter is seen more particularly in the parts for the Princess and Lucifer. Traces of the set number are still found even in the Czech composer's last opera.

Dvořák uses motifs to suggest groups of people, and variants on them to represent specific characters. The peasants' theme is found in a variety of forms, and among them is one showing Jirka in a defiant mood and another portraying the oppression of the people (Exx. 6a and 6b). Besides Kate's use of a diminution of this basic theme, her garrulous nature is vividly depicted when she takes over, in addition, a bagpipe melody, which in turn undergoes further transformations in the ballet performed for her benefit in hell. The angular hell motive:

Ex. 7.

is put to excellent use. It appears in diatonic form in the fantastic Lucifer melody, which runs for eleven beats of $\frac{3}{4}$ time and is immediately repeated. Similarly it occurs in Marbuel's description of his fine red castle, strikingly scored for cor anglais, bass clarinet, bassoon, 'cellos, tubas and harp. When the villagers denounce their feudal overlord the Princess, and her steward, this motif is interjected to suggest the fate that awaits them.

If the Princess's pentatonic theme, sketched by Dvořák in America, is intended to express her penitence, it is hardly adequate for the purpose. It is perhaps unfortunate, too, that although there are bitter references to her several times in the first two acts, at which the above-mentioned oppression theme occurs, no personal motif is heard until the last act, when she appears for the first time. It does not seem to have occurred to Dvořák to find a theme for her that would portray her basic character and which could then be changed to suggest her fear and remorse. These are suggested in other ways. It is strange too that Lucifer should pronounce judgment on the Princess as if it were a somewhat unpleasant duty, instead of showing relish at the promise of securing such a distinguished victim to augment his kingdom. If Dvořák's devils were less kindly creatures, scaring Marbuel and saving the Princess would make an even stronger dramatic impact in the one act that is genuinely dramatic. The second act could have been brought to a more effective climax if Kate's dance with Jirka had lasted a little longer. The brilliant ballet that precedes this, in which Dvořák yet again displays his exceptional genius in the composition of dances, tends to overshadow this final stroke of drama, and Kate is danced out of hell without much rise in the emotional temperature. Even if the opera occasionally lacks the pure essence of Dvořák, everywhere else it shows many facets of the composer's genius, notably in the freshness of its inspiration, the richness of resource and the lively reaction to dramatic stimuli. The work is without question the composer's finest comic opera.

RUSALKA

Dvořák was anxious to follow *Kate and the Devil* with another opera as soon as possible. Having obtained a libretto by Karel Pippich, *The Death of Vlasta*, he began sketching some themes, but made very little progress.[1] Hearing that Nedbal, Foerster and Suk had rejected a libretto written by Jaroslav Kvapil, a young man who was too timid to approach a composer as renowned as Dvořák to find out if he would be interested in it, and that Šubert, the Director of the National Theatre, warmly recommended him to make use of it, Dvořák read *Rusalka* and was captivated by it. Kvapil's plot derives mainly from de la Motte Fouqué's *Undine*, with additions from Andersen's *Little Mermaid*, and occasional suggestions from Hauptmann's *Sunken Bell*, the French Mélusine legend, and possibly also from von Steinsberg's *The Dumb Forest Maiden*. Kvapil stated that Bertald and Huldbrand in Fouqué's tale were the models for his Princess and Prince, and that the suggestion that Rusalka should be tempted to kill the Prince came direct from Andersen. The *Undine* operas of E. T. A. Hoffmann and Lortzing exercised no direct influence, even though Kvapil, and of course Dvořák, knew the latter. Dargomizhsky's *Russalka*, based on a ballad of Pushkin, is totally unrelated. As a great admirer of Erben and of the folk-lore of his country, the librettist succeeded in absorbing these fairy tales of other lands,

---

[1] This libretto was soon set by Ostrčil, and his opera was publicly performed in 1904.

and presenting them in a characteristically Czech setting, and in the spirit of Erben.

Dvořák began sketching the first act of his new opera on April 21st, 1900. The full score occupied him from June 28th until November 27th that year. Kovařovic conducted the first performance at the Prague National Theatre on March 31st, 1901, and the work was an immediate success, the greatest that Dvořák ever experienced in a work for the stage. *Rusalka* has always been accepted by the people of Czechoslovakia as one of the very few best-loved Czech operas, and an essential part of their national artistic heritage. Hearing of its outstanding success, Mahler planned to perform it in Vienna; it was rehearsed, and after some delays it was to be ready for production in March 1902. Mahler had secured better terms than usual for Dvořák, and the composer made numerous visits to the Austrian capital to ensure that everything possible would be done to make the performance a success. However, he seems to have been suspicious in some way, and did not sign his contract. W. Hesch, who was to have sung the Water Goblin, fell ill, and the production was postponed until the next season, but it did not take place. The first performance abroad was given in Slovene at Ljubljana in the spring of 1908, three years after M. Urbánek had published the vocal score. In the same year it was performed at Zagreb. *Rusalka* was given in Vienna in the autumn of 1910 by the Brno Company, but it did not make any further progress abroad until the Bratislava National Theatre Company presented it in Barcelona (21. II. 1924) and Madrid (15. III. 1924), and the Olomouc Opera Company repeated it in Vienna (9. V. 1924), where it made a deep impression.

It is probably true to say that Dvořák was enchanted when he wrote *Rusalka*. He was fascinated by the libretto, and became completely absorbed in creating in the most vivid way possible the fantastic atmosphere of the realm of nixies and water sprites, of witches and forest fairies. A measure of his success is that, in contrast, the world of mortals recedes into the background and appears less real, and we find that our sympathies are almost wholly with Rusalka and her father the Water Goblin, and to a lesser extent with the Prince and Ježibaba the witch. The imperious foreign Princess is an entirely unsympathetic character. It was an admirable idea of Kvapil's to introduce the comic Forest Ranger and Scullion to purvey the latest Court gossip, and to comment on and keep the audience informed about the state of the Prince's relationship with Rusalka, thereby taking over some of the functions of a Greek chorus.

The forest folk in general, fairies and witch, share the staccato motif with which the first act opens. In addition to this Ježibaba acquires a personal theme that grows out of a fragment of her incantation, and which later takes on what Šourek describes as the 'nature rhythm'. The repeated notes of the collective 'forest' theme link it with the Water Goblin's motif, which as Šourek has pointed out, was in all probability a musical expression of the 'brekekekes krak krak' of Hauptmann's Nickelmann:

Ex. 8.

This theme is splendidly used to suggest the grotesque ruler of the water kingdom, and his deep forebodings of the tragedy that will result from his daughter's desire to be granted human form and a soul in exchange for the power of speech, coupled with the threat of damnation if the Prince is untrue to her.

The meaning of Dvořák's motifs is not always clear. The three chromatically descending Wagnerian chords may represent sorrow and foreboding, and the tremulous rising figure may suggest the water spirits' fear for Rusalka, but if so why is the second of these heard so early in the opera before her aspirations are known?[1] Rusalka's curse motif is all the more effective for being sparingly used. Telling use is made of a four-note theme that seems to suggest the magical allurements of the water kingdom and its inhabitants, and more specifically the fatal magnetic attraction that Rusalka exerts over the Prince. As he is dying in her arms it is played by treble woodwind and strings as in ex. 9. (See also ex. 4b on p. 62).

The Rusalka theme is to be found in three slightly different versions in Dvořák's American sketch books. This beautiful melody at last found its place as the central pivot of his greatest opera after it had haunted him for some years without a use having been found for it. Dvořák made the most of the chances it offered him for continuous lyrical expression, and also moulded it and modified it to meet the changing dramatic situations, with one notable exception. If we compare the way this theme is scored when Rusalka first appears with that when the distraught Prince searches her out in the last act, we find that the second time the orchestration is a little fuller than before, and that no recognition has been made of the fact that she has been changed into a will-o'-the-wisp. Since Dvořák did not try to surmount the problem of having a dumb heroine in a way similar to Weber's in *Sylvana*, a love duet was only possible in the last act, after she had recovered her speech.

It would have been preferable if the trio in $\frac{6}{8}$ time in the third act for the forest fairies had been less like the chorus at the castle, and it is a pity that

[1] Both motifs occur on p. 34 of the Orbis vocal score, shortly after the Water Goblin has appeared for the first time.

Ex. 9.

the Water Goblin repeats the wedding guests' song. Judging by the polonaise rhythms, the Princess was probably Polish, yet we find her inconsistent, sometimes singing in Italian style. A few cadences are rather too conventional, and occasionally Wagnerian harmony rears its head too obviously. But these are small points. The unfolding of the drama is spacious, and through much of it the note of tragedy can be detected. This, however, is tempered periodically with teasing dances of fairies and other diversions. In the work as a whole it is the rich combination of the lyrical with the fantastic that makes *Rusalka* unique among Dvořák's operas.

ARMIDA

In his reminiscences Kvapil related the following: 'Early on the Monday following the première of *Rusalka* Dvořák came to see us in the theatre office. He was in a very good humour. When he saw me he immediately said: "Now quick, quick—a new libretto!" I replied: "I haven't one, Master!" And he said: "Then write something quickly while I'm in the mood! And provide a nice role for Maturová!"'[1] Kvapil promised to write one, but failed to do so. While hunting in the theatre archives the composer came across a libretto of *Cinderella* that Hostinský had written for Rozkošný, whose opera on this subject had been performed in 1885. Hostinský gave Dvořák his permission to use the libretto provided Rozkošný agreed, but nothing more was

[1] Maturová had sung the part of Rusalka at the first performance, and she also took the leading role when *Armida* was presented.

288

heard of the matter. Fifteen months passed without a suitable subject being found. Ultimately, following in the footsteps of some fifty other composers, Dvořák decided to compose *Armida*, using a libretto that Jaroslav Vrchlický had written for Kovařovic, who had abandoned his project shortly after completing the first act. Before the libretto had reached Dvořák's hands Bendl and Fibich had given it their consideration.

It was surprising that, for the first time since *Alfred*, Dvořák should have chosen a subject that was not Slavonic. But good texts were scarce, and he may have felt under a slight obligation to the distinguished Czech poet, whose book for an oratorio, *St. Ethelbert*, he had so recently rejected. With *Rusalka* a great success and likely to be performed in Vienna, he may well have been tempted to select so famous a subject in order to try to make a stronger bid for operatic fame in the world's leading opera houses. Undoubtedly, following *Rusalka*, the powerful love drama appealed to him, as also did the religious theme and the scenes in Armida's magic gardens. Furthermore he was reminded of *Parsifal*, and more especially *Tannhäuser*, which he believed to be Wagner's greatest opera. Wagner was becoming an increasingly strong attraction to him at that time. When Richter wrote saying: 'Shan't I perhaps see you at Bayreuth? *You musn't fail to be there!*', he replied, 'It is my dearest wish to go to Bayreuth this year, but it is so difficult to get there!'[1]

Could *Armida* possibly become a Czech *Tannhäuser*?

Progress on the opera did not proceed entirely smoothly at first, and it took Dvořák from March 11th, 1902, until June 4th the following year to complete the sketch of the four acts. He was at work on the full score from September 2nd, 1902, until June 29th, 1903. The overture was finished on August 23rd. Finding the libretto overlong he asked Vrchlický to shorten it to three acts, but could not get him to agree. He was disappointed that Picka, and not Kovařovic, the chief conductor, was to conduct his opera at the National Theatre, and several times he had arguments with the former during rehearsals. When the first performance took place on March 25th, 1904, it was not a success.[2] Emanuel Chvála, the critic, complained that the scenic arrangements were unimaginative and primitive, especially in the magical scenes, and so did much to destroy the illusion. Vrchlický has been blamed for his hasty versification. This fault was not observed by the critics from abroad, who bestowed greater praise on the opera than the Czechs. The opera has seldom been revived, which is unfortunate. It was not until

[1] 24. I. 1902; 11. II. 1902.
[2] According to Otakar Dvořák, the composer's son, the reason that Kovařovic refused to conduct the work himself was that he had at one time started to set the same libretto. Eventually he realized that by his refusal he had done Dvořák a serious injury. I am indebted to Dr. Richard Stretti for this information.

February 19th, 1961, when it was performed at Bremen, that it was given for the first time outside Czechoslovakia.

Vrchlický, who had at an earlier date made a complete translation of *Gerusalemme liberata*, departed far more from Tasso's original than Quinault had. He makes Armida hesitant to go into the Crusader's camp until Ismen, by means of his magical powers, conjures up a picture of it, in which she recognizes Rinaldo whom she has dreamed about and to whom she has already lost her heart. Rinaldo, instead of repelling Armida's seductive charms, falls deeply in love and escapes with her from the camp. Ismen, too, is in love with her, and to further his schemes it is he who gives the archangel Michael's diamond shield to Ubald and Sven to break the hold the enchantress has on Rinaldo, and Ismen, not Armida herself, destroys her magic palace and gardens. Quinault had finished this libretto with the broken-hearted Armida intending to perish buried in the ruins of her palace. Vrchlický takes the drama further, and brilliantly substitutes for her meek submission after her attempted suicide near the battlefield (Canto XX) a fight similar to that between Tancred and Clorinda (Canto XII). As a result of these changes Rinaldo emerges as a rather more convincing character than in Lully's and Gluck's operas. He enslaves himself to Armida voluntarily when on home ground, and not when held as her captive on an enchanted island surrounded by sirens. He kills her unwittingly, but with her connivance.

The amount of wizardry in the third act strikes the modern opera-goer as excessive. Apart from the talisman used by the two knights, Ismen destroys the palace, which is then immediately rebuilt because of the power of Armida's love for Rinaldo, but finally, when she is grief-stricken at his departure, the monarch of Syria is able to repeat his work of devastation. This incredible series of events has been introduced because his love has been thwarted, but something closer to Tasso would be preferable, and less spectacular evidence of his rage would carry greater conviction. At Bremen the experiment was tried of eliminating from the opera all use of magic arts, but this is not the best solution. The drama is stronger if rare feminine beauty, aided by witchcraft, is opposed by Christian loyalty and faith just when the lovers' passion reaches its climax, and proves to have insufficient power to overcome them.[1]

Dvořák's profound veneration for Wagner is more clearly seen in *Armida* than in any other work of his. We find extensive passages that are reminiscent

---

[1] It is not essential that the shield should possess magical properties: as a sacred symbol it could serve to work on Rinaldo's conscience and so bring about a similar result. Although advocating the retention of a limited amount of sorcery in Dvořák's opera, I am convinced that Wagner was wrong to rely on a love potion to stimulate the unquenchable passion of Tristan and Isolde.

of the German composer's harmonic style, and others in which he imitates his methods of handling the orchestra. There is greater reliance on *leitmotive* than in *Rusalka*, and Dvořák's Cross motif is a near quotation of the beginning of the Grail theme. The influence of Verdi and Meyerbeer, about whom he made favourable remarks, may also be seen in the choral scenes, in the use of brass, and also sometimes in the vocal lines. Elsewhere there are reminders of Dvořák's American style, as in Armida's delightful 'I hurried after a slender gazelle', sung when in a trance, and more especially in the molto tranquillo section of her duet with Rinaldo in the second act. There are not many opportunities for the use of dance elements except in the charming magic garden scenes, in which the composer had no difficulty in creating the right atmosphere. Oddly enough, here fairies and cupids sport to the strains of a waltz derived from the Ismen theme. The motifs are usually used consistently, but we observe that the expected Cross theme is absent when Armida is baptized. It is understandable that it might be appropriate to use the love theme when Rinaldo is moody and apathetic before he has ever seen Armida, but there is no explanation why the theme representing the Cross and the liberation of Jerusalem should at one point be used to suggest her power.[1] A siren song, later used in the magic shield scene and also when Rinaldo prays, may be presumed to represent supernatural power, either pagan or Christian.

Some of the transformations of themes suggest Liszt's influence rather than Wagner's. Metamorphosis is an outstanding feature of this opera, and is perhaps seen at its best when Rinaldo's theme in its heroic form (*a*) is compared with versions heard during his fine soliloquy, when he lies exhausted after having been rescued by the two knights (*b*), and when he recovers his full stature as a noble warrior, significantly presented in a minor key (*c*) (Exx. 10a, 10b and 10c). There is a hint of the dark mood of the last act of *Tristan* in the second of these quotations, in which the love motif is relegated to the lower strings and the Crusaders' theme is played in disembodied form by a muted trumpet. Ismen is clearly drawn, and is at his best when in the disguise of an old man he sings 'On the threshold of vile deserts'. With Maturová in mind, Dvořák put much of his finest music into the name part, and into her final duet with Rinaldo.

When he wrote *Armida* Dvořák was at the height of his powers, but the subject offered him personally rather less opportunities than *Rusalka*. Just as one would expect, it shows him seeking out fresh solutions to operatic problems, for he disliked repeating himself and was not one to rest on his laurels. Some people may be uneasy at the distance he travelled along the Wagnerian path, since they notice less of the familiar Dvořák, but if they

---

[1] Orbis vocal score, p. 234.

look more carefully, they will discover that only he could have written it. This work, in fact, represents the extreme to which the composer went in the direction he chose for himself. It was written in all sincerity, in a quasi-realist style he had made his own, and must be regarded as representative of him in the final stage of his career. Since he poured into this work so much fine music it is absurd that it should be so sadly neglected.

On August 31st, 1903, Dvořák began to make some preliminary sketches for yet another opera, *Horymír*, on a libretto by Rudolf Stárek, but they remain fragments. Among them is the following eloquent theme:[1]

Ex. 11.

Smetana had a more innate theatrical sense than Dvořák, but through determination and perseverance the younger man overcame most of his operatic problems, though he was never able to bring about sudden electrifying dramatic changes as Verdi could. Primarily his strength lay in lyricism, coupled with a lively and rich imaginative sense and a keen feeling for tonal colouring and vital rhythm, but he was able finally to show that he possessed considerable dramatic power. Having a feeling for formal balance, he needed time to establish a mood, and clearly seen here is his experience of instrumental forms, which for a Czech was unrivalled. Consequently his work has a feeling of spaciousness, but from the strictly dramatic angle it tends towards prolixity. Smetana had tended to idealize his characters, whereas Dvořák presented his with a stronger sense of realism. In his later years he was generally fortunate over his libretti, more so perhaps than his compatriot. Even though Dvořák is not one of the world's greatest dramatic composers, he takes his place with Smetana and Janácek as one of the three leading operatic composers of his country. It is not sufficiently well known outside his own country that his operas are a rich storehouse and offer many fine rewards.

[1] Quoted from Šourek's *Život a dílo Antonína Dvořáka*, Vol. IV.

Appendix I

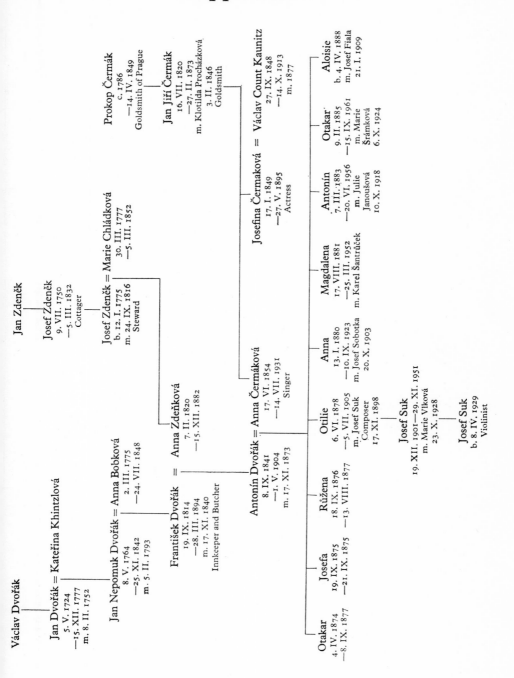

Appendix II

FRANZ SCHUBERT
by Antonín Dvořák
(In co-operation with Henry T. Finck)

IN less than three years, on January 31st, 1897, a century will have elapsed since Franz Schubert was born, and sixty-nine years since he died. He lived only thirty-two years, yet in this short time—or, more accurately in eighteen years—he wrote more than eleven hundred compositions. This fact, in itself sufficiently astounding, becomes more so when we consider the conditions of his life as described by his biographers—his poverty and privations, from his early years, when we find him suffering from hunger and cold, and unable to buy music-paper to write down his inspirations, to his last year, when typhoid fever ended his career and left his heirs about ten dollars, not enough to pay for his funeral expenses—and no wonder, since even in his last years twenty cents was considered pay enough for some of those songs on which many publishers have since grown rich.

Surprise has often been expressed that the Viennese (among whom he lived) and the publishers should not have appreciated him more substantially; yet it is not difficult to find reasons for this in the circumstances of the case. While a pianist or singer may find immediate recognition, a composer, especially if he has so original a message to deliver as Schubert, has to bide his time. We must bear in mind how very young he was when he died. Dr. Hanslick has urged, in defence of the Viennese, that only seven years elapsed between the publication of Schubert's first works and his death, and that during his lifetime he became known chiefly as a song composer; and songs were at that time not sung at public concerts, but only in the domestic circle. Moreover, Rossini on the one hand, and Beethoven on the other, overshadowed the modest young Schubert, and it is significant that Beethoven himself did not discover his genius till the year of his own death. As regards Schubert's orchestral works, we must remember that orchestras were not at that time what they are today. The best Viennese organization, the Gesellschaft der Musikfreunde, found the Symphony in C 'too long and too difficult' at the rehearsal and substituted an earlier work. This was in 1828, the year of the composer's death. Ten years later the zealous Schumann discovered the great Symphony in C and took it to Leipsic, where the equally enthusiastic Mendelssohn secured for it a noteworthy success. In Vienna too it was taken up again in the following year, but only two movements were given, and these were separated by a Donizetti aria! Three years later Habeneck attempted to produce this symphony in Paris, but the band rebelled over the first movement, and the same result followed in London, two years later still, when Mendelssohn put it in rehearsal for a Philharmonic concert. These things seem strange to us, but they are historic facts and help to explain why Schubert, with all his melody and spontaneity, made his way so slowly to popular appreciation. He was young, modest, and unknown, and musicians did not hesitate to slight a symphony which they would have felt bound to study, had it borne the name of Beethoven or Mozart.

But his fame has grown steadily from year to year, and will grow greater still in the next century. Rubinstein has, perhaps gone farther than any one, not only in including Schubert in the list of those he considers the five greatest composers—Bach, Beethoven, Schubert, Chopin, Glinka—but in exclaiming, 'Once more, a thousand times more, Bach, Beethoven and Schubert are the highest summits in music' (*Die Musik und Ihre Meister*, p. 50). I am asked whether I approve of this classification. Such questions are very difficult to answer. I should follow Rubinstein in including Schubert in the list of the very greatest composers, but I should not follow him in omitting Mozart. Schubert and Mozart have much in common; in both we find the same delicate sense of instrumental colouring, the same spontaneous and irrepressible flow of melody, the same instinctive command of the means of expression, and the same versatility in all the branches of their art. In their amazing fertility, too, they were alike; and herein lay, and still lies, one of the greatest impediments to their popular appreciation. The longer I live, the more I become convinced that composers, like authors, mostly follow the impulse of writing too much. There are a few exceptions, like Berlioz and Chopin—not to forget Wagner, who condensed all his genius into ten great music-dramas. Would it not have been better for their immortality and the perpetual delight of mankind, had Rossini written ten operas instead of forty, Donizetti seven instead of seventy? Even Bach's magnificent cantatas would have had a better chance of appreciation if there were not quite so many (the first 34 volumes of Bach's collected works contain 160 of them). At the same time we should be sorry to lose a single one of them.

If we are often amazed at the prevailing ignorance and neglect of many of the great works of the masters, we are at the same time obliged to confess that they themselves are largely to blame; they have given us too much. However, it is easier to give advice than to follow it. There is in creative minds an impulse to write, which it is difficult to curb, and this was especially the case with Schubert, whose genius was like a spring which nothing but exhaustion could stop from flowing. Fortunately the works of the great masters have at last been made accessible in complete editions; the Schubert collection is just being completed by Breitkopf and Härtel. It contains many gems unknown to the public, or even to the profession; and it now behoves artists and conductors to select from this embarrassing wealth what most deserves revival.

Schubert contributed to every form of his art; he was, as I have said, as versatile as Mozart, to whom he bears so many points of resemblance. But in one respect these two masters differ widely. Mozart was greatest in the opera, where Schubert was weakest. Schubert's attempts to exercise his genius and improve his fortunes by writing operas came at an unpropitious moment— a time when Vienna was so Rossini-mad that even Beethoven was discouraged from writing for the stage. It took several rebuffs to discourage Schubert; indeed, though all his attempts failed, he is said to have had further operatic projects at the time of his last illness. He was always unlucky with his librettos, which are, without exception, inadequate. There were other untoward circumstances; yet the chief cause of his failure lay, after all, in the nature of his genius, which was lyrical, and not dramatic, or, at any rate, not theatrical. When Liszt produced 'Alfonso und Estrella' at Weimar in 1854, it had only a *succès d'estime*, and Liszt himself confessed that its performance must be regarded merely as *ein Act der Pietät*, and an execution of historic justice. He called attention to the strange fact that Schubert, who in his songs contributed such picturesque and expressive accompaniments, should in this opera have assigned to the instruments such a subordinate rôle that it seemed little more than a pianoforte accompaniment arranged for the orchestra. At the same time, as Liszt very properly adds, Schubert influenced the progress of opera *indirectly*, by showing in his *songs* how closely poetry can be wedded to music, and that it can be emotionally intensified by its impassioned accents. Nor must we overlook the fact that there are in these Schubert operas not a few melodies, beautiful as such, which we can enjoy at home or in the concert hall. These melodies were too lyrical in style to save the operas; they lacked also the ornamental brilliancy and theatrical dash which enabled Rossini to succeed temporarily with poor librettos, and with a less genuine dramatic instinct than Schubert has shown in some of his songs such as the 'Erl King' and especially the 'Doppelgänger' where we come across chords and modulations that affect us like the weird harmonies of *Ortrud's* scenes in *Lohengrin*.

Besides the opera there is only one department of music in which Schubert has not in some of his efforts reached the highest summit of musical achievement. His sacred compositions, although very beautiful from a purely musical point of view, usually lack the true ecclesiastical atmosphere—a remark which may be applied, in a general way, to Haydn and Mozart, too. To my mind, the three composers who have been most successful in revealing the inmost spirit of religious music are Palestrina, in whom Roman

Catholic music reaches its climax; Bach, who embodies the Protestant spirit; and Wagner, who has struck the true ecclesiastical chord in the Pilgrims' Chorus of *Tannhäuser*, and especially in the first and thirds acts of *Parsifal*. Compared with these three masters, other composers appear to have made too many concessions to worldly and purely musical factors—of course, not without exceptions. One of these exceptions is Mozart's Requiem, especially the 'Dies Irae', which moves us as few compositions do, and attunes the soul to reverence and worship. Such exceptions may also be found among Schubert's sacred compositions. *Miriam's Song of Victory* is a wonderful work, as are some of his masses. In the Psalms, too, he has achieved great things, especially the one for female voices in A flat major, which is celestial without worldly admixtures. It must not be forgotten, too, that the notions as to what is truly sacred in music may differ somewhat among nations and individuals, like the sense of humour. To the Viennese of their time the masses of Haydn, Mozart and Schubert probably did not seem too *gemüth-lich*, as the Germans say—too genial and sentimental. As for Schubert himself, although he was one of the most modest of men, he was thoroughly convinced of the truly devotional character of his church music. We know this from a letter he wrote to his parents in 1825, and in which occurs the following passage:

' Surprise was also expressed at my piety, to which I have given expression in a hymn to the Holy Virgin, and which, as it seems, moves everyone to devotion. I believe this comes of the circumstances that I never force myself into a devout attitude, and never compose such hymns or prayers unless I am involuntarily overcome by it; but in that case it usually happens to be the genuine spirit of devotion.'

Schubert's chamber music, especially his string quartets and his trios for pianoforte, violin and violoncello, must be ranked among the very best of their kind in all musical literature. Of the quartets, the one in D minor is, in my opinion, the most original and important, the one in A minor the most fascinating. Schubert does not try to give his chamber music an orchestral character, yet he attains a marvellous variety of beautiful tonal effects. Here, as elsewhere, his flow of melody is spontaneous, incessant and irrepressible, leading often to excessive diffuseness. Like Chopin and Rossini, Schubert has frequently shown how a melody may be created which can wonderfully charm us even apart from the harmonic accompaniment which naturally goes with and enriches it. But he was accused by his contemporaries of neglecting polyphony, or the art of interweaving several melodious parts into a contrapuntal web. This charge, combined with a late study of Handel's scores, induced him shortly before his death to plan a course of counterpoint with Sechter. No doubt his education in counterpoint had been neglected.

It is not likely, however, that such study would have materially altered his style. This was too individual from the beginning to undergo much change, for Schubert did not outgrow his early style so noticeably as did Beethoven and Wagner, for example. Besides, Schubert had no real need of contrapuntal study. In his chamber music, as in his symphonies, we often find beautiful specimens of polyphonic writing—see, for instance, the andantes of the C major Quintet and of the D minor Quartet—and though his polyphony be different from Bach's or Beethoven's, it is none the less admirable. Mendelssohn is undoubtedly a greater master of polyphony than Schubert, yet I prefer Schubert's chamber music to Mendelssohn's.

Of Schubert's symphonies, too, I am such an enthusiastic admirer that I do not hesitate to place him next to Beethoven, far above Mendelssohn, as well as above Schumann. Mendelssohn had some of Mozart's natural instinct for orchestration and gift for form, but much of his work has proved ephemeral. Schumann is at his best in his songs, his chamber music and his pianoforte pieces. His symphonies, too, are great works, yet they are not always truly orchestral; the form seems to hamper the composer, and the instrumentation is not always satisfactory. This is never the case with Schubert. Although he sometimes wrote carelessly, and often diffusely, he is never at fault in his means of expression, while mastery of form came to him spontaneously. In originality of harmony and modulation, and in his gift of orchestral colouring, Schubert has had no superior. Dr. Riemann asserts with justice that in their use of harmony both Schumann and Liszt are descendants of Schubert; Brahms, too, whose enthusiasm for Schubert is well known, has perhaps felt his influence; and as for myself, I cordially acknowledge my great obligations to him.

I have just observed that mastery of form came to Schubert spontaneously. This is illustrated by his early symphonies, five of which he wrote before he was twenty, at which, the more I study them, the more I marvel. Although the influence of Haydn and Mozart is apparent in them, Schubert's musical individuality is unmistakable in the character of the melody, in the harmonic progressions, and in many exquisite bits of orchestration. In his later symphonies he becomes more and more individual and original. The influence of Haydn and Mozart, so obvious in his earlier efforts, is gradually eliminated, and with his contemporary, Beethoven, he had less in common from the beginning. He resembles Beethoven, however, in the vigour and melodious flow of his basses; such basses we find already in his early symphonies. His *Unfinished Symphony* and the great one in C are unique contributions to musical literature, absolutely new and original, Schubert in every bar. What is perhaps most characteristic about them is the song-like melody pervading them. He introduced the song into the symphony, and made the transfer so skilfully that Schumann was led to speak of the resemblance to the human voice (Aehnlichkeit mith dem Stimmorgan) in these orchestral parts.

Although these two symphonies are by far the best of Schubert's, it is a pity that they alone should be deemed worthy [of] a place in our concert programmes. I played the sixth in C major and No. 5 in B [sic] major a dozen times with my orchestral pupils at the National Conservatory last winter; they shared my pleasure in them, and recognized at once their great beauty.

It was with great pleasure and feelings of gratitude that I read not long ago of the performance in Berlin of the B [sic] major Symphony by Herr Weingartner, one of the few conductors who have had the courage to put this youthful work on their programmes. Schubert's fourth too, is an admirable composition. It bears the title of *Tragic Symphony*, and was written at the age of nineteen, about a year after the "Erl King". It makes one marvel that one so young should have had the power to give utterance to such deep pathos. In the adagio there are chords that strikingly suggest the anguish of Tristan's utterances; nor is this the only place wherein Schubert is prophetic of Wagnerian harmonies. And although partly anticipated by Gluck and Mozart, he was one of the first to make use of an effect to which Wagner and other modern composers owe many of their most beautiful orchestral colours—the employment of the brass, not for noise, but played softly, to secure rich and warm tints.

The richness and variety of colouring in the great Symphony in C are astounding. It is a work which always fascinates, always remains new. It has the effect of gathering clouds, with constant glimpses of sunshine breaking through them. It illustrates also, like most of Schubert's compositions, the truth of an assertion once made to me by Dr. Hans Richter—that the greatest masters always reveal their genius most unmistakably and most delightfully in their slow movements. Personally I prefer the *Unfinished Symphony* even to the one in C; apart from its intrinsic beauty, it avoids the fault of diffuseness.

If Schubert's symphonies have a serious fault it is prolixity; he does not know when to stop; yet, if the repeats are omitted, a course of which I thoroughly approve, and which, indeed, is now generally adopted, they are not too long. Schubert's case, in fact, is not an exception to, but an illustration of, the general rule that symphonies are made too long. When Bruckner's eighth Symphony was produced in Vienna last winter, the Philharmonic Society had to devote a whole concert to it. The experiment has not been repeated anywhere, and there can be no doubt that this symphony would have a better chance of making its way in the world if it were shorter. This remark has a general application. We should return to the symphonic dimensions approved by Haydn and Mozart. In this respect Schumann is a model, especially in his B flat major and D minor Symphonies; also in his chamber music. Modern taste calls for music that is concise, condensed and pithy.

In Germany, England and America, Schubert's instrumental works, chamber and orchestral, have long since enjoyed a vogue and popularity which have amply atoned for their neglect at first. As for the French, they have produced two Schubert biographies, but it cannot be said that they have shown the same general sympathy for this master as for some other German composers, or as the English have, thanks largely to the enthusiastic efforts of my esteemed friend Sir George Grove. It is on record that after Habeneck had made an unsuccessful effort (his musicians rebelled at the rehearsal) to produce the great Symphony in C at a Conservatoire concert no further attempt was made with Schubert's orchestral compositions at these concerts for forty years.

This may help to explain the extraordinary opinion of the eminent French critic, Fétis, that Schubert is less original in his instrumental works than in his songs, the popularity of which, too, he declared to be largely a matter of fashion! The latter insinuation is of course too absurd to call for comment today, but as regards the first part of his criticism I do not hesitate to say that greatly as I esteem Schubert's songs, I value his instrumental works even more highly. Were all his compositions to be destroyed but two, I should say, save the last two symphonies.

Fortunately we are not confronted by any such necessity. The loss of Schubert's pianoforte pieces and songs would indeed be irreparable. For although much of their spirit and substance has passed into the works of his imitators and legitimate followers, the originals have never been equalled in their way. In most of his works Schubert is unique in melody, rhythm, modulation and orchestration, but from a formal point of view he is most original in his songs and his short pieces for piano. In his symphonies, chamber music, operas and sacred compositions, he follows classical models; but in the *Lied*, the *Musical Moment*, the Impromptu, he is romanticist in every fibre. Yet he wrote no fewer than twenty-four sonatas for pianoforte, two or four hands, in which he follows classical models, and we can trace the influence of Beethoven's style even in the three which he wrote in the last year of his life. This seems strange at first when we consider that in the *Lied* and the short pianoforte pieces he betrayed no such influence even in his earliest days. The 'Erl King' and 'The Wanderer', written when he was eighteen and nineteen respectively, are Schubert in every bar, whereas the piano sonatas and symphonies of this period are much more imitative, much less individual. One reason for this, doubtless, is that just as it is easier to write a short lyric poem than a long epic, so it is easier for a young composer to be original in short forms than in the more elaborate sonata and symphony; and we must remember that Schubert died at thirty-one.

APPENDIX II

But there was another reason. The tendency of the romantic school has been towards short forms, and although Weber helped to show the way, to Schubert belongs the chief credit of originating the short models of pianoforte pieces which the romantic school has preferably cultivated. His *Musical Moments* are unique, and it may be said that in the third Impromptu (op. 90) lie the germs of the whole of Mendelssohn's *Songs without Words*. Schumann has remarked that Schubert's style is more idiomatically pianistic (claviermässig) than Beethoven's, and this is perhaps true of these short pieces. Yet it can hardly be said that either Schubert or Schumann was in this respect equal to Bach or Chopin, who of all composers have written the most idiomatically for the piano. I cannot agree with Schumann in his rather depreciatory notice of Schubert's last sonatas. (He speaks of 'greater simplicity of invention', 'a voluntary dispensing with brilliant novelty', and connects this with Schubert's last illness.) I would not say that Schubert is at his best in these sonatas as a whole, but I have a great admiration for parts of them, especially for the last one in B flat with the exquisite andante in C sharp minor. Taking them all in all, I do not know but that I prefer his sonatas even to his short pieces for the piano. Yet they are never played at concerts.

Just as the Impromptus and *Musical Moments* were the source of the large crop of romantic short pieces, so Schubert's charming waltzes were the predecessors of the Lanner and Strauss dances on the one hand, and of Chopin's waltzes on the other. There is an astounding number of these Schubert dance pieces; they are charming as originally written, and Liszt has given some of them a brilliant setting for the concert hall. In this humble sphere, as in the more exalted ones we have discussed, historians have hardly given Schubert full credit for his originality and influence.

In Schubert's pianoforte music, perhaps even more than in his other compositions, we find a Slavic trait which he was the first to introduce prominently into art-music, namely the quaint alternation of major and minor within the same period. Nor is this the only Slavic or Hungarian trait to be found in his music. During his residence in Hungary, he assimilated national melodies and rhythmic peculiarities, and embodied them in his art, thus becoming the forerunner of Liszt, Brahms and others who have made Hungarian melodies an integral part of European concert music. From the rich stores of Slavic folk music, in its Hungarian,[1] Russian, Bohemian and Polish varieties, the composers of today have derived, and will continue to derive, much that is charming and novel in their music. Nor is there anything objectionable in this, for if the poet and the painter base much of their best art on national legends, songs and traditions, why should not the musician?

[1] Here he presumably means Slovak.

And to Schubert will belong the honour of having been one of the first to show the way.

Perhaps the luckiest accident in Schubert's life was his acquaintance and friendship with the famous tenor Vogl. This was brought about deliberately by his friends, in order to secure for his songs the advantage of that singer's artistic interpretations. Vogl at first pretended to be 'tired of music', and showed some indifference to his modest young accompanist's songs; but this was soon changed to interest, followed by genuine enthusiasm. Thus it came about that these songs were gradually made familiar in Viennese social circles. Schubert himself sang, though only with a 'composer's voice'; but he must have been an admirable accompanist. In a letter to his parents he says: 'I am assured by some that under my fingers the keys are changed to singing voices, which, if true, would please me greatly.' This, written only three years before his death, illustrates his great modesty. In some recently published reminiscences by Josef von Spaun[1] it is related how, when Vogl and Schubert performed together at soirées in Vienna, the ladies would crowd about the tenor, lionizing him and entirely ignoring the composer. But Schubert, instead of feeling annoyed or jealous, was actually pleased. Adoration embarrassed him, and he is known to have dodged it once by escaping secretly by the back door.

Little did the Viennese dream that the songs thus interpreted for them by Schubert and Vogl would create a new era in music. In the *Lied* or lyric song, not only is Schubert the first in point of time, but no one has ever surpassed him. Haydn, Mozart and Beethoven did indeed write a few songs, but merely by the way, and without revealing much of their genius or individuality in them. But Schubert created a new epoch with the *Lied*, as Bach did with the piano, and Haydn with the orchestra. All other song writers have followed in his footsteps, all are his pupils, and it is to his rich treasure of songs that we owe, as a heritage, the beautiful songs of such masters as Schumann, Franz and Brahms. To my taste the best songs written since Schubert are the *Magelonen-Lieder* of Brahms; but I agree with the remark once made to me by the critic Ehlert that Franz attained the highest perfection of all in making poetry and music equivalent in his songs.

In the best of Schubert's songs we find the same equivalence of poem and music, and it was lucky that Vogl was an artist who, as Spaun says, 'sang in such a way as to interest his hearers not only in the music, but also in the poem', which so few singers do. In the absence of singers who could imitate Vogl in this respect, Liszt was justified in arranging these songs for the pianoforte, whereby he greatly accelerated their popularity. To hear the real Schubert, however, we must have the voice and the poem too, so that we may note how closely the poem and the music are amalgamated, and how

---

[1] *Classisches und Romantisches aus der Tonwelt*, von La Mara. 1892.

admirably the melodic accent coincides with the poetic. In this respect Schubert marks a great advance over his predecessors. He was almost as adverse to word repetitions as Wagner, whom he also resembles in the powerful emotional effects he produces by his modulations, especially in his later songs.

Schubert's melodic fount flowed so freely that he sometimes squandered good music on a poor text, as is shown in his operas and in some of his songs. Usually, however, the best poems evoked the best music from his creative fancy. His fertility is amazing. It is known that he composed as many as eight songs in one day, and ninety-nine in one year (1816), while the whole number of his songs exceeds six hundred. The best of these songs are now so universally known, and have been so much discussed, that it is difficult to offer any new comment on them.

There is only one more point to which attention may be called here— Schubert's power of surrounding us with the poetic atmosphere of his subject with the very first bars of his *Lieder*. For such a stroke of genius recall his song 'Der Leiermann', the pathetic story of the poor hurdy-gurdy player whose plate is always empty, and for whose woes Schubert wins our sympathy by his sad music—by that plaintive monotonous figure which pervades the accompaniment from beginning to end, bringing the whole scene vividly before our eyes and keeping it there to the end. Before Schubert no song writer had conceived such an effect; after he had shown the way others eagerly followed in his footsteps.

[Reprinted from *The Century Illustrated Monthly Magazine*, New York, 1894. The text is reproduced exactly as it appeared originally, without any attempt being made to correct factual errors.]

LETTER FROM SIR GEORGE GROVE

July 15th, 1894
Lower Sydenham, S.E.
London.

Dear Master,

I only saw your article on Schubert last night, and I lose no time in asking you to accept my best and warmest thanks for it. It is certainly the best and the most interesting thing that has been written upon that great musician; and every student and every amateur should be grateful to you for thus throwing the light of your genius upon the career and works of your fellow-composer.

I shall read and re-read it until I know it by heart! Let me thank you especially for what you say of his pianoforte music and his orchestral compositions. The pianoforte sonatas and pieces may not be as good 'teaching pieces' as those of Beethoven and others; but surely they are too much neglected by the teachers. Even if they do not form the fingers as readily as other compositions, surely the poetry and pathos which they contain must be good food for the imagination and intellect of young students.

As to the orchestral works I am *most* grateful to you. I was fortunately able, long before Breitkopf's great edition was thought of, to get copies of all the symphonies for the Crystal Palace. There they were all played in order in 1880–81, and excited the greatest interest. You do not mention the Rosamunde entractes; but dear Master, pray look at the one in H moll and see how noble, how melodious, how dignified and beautiful it is! Surely he has written nothing finer anywhere!

How completely what you say of the value of the use of national music to composers (page 345) is confirmed by the discovery of the use which Beethoven made of Slavonic tunes in the Pastoral Symphony (see Professor Kuhatsch's collection, Agram 1878–81, and Siegmann's[1] *Allg. Musik Zeitung*, Oct. 6, 13, 20, 1893). But I must not go on like this. Let me only ask you where you found what you say about two movements of the great symphony being performed in Vienna with an opera air between them; I can find no notice of this in *A. Musik Zeitung* of that date. The performances are mentioned in 1828 and 1829, but apparently of the entire work (see Vol. 31—p. 75 and 296). Also the story of Habeneck—I should be very glad to have a reference to. Now dear Mr. Dvorshák I must stop. I hope you are well and happy and that Mrs. Dvorshák is as well and charming as ever. Your works are as great favourites in London as ever. I heard a splendid performance of the Symphony in G, and shall soon hear the last one.

With my respectful homage to Madame and my most affectionate wishes to you, believe me,

Yours most sincerely,
G. Grove

---

[1] Siegmann was not editor of this periodical, but of *Neue Musikerzeitung*.

Appendix III

CATALOGUE OF COMPLETED WORKS

THIS catalogue has been compiled from J. Burghauser's *Antonín Dvořák Thematic Catalogue* (Prague 1960), which should be consulted if more detailed information is required. After the opus number (if any) and title of each work, and in some cases additional information, will be found: (i) the Burghauser catalogue number preceded by the letter 'B.', (ii), the year or years of composition (or revision), and (iii) the name of the publisher of the earliest edition, together with date of publication. Publishers' names will be found abbreviated as follows:

BB.	Bote & Bock, Berlin.	O.	Orbis, Prague.
BH.	Breitkopf & Härtel, Leipzig.	S.	N. Simrock, Berlin.
Cr.	Cranz, Leipzig.	Sch.	Schlesinger, Berlin.
FAU.	F. A. Urbánek, Prague.	St.	Starý, Prague.
H.	Hofmeister, Leipzig.	SV.	Critical Edition of Dvořák's
Ha.	Hainauer, Breslau (Wróclaw).		Works, Prague.
HM.	Hudební matice, Prague.	UE.	Universal Edition, Vienna.
MU.	M. Urbánek, Prague.	V.	J. R. Vilímek, Prague
N.	Novello, Ewer & Co., London.		

A. ORCHESTRAL WORKS
I. SYMPHONIES

Op.

- 1. Symphony in C minor (*The Bells of Zlonice—Zlonické zvony*). B.9. 1865. SV.1961.
4   2. Symphony in B flat major. B.12. 1865. SV.1959.
10 3. Symphony in E flat major. B. 34. 1873. S. 1912.
13 4. Symphony in D minor. B.41. 1874. S. 1912.
76 5. Symphony in F major (op. 24). B.54. 1875, revised 1887. S. 1888 (no. 3).
60 6. Symphony in D major (op. 58). B. 112. 1880. S. 1882 (no. 1).
70 7. Symphony in D minor. B.141. 1884–85. S. 1885 (no. 2).
88 8. Symphony in G major. B.163. 1889. N. 1892 (no. 4).
95 9. Symphony in E minor (*From the New World—Z Nového světa*). B.178. 1893. S. 1894 (no. 5).

II. OVERTURES, RHAPSODIES AND SYMPHONIC POEMS

Op.

1   *Tragic* (*Dramatic*), overture (originally for *Alfred*). B.16a. 1870. S. 1912.
(12) Overture in F major (originally for *King and Charcoal Burner*, 1st version). B.21a. 1871. Unpublished.

APPENDIX III

(21) *Romeo and Juliet*, overture. B.35. 1873. Lost.
14   Symphonic Poem (Rhapsody in A minor). B.44. 1874. S. 1912.
45   *Slavonic Rhapsodies*, no. 1 in D major, no. 2 in G minor, no. 3 in A flat major. B.86. 1878. S. 1879.
25   *Vanda*, overture. B. 97. 1879. Cr. 1885.
(62) *My Home* (My Country—*Domov můj*), overture (overture to *J. K. Tyl*). B.125a. 1882. S. 1882.
67   *Hussite* (*Husitská*), overture. B.132. 1883. S. 1884.
91   *In Nature's Realm* (*V přírodě*), overture. B.168. 1891. W. 1894.
92   *Carnival*, overture. B.169. 1891. S. 1894.
93   *Othello*, overture. B.174. 1891–92. S. 1894.
     (Opp. 91–93 form the *Triple Overture*, formerly entitled *Nature, Life and Love*.)
107 *The Water Goblin* (*Vodník*), symphonic poem. B.195. 1896. S. 1896.
108 *The Noon Witch* (*Polednice*), symphonic poem. B.196. 1896. S. 1896.
109 *The Golden Spinning Wheel* (*Zlatý kolovrat*), symphonic poem. B.197. 1896. S. 1896.
110 *The Wild Dove* (*Holoubek*), symphonic poem. B.198. 1896. S. 1899.
111 *Heroic Song* (*Píseň bohatýrská*), symphonic poem. B.199. 1897. S. 1899.

III. Serenades and Suites
Op.
22   Serenade in E major, for string orchestra. B.52. 1875. BB. 1879. (Pianoforte duet: St. 1877).
44   Serenade in D minor, for wind instruments. B.77. 1878. S. 1879.
39   *Czech Suite*, in D major, for orchestra. B.93. 1879 Sch. 1881.
98b Suite in A major, for orchestra. B. 190. 1895. S. 1911.

IV. Works for Solo Instrument and Orchestra
Op.
11   *Romance* in F minor, for violin and orchestra. B.39. 1873/77 (?) S. 1879.
33   Pianoforte Concerto in G minor. B.63. 1876. Ha. 1883.
49   *Mazurek*, for violin and orchestra. B.90. 1879. S. 1879.
53   Violin Concerto in A minor. B.96 and 108. 1879, revised 1880 and 1882. S. 1883.
94   Rondo in G minor, for 'cello and orchestra. B.181. 1893. S. 1894.
68/5 *Silent Woods* (*Klid*), for 'cello and orchestra. B.182. 1893. S. 1894.
104 Violoncello Concerto in B minor. B.191. 1894–95. S. 1896.
     NOTE.—The Violoncello Concerto of 1865 was not orchestrated. It appears under the heading 'Chamber Music'.

V. Dances
Op.
–   *The Woman Harpist* (*Harfenice*), polka. B.4. 1860 (?) Lost.
–   (?) Polka and Gallop. B.5–6. 1861/62 (?) Lost.
28   Two Minuets. Orchestral version of B.58. 1876 (?) Piano version: St. 1879.
46   *Slavonic Dances*, 1st series. B.83. 1878. S. 1878.

APPENDIX III

54   *Festival March.* B.88. 1879. St. 1879.
-   *Prague Waltzes.* B.99. 1879. Pianoforte version only published: FAU. 1880.
-   Polonaise in E flat major. B.100. 1879. Pianoforte duet version only published: FAU. 1883.
-   Polka 'For Prague Students'. B.114. 1880. Pianoforte version only published: St. 1882.
-   Gallop (Kvapík). B.119. 1881 (?) Pianoforte version only published: St. 1882.
72   *Slavonic Dances,* 2nd series. B. 147. 1886–87. S. 1887.

VI. Miscellaneous Works

Op.
-   *Intermezzi (Meziaktní skladby).* B.15. 1867. Unpublished.
-   *Three Nocturnes.* B.31. 1872. Unpublished—ms. incomplete.
40   *Nocturne* in B major, for strings. B.47. 1875 (?) revised 1882/83 (?) BB. 1883.
78   *Symphonic Variations* (op. 28). B.70. 1877. S. 1888.
59   *Legends.* B. 122. 1881. S. 1882.
66   *Scherzo capriccioso.* B.131. 1883. BB. 1884.
-   *Fanfares* (four trumpets, timpani). B.167. 1891. Unpublished.

B. CHAMBER MUSIC
I. Works for Five or More Instruments

Op.
1   String Quintet in A minor. B.7. 1861. HM. 1943.
-   Clarinet Quintet in B flat minor, for clarinet and string quartet. B.14. 1865/69 (?) Lost.
5   Pianoforte Quintet in A major. B.28. 1872. SV. 1959.
(22)   Octet (Serenade), for clarinet, bassoon, horn, two violins, viola, double bass and piano. B. 36. 1873. Lost.
77   String Quintet in G major, for string quartet and double bass (op. 18). B.49. 1875. S. 1888.
48   String Sextet in A major, for two violins, two violas, two violoncellos. B.80. 1878. S. 1879.
81   Pianoforte Quintet in A major. B.155. 1887. S. 1888.
97   String Quintet in E flat major. B.180. 1893. S. 1894.

II. String Quartets

Op.
2   1.   String Quartet in A major. B.8. 1862. HM. 1948.
-   2.   String Quartet in B flat major. B.17. 1869 (?) SV. 1962.
-   3.   String Quartet in D major. B. 18. 1870 (?) SV. 1964.
-   4.   String Quartet in E minor. B.19. 1870 (?) Unpublished.
9   5.   String Quartet in F minor. B.37. 1873. Ms. missing; original version unpublished. Arranged Raphael: BH. 1929.
12   6.   String Quartet in A minor. B.40. 1873. Unpublished.
16   7.   String Quartet in A minor. B.45. 1874. St. 1875.
80   8.   String Quartet in E major (op. 27). B.57. 1876. S. 1888.
34   9.   String Quartet in D minor. B.75. 1877. Sch. 1880.
51   10.   String Quartet in E flat major. B.92. 1878–79. S. 1879.

APPENDIX III

54   Two Waltzes (Nos. 1 and 4 of the set for piano). B.105. 1880 (?) S. 1911.

–   Quartet Movement in F major. B.120. 1881. O. 1951.

61 11.   String Quartet in C major. B.121. 1881. S. 1882.

–   *Cypresses* (arrangements of 12 songs from the Cycle of 1865: Nos. 6, 3, 2, 8, 12, 7, 9, 14, 4, 16, 17 and 18; see Songs below.) B.152. 1887. HM. 1921 (except nos. 10 and 12); complete: SV. 1957.

96 12.   String Quartet in F major (*The American*). B.179. 1893. S. 1894.

106 13.   String Quartet in G major. B.192. 1895. S. 1896.

105 14.   String Quartet in A flat major. B.193. 1895. S. 1896.

III. Quartets with Piano (or Harmonium)

Op.

23   Piano Quartet in D major. B.53. 1875. Sch. 1880.

47   *Bagatelles* (*Maličkosti*), for two violins, violoncello and harmonium. B.79. 1878. S. 1880.

87   Piano Quartet in E flat major. B.162. 1889. S. 1890.

IV. Trios

Op.

(13)   Two Pianoforte Trios. B.25–26. 1871/72 (?) Lost.

21   Pianoforte Trio in B flat major. B.51. 1875. Sch. 1880.

26   Pianoforte Trio in G minor. B.56. 1876. BB. 1879.

65   Pianoforte Trio in F minor. B.130. 1883. S. 1883.

74   Terzetto in C major, for two violins and viola. B. 148. 1887. S. 1887.

75a   *Drobnosti* (*Miniatures*), for two violins and viola. B.149. 1887. HM. 1945.

–   *Gavotte* for Three Violins. B. 164. 1890. V. 1890.

90   *Dumkas* (*Dumky Trio*), for pianoforte trio. B.166. 1890–91. S. 1894.

V. Works for Violin and Pianoforte

Op.

(19)   Sonata in A minor. B.33. 1873. Lost.

11   *Romance* in F minor. B.38. 1873/77 (?) Arranged Zubatý: S. 1879. Original version: SV. 1955.

40   *Nocturne* in B major. B.48. 1875/83 (?) BB. 1883.

(24)   *Capriccio*. B.81. 1878. Original version unpublished. Arranged Raphael: BH. 1929.

49   *Mazurek*. B.89. 1879. S. 1879.

57   Sonata in F major. B.106. 1880. S. 1880.

15/1   *Ballad* in D minor. B.139. 1884. Magazine of Music 1884: FAU. 1885.

75   *Romantic Pieces*. B.150. 1887. S. 1887.

–   *Slavonic Dance* in E minor (from op. 46). B.170. 1891 (?) Unpublished.

100   Sonatina in G major. B.183. 1893. S. 1894.

VI. Works for Violoncello and Pianoforte

Op.

–   Concerto in A major. B.10. 1865. Original version unpublished; arranged Raphael: BH. 1929.

(10)   Sonata in F minor. B.20. 1871. Piano part lost; 'cello part missing.

APPENDIX III

- *Polonaise* in A major. B.94. 1879. UE. 1925.
94 Rondo in G minor. B.171. 1891. S. 1894.
- *Slavonic Dance* in G minor (from op. 46). B.172. 1891. Unpublished.
68/5 *Silent Woods (Klid)* (from op. 68 for piano.) B. 173. 1891. S. 1894.

C. PIANOFORTE WORKS
I. PIANO SOLO

Op.
- *Forget-me-not Polka (Polka pomněnka)*. B.1. 1855/56 (?) Unpublished.
- Polka in E major. B.3. 1860. Unpublished.
- Potpourri on *King and Charcoal Burner* (1st version). B.22. 1871/3 (?) St. 1873.
- Potpourri on *King and Charcoal Burner* (2nd version). B.43. 1874/75 (?) Wetzler 1875.
28 Two Minuets. B.58. 1876 (?) St. 1879.
35 *Dumka* in D minor. B.64. 1876. BB. 1879.
36 Theme and Variations. B. 65. 1876. BB. 1879.
41 *Scottish Dances (Škotské tance)*. B.74. 1877. St. 1879.
42 *Furiants*. B.85. 1878. BB. 1879.
8 *Silhouettes*. B.32 and 98. 1870/72 (?) and 1879. H. 1880.
54 Waltzes (Valčíky). B.101. 1879–80. S. 1880.
56 *Eclogues*. B.103. 1880. HM. 1921.
- *Album Leaves (Lístky do památníku)*. B.109. 1880. Nos. 2–4: HM. 1921; No. 1 unpublished.
52 *Pianoforte Pieces (Klavírní skladby)*. B.110. 1880. Nos. 1–4: H. 1881; No. 5: HM. 1921; complete (nos. 1–6): SV 1961.
56 Mazurkas. B.111. 1880. BB. 1880.
- *Moderato* in A major. B.116. 1881. HM.1921.
- *Question (Otázka)*. B.128a. 1882. Unpublished.
- *Impromptu* in D minor. B.129. 1883. V. 1883.
12 *Dumka and Furiant*. B.136–7. 1884. *Furiant*: Magazine of Music 1884; both pieces: FAU. 1885.
- *Humoresque* in F sharp major. B.138. 1884. FAU. 1884.
- *Two Little Pearls (Dvě perličky)*. B.156. 1887. FAU. 1888.
- *Album Leaf*. B.158. 1888. Unpublished.
85 *Poetic Tone Pictures (Poetické nálady)*. B.161. 1889. S. 1889.
98 Suite in A major. B.184. 1894. S. 1894.
101 *Humoresques*. B.187. 1894. S. 1894.
- *Lullaby (Ukolébavka)* and *Capriccio*. B.188. 1894. S. 1911.

II. PIANO DUET

Op.
46 *Slavonic Dances*, 1st series. B.78. 1878. S.1878.
59 *Legends*. B.117. 1880–81. S. 1881.
68 *From the Bohemian Forest (Ze Šumavy)*. B.133. 1883–84. S. 1884.
72 *Slavonic Dances*, 2nd series. B.145. 1886. S. 1886.

APPENDIX III

D. ORGAN

Op.

– 5 Preludes and 3 Fugues. B.302. 1859. Prelude 1 and Fugue 1: Státní nakladatelství. 1954.

E. OPERAS AND INCIDENTAL MUSIC

Op.

(1 ?) *Alfred.* Heroic opera in three acts. Libr. by K. T. Körner. B.16. 1870. Unpublished, but see Overtures.

(12) *King and Charcoal Burner (Král a uhlíř).* 1st version. Comic opera in three acts. Libr. by B. J. Lobeský (B. Guldener). B.21. 1871. Unpublished.

14 *King and Charcoal Burner.* 2nd version. Comic opera in three acts. Libr. by B. Guldener. B.42, (115) and 151. 1874, revised 1887. Vocal score: HM. 1915.

17 *The Stubborn Lovers (Tvrdé palice).* Comic opera in one act. Libr. by J. Štolba. B.46. 1874. Vocal score: S. 1882.

25 *Vanda.* Tragic opera in five acts. Libr. by V. Beneš-Šumavský. B.55. 1875. Unpublished, but see Overtures.

37 *The Cunning Peasant (Šelma sedlák).* Comic opera in two acts. Libr. by J. O. Veselý. B.67. 1877. S. 1882.

62 *Josef Kajetán Tyl.* Overture and incidental music to the play by F. F. Šamberk. B.125. 1881–82. S. 1882.

64 *Dimitrij.* Historic opera in four acts. Libr. by M. Červinková-Riegrová. B.127 and 186. 1881–82, revised 1883, 1885 and 1894–95. Vocal score: 1885 version, St. 1886; 1st version revised Kovařovic, HM. 1912.

84 *The Jacobin.* Opera in three acts. Libr. by M. Červinková-Riegrová. B.159 and 200. 1887–88, revised 1897. Vocal score: 1st version revised Kovařovic, HM. 1911; 2nd version, HM. 1941 (?).

112 *Kate and the Devil (Čert a Káča).* Opera in three acts. Libr. by A. Wenig. B. 201. 1898–99. Vocal score: MU. 1908.

114 *Rusalka.* Lyric fairy tale in three acts. Libr. by J. Kvapil. B.203. 1900. Vocal score: MU. 1905: Full score: SV. 1960.

115 *Armida.* Opera in four acts. Libr. by J. Vrchlický. B.206. 1902–03. Vocal score: O. 1941.

F. CHORAL MUSIC

I. MASSES, ORATORIOS AND CANTATAS

Op.

– Mass in B flat major. B.2. 1857/59 (?) Lost.

30 Hymnus: *The Heirs of the White Mountain (Dědicové bílé hory).* Poem by V. Hálek. Mixed chorus and orchestra. B.27, 102 and 134. 1872, revised 1880 and 1884. N. 1885.

58 *Stabat Mater.* Soprano, contralto, tenor and bass soli, chorus and orchestra. B.71. 1876–77. S. 1881.

79 149th Psalm. Male voice chorus and orchestra: B.91. 1879. Unpublished. Mixed chorus and orchestra: B.154. 1887. S. 1888.

69 *The Spectre's Bride (Svatební košile).* Ballad by K. J. Erben. Soprano, tenor and bass (baritone) soli, chorus and orchestra. B.135. 1884. N. 1885.

71   *St. Ludmila.* Libretto by J. Vrchlický. Soprano, contralto, tenor and bass soli, chorus and orchestra. B.144 (Recits. for stage perf., B.205, 1901). 1885–86. N. 1887.

86   Mass in D major. Soloists, or semi-chorus, and mixed choir. Organ accompaniment: B.153. 1887. Unpublished. Orchestral accompaniment: B.175. 1892. N. 1893.

89   Requiem Mass. Soprano, contralto, tenor and bass soli, chorus and. orchestra. B. 165. 1890. N. 1891.

103   *Te Deum.* Soprano and bass soli, mixed chorus and orchestra. B.176. 1892. S. 1896.

102   *The American Flag (Americký prapor).* Poem by J. R. Drake. Contralto, tenor and bass soli, mixed chorus and orchestra. B.177. 1892–93. Vocal score: Schirmer 1895. Full score unpublished.

113   *Festival Song (Slavnostní zpěv).* Poem by J. Vrchlický. Mixed chorus and orchestra. B.202. 1900. Vocal score (pianoforte duet accompaniment): MU. 1902.

II. SMALL CHORAL WORKS AND PART-SONGS
(i) FEMALE VOICES

Op.

32   *Moravian Duets* (op. 32, nos. 2, 5 and 10; op. 29, nos. 2 and 3.) Unaccompanied. B.107. 1880. Unpublished.

(ii) MALE VOICES

–   *Choral Songs for Male Voices.* Unaccompanied. B.66. 1877. HM. 1921.
    1. 'The Ferryman' ('Převozníček')   ⎫ Moravian folk
    2. 'The Beloved as Poisoner' ('Milenka travička')   ⎬ poems.
    3. 'The Fiddler' ('Huslař'). V. Hálek.

41   *Bouquet of Czech Folk-Songs.* Czech and Moravian folk poems. Unaccompanied. B. 72. 1877. Nos. 1–3: privately printed, n.d.; HM. 1921. No. 4 unpublished.
    1. 'The Betrayed Shepherd' ('Zavedený ovčák').
    2. 'The Sweetheart's Resolve' ('Úmysl milenčin').
    3. 'The Guelder Rose' ('Kalina').
    4. 'The Czech Diogenes' (Český Diogenes').

–   *The Song of a Czech (Píseň čecha).* Poem by F. J. Vacek-Kamenický. Unaccompanied. B.73. 1877 (?) HM. 1921.

43   *From a Bouquet of Slavonic Folk-Songs (Z kytice národních písní slovanských).* Piano accompaniment. B.76 1877–78. Piano duet accompaniment arranged Zubatý: St. 1879.
    1. 'Sorrow' ('Žal'). Slovak folk poem.
    2. 'Miraculous Water' ('Divná voda'), Moravian folk poem.
    3. 'The Girl in the Woods' ('Děvče v háji'), Slovak folk poem.

27   *Five Choral Songs (Pět sborů pro mužské hlasy).* Lithuanian folk poems. Unaccompanied. B.87. 1878. FAU. 1890.
    1. 'Village Gossip' ('Pomluva').
    2. 'Dwellers by the sea' (Pomořané).
    3. 'The Love Promise' (Přípověd lásky').

4. 'The Lost Lamb' ('Ztracená ovečka').
5. 'The Sparrow's Party' ('Hostina').

(iii) MIXED VOICES

29 *Four Part-Songs for Mixed Choir* (*Čtyři sbory pro smíšené hlasy*). Unaccompanied. B.59. 1876. St. 1879.
    1. 'Evening's Blessing' ('Místo klekání') ⎤ A. Heyduk.
    2. 'Cradle Song' ('Ukolébavka') ⎦
    3. 'I don't say it' ('Nepovím') ⎤ Moravian folk poems.
    4. 'Forsaken' ('Opuštěný') ⎦

63 *In Nature's Realm* (*V přírodě*). Poems by V. Hálek. Unaccompanied. B.126. 1882. Cr. 1882.
    1. 'Songs to my soul have drifted down' ('Napadly písně . . .').
    2. 'Hark! in the wood sweet bells are ringing' ('Večerní les . . .').
    3. 'Lo, before me spreads the rye field' ('Žitné pole . . .').
    4. 'Pretty white birch tree leapt with joy' ('Vyběhla bříza . . .').
    5. 'Come! gaily trip it, loudly carol!' ('Dnes do skoku . . .').

28 *Hymn of the Czech Peasants* (*Hymna českého rolnictva*). Poem by K. Pippich. With orchestral accompaniment. B.143. 1885. Piano duet accompaniment arranged Zubatý: FAU. 1885.

G. SONGS
I. PIANO ACCOMPANIMENT

Op.

– *Cypresses* (*Cypřiše*). Poems by G. Pfleger-Moravský. B.11. 1865. No. 11 publ. unrevised in *Dvořákova čítanka*, 1929. For others, see op. 2, *Six Songs* (B.123), op. 83 and *Cypresses* (for string quartet).
    1. 'Sing fervent songs at nightfall' ('Vy vroucí písně . . .').
    2. 'When thy sweet glances on me fall' ('V té sladké moci . . .').
    3. 'Death reigns in many a human breast' ('V tak mnohém srdci . . .').
    4. 'Thou only dear one, but for thee' ('Ó duše draha . . .').
    5. 'Oh what a perfect golden dream!' ('Ó byl to krásný . . .').
    6. 'I know that on my love to thee' ('Já vím, že v sladké . . .').
    7. 'O charming golden rose' ('O zlatá růže . . .').
    8. 'Never will love lead us to that glad goal' ('Ó, naší lásce . . .').
    9. 'I wander oft past yonder house' ('Kol domu se . . .').
    10. 'Tormented oft by doubt am I' ('Mne často týrá . . .').
    11. 'My heart, often in pain, is plunged in sadness' ('Mé srdce často . . .').
    12. 'Here gaze I at that dear letter' ('Zde hledím . . .').
    13. 'Ev'rything's still in valley and mountain' ('Na horách ticho . . .').
    14. 'In deepest forest glade I stand' ('Zde v lese . . .').
    15. 'Painful emotions pierce my soul' ('Mou celou duší . . .').
    16. 'There stands an ancient rock' ('Tam stojí stará skála . . .').
    17. 'Nature lies peaceful in slumber and dreaming' ('Nad krajem vévodí . . .').
    18. 'You are asking why my songs are raging' ('Ty se ptáš . . .').

– *Two Songs for Baritone* (*Dvě písně pro baryton*). Poems by A. Heyduk. B.13. 1865. Unpublished.

1. 'If dear maiden you upon a throne were seated' ('Kdybys, milé děvče . . .').
2. 'If you were born to be a song' ('A kdybys písní stvořená . . .').
- *Songs to Words by Eliška Krásnohorská.* B.23. 1871. Nos. 2 and 4: Sch. 1880. Complete: SV. 1959.
    1. 'The Reason' ('Proto').
    2. 'Obstacles' ('Překážky').
    3. 'Meditation' ('Přemítaní').
    4. 'Lime Trees' ('Lípy').
    NOTE—A fifth song, 'Remembrance' ('Vzpomínání'), was left incomplete.
5 *The Orphan (Sirotek).* Ballad by K. J. Erben. B. 24. 1871. FAU. 1883.
- *Rosmarine (Rosmarýna).* Poem by K. J. Erben. B24a. 1871(?) SV. 1962.
6 *Four Songs on Serbian Folk Poems.* Transl. S. Kapper. B.29. 1872(?)
    S. 1879 (German and English words only).
    1. 'The Maiden and the Grass' ('Panenka a tráva').
    2. 'Warning' ('Připamatování').
    3. 'Flowery Omens' ('Výklad znamení).
    4. 'No Escape' ('Lásce neujdeš').
7 *Songs from the Dvůr Králové Manuscript* (i.e. Königinhof MS.). B.30. 1872.
    No. 3 in periodical *Dalibor,* 1873. Complete: St. 1873.
    1. 'The Cuckoo' ('Zezhulice').
    2. 'The Forsaken Maiden' ('Opuščená').
    3. 'The Lark' ('Skřivánek').
    4. 'The Rose' ('Růže').
    5. 'Flowery Message' ('Kytice').
    6. 'The Strawberries' ('Jahody').
3,9, *Evening Songs (Večerní písně).* Poems by V. Hálek. B.61. 1876. Nos. 1–4:
31 H.1881 (op. 3); nos. 5–6: Sch. 1880 (op. 9. Nos. 3 and 4); nos. 7–11: FAU.
    1883 (op. 31). No. 12 unpublished.
    1. 'The stars that twinkle in the sky' ('Ty hvězdičky tam . . .').
    2. 'I dreamed last night that you were dead' ('Mně zdálo se . . .').
    3. 'I am that knight of fairy tale' ('Já jsem ten rytíř . . .').
    4. 'When God was in a happy mood' ('Když Bůh byl nejvíc . . .').
    5. 'The soughing of the trees has ceased' ('Umlklo stromů . . .').
    6. 'The spring came flying from afar' ('Přilítlo jaro . . .').
    7. 'Visions of heaven I fondly paint' ('Když jsem se díval . . .').
    8. 'This would I ask each tiny bird' ('Vy malí, drobní ptáčkové . . .').
    9. 'Like to a linden tree am I' ('Jsem jako lípa . . .').
    10. 'All ye who are oppressed' ('Vy všichni, kdo . . .').
    11. 'All through the night that bird sings' ('Ten ptáček . . .').
    12. 'Thus as the moon in heaven's dome' ('Tak jak ten měsíc . . .').
50 *Three Modern Greek Poems (Tři novořecké basně).* Transl. V. B. Nebeský.
    B.84. 1878. Ha. 1883.
    1. 'Kolja' ('Klepht Song').
    2. 'Nixies' ('Ballad').
    3. 'Parga's Lament' ('Heroic Song') ('Žalozpěv Pargy').
55 *Gipsy Melodies (Cigánské melodie).* Poems by A. Heyduk. B. 104. 1880.
    S. 1880.

1. 'My song of love rings through the dusk' ('I chant my lay . . .') ('Má píseň zas . . .').
2. 'Hey! Ring out, my triangle' ('Aj! Kterak trojhranec . . .').
3. 'All round about the woods are still' ('A les je tichý . . .').
4. 'When my mother taught me' ('Songs my mother taught me') ('Když mne stará matka . . .').
5. 'Come and join the dancing' ('Tune thy strings, O gipsy!') ('Struna naladěna . . .').
6. 'Wide the sleeves and trousers' ('In his wide and ample . . .') ('Široké rukávy . . .').
7. 'Give a hawk a fine cage' ('Cloudy heights of Tatra') ('Dejte klec jestřábu . . .').

NOTE—The first lines quoted are from the Critical Edition. Those shown in parenthesis are from the Simrock edition.

2   *Six Songs* (*Šest písní*). Poems by G. Pfleger-Moravský. B.123–124. 1881/82 (?) Nos. 1, 2, 6 and 5: St. 1882, as 'Four Songs'. Complete: SV. 1959. Revision of *Cypresses*, nos. 1, 5, 9, 8, 13 and 11. (See above.)

—   *The Wild Duck* (*Kačena divoká*) Folk poem. B.140. 1884. Lost.

—   *Two Songs* (*Dvě písně*). Czech folk poems. B.142. 1885. HM. 1921.
     1. 'Lullaby' ('Ukolébavka').
     2. 'Hindrance to Piety' ('Překážka v pobožnosti').

73   *In Folk Tone* (*V národním tónu*). B.146. 1886. S. 1887.
     1. 'Fond good night, darling girl' ('Dobrú noc, má milá').   ⎱ Slovak
     2. 'When a maiden was a-mowing' ('Žalo dievča, žalo trávu'). ⎰ folk
                                                      poems
     3. 'Nothing can change for me' ('Ach není, není tu'). Czech folk poem.
     4. 'I have a faithful mare' ('Ej, mám ja koňa faku'). Slovak folk poem.

82   *Four Songs* (*Čtyři písně*). Poems by O. Malybrok-Stieler. B.157. 1887–88. S. 1889.
     1. 'Leave me alone . . .' ('Kéž duch můj sám . . .').
     2. 'Over her Embroidery' ('Při vyšívání').
     3. 'Spring-tide' ('Jaro').
     4. 'At the Brook' ('U potoka').

83   *Love Songs* (*Písně milostné*). Poems by G. Pfleger-Moravský. B.160. 1888 S. 1889. Revision of *Cypresses*, nos. 8, 3, 9, 6, 17, 14, 2 and 4. (See above.)

99   *Biblical Songs* (*Biblické písně*). Text: Bible of Králíky. B.185. 1894. S. 1895.
     1. 'Darkness and thunderclouds . . .' ('Oblak a mrákota . . .').
     2. 'Lord my shield, my refuge' ('Skrýše má a paveza má . . .').
     3. 'Hear, oh hear my prayer, Lord' ('Slyš, ó Bože . . .').
     4. 'Oh, my shepherd is the Lord' ('Hospodin jest můj pastýř').
     5. 'Songs of gladness will I sing Thee' ('Bože! Bože! Píseň novou').
     6. 'Hear, O Lord, my bitter cry' ('Slyš, ó Bože, volání mé').
     7. 'By the shore of the river Babylon' ('Při řekách babylonských').
     8. 'O Lord, have mercy and turn Thou . . .' ('Popatřiž na mne . . .').
     9. 'My eyes will I to the hills lift up' ('Pozdvihuji oči svých . . .').
     10. 'Oh, sing unto the Lord a joyful song' ('Zpívejte Hospodinu . . .').

—   'Lullaby' ('Ukolébavka'). Poem by F. L. Jelínek. B.194. 1895. Periodical, *Květy mládeže*, 1896.

APPENDIX III

- *Song from 'The Smith of Lešetín'* (*Zpěv z lešetínského kováře*). Poem by S. Čech. B.204. 1901. S. 1911.

II. ORGAN ACCOMPANIMENT

Op.
19b   *Ave Maria*, for contralto (or baritone). B.68. 1877. St. 1883.
  –   *Hymnus ad Laudes in festo Sanctae Trinitatis*. B.82. 1878. Sodalitas s. Cyrilli, Prague 1911, revised J. Suk.
19b   *Ave maris stella*. B.95. 1879. St. 1883.

III. ORCHESTRAL ACCOMPANIMENT

Op.
(50)   *Three Modern Greek Poems*. B.84a. 1878. Unpublished. (See above.)
 3   *Evening Songs* (nos. 3 and 3). B.128. 1882. Unpublished. (See above.)
99   *Biblical Songs* (nos. 1–5). B.189. 1895. Transposed for soprano: S. 1929 (with nos. 6–10, arranged Zemánek).

H. VOCAL DUETS
I. PIANO ACCOMPANIMENT

Op.
20   *Moravian Duets* (*Moravské dvojzpěvy*), for soprano (contralto) and tenor. Moravian folk poems. B.50. 1875. S. 1879.
    1. 'Destined' ('Proměny').
    2. 'The Parting' ('Rozloučení').
    3. 'Poverty' ('Chudoba').
    4. 'The Last Wish' ('Vuře šuhaj, vuře').
32   *Moravian Duets*, for soprano and contralto. Moravian folk poems. B.60 and 62. 1876. Nos. 1–5: St. 1876 (op. 29). Nos. 6–13: St. 1876 (op. 32). Nos. 1–13: S. 1878 (as op. 32). Complete: SV. 1955.
    1. 'From thee now I must go' ('A já ti uplynu').
    2. 'Fly, sweet Songster' ('Velet', vtáčku').
    3. 'The Slighted Heart' ('Dyby byla kosa nabróšená').
    4. 'Parting without Sorrow' ('V dobrým sme se sešli').
    5. 'The Pledge of Love' ('Slavíkovský polečko malý').
    6. 'Forsaken' ('Holub na javoře').
    7. 'Water and Tears' ('Voda a pláč').
    8. 'The Modest Maid' ('Skromná').
    9. 'The Ring' ('Prsten').
    10. 'Grass, be green!' ('Zelanaj se, zelanaj').
    11. 'Captured' ('Zajatá').
    12. 'Comfort' ('Neveta').
    13. 'The Wild Rose' ('Šípek').
    14. 'The Soldier's Farewell' ('Život vojenský').
38   *Moravian Duets*, for soprano and contralto. Moravian folk poems. B.69. 1877. S. 1879.
    1. 'Hoping in Vain' ('Možnost').
    2. 'Greeting from Afar' ('Jablko').
    3. 'The Crown' ('Věneček').

APPENDIX III

4. 'The Smart' ('Hoře').
- *There on our roof* . . . (*Na tej našej střeše* . . .), for soprano and contralto. Moravian folk poem. B.118. 1881. St. 1882 (Umělecká beseda Album).

II. ORGAN ACCOMPANIMENT

Op.
19a   *O sanctissima dulcis Virgo Maria!*, for contralto and baritone. B.95a. 1879. St. 1883.

III. UNACCOMPANIED

Op.
-   *Child's Song (Dětská píseň)*. Poem by Š. Bačkora. B.113. 1880. In periodical *Hudební výchova*, 1956.

DVOŘÁK'S ARRANGEMENTS OF MUSIC BY OTHERS

Two Irish Songs (Dvě irské písně), for male voice choir.[1] B.601. 1878. Unpublished.
1. 'Můj Konnor má tváře jak červená růže'. (Dear Connor).
2. 'Nuž zdobte se kvítím, ať zaplane zář'.
Hungarian Dances, Nos. 17–21 (Brahms), orchestrated by Dvořák. B.602. 1880. S. 1881.
Russian Songs (Ruské písně), for two female voices and piano, arranged from folk-songs in M. Bernard's collection *Pyesni ruskoga naroda* (Petersburg 1866). B.603. 1883 (?) O. 1951.
1. 'Povylétla holubice pode strání' ('Вылетала голубина').
2. 'Čím jsem já tě rozhněvala' ('Чем тебя я огорчила?').

[1] Šourek states that Dvořák was asked to make these arrangements by Srb-Debrnov, who might have written the Czech verses himself. It is possible that the first song may have been derived directly or indirectly either from *Maver's Collection of Genuine Irish Melodies and Songs*, Glasgow 1877, p. 142, or from Maver's source, for Dvořák's melody resembles that version more closely than any other I have seen. I am grateful to Dr. Donal O'Sullivan for identifying the second song, and for the information that follows on the origin of the two songs:
(i) It is highly probable that both the words and the music of 'The Dear Irish Boy' ('The Wild Irish Boy') were written by John Barton c. 1800. According to Henry Hudson (1842), musical editor of *The Citizen, or Dublin Monthly Magazine*, this song was published by Thomas S. Cooke, who was active as a publisher c. 1810. Originally the words began 'My Connor—his cheeks are as ruddy as the morning', but another early version commences, 'Oh my Connor his cheeks are like the rose' (S. Holden, 1806), which is similar to the first line of the Czech translation. By 1841 the melody had been given new words by Desmond Ryan, beginning 'Oh! weary's on money—and weary's on wealth' (F. N. Crouch).
(ii) The second melody is an adaptation of the genuine folk-song 'Contented Am I', better known as 'Noch bonin shin doe', which is a corruption of 'Nach baineann sin dó'. This was published by Frederick W. Horncastle in *Music of Ireland* (London 1844) and re-published, with new verses by Thomas Davis, as 'The Battle Eve of the Brigade' in *The Spirit of the Nation* (1845). The Czech verses, which begin 'Ho! adorn yourself with flowers . . .' are neither a translation of the folk poem nor of the verses of Davis.

3. 'Mladá, pěkná krasavice' ('Белолица, круглолица').
4. 'Cožpak, můj holoubku' ('Ах, что ж ты, голубчик').
5. 'Zkvétal, zkvétal v máji květ' ('Цвели, цвели цветики').
6. 'Jako mhou se tmí' ('Ах, как пал туман').
7. 'Ach, vy říčky šumivé' ('Ах, реченьки, реченьки').
8. 'Mladice ty krásná' ('Молодка, молодая').
9. 'Po mátušce, mocné Volze' ('Вниз по матушке по Волге').
10. 'Na políčku bříza tam stála' ('Во поле берёза стояла').
11. 'Vyjdu já si podle říčky' ('Выйду я на реченьку').
12. 'Na tom našem náměstí' ('Как у нас на улице').
13. 'Já si zasil bez orání' ('Я посеял конопельку').
14. 'Oj, ty luční kačko malá' ('Ах, утушка луговая').
15. 'V poli zrají višně' ('Гей, у поли вышня').
16. 'Oj, kráče havran černý' ('Ой, кряче, черненький ворон').

Ha, ta láska (Ah, the love . . .), song by Josef Lev, orchestrated by Dvořák. B.604. 1880/84? Unpublished.

Old Folks at Home (Stephen Foster) arranged for soli, mixed chorus and orchestra. B.605. 1893–94. Unpublished.

Vysoká Polka (anon), arranged for piano. B.606. 1902. Unpublished.

COMPLETE EDITION OF DVOŘÁK'S WORKS

Most of Dvořák's music is now available in the authentic Critical Edition which was launched by Otakar Šourek on the 50th anniversary of the composer's death. Practically the whole of the instrumental music has already been published, including several works for the first time. Very many of the songs and the most important choral compositions have appeared, but progress on the operas is less far advanced. The vocal works are being provided with new translations in English and German which adhere closely to the original Czech text, and it is hoped that these will supersede the unsatisfactory translations, such as those Troutbeck made for *The Spectre's Bride* and *St. Ludmila*, which are found in earlier editions.

Appendix IV

WORKS IN ORDER OF COMPOSITION

Most of Dvořák's manuscripts are dated, so that except in cases where a manuscript has been lost it is normally possible to arrange his works in chronological order with considerable certainty. In the table that follows each work is, as far as possible, placed within the year or years in which it was composed, and the date given after each work is the date of completion. In the case of bigger works, however, the date of commencement is also shown. It will be noticed that in a few cases in which composition was spread over more than one year, shorter works that were composed simultaneously and were completed first will be listed immediately after these, but the dates cited should make this clear. Apart from this the works are arranged in order of completion. Oblique strokes imply uncertainty.

1855/56	*Forget-me-not Polka* (pianoforte).
1857/59	Mass in B flat major.
1859	Preludes and Fugues (organ).
1860	Polka in E major (pianoforte). February 27.
	The Woman Harpist (orchestra). (?)
1861	String Quintet in A minor, op. 1. (?)
1861/62	Polka and Gallop (orchestra). (?)
1862	String Quartet in A major, op. 2. March.
1863–64	Compositions of these years destroyed.
1865	1st Symphony, *The Bells of Zlonice*. Feb. 14–March 24.
	'Cello Concerto in A major (violoncello and pianoforte). June 30.
	Cypresses Song Cycle. July 27.
	2nd Symphony in B flat major, op. 4. August 1–October 9.
	Two Songs for Baritone. October 24.
1865/69	Clarinet Quintet in B flat minor. This and other compositions of these years were destroyed.
1867	*Intermezzi* (orchestra). February 5.
1869/70	String Quartet in B flat major (?)
	String Quartet in D major (?)
1870	*Alfred* (opera in three acts). May 26–October 19.
	String Quartet in E minor. December 1870 (?)
1871	'Cello and Piano Sonata in F minor. January 4.
	Krásnohorská, songs. November.
	King and Charcoal Burner (opera in three acts, 1st version). April–December 20.
	The Orphan (ballad, voice and pianoforte). November/December (?)

Rosmarine (song) (?)

1871/72 Two Pianoforte Trios. (?)

1871/73 Potpourri on *King and Charcoal Burner*. (?)

1872 Hymnus: *The Heirs of the White Mountain*, op. 30. June 3.
Piano Quintet in A major, op. 5. August (?)
Four Songs on Serbian folk poems, op. 6. September (?)
Songs from the Dvůr Králové Ms., op. 7. September 21.
Three Nocturnes (orchestra). October (?)

1870/72 *Silhouettes* (pianoforte). (?)

1873 Violin and Piano Sonata in A minor. January.
3rd Symphony in E flat major, op. 10. April–July 4.
Romeo and Juliet (overture). July.
Octet (Serenade) (wind and strings). September.
String Quartet in F minor, op. 9. October 4.
String Quartet in A minor, op. 12. December 5.

1873/77 *Romance* in F minor, op. 11 (violin and pianoforte; also violin and
orchestra. (?)

1874 4th Symphony in D minor, op. 13. January 1–March 26.
Symphonic Poem (Rhapsody in A minor), Op. 14. September 12.
String Quartet in A minor, op. 16. September 24.
King and Charcoal Burner (opera in three acts, 2nd version). April 17–
November 3.
The Stubborn Lovers, op. 17 (opera in one act). September–December
24; overture (?)

1874/75 Potpourri on *King and Charcoal Burner*, 2nd version. (?)

1875 Nocturne in B major, op. 40 (string orchestra). January (?)
String Quintet in G major, op. 77. March.
Moravian Duets, op. 20 (soprano and tenor). March (?)
Piano Trio in B flat major, op. 21. April 14 (?)
Serenade in E major, op. 22 (string orchestra). May 14.
Piano Quartet in D major, op. 23. June 10.
5th Symphony in F major, op. 76. June 15–July 23.
Vanda, op. 25 (opera in five acts). August 9–December 22.

1876 Piano Trio in G minor, op. 26. January 20.
String Quartet in E major, op. 80. February 4.
Two Minuets, op. 28 (orchestra; also pianoforte). February (?)
Four Part-Songs for Mixed Choir, op. 29. February (?)
Moravian Duets, op. 32 (soprano and contralto). May 17–July 13.
Evening Songs, opp. 3 and 9. July (?)
Piano Concerto, op. 33. August–September 14.
Dumka, op. 35 (pianoforte). December.
Theme and Variations, op. 36 (pianoforte). December.

1876–77 *Stabat Mater*, op. 58. Sketch: February 19–May 7, 1876; score complete: November 13, 1877.

1877 Choral Songs for Male Voices. January 16.
The Cunning Peasant, op. 37 (opera in two acts). February–July (?)
Ave Maria, op. 19b (contralto and organ), July 24.
Moravian Duets, op. 38 (soprano and contralto). August (?)
Symphonic Variations, op. 78 (orchestra). August 6–September 28.

Bouquet of Czech Folk-Songs, op. 41 (male voice choir). November (?)
The Song of a Czech (male voice choir). November (?)
Scottish Dances, op. 41 (pianoforte). November/December (?)
String Quartet in D minor, op. 34. December 18.

1877–78 *From a Bouquet of Slavonic Folk-Songs*, op. 43 (male voice choir). January 6, 1878.

1878 Serenade for Wind Instruments, op. 44. January 18.
Slavonic Dances, op. 46, 1st series (pianoforte duet). March 18–May 7.
Bagatelles, op. 47 (two violins, violoncello, harmonium). May 12.
Sextet, op. 48. May 27.
Capriccio (violin, pianoforte). June (?)
Hymnus ad Laudes in festo Ss. Trinitas (voice, organ). August 14.
Slavonic Dances, op. 46, 1st series (orchestra). April–August 22.
Three Modern Greek Poems, op. 50 (voice, pianoforte). August 22.
Three Modern Greek Poems, op. 50 (voice, orchestra). August/September (?)
Furiants, op. 42 (pianoforte). September 25.
Three Slavonic Rhapsodies, op. 45 (orchestra). I: March 17; II: September 18; III: December 3.
Five Choral Songs, op. 27 (male voice). December 12.

1878–79 String Quartet in E flat major, op. 51. December 25, 1878–March 28, 1879.

1879 *Festival March*, op. 54 (orchestra). January/February (?)
Mazurek, Op. 49 (viola, pianoforte). February; (viola, orchestra) February 15.
149*th Psalm*, op. 52 (male voice choir, orchestra). February 24.
Czech Suite, op. 39 (orchestra). April (?)
Polonaise in A major (violoncello, pianoforte). June (?)
Ave Maris Stella, op. 19b (voice, organ). September 4.
O Sanctissima . . ., op. 19a (contralto, baritone, organ). September 6.
Violin Concerto, op. 53, 1st version. July 5–Mid-September.
Vanda, op. 25, overture. October (?)
Silhouettes, op. 8 (pianoforte). October (November (?))
Prague Waltzes (orchestra). December 12.
Polonaise in E flat major (orchestra). December 24.

1879–80 Waltzes, op. 54 (pianoforte). January 17, 1880.

1880 *The Heirs of the White Mountain* (revised). January 15.
Eclogues, op. 56 (pianoforte). February 7.
Gipsy Melodies, op. 55 (voice, pianoforte). February 23 (?)
Two Waltzes, op. 54 (string quartet). February (?)
Violin and Piano Sonata in F major, op. 57. March 17.
Five Moravian Duets, arranged for women's choir. March 19.
Violin Concerto (revised). April 4–May 25.
Album Leaves (pianoforte). June (?)
Piano Pieces, op. 52. June (?)
Mazurkas, op. 56 (pianoforte). June (?)
6th Symphony in D major, op. 60. August 27–October 15.
Child's Song (vocal duet). November 14.
Polka, 'For Prague Students'. December 14.

1880–81 *Ballad of King Matthias*, new version (for *King and Charcoal Burner*). January 1881 (?)
       Legends, op. 59 (pianoforte duet). March 22, 1881.
1881 Moderato in A major (pianoforte). February 3.
       'There on our roof . . .' (*Moravian Duet*). March/May (?)
       Quartet Movement in F major. October 9.
       String Quartet in C major, op. 61. November 10.
       Legends, op. 59 (orchestral version). December 9.
       Gallop in E major (orchestra). December (?)
1881–82 *Six Songs* (*Pfleger-Moravský*). (?)
       Josef Kajetán Tyl, op. 62 (overture and incidental music). January 23, 1882.
       Dimitrij, op. 64 (opera in four acts). May 8, 1881–September 23, 1882.
1882 *In Nature's Realm*, op. 63 (mixed choir), January 27.
       Two Evening Songs, op. 3 (voice, orchestra). November 24.
       Question (pianoforte). December 13.
1883 Impromptu in D minor (pianoforte). January 16.
       Scherzo capriccioso, op. 66 (orchestra). May 2.
       Piano Trio in F minor, op. 65. February 4–May (?)
       Hussite, op. 67, overture. September 9.
1883–84 *From the Bohemian Forest*, op. 68 (pianoforte duet). January 12, 1884.
       The Heirs of the White Mountain, final revision. May 3.
       Dumka and Furiant, op. 12 (pianoforte). September (?)
       Humoresque in F sharp major (pianoforte). (?)
       Ballad in D minor, op. 15–I (violin, pianoforte). September/October (?)
       'The Wild Duck' (song). September/October (?)
       The Spectre's Bride, op. 69 (cantata). May 26–November 27.
1884–85 7th Symphony in D minor, op. 70. December 13, 1884–March 17, 1885.
1885 Two Songs (folk poem texts). May 2.
       Hymn of the Czech Peasants, op. 28 (mixed chorus, orchestra). August 13.
1885–86 *St. Ludmila*, op. 71 (oratorio). September 17, 1885–May 30, 1886.
       Slavonic Dances, op. 72, 2nd series (pianoforte duet). July 9.
       In Folk Tone, op. 73 (songs). September 13.
1886–87 *Slavonic Dances*, op. 72, 2nd series (orchestra). January 5, 1887.
1887 Terzetto, op. 74 (two violins, viola). January 14.
       Drobnosti, op. 75a (two violins, viola). January 18 (?)
       Romantic Pieces, op. 75 (violin, pianoforte). January 25.
       King and Charcoal Burner (opera, final revision). February–March.
       Cypresses (string quartet). May 21.
       Mass in D major, op. 86 (soli, chorus, organ). March 26–June 17.
       149*th Psalm*, op. 79 (version for mixed choir). July (?)
       Piano Quintet in A major, op. 81. August 18–October 3.
       Two Little Pearls (pianoforte). December (?)
1887–88 *Four Songs* (*Malybrok-Stieler*), op. 82. January 5, 1888.
       The Jacobin, op. 84 (opera in three acts). November 10, 1887–November 18, 1888.
1888 *Album Leaf* (pianoforte). July 21.
       Love Songs, op. 83. December.

1889   *Poetic Tone Pictures* (pianoforte). June 6.
          Piano Quartet in E flat major, op. 87. August 19.
          8th Symphony in G major, op. 88. August 26–November 8.
1890   Gavotte for three violins. August 19.
          Requiem Mass, op. 89. January 1–October 31.
1890–91   *Dumky Trio*, op. 90. November 1890–February 12, 1891.
1891   *Fanfares*. April 30.
          In Nature's Realm, op. 91 (overture). March 31–July 8.
          Carnival, op. 92 (overture). July 28–September 12.
          Slavonic Dance in E minor (arranged violin and pianoforte). December (?)
          Rondo in G minor, op. 94 (violoncello, pianoforte). December 26.
          Slavonic Dance in G minor (arranged violoncello and pianoforte). December 27.
          Silent Woods (arranged violoncello and pianoforte). December 28.
1891–92   *Othello*, op. 93 (overture). November 1891–January 18, 1892.
1892   Mass in D major, op. 86, version with orchestral accompaniment. March 24–June 15.
          Te Deum, op. 103. June 25–July 28.
1892–93   *The American Flag*, op. 102 (cantata). August 3, 1892–January 8, 1893.
1893   9th Symphony in E minor (*From the New World*), op. 95. January 10 –May 24.
          String Quartet in F major, op. 96. June 23.
          String Quintet in E flat major, op. 97. August 1.
          Rondo in G minor (version for violoncello and orchestra). October 22.
          Silent Woods (version for violoncello and orchestra). October 28.
          Violin and Piano Sonatina in G major, op. 100. December 3.
1894   Suite in A major, op. 98 (pianoforte). March 1.
          Biblical Songs, op. 99. March 26.
          Humoresques, op. 101 (pianoforte). August 27.
          Lullaby and *Capriccio* (pianoforte). September 7.
1894–95   *Dimitrij* (opera, revised). April 9, 1894–January 30, 1895 (?)
          'Cello Concerto in B minor, op. 104. November 8, 1894–February 9, 1895.
1895   *Biblical Songs* (nos. 1–5 with orchestral accompaniment). January 8.
          Suite in A major, op. 98b (version for orchestra). February (?)
          'Cello Concerto in B minor, op. 104 (revised). June 11.
          String Quartet in G major, op. 106. Before November 11–December 9.
          'Lullaby' (song). December 20.
          String Quartet in A flat major, op. 105. March 26–December 30.
1896   *The Water Goblin*, op. 107 (symphonic poem). January 6–February 11.
          The Noon Witch, op. 108 (symphonic poem). January 11–February 27.
          The Golden Spinning Wheel, op. 109 (symphonic poem). January 15–April 25.
          The Wild Dove, op. 110 (symphonic poem). October 22–November 18.
1897   *Heroic Song*, op. 111 (symphonic poem). August 4–October 25.
          The Jacobin (opera, revised version). February 17–December 7.
1898–99   *Kate and the Devil*, op. 112 (opera in three acts). May 5, 1898–February 27, 1899.

1900   *Festival Song*, op. 113 (chorus and orchestra). April 17.
        Rusalka, op. 114 (opera in three acts). April 21–November 27.
1901   Song from *The Smith of Lešetín*. August 6.
        Recitatives for stage performance of *St. Ludmila*. August 17.
1902–03 *Armida*, op. 115 (opera in four acts). March 11, 1902–August 23, 1903.

Appendix V

SELECT BIBLIOGRAPHY

By far the most comprehensive Dvořák bibliography ever published appears in J. Burghauser's *Antonín Dvořák Thematic Catologue*, pp. 401-458.

I. BOOKS

BACHTÍK, Josef: *Antonín Dvořák dirigent* ('A. D. Conductor'). Prague 1940.
Dvořákovy Slovanské tance ('D.'s Slavonic Dances'). Prague 1947.

BELZA, Igor: *Antonín Dvorzhak*. Moscow 1949.

BOESE, Helmut: *Zwei Urmusikanten, Smetana—Dvořák*. Vienna 1955.

BRÁFOVÁ, Libuše: *Rieger, Smetana, Dvořák*. Prague 1913.

BURGHAUSER, Jarmil: *Antonín Dvořák Thematic Catalogue* (in Czech, German and English). Prague 1960.

—— *Orchestrace Dvořákových Slovanských tanců* (The Orchestration of D's. Slavonic Dances). Prague 1959.

—— *Antonín Dvořák*. Prague 1966. (Includes catalogue of works and editions, discography and multilingual bibliography.)

COLLES, Henry C.: *Oxford History of Music*, Vol. VII, 'Symphony and Drama' (esp. chapters 4 and 7). London 1934.

FISCHL, Viktor (editor): *Antonín Dvořák: his Achievement*. London 1943. (Contributors: G. Abraham, M. Carner, H. C. Colles, H. Cohen, A. Desmond, T. Dunhill, E. Evans, V. Fischl., J. Harrison, F. Howes, E. Walker).

FRIC, Ota: *Antonín Dvořák a Kroměříž* ('A. D. and K.'; includes letters). Kroměříž 1946.

HADOW, W. Henry: *Studies in Modern Music*, Second Series. London 1895.

HOFFMEISTER, Karel: *Antonín Dvořák*. Prague 1924. Transl. R. Newmarch, London, 1928.

HOŘEJŠ, Antonín: *Antonín Dvořák, sein Leben und Werk in Bilden*.

—— *Antonín Dvořák, the Composer's Life and Work in Pictures*. Also French, Hungarian and Polish translations. Prague 1955.

KULL, Hans: *Dvořáks Kammermusik*. Berne 1948.

KVĚT, Jan M.: *Mladí Antonína Dvořáka* ('The Youth of A. D.'). Prague 1943.

LEITNER, Karel: *Antonín Dvořák jak učil* ('A D. as he taught'). New York 1943.

NEWMARCH, Rosa: *The Music of Czechoslovakia*. London 1942.

PURDY, Claire L.: *Antonín Dvořák, Composer from Bohemia*. New York 1950.

RACEK, Jan: *Antonín Dvořák a Morava* ('A. D. and Moravia'). Prague 1941.

ROBERTSON, Alec: *Dvořák*. London 1945.

—— *Antonín Dvořák. Leben und Werk*, transl. A. E. Cherbuliez. Zurich 1947.

SAKKA, Keisei: *Dvořák*. Tokyo 1963.

SIRP, Hermann: *Anton Dvořák*. Potsdam 1939.

ŠOUREK, Otakar:

1. *Dvořák's Werke. Ein vollständiges Verzeichnis*. Berlin 1917.

APPENDIX V

2. *Život a dílo Antonína Dvořáka* ('Life and Work of A. D.') 4 vols. Prague 1916–1933. I, 3rd edn. 1955; II, 3rd edn. 1956; III, 2nd edn. 1957; IV, 2nd edn. 1958.
3. *Antonín Dvořák.* Prague 1929. 4th edn. 1947. *Antonín Dvořák. His Life and Works.* Engl. transl. 1952. *Antonín Dvořák. Sein Leben und sein Werk.* Transl. P. Eisner, 1953. Also transl. into many other languages.
4. *Dvořákovy symfonie.* Prague 1922. 3rd edn. 1948.
5. *Dvořákovy skladby orchestrální*, 2 vols. Prague 1944–46. The following are abridged translations of Nos. 4 and 5: *Antonín Dvořák Werkanalysen I. Orchesterwerke.* Transl. P. Eisner, 1954. *The Orchestral Works of Antonín Dvořák.* Transl. R. F. Samsour, 1956.
6. *Dvořákovy skladby komorní.* Prague 1943. 2nd edn. 1949. Abridged translations: *Antonín Dvořák Werkanalysen II. Kammermusik.* Transl. P. Eisner, 1954. *The Chamber Music of Antonín Dvořák.* Transl. R. F. Samsour, 1956.
7. *Dvořák ve vzpomínkách a dopisech.* Prague 1938. 9th edn. 1951. *Antonín Dvořák. Letters and Reminiscences.* Transl. R. F. Samsour, 1954. *Antonín Dvořák in Briefen und Erinnerungen.* Transl. B. Eben, 1955. *Dvorzhak v pismakh i vospominaniyakh.* Transl. L. A. Alexandrova, Moscow 1964. This Russian translation includes some documents that do not appear in the three books listed above.
8. *Antonín Dvořák přátelům doma* ('A. D. to his friends at home'. 395 letters). Prague 1941.
9. *Antonín Dvořák a Hans Richter* ('A. D. and H. R.' Letters and commentary). Prague 1942. Selections transl. by R. Newmarch: 'The Letters of Dvořák to Hans Richter', in *Musical Times*, Vol. 73, 1932, pp. 605–9, 698–701, 795–7.

ŠOUREK, O. and STEFAN, P.: *Dvořák. Leben und Werk.* Vienna 1935.
ŠPELDA, Antonín: *Dr. Antonín Dvořák a Plzeň* ('Dr. A. D. and Pilsen'; includes documents). Pilsen 1941.
STEFAN, Paul: *Anton Dvořák.* Transl. Y. W. Vance from Šourek and Stefan. New York 1941.
SYCHRA, Antonín: *Estetika Dvořákovy symfonické tvorby* ('The aesthetic of D.'s symphonic works'). Prague 1959.
TOMEK, Ferdinand: *Dr. Ant. Dvořák a olomoucký 'Žerotín'* ('Dr. A. D. and the Olomouc Žerotín choral society'). Olomouc 1929.
ZUBATÝ, Josef: *Ant. Dvořák. Eine biographische Skizze.* Leipzig 1886.

VARIOUS AUTHORS:

Antonín Dvořák. Umělecká beseda, Prague 1912. (Contributors: B. Kalenský, F. V. Krejči, E. Chvála, K. Knittl, J. Boleška, K. Hoffmeister, O. Hostinský, K. Stecker, J. Borecký, B. Vendler, R. Zamrzla, V. Müller.)
Dvořákův sborník Hudební revue (Memorial volume). Prague 1911. (Contributors: A. Sova, K. Hoffmeister, K. Kovařovic, K. Stecker, J. E. S. Vojan, J. B. Foerster, J. Kvapil, O. Šourek, L. Janáček, J. Löwenbach, F. A. Šubert, O. Nebuška, V. J. Novotný, J. Michl, M. Kalbeck, A. Wenig, F. Vach, R. Reissig, V. Novák, J. Faměra, F. Spilka, O. Nedbal, K. Weis, J. Zubatý.

II. MICROFILM

ABORN, M. Robert: *The Influence on American Musical Culture of Dvořák's Sojourn in America.* Ann Arbor: University Microfilms, no. 65-10,798 (positive film and Xerox) 1965. Abstract in: *Dissertation Abstracts*, XXVI, 5, Nov. 30, 1965. Indiana University dissertation, 337 pp.

III. ARTICLES, ESSAYS AND CRITICISM

ABRAHAM, Gerald: 'Czechoslovakia'. In Stevens, Denis (editor): *A History of Song*. London 1960.

ALTMANN, Wilhelm: Antonín Dvořák im Verkehr mit seinem Verleger Fritz Simrock'. In *Die Musik* X (Band XL), Berlin 1910–11, pp. 259–292, 346–353. Also in *N. Simrock Jahrbuch* II, Berlin 1929.

BENNETT, Joseph: 'The Music of Anton Dvořák'. In *Musical Times* XXII, 1881, pp. 165–9, 236–9.

—— 'Anton Dvořák'. In *Musical Times* XXV, 1884, pp. 189–192.

CLAPHAM, John: 'Dvořák and the Impact of America'. In *Music Review*, XV, 3, 1954.

—— 'Dvořák and the Philharmonic Society'. In *Music and Letters* XXXIX, 2, 1958. (Incl. unpubl. letters.)

—— 'The Evolution of Dvořák's Symphony "From the New World"'. In *Musical Quarterly* XLIV, 2, 1958.

—— 'Dvořák at Cambridge'. In *Monthly Musical Record* LXXXIX, 1959, pp. 135–142.

—— 'Blick in die Werkstatt eines Komponisten: die beiden Fassungen von Dvořáks Klaviertrio F moll'. In *Musica* XIII, 10, Kassel 1959.

—— 'The Progress of Dvořák's Music in Britain'. In *Music Review* XXI, 2, 1960.

—— 'Dvořák's Symphony in D minor: the Creative Process'. In *Music and Letters* XLII, 2, 1961.

—— 'The National Origins of Dvořák's Art'. In *Proceedings of the Royal Musical Association* LXXXIX, 1962/63.

—— 'Dvořák's Visit to Russia'. In *Musical Quarterly* LI, 3, 1965.

COLLES, Henry C.: 'Antonín Dvořák, 1. Opera at Home; 2. Song and Symphony in England; 3. 'In the New World'. In *Musical Times* LXXXII, 1941, pp. 130–3, 173–6, 209–11.

DVOŘÁK, Antonín: 'Franz Schubert' in collab. H. T. Finck. In *Century Illustrated Monthly Magazine* XLVIII, 3, New York 1894.

—— 'Music in America' in collab. E. Emerson. In *Harper's New Monthly Magazine* XC, New York 1895. Also in Morgenstern, S.: *Composers on Music*, New York 1956, London 1958.

EHLERT, Louis: (Slavonic Dances; Moravian Duets). In *Nationalzeitung*, Berlin, 15. XI. 1878. Also in *Politik* (in German), Prague, 17. XI. 1878.

—— 'Anton Dvořák'. In *Westermanns Illustrierte Monatshefte*, Brunswick, 1880, pp. 232–8.

EVANS, Ramona: 'Dvořák at Spillville'. In *The Palimpsest* XI, 3, Iowa City, 1930.

HANSLICK, Eduard: 'Concerte, Componisten und Virtuosen . . . 1870–1885'. 3rd. edn. Berlin 1896.

—— 'Aus dem Tagebuch eines Musikers' (1885–1891). Berlin 1892.

—— 'Fünf Jahre Musik (1891–1895)'. 3rd edn. Berlin 1896.

—— 'Am Ende des Jahrhunderts'. 3rd edn. Berlin 1899.

HELY-HUTCHINSON, Victor: 'Dvořák the Craftsman'. In *Music and Letters* XXII, 4, 1941.

JANÁČEK, Leoš: 'České proudy hudební' ('The Czech musical streams'). In *Hlídka* II (XIV), Brno 1897, pp. 285–92, 454–9, 594–600, and *Hlídka* III (XV), Brno 1898, pp. 277–82.

JARKA, V. Hanno: 'Příspěvek k vídeňské korespondenci Antonína Dvořáka' ('A Contribution to A. D.'s Viennese Correspondence'; Mandyczewski letters). In *Hudební revue* VII, Prague 1914, pp. 376–392.

KINSCELLA, Hazel G.: 'Dvořák and Spillville, forty years after'. In *Musical America* LIII, 10, New York 25. V. 1933. Reprinted in *Music on the Air*, New York 1934.

KISELEV, Vasili A.: 'Antonin Dvorzhak v Rossii' (A. D. in Russia'). In *Sovetskaya musika* 1951, No. 11.

—— 'Perepiska A. Dvorzhaka s V. I. Safonovim' (Correspondence of A. D. with V. I. Safonov). In *Kratkie soobshcheniya* no. 17, Instituta Slavyanovedeniya Akademii Nauk, USSR, 1955.

KREHBIEL, Henry E.: 'Antonín Dvořák'. In *Century Illustrated Monthly Magazine* XLIV, 5, New York 1892.

—— 'Antonín Dvořák'. In *The Looker-On*, New York 1896, pp. 261–271.

NOVÁK, Vitězslav: 'Antonín Dvořák'. In *Tempo* VIII, Prague 1929. Also in *Muzyka* VI, Warsaw 1929.

ROBERTSON, Alec: 'Antonín Dvořák'. In Hill, Ralph (editor): 'The Symphony'. London 1949.

ŠOUREK, Otakar: 'Z neznámých dopisů Antonína Dvořáka nakladateli Simrockovi' (Unknown letters of A. D. to the publisher Simrock). In *Smetana* XXXVII, Prague 1944, pp. 119–123, 131–135.

ŠOUREK, O. and STEFAN, P.: 'Konservatoriumsdirektor Anton Dvořák über amerikanische Volksmusik'. In *Musikblätter des Anbruch* XVI, Vienna 1934.

STEFAN, Paul: 'Why Dvořák would not return to America' (Letters). In *Musical America* LVIII, New York 25. II. 1938. Five letters additional to this series appear in: Šourek, Otakar: 'Neznámé dopisy Dvořákovy'. In *Národní divadlo moravsko-slezské*, Ostrava 5. IV. 1940.

SUK, Josef: 'Aus meiner Jugend. Wiener Brahms-Erinnerungen'. In *Der Merker* II, Vienna 1910, p. 147. Czech translation: 'Několik vzpomínek'. In *Národní a Stavovské divadlo* VI, Prague 3. VI. 1929. Reprinted in *Národní divadlo* XVIII, 13, Prague 1941.

TAYLOR, Sedley: 'Dvořák'. In *Cambridge Review*, 11. VI. 1891.

THURBER, Jeannette M.: 'Dvořák as I knew him'. In *The Etude* XXXVII, 11, Philadelphia 1919.

TOVEY, Donald F.: *Essays in Musical Analysis* II, III, IV. London 1935–1936.

IV. FOLK-SONG COLLECTIONS

ALLEN, William F.: *Slave Songs of the United States*. New York 1867.

BAKER, Theodor: *Über die Musik der Nordamerikanischen Wilden*. Leipzig 1882.

BARTOŠ, František: *Národní písně moravské* ('Moravian National Songs'). Brno 1889. New edn. in collaboration with L. Janáček, 1901.

CURTIS, Natalie: *The Indians' Book*. New York 1907.

ERBEN, Karel J.: *Prostonárodní české písně a říkadla, s nápěvy* ('National Czech Songs and Proverbs'). Prague 1842. 3rd edn. 1862–64.

APPENDIX V

Kuba, Ludvík: *Slovanstvo ve svých zpěvech* ('The Slavonic Lands in their Songs'). Prague 1884–1929. 16 volumes, the first three of which contain Czech, Moravian and Slovak songs respectively.

Slovenské spevy ('Slovak Songs') I–III. Turč sv. Martin 1880–1899.

Sušil, František: *Moravské národní písně* ('Moravian National Songs'). Brno 1835. 3rd edn. 1860.

ADDENDA

Publication of this book progressed too rapidly for the following discoveries to be taken into account:

(i) (P. 17, lines 16–18). The contract in its final form was posted to Dvořák from London on December 21st 1891, and was very probably signed by him on the 23rd or 24th.

(ii) (P. 21, lines 5–7). According to the contract signed on April 28th 1894, Dvořák agreed to continue as Director for *two* years, i.e. for a 6-month period during 1894–95 and an 8-month period in 1895–96. Owing to the family reasons set out fully in his letter to Mrs. Thurber of August 17th 1895, he was unable to fulfil his obligations in accordance with the terms of this contract, and he did not return to America for the 8-month period.

General Index

331

GENERAL INDEX

hajduch, 142
'Hajej, můj andílku', 47
Hálek, Vítězslav, 226, 230, 242, 265, 312, 313, 314
Hallé, Sir Charles, 131, 169, 200, 247, 256
Hallé, Lady (see Norman-Néruda)
Halski, C. R., 206
Hancke, Franz, 4
Handel, 176, 245, 246, 251, 253, 299
Hanka, Václav, 230
Hanslick, Eduard, 8, 10, 15, 22, 64, 131, 132, 154, 276, 279, 296
Hanslick, Sophie, 234
Harrison, Julius, 72, 75, 86
Harte, Bret, 87
Hartnoll, P., 114
Hauptmann, Gerhart, 285, 287
Hausmann, R., 108
Haydn, 46, 144, 160, 205, 245, 298, 299, 300, 301, 304
'Hej, Slované!', 161
Hellmesberger, Joseph, 172, 173, 175
Hely-Hutchinson, Victor, 27
Herbeck, Johann, 8, 64
Herbert, Victor, 103
Hersee, Henry, 100
Hesch, W., 286
Heyduk, Adolf, 227, 232, 263, 264, 314, 315
Hill, Ralph, 98
Hlávka, Josef, 87, 253, 254
Hlávková, Zdeňka Havelková-, 194, 254
Hnátek, Josef, 26
Hoffmann, Baron, 10, 279
Hoffmann, Karel, 184
Hofmeister, 214
Holden, S., 318
'Hop, holka, svlíkej kabát', 139
'Hop škrk Helena', 140
Hoppe, Olga, 212
Horncastle, F. W., 318
'Hospodine, pomiluj ny', 253
Hostinský, Otakar, 288
'Hrály dudy u Pobudy', 193
Hřimalý, V. and J., 189
Hruška, František, 244
Hudební rozhledy, xv
Hudson, Henry, 318
Hus, John, 111, 246
Hussite Chorale (see 'Ye who are warriors of God')
Hyatt King, A., xiv

'I go out on the hillock', 208–209

'Já tu nebudu!', 46, 143
Jacopone da Todi, 245
Janáček, 52, 117, 118, 123, 137, 218, 242, 244, 293
Jauner, Franz, 10, 272
Jelínek, F. L., 238, 316
'Jeszcze Polska nie zginęła' 162
Jiránek, Josef, 190
Jirásek, Alois, 280
Joachim, Amalia, 232
Joachim, Joseph, 9, 99–101, 108, 131, 169, 172, 173, 194
Johnson, A., 90

Káan, Jindřich, 261
Kamenický, F. J., 265, 313
Kapper, S., 229
Katya Kabanová, 52
Kaunitz, Václav Count, 12, 225
Kaunitzová, Josefina, née Čermáková (see Čermáková)
'Kdybys byl, Honzíčku', 199
'Když jsi ty, sedláčku, pán', 202
'Kde domov můj?', 110, 133, 275
Keller, Robert, 100
Khomyakov, 275
Kinsky, Count, 4
Kiss, The, 47, 273
klatovák, 139
Kleist, B. H. W. von, 279
Klimeš, J., 194
Klusáková, Olga, xiv
Knaben Wunderhorn, Des, 246
Kneisel Quartet, 180, 181
Knittl, Zdeněk, 26, 242, 245
Körner, K. T., 267, 312
kolo, 137, 144
kolomajka, 142
kolovrat, 138
Komzák, Karel, 5, 137, 144
Konopásek, Prokop, 269
Kopta, Václav, 191
Kovařík, Josef, J., 18, 19, 181
Kovařovic, Karel, 200, 286, 289, 312
Kovařovic, Tomáš, 193
kozáček, 138
kozácká, 142
Kozánek, Emil, 86, 212
krakowiak, 138
Krásnohorská, Eliška, 226, 229, 230, 315
Krehbiel, Henry E., 88

333

Index of Works